Excluded Ancestors, Inventible Traditions

HISTORY OF ANTHROPOLOGY

Excluded Ancestors, Inventible Traditions

ESSAYS TOWARD
A MORE INCLUSIVE
HISTORY OF ANTHROPOLOGY

Edited by

Richard Handler

HISTORY OF ANTHROPOLOGY
Volume 9

THE UNIVERSITY OF WISCONSIN PRESS

The University of Wisconsin Press
2537 Daniels Street
Madison, Wisconsin 53718

3 Henrietta Street
London WC2E 8LU, England

Library of Congress Cataloging-in-Publication Data
Excluded ancestors, inventible traditions : essays toward a more
inclusive history of anthropology / edited by Richard Handler.
pp.   cm.—(History of anthropology : v. 9)
Includes bibliographical references and index.
ISBN 0-299-16390-3 (cloth: alk. paper)
1. Ethnology—History.
I. Handler, Richard, 1950-.   II. Series.
GN308.E9   2000
305.8'009—dc21   99-35054

Information for Contributors

Normally, every volume of *History of Anthropology* will be organized around a particular theme of historical and contemporary anthropological significance, although each volume may also contain one or more "miscellaneous studies," and there may be occasional volumes devoted entirely to such studies. Since volume themes will be chosen and developed in the light of information available to the Editorial Board regarding research in progress, potential contributors from all areas in the history of anthropology are encouraged to communicate with the editor concerning their ongoing work.

Manuscripts submitted for consideration to HOA should be typed twenty-six lines to a page with 1¼-inch margins, with *all* material double-spaced, and documentation in the anthropological style. For exemplification of stylistic details, consult the published volumes; for guidance on any problematic issues, write to the editor. Unsolicited manuscripts will not be returned unless accompanied by adequate postage. All communications on editorial matters should be sent to the editor:

Richard Handler
Department of Anthropology
University of Virginia
Brooks Hall
Charlottesville, Virginia 22904-4120 U.S.A.

HISTORY OF ANTHROPOLOGY

Pauline Turner Strong
Department of Anthropology, University of Texas–Austin
Bruce Trigger
Department of Anthropology, McGill University
Patrick Wolfe
Europe-Australia Institute, Victoria University of Technology

Contents

Excluded Ancestors,
Inventible Traditions

BOUNDARIES
AND TRANSITIONS

This is the first volume of *History of Anthropology* under the second editor of the series. As such, it may someday be viewed as a document illustrative of that historical process Weber termed the routinization of charisma. Whether *HOA*'s founding editor, George Stocking, would consider himself a charismatic leader is an open question; but few would dispute (though there must be some who would, which is an important caveat, given the theme of the present volume) that Stocking is the leading practitioner in a dynamic subfield of anthropology, the history of anthropology, one that he has been largely responsible for moving from the margins to the center of the discipline.

Already in 1904 Boas had presented a paper on the history of anthropology, and Tylor's 1910 essay on "Anthropology" in the eleventh edition of the *Encyclopaedia Britannica* presents its subject matter through a historical narrative (Boas 1906; Tylor 1910). Since Boas and Tylor, anthropologists have occasionally pursued the genre (for example, Lowie 1937), but, as Stocking has noted (1966), we find the subfield beginning to "take off" only in the 1960s. To assist that process, Stocking founded the *History of Anthropology Newsletter* (in 1973) to inform practitioners of new or newly noticed publications, dissertations, and sources relevant to their work and *HOA* (in 1983) as a venue for the publication of scholarly work in the subdiscipline. The success of *HOA* — its growing readership, the considerable interest each new volume seems to arouse in the small world of institutionalized anthropology, the frequency with which it is cited, and the willingness of its publisher to continue it after Stocking retired from the editorship — makes it fair to say the series is now institutionalized. Whether history of anthropology as a subfield is also institutionalized, or even what it means to say so, is less certain, but Stocking has explicitly commented on "the crucial role a journal . . . can play" in the process of disciplinary institutionalization (1966:289). In any case, there is no doubt that at present, a small but growing number of both anthropologists and historians would claim to "do" history of anthropology, either exclusively or as an important part of their professional work; that there are venues for such work; and that expertise in the subfield can be an asset in the job market of both disciplines.[1]

The role of the history of anthropology in relation to the wider discipline, anthropology, can be construed in several ways. Stocking is fond of referring to Hallowell's notion of the history of anthropology as an anthropological project (Hallowell 1965; Stocking 1983:7; also Stocking 1966:286). In this view, history and anthropology are akin in their fundamental aim—to understand particularly situated human meaning-worlds and events—however distinct the two disciplines may be in terms of method and disciplinary culture. Thus to interpret or explain past anthropological practices in relation to specific cultural-historical moments should be business as usual for anthropologists accustomed to empirical research in local communities and situations, despite the necessity of relying on archival rather the field research (though the collection of oral histories to some extent bridges the methodological gap). Indeed, the historical contextualization of past anthropological work should be a valuable resource for anthropological self-critique. On the other hand, reflexive critique can be construed as a sign of disciplinary decay. In this negative view of current developments, one can say that the larger discipline, however securely institutionalized it may be, has exhausted itself intellectually—its object of study, whether conceived as "culture" or exotic others, having vanished or been declared to have been inappropriately objectified in the first place. Left without a real-world object to legitimize it as a scientific field of study, anthropology must now cannibalize itself, taking itself (its history, its methods, its epistemology) as its principal subject matter.

We can also think about the role of the history of anthropology in relationship to current theory-making and teaching in anthropology. As we know from the large body of recent literature on history and the politics of culture, history can be used both to bolster and to contest hegemonic institutions and orders. Stocking has commented in several places on the "whiggishness" of much disciplinary history, as practitioners read and write the history of their discipline as a prelude to the triumph of their own theoretical positions (1966:284–85, 1968:1–12). In the hands of securely institutionalized "winners" (those, for example, with tenured positions at elite universities), this sort of "mythistorical" (Stocking 1992:214) justification of their own theoretical agenda becomes a defense of an established canon. On the other hand,

---

1. In this discussion, the term "subfield" refers not to anthropology's four fields (the Boasian sacred bundle) but to areas of interest less inclusive than those, such as political, medical, and psychological anthropology, or historic archeology. This discussion also presupposes that history of anthropology has a higher profile as a recognizable subfield within anthropology than it does within history—in which the history of various disciplines is a concern within intellectual history.

those who see themselves as excluded from the anthropological establishment, however defined, can use the history of anthropology to resurrect forgotten ancestors (in effect, to create them) and to forge alternative anthropological pasts that suggest alternative canons (cf. Behar 1995; Strong 1997).[2]

The notion of a canon is precisely what is at issue in the present volume: to speak of "excluded ancestors" and to work "toward a more inclusive" discipline assumes that the boundaries of that discipline, and the roster of accepted, acceptable, and/or canonized practitioners/ancestors, can be specified and agreed upon. Such assumptions, with regard both to anthropology and to the history of anthropology, are easily challenged.

Taking first the case of the wider discipline, anthropology, we can ask: who belongs in "the history of anthropology?"—or, even, "which different histories of anthropology include which different ancestors?" For example, in my department at the University of Virginia, beginning graduate students are required to take a sequence of three "core" courses covering (roughly speaking) the history of anthropological theory, contemporary theory, and "classic" or otherwise exemplary ethnographic monographs. These courses rotate among the faculty, who agree that each person teaching any of these courses will use an idiosyncratic selection of "must-read" authors—indeed, that it would be futile to attempt to put together a "master" reading list and a master narrative for the history of the discipline, precisely because faculty in the department (not to mention students) will disagree about who the must-read authors are. The situation is similar in many other departments.

From within a department such as mine, different canonical reading lists are understood as a function of different theoretical orientations and, secondarily, different ways of telling the history of anthropology. The boundary between such positions—between, for example, British functionalism and American cultural anthropology—can be clearly drawn, though it is not necessarily contentious. Yet what appears from within a conventional anthropology department to be a range of distinctive opinions concerning the canon may well seem, from various perspectives outside such departments, to be a high degree of agreement. British functionalism and American cultural anthropology are, after all, varieties of the synchronic structuralism that became hegemonic in anthropology in the early twentieth century (Stocking 1995:944–51; Wolfe 1999:43–68). And outsiders might well attribute

2. In Stocking's initial discussion (1968:1–12), "whiggish history" is presented as a variety of presentism, an epistemological and historiographical position opposed to historicism. In the current discussion, I am treating whiggishness as a tendency to use history to justify an established approach, and opposing it to revisionism. The two distinctions, presentism/historicism and status quo/revisionist, probably crosscut each other in interesting ways, but that is beyond the scope of this argument.

the similarity of such orientations, and of institutionalized anthropological praxis in general, to the social homogeneity of conventional anthropology departments—their tendency to recruit their faculty from a narrow range of graduate-degree-granting institutions, which in turn recruit students and faculty from a narrow range of social groups.

Over time (or, "throughout the history of anthropology"), the social criteria for recruitment into and exclusion from the ranks of professional anthropology change. With the possible exception of certain sectarian universities, we would not today expect, in the Anglo-American world, to find religious affiliation used as such a criterion, though of course for Boas and his students anti-Semitism was a considerable barrier. In the past 20 years, barriers of race, gender, sexual orientation, and to a lesser extent class have become more visible and problematic, but a comprehensive list of criteria of inclusion/exclusion would include more than those. Stocking e-mailed (12/7/98) such a list to me as we were discussing plans for the current volume: "Imagine a category grid or list of types of excluded people: gays, lesbians, Native Americans, African Americans, Third Worlders, informants, shamanistic marginals, women, [those from] nonelite schools, great teachers without publications, Catholics or other nonsecular anthropologists, [those aligned with] nonhegemonic traditions, non-Anglophone anthropologists (who, in terms of an international discipline, are an excluded category)." Note that such categories vary in the degree to which they transcend, or are particular to, anthropology. Informants, shamanistic marginals, and missionaries are peculiarly anthropological "others," as are Native Americans, though the latter are also marginalized in most domains in North and South American societies. Inequality structured in terms of race, gender, sexuality, and class is, of course, prevalent far beyond the boundaries of professional anthropology; but we should keep in mind the ways in which the very existence of anthropology, institutionalized as a science of "others," can reinforce (even as most of its practitioners deplore) hegemonic processes of "othering."

A different though related way to construe canons and disciplinary boundaries concerns institutionalized anthropology's antecedents. Core courses in anthropology typically include writers who would not have been classified as anthropologists in their time, or authors who worked before anthropology existed as an institutionalized discipline. The "origins" of anthropology cannot be traced with certainty; indeed, they must be reconstructed retrospectively, in an imaginative process that can pull in all sorts of "ancestors." As Stocking has noted, "the boundaries of anthropology have always been problematic" and the discipline defies conventional origin stories of genealogical branchings: "anthropology may best be visualized historically as originating by processes of fusion rather than fission," with antecedents drawn from older traditions of scholarship in "natural history, philology, . . . moral philosophy, . . . [and] antiquarianism" (1996:933, 936).[3]

Given the indeterminacy of anthropology's boundaries, history-making matters. Historians of anthropology can bring to light the work of anthropological practitioners who may have been marginalized in their time and subsequently erased from disciplinary memory. As one of many examples, consider Sally Cole's recent work (1995) on Ruth Landes. Landes' name is hardly unknown to students of Boasian anthropology, but, as Cole notes, "she did not receive recognition in her lifetime," "was effectively excluded" (by Melville Herskovits) "from participation in African American culture studies in anthropology," and, all in all, must be considered "a historical casualt[y] of the process of disciplinary professionalization" (1995:168–69, 176–77). In Cole's account, Landes' differences vis-à-vis the disciplinary mainstream were theoretical and methodological, but those differences were magnified by the way in which gender and sexuality intersected with Landes' career.[4]

Beyond resurrecting forgotten practitioners, historians of anthropology can also, in effect, alter the disciplinary past such that anthropologists today must take into account or even canonize scholars who during their lifetimes did not consider themselves to be anthropologists. The recent inclusion of W. E. B. Du Bois in some versions of today's anthropological canon is a case in point. Du Bois was broadly trained in the social sciences—history, political economy, sociology—but not in anthropology. Yet his work on race, identity, the politics of race, and the racialized politics of culture must (or so it seems now) be read in conjunction with the work of Boasian anthropologists, with many of whom, of course, Du Bois was in contact. As a mere matter of fact, Du Bois was not much involved in institutionalized anthropology, but his relationships to people who were, and the importance of his work in the domains where those anthropologists also worked, make him a central figure in at least some tellings of the history of American anthropology (Baker 1998:99–126; Harrison 1992; Liss 1998; Williams 1996).

The present volume of HOA has been organized to highlight the issue of historical inclusion and exclusion, but it must be understood that no single

3. Kroeber thought that such processes of historical fusion distinguished the superorganic from the organic realm: "The tree of life is eternally branching, and never doing anything fundamental but branching, except for the dying-away of branches. The tree of human history, on the contrary, is constantly branching and at the same time having its branches grow together again" (1952:86).

4. Of obvious relevance here, but beyond the scope of the present discussion, are questions about "the gender of theory" (Lutz 1995) or, more generally, the relationship between people's social positioning and the types of intellectual work they do, are expected to do, or are permitted to do.

collection of essays could address all the categorical omissions (not to mention individual forgotten ancestors) we might imagine. Four of the essays focus on people who are probably unknown to most anthropologists today. John William Jackson, the members of the Hampton Folk-Lore Society, Charlotte Gower Chapman, and Lucie Varga (in the papers by Peter Pels, Lee Baker, Maria Lepowsky, and Ronald Stade) were connected more or less securely to the anthropological establishments of their day, but they were for different reasons marginal figures. By contrast, Marius Barbeau and Sol Tax (in the papers of Frances Slaney and George Stocking), were centrally located within, respectively, Canadian and American anthropological institutions, but because they chose to work as (roughly speaking) cultural and academic entrepreneurs rather than theorists, they are frequently omitted from canonizing discourses (for the example of Margaret Mead in this regard, see Lutkehaus 1995). The final essay of the volume focuses not on an individual but on a "classic" ethnographic area, as Doug Dalton considers the place of Highland New Guinea in the anthropological imagination.

The present collection, then, brings various excluded ancestors, "inventible" traditions, and marginalized work into a new (however fleeting) limelight, and it also raises questions about the processes of inclusion and exclusion that, over time, do much to constitute "the history of anthropology." That this, or any other volume, could never be exhaustive suggests that the same processes (of inclusion and exclusion) that affect the discipline of anthropology also affect history of anthropology as a subfield. (The subtitle of the current volume, "Essays Toward a More Inclusive History of Anthropology," can refer either to anthropology's history or to the subfield that studies it.)

The elicitation, discovery, selection, and/or grooming of other people's work that is so central to editorial work is at once serendipitous and structured. The metaphor of a marketplace of ideas is apt, but only if we remember that the freedom of markets is limited. An established academic journal has a certain visibility, and a range of scholars in fields the journal is relevant to will have an interest in publishing their work in it. But there is no doubt that an editor's situated knowledge of ongoing work plays a role in encouraging potential contributors. The importance of such encouragement—"elicititation" and "discovery"—is magnified in the case of *HOA* by its "themed" format. *HOA*'s inaugural editorial defined that format in these terms: "periodic booklength volumes organized around particular themes announced and developed in advance" (Stocking 1983:7). A journal organized solely in terms of preselected themes is something of a rarity. In contrast to most journals, then, which periodically (and, usually, much more frequently than *HOA*) publish essays grouped mainly on the basis of disciplinary or subdisciplinary identifications, *HOA* seeks to organize work *within* a subdiscipline (and a small one, at that) such that only a small portion of ongoing work in the subfield can be relevant for a particular volume. This means that an editor's choice of a theme has weighty gate-keeping consequences. Moreover, in practice, themes depend on an editor's knowledge of available work—which means that an editor's participation in disciplinary networks will influence the choice of themes and thus the selection of work for publication.[5]

Acknowledging the constraints posed by the themed format, HOA from the outset made use of the category of "miscellaneous studies"—to accommodate work not related to a volume's theme—and held out the possibility of the publication of "an occasional miscellaneous volume" (Stocking 1983:7). There has not yet been such a miscellaneous volume (indeed, there have been only two miscellaneous essays in the first nine volumes), nor is it my intention to abandon the themed format. I will welcome, however, readers' suggestions not just for individual essays but for volume themes. If HOA is indeed institutionalized, as seems surely to be the case, one benefit of institutionalization should be a broad and interested readership who will contribute their work, their ideas, and their criticisms to the series. With such a readership, we can perhaps avoid the perils of Weberian routinization for some time to come.

Acknowledgments

Matti Bunzl, Julia Liss, Daniel Segal, George Stocking, and Pauline Turner Strong read an earlier version of this draft; their lively discussion of the relationship of the history of anthropology to both history and anthropology, and of HOA as a project and a possibility, informs but transcends this introductory essay. I am also grateful to the editors and staff of the University of Wisconsin Press for their ongoing commitment to HOA and for much practical help and advice.

References Cited

Baker, L. D. 1998. *From savage to Negro: Anthropology and the construction of race, 1896–1954.* Berkeley, Calif.
Behar, R. 1995. Introduction: Out of exile. In *Women writing culture,* ed. R. Behar & D. A. Gordon, 1–29. Berkeley, Calif.

5. The relationship of a volume's theme to its contents is more complicated than this paragraph suggests, since ongoing work and available material influence an editor's choice of themes. As Stocking put it in an e-mailed message (GWS/RH 3/4/99) concerning this problem, the themed format "was hard to realize in practice." Thus "to one extent or another the thematic unity [of particular volumes] was ex post facto rather than a priori—a matter of finding unity in diverse materials, or modifying the theme to fit the materials that happened to become available." The point remains, however, that an editor's knowledge of disciplinary networks has gate-keeping implications.

Boas, F. 1906. The history of anthropology. In *The shaping of American anthropology, 1883–1911: A Franz Boas reader*, ed. G. W. Stocking, Jr., 1974: 23–36. Chicago.

Cole, S. 1995. Ruth Landes and the early ethnography of race and gender. In *Women writing culture*, ed. R. Behar & D. A. Gordon, 166–85. Berkeley, Calif.

Hallowell, A. 1965. The history of anthropology as an anthropological problem. In *Contributions to anthropology: Selected papers of A. Irving Hallowell*, ed. R. D. Fogelson, 1976: 21–35. Chicago.

Harrison, F. V. 1992. The Du Boisian legacy in anthropology. *Critique of Anthropology* 12:239–60.

Kroeber, A. L. 1952. *The nature of culture*. Chicago.

Liss, J. E. 1998. Diasporic identities: The science and politics of race in the work of Franz Boas and W. E. B. Du Bois, 1894–1919. *Cultural Anthropology* 13:127–66.

Lowie, R. H. 1937. *The history of ethnological theory*. New York.

Lutkehaus, N. C. 1995. Margaret Mead and the "Rustling-of-the-wind-in-the-palm-trees school" of ethnographic writing. In *Women writing culture*, ed. R. Behar & D. A. Gordon, 186–206. Berkeley, Calif.

Lutz, C. 1995. The gender of theory. In *Women writing culture*, ed. R. Behar & D. A. Gordon, 249–66. Berkeley, Calif.

Stocking, G. W., Jr. 1966. The history of anthropology: Where, whence, whither? *Journal of the History of the Behavioral Sciences* 2(1):281–90.

Stocking, G. W., Jr. 1968. *Race, culture, and evolution: Essays in the history of anthropology*. New York.

Stocking, G. W., Jr. 1983. History of anthropology: Whence/whither. In *Observers observed: Essays on ethnographic fieldwork*, ed. G. W. Stocking, Jr. HOA 1:3–12. Madison, Wis.

Stocking, G. W., Jr. 1992. *The ethnographer's magic and other essays in the history of anthropology*. Madison, Wis.

Stocking, G. W., Jr. 1995. Delimiting anthropology: Historical reflections on the boundaries of a boundless discipline. *Social Research* 62:933–66.

Strong, P. T. 1997. On centers and their margins: George Stocking's significance for feminist histories of anthropology. Paper presented at the annual meeting of the American Anthropological Association, Washington, D.C.

Tylor, E. B. 1910. Anthropology. *Encyclopaedia Britannica*, 11th ed., Vol. 2:108–19.

Williams, V. J. 1996. *Rethinking race: Franz Boas and his contemporaries*. Lexington, Ky.

Wolfe, P. 1999. *Settler colonialism and the transformation of anthropology: The politics and poetics of an ethnographic event*. London.

OCCULT TRUTHS

Race, Conjecture, and Theosophy
in Victorian Anthropology

PETER PELS

To social scientists, the occult is usually an object of study, and most of them will laugh at, or be offended by, the idea that it actually has contributed, and does contribute, to the construction of social scientific epistemology. Yet anthropology has a far tighter relationship with the occult than most prac-titioners know. In the twentieth century, the probably fraudulent work of Carlos Castaneda (1968, 1971) not only has been succeeded by a number of genuine sorcerer's apprentices (Stoller & Olkes 1987; Turner 1992; Van Binsbergen 1991), but also was preceded by the occult inspirations of Ba-taille's and Leiris' "surrealist" ethnography (Clifford 1981; Webb 1976:417–27), the tremendous influence of Frazer's *The Golden Bough* on modern oc-cultists (Gould 1990; Luhrmann 1989a:394), the belief in fairies of the folk-lorist Evans-Wentz (1911), and the interest in psychical phenomena of some of the first professional anthropologists in Britain, William McDougall and William Rivers in particular (Mauskopf & McVaugh 1980; Rivers 1912). The genealogy of occult interfaces with anthropology in the nineteenth century includes Kipling's fusion of ethnology, secret service, and Tibetan wisdom in *Kim*, Andrew Lang's interest in psychical research (Lang 1895), the not-always-unbelieving preoccupation of folklorists with ghosts, fairy tales, and other mysteries (Dorson 1968), and the concern with Spiritualism of Edward Tylor, Alfred Wallace, and a number of other Victorian anthropologists (Pels

Peter Pels lectures at the Research Centre Religion and Society of the University of Amsterdam, Netherlands. He has published widely on the anthropology of colonial-ism and the history of anthropology. He is currently working on two books, one about the introduction of the secret ballot to late colonial Tanganyika, the other on anthro-pology and the occult in the nineteenth and twentieth centuries.

11

1995; Stocking 1971). All this was prefigured in the late eighteenth century by Diderot's and Herder's interest in, and philosophical use of, shamanism (Flaherty 1992).[1]

The era of Diderot and Herder produced a notion that would develop into another important contribution of anthropology to occult thinking: that of an "Aryan" race. Emerging from the "oriental renaissance" in the late eighteenth and early nineteenth centuries, it developed into one of the intellectual points of departure of the Theosophical Society, which provided Western culture with the occult masters who manifested themselves in the prototype of the Western guru, Madame Blavatsky (Washington 1993). About the same time that the Theosophical Society was founded (1875), the originally "oriental" Aryan was transformed into the blond and blue-eyed image of what was to become one of the most frightening forms of modern racism (Poliakov 1971:264). This coincidence has never been questioned by historians of anthropology. It cannot be explained by the invention of an "Aryan Myth" (Poliakov 1971), for if the "Aryan" was the main racial category within which early-nineteenth-century Europeans formulated their differing notions of selfhood (just as "the Negro" was their predominant "other": see Curtin 1964), the diversity of the category's deployments does not allow for easy generalizations about racism, occultism, and their mutual relationship (see Leopold 1974). Moreover, the investigation of such relationships was prevented by the tendency of the disciplinary history of anthropology and psychology— the history for the profession by the profession—to declare racism and occultism out of bounds, as "pseudo-science" (Leahey & Leahey 1983; Stocking 1968:42).

The label "pseudo-science" indicates a point at which the boundaries of the discipline and its scientific authority are being debated—a point, therefore, where the construction of these boundaries can be studied critically (Pels & Salemink 1994:5). This essay makes such an attempt, by zooming in on the career of an—perhaps rightly—excluded ancestor, as a way to inquire into both the prehistory of this idea of a "pseud-oscience," and the relationships between racism, occultism, and anthropology. The work of John William Jackson, itinerant phreno-mesmerist lecturer, takes one into the border zone of a barely professionalized anthropology. On the one hand, his work took place in the sphere of what we now classify as occultism, and he has been regarded as a predecessor of Theosophy (Leopold 1974:586–87). On the other, he started to contribute to the pages of the *Anthropological Review* in 1863, and his polygenist ideas are regularly cited as representative of the racism

1. This overview sketches the outline of a book on the history of anthropology and the occult on which I have been working. Earlier statements on the topic can be found in Pels (1995) and Van Dijk & Pels (1996).

Frontispiece photo of John Jackson, taken from his *Lectures on Mesmerism*, 2d ed., 1856. (Courtesy of the Whipple Library, University of Cambridge, Department of History and Philosophy of Science. I thank Alison Winter and George Stocking for their help in providing photographs for this essay.)

of the Anthropological Society of London as a whole (Biddiss 1979:14) and sometimes even mistakenly attributed to its president, James Hunt (Rainger 1978:56, 63; Weber 1974:n. 22). Therefore, Jackson is situated at the intersection of fault lines dividing the British scientific community, divisions which, as I hope to show, are crucial for understanding the process of professionalization in which natural-scientific knowledge and general culture were divorced from each other (Shapin & Thackray 1974:11).

Jackson's career will show a dimension of the appeal of anthropology to a lower-middle-class audience which disciplinary history usually leaves out of consideration. Apart from thus questioning one of the ways in which the history of anthropology has actively constructed a measure of ignorance about its own past (its racist past in particular), it also, and more important, brings out a struggle over the social composition of anthropological expertise. Jackson's efforts to gain entrance to scientific circles took place near the end of the process that saw the rise to prominence of the British "intellectual aristocracy" of Darwins, Huxleys, and Tyndalls (Annan 1955). In his more plebeian and democratic approach to method—a method founded on conjecture or "medical semiotics" (Ginzburg 1983)—Jackson resembled a group of lower-middle-class intellectuals in the first half of the century that resisted the claims of these ascendant "aristocrats" and their reliance on the methods, language, and institutions of medical anatomy. A study of Jackson's career thus also contributes to the recently emerging history of the cultural politics of method (Dirks 1993; Fabian 1983; Ludden 1993), and thereby allows a sharper focus on the social history of an important phase in the professionalization of anthropology.

I shall discuss the relationship between race, the occult, and scientific authority in Victorian anthropology in three steps: first, by putting it in the context of the tensions between the elite medical authority of the intellectual "aristocrats" and Jackson's more "plebeian" ideas on phrenology and mesmerism, tensions often mediated by the conjectural method common to both medical semiotics and other sciences.[2] My second step is to consider Jackson's polygenism and the place of race in the contemporary rivalry between the Anthropological Society of London and the Ethnological Society of London (for which a comparison with Francis Galton's equally racist statistics will help). In the third section I will compare Jackson's notion of "theosophy" with the way in which Friedrich Max Müller and Helena Petrovna Blavatsky used the term. Both developed an interest in the Aryan race, the spiritual determi-

2. I use "aristocratic" and "plebeian" here to indicate the two sides of a struggle, taking place mostly among the middle classes, over the accessibility of the modes of production of knowledge. "Aristocrats" mostly stressed the importance of existing institutions of learning (although they, too, wanted to reform the traditional Oxbridge establishment) while "plebeians" emphasized those methods and techniques that were accessible to the autodidact and self-taught.

nation of historical evolution, and the "religion of the future" comparable to Jackson's, yet Müller's and Blavatsky's ideas on "theosophy" seem to be set at a later stage, when the professional authority of science had been accepted as a fact. This comparison of Jackson, Blavatsky, and Müller will raise, in conclusion, the question of what kind of assumptions of authority underlie the anthropological excommunication of Jackson (and others), and suggest that the qualification of both racism and occultism as "pseudo-science" runs along parallel lines.

Phreno-mesmerism and the Democracy of Medical Conjecture

John William Jackson (1809–71) was born in the west of England, the ninth and sole surviving child of Mary Pine and John Jackson.[3] His mother, a deeply religious Wesleyan, was disinherited by her father, a daring and radical newspaperman, for marrying Jackson, a gentleman of means from a family of Navy background. John William was also intended for a Navy career, but a cricket injury lamed him at the age of 13, and until his father's premature death in 1832 he was educated at home. Following that, John moved to London with his mother. Determined to become a writer, he educated himself at the British Museum, regularly making a fruitless round of publishers with his writings. Around 1839, he lost whatever fortune he had in unfortunate speculations, and he and his mother spent the last three-and-a-half years of her life in poverty. Some years after her death, illness and poverty drove Jackson from London to Bridgeport, where he apparently had some success in lecturing, and where he met, in 1848, William Davey, a practical mesmerist, with whom he started to tour the west of England with phreno-mesmerist demonstrations. The two also went to Dublin, where Jackson published his *Lectures on Mesmerism* (1851), which attracted the favorable attention of John Elliotson, editor of *The Zoist* and leader in the phreno-mesmerist field. Jackson and Davey wandered around Ireland lecturing for several years, Jackson supplementing his income by occasional journalism. In 1855, they settled in Edinburgh, where they lectured and ran a phreno-mesmeric clinic until Davey's death in 1858.

Mesmerism and phrenology are nowadays included among occult sciences (Leahey & Leahey 1983:91–156; Webb 1974:23–25). This assessment dates, at least in the case of mesmerism, from the late nineteenth century (Blavatsky 1877:I, 165; Waite 1891:227–46). Since our present-day understanding

---

3. If not otherwise indicated, biographical information is taken from E. B. Jackson (1875) and Cooter (1989:182).

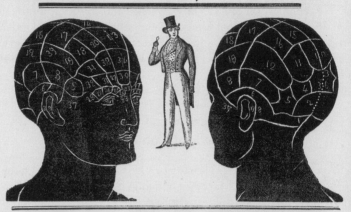

TOWN HALL, CHARD.

Mr. DAVEY

Who has just concluded a Course of Nine Lectures at Tiverton, respectfully announces to the Gentry and Public generally of CHARD, and its Vicinity, that he will deliver a Course of

THREE EXPERIMENTAL LECTURES,

ON THE UTILITY OF

MESMERISM

PHRENOLOGY,

SYMPATHY & MINERAL MAGNETISM,

AT THE ABOVE HALL, KINDLY LENT FOR THE OCCASION,

On Tuesday 8th, Thursday 10th & Friday 11th December, 1846,

TO COMMENCE AT SEVEN O'CLOCK, P. M.

That all persons may have an opportunity of witnessing the greatest wonder of the age, the price of Admission will be reduced one-half, viz. RESERVED SEATS, 1s.; SECOND CLASS, 6d.; BACK SEATS, 3d.

THE LECTURER

Will explain in his preparatory Lectures the locality, use, and abuse of the Organs, and the application of Mesmerism to human welfare, and exhibit a number of Busts, whose characters are before the Public. He will then undertake to produce Mesmeric Sleep, Rigidity of the Limbs, Power of Attraction and Repulsion, and the Transmission of Sympathetic Feelings. He will also demonstrate Phrenology, by exciting the Organs while in a state of Coma. The sleepers will perform Vocal and Instrumental Music, Dancing, Talking, Nursing, Eating, Drinking, and other feelings of mirth, imitation and independence, even up to the highest manifestations of benevolence, veneration and sublimity, while in the Mesmeric Sleep.

Mr. D. will be accompanied by Miss Henly, daughter of the late Capt. Henly, from Newton-Abbot, born Deaf and Dumb; and he feels confident of bringing into action those faculties which have been dormant from her birth, by the aid of Phreno-Mesmerism.

"FACTS ARE STUBBORN THINGS."

AS WILL BE SEEN BY THESE EXTRACTS AND TESTIMONIALS.

Flyer advertising Davey's mesmerism lectures, 1846.

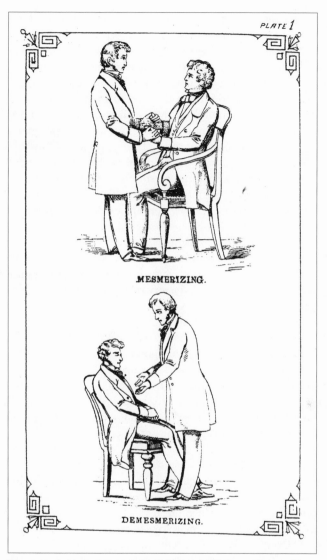

PLATE 1

MESMERIZING.

DEMESMERIZING.

Drawings of mesmerism in progress, taken from W. Davey *Illustrated Practical Mesmerism*, ed. J. W. Jackson (London 1862).

of the "occult" was formulated in more or less the same period, this qualification does not give an adequate idea of the status of these two paradigms in many people's minds during the first half of the nineteenth century. At that time, phrenology and mesmerism figured prominently in debates about scientific authority, particularly where they defined access to a "Republic of Science" that promised to be anti-authoritarian and meritocratic (Shapin & Thackray 1974:5). Both phrenology and mesmerism were important assets of a plebeian "democratic epistemology," "a definition of knowledge as open to anybody," (Barrow 1986:146) that resisted the increasing closure of the scientific—particularly the medical—professional establishment. Roger Cooter's description of both phrenology and mesmerism as "anti-occult," that is, opposed to the perceived obscurantism of the Royal Society and Oxbridge establishments, is therefore just as, perhaps even more, accurate (Cooter 1978:72).

One may distinguish three meanings of the "occult" as they were developed after the seventeenth century. The most common twentieth-century meaning is that of the occult as a secret European magical tradition going back to Neo–Platonism and the Mystery religions (Luhrmann 1989a; Webb 1974:194): I call this *occult tradition*. The second one is that of the occult as rejected knowledge, a collection of paradigms no longer accepted by the knowledge establishment (Leahey & Leahey 1983; Webb 1974:191). This is the *occult opposition*, which may, at certain points in time, merge with the occult tradition, as is currently the case with sciences like astrology, alchemy, and mesmerism. The occult opposition is the product of historically specific occultization processes in European culture. Yet it often plays a role, together with the occult tradition, in similarly specific sequences of de-occultization, such as those that occurred during the occult revival of the 1960s and 1970s (Marty 1970; Tiryakian 1973; Truzzi 1972), and whose influence can be traced in the anthropology of Carlos Castaneda and Paul Stoller, among others. Lastly, there is a notion of the occult as something inaccessible to human perception (Hutchinson 1982). Although less common nowadays, this idea was crucial during the Scientific Revolution. Such *occult qualities* are still part of medical terminology, of symptomatology in particular (see Salmasi & Nicolaides 1991).[4] Coupled with the usually negative connotations of the occult tradition or opposition, "occult" may also indicate an unintelligible quality, as when the Cartesians accused the Newtonians of using an "occult quality" like gravity for purposes of explanation (Hutchinson 1982:250–53). In the theory and practice of phreno-mesmerism, the empirically tangible signs of

4. The *Oxford English Dictionary* lists other meanings of the occult, such as hidden lines in a drawing or things unintelligible to human understanding; these definitions are obsolete or not germane to my argument.

race were made subordinate to its occult qualities in terms of innate character and natural disposition.

In the course of the nineteenth century, mesmerism and phrenology were progressively occultized, and by the time of Jackson's death in 1871 they had largely become part of an occult opposition. Mesmerism, in particular, was adopted by adherents of European occult traditions, either through the mediation of spiritualism (in the case of Blavatsky's Theosophy: see Braude 1989:146, 178; Owen 1989:119, 124) or through its direct adoption as a magical technique (by, for instance, Aleister Crowley: see Grant 1972:10). But at the time that John Jackson was working as a phreno-mesmerist lecturer, this process of occultization was still in full swing. Both paradigms were part of a political battle over scientific expertise—medical expertise in particular. The battleground for both parties was, to a large extent, the field of the conjectural method or medical semiotics (Ginzburg 1983), which, by hypothesizing invisible causes from perceived minute effects, was very much engaged with occult qualities. While phrenology or "cerebral physiology" was a form of the conjecture of character, insanity, or criminality from perceived "bumps" on the head, mesmerism was the main source of hypotheses about imponderable or occult qualities, especially in medical and psychological speculations about the mysterious agentive force that could explain trances and communications through mediums. Of the two, phrenology was the more respectable and the more conspicuously "open" in its method of reading character, while mesmerism was from its inception more mysterious and scandalous, especially since its experiments involved not just occult agency, but also employed mostly female mediums, whom trance rendered passive to the mesmerizer— a situation with clear sexual connotations.

Franz Joseph Gall's phrenology had been introduced in England by J. G. Spurzheim and made into a mainstay of middle-class self-fashioning by George Combe, particularly through his *The Constitution of Man* (1828). Here Combe argued that it was possible to divine individual and racial character because a person's head displayed to the trained eye indications of the extent to which someone possessed specific mental "functions" or "faculties." The paradigm rose on the wave of an increasingly powerful middle class by extolling—in the idea of individual character and "fitness" for specific societal roles—a naturalized version of the social fragmentation and divisions of labor of emergent industrial society (Shapin 1979:61). Moreover, Combe's theory also appealed to working-class ideologues, for whom the idea of the brain as a "republic" of qualities provided a radically materialist alternative to existing—largely ecclesiastical—moral authorities and hierarchies (Cooter 1978:185–86). And, of course, phrenology was a tremendous boost for the rising class of medical professionals, since it promised independence from a clerically dominated intelligentsia by providing a translation of abstract metaphysical categories into observable and material "organs" of the mind (Cooter 1978:32).

In the 1890s, however, when a number of phrenology's major presuppositions had been included in scientific orthodoxy, one of its leading adherents complained that it had been "cold-shouldered by the scientific classes, especially the medical" because it didn't pay and was clerically disreputable (Cooter 1978:257, 259). Although the medical establishment had a lot to gain from the philosophical possibilities of phrenology, and although phrenology in the 1830s could count on the support of The Lancet and major medical practitioners (De Giustino 1975:41), it was never fully accepted by the medical establishment, at least partly because it militated against one of the mainstays of medical authority: anatomy. As George Combe put it in his Elements of Phrenology of 1819: "The anatomist might dissect the olfactory nerves, till his eyes grow dim with age, and never discover that these nerves perform the functions of smell . . . He might dissect every organ of the body, but could never, from the anatomical structure of any one of them, infer the functions it performs in the living body" (quoted in De Giustino 1975:34). Phrenology was, indeed, a "physiology," a doctrine of the functions and actions of human beings, rather than their structure or anatomy (cf. Huxley 1860:354). And as the French physiocrat Cabanis put it, the secrets of the living body were always out of reach. Thus the impossibility of eliminating the qualitative and the individual in the observation of living disease made any practitioner fall back on conjecture (Ginzburg 1983:100).

Of course, conjecture had been disciplined medically by subsuming the observation of symptoms under clinical labeling, which produced a repetition of results that compensated for the uncertainties of conjecture identified by Cabanis. However, uncertainty about the occult causes of disease remained fundamental and obscured by a mystique of the good doctor's tactile intuition (Foucault 1963). Another strategy of professional closure was the collection of medical statistics, which again required a clinical establishment to be effective (see Hacking 1990). Yet this was precisely the kind of institutional closure by the "caste" of trained and diplomaed professionals that many plebeian healers resented (Barrow 1986:175). Symptomatology as such—"the discipline which permits diagnosis on the basis of superficial symptoms or signs, often irrelevant to the eye of the layman" (Ginzburg 1983:87)—could not be completely monopolized by the medical establishment, for if the criteria for the relevance of observed symptoms and conjectured causes were in dispute, those that distinguished between "professional" and "layman" were also in doubt. In this context, John Jackson's standpoint, that reasoning about structure is subordinate to knowledge about function, and that anatomy (which researched structure) is not the best indicator nor the foremost tool of ethnology, becomes a distinctly political remark. According to Jackson, a far more penetrating insight was produced by conjecturing "character" or "race" from the observation of bumps on the head, guided by the findings of "cerebral physiology" (1863: 13, 27, 96–97).[5] Significantly, the comparative anatomist Thomas Huxley inverted the emphasis on function and structure (1881: 145–46).

Phrenologists from Gall onward wanted to escape the metaphysics of mental philosophy (De Giustino 1975: 13–14). But they introduced their own metaphysics of "character" and "race" by insisting on the necessity to form conjectures of imponderable causes, a necessity that also allowed for a considerable amount of intellectually democratic speculation. This move in turn was aggravated by mesmerism, for if phrenology by itself did not postulate anything more mysterious than "character" or "function," mesmerism definitely pulled conjecture into the realm of the extraordinary and mysterious (Barrow 1986: 75). The "mesmeric mania" of the 1840s centered to a large extent on the figure of John Elliotson, leader of the London phrenologists, whose already tense relationship with the Edinburgh phrenologists under George Combe was definitely broken when Elliotson *cum suis* ventured into mesmerism (De Giustino 1975: 94ff.). Elliotson, a professor at University College Hospital, had been put forward by *The Lancet* as a prime emblem of the leveling and meritocratic possibilities of the "Republic of Science," and of a medical career in particular. When he subsequently turned to mesmerism in combination with phrenology, however, Thomas Wakley, the editor of *The Lancet,* deserted him and sometime later he was also barred from lecturing at the clinic. This forced Elliotson to continue mesmerist experiments at home and start his own journal, *The Zoist,* in 1843, to which Jackson contributed (1854).

Mesmerism had already from its inception been associated with scandal, fraud, and abuse of the seemingly will-less mesmerisee (Darnton 1968). Elliotson didn't make his experiments more acceptable after he allowed speculations to be voiced about clairvoyance on the part of his prime subjects, the O'Key sisters, despite the support of respected figures like Charles Dickens, Herbert Spencer, Harriet Martineau, and the bishop of Dublin, Richard Whately (De Giustino 1975: 99; Kaplan 1975: 50, 57). Phrenology merely gave access to knowledge of a person's character, his "normal state"—and by calling it "normal," it simultaneously *described* and *prescribed* it (cf. Hacking 1990: 160ff.). But the trance induced by the mesmeriser, and the surprising manipulations of the mesmerisee possible in this state, suggested that this was

5. Colonial administrator–ethnologists displayed a similar predilection toward using a physiology of appearance as a criterion of ethnic identity, in opposition to the established medics' espousal of comparative anatomy (Pels 1999). I have not yet been able to trace Jackson's *Lectures in Phrenology,* printed privately in 1853, so I cannot check except by his later publications to what extent he reproduced common phrenological assumptions.

an "abnormal state," and moreover, one that could not simply be designated as pathological and negatively evaluated as deviant (Weber 1974:273). Jackson was not alone in thinking that the occasional clairvoyant in mesmerist experiments was a sign of nothing more than an as yet insufficiently realized human potential, comparable to extraordinary seers and prophets (Jackson 1859). Moreover, these abnormal effects, from which even the adherents of mesmerism itself did not know exactly what to conclude, were replicable by experiment. According to its adherents, mesmerism bore the seal of the Master of Verulam, Francis Bacon, who had, indeed, urged the study of the occult as a "prerogative instance" of the new inductive philosophy (Clark 1984:355).

Of course, the phrenological notions of "character" and "function" were as little exact as the wildest imaginings of mesmerists and just as imponderable as the latter's musings on communication through "mesmeric fluid" or "odic force." Adherents of mesmerism frequently relied on the analogy with electricity to state their case—Jackson, for instance, said the relationship between actor and actee in a mesmeric experiment was like "the positive and negative poles of the human battery" (1851:13)—and this claim was to some extent justified, because electricity, like gravity once, was an occult quality in contemporary science. Many imponderable causes would remain occult no matter how many experiments were held, especially within a plebeian "democratic epistemology," where everyone tried for himself, and experimentation—often domestic—had little chance of being authoritatively replicated (Barrow 1986:178). Plebeian experiments did not build up an experimental history of testing and remained ambiguous about the fundamental nature of matter: hence Jackson's wavering between spiritualist and materialist arguments (1851:43, 59). At the same time, imponderable causes were sufficiently flexible to produce satisfaction of most practitioners' and clients' criteria. As Roger Cooter points out, phrenology was like astrology, in providing an exceedingly practical answer to "the first question of philosophy": "what should we do with our lives" (1978:176).

Thus, phrenology promised to divine character, while mesmerism went beyond that to clairvoyance. Indeed, Carlo Ginzburg traced back the conjectural or semiotic method to practices of divination (1983:89-90), thus offering an interesting insight into the moral economy in which nineteenth-century sciences were set. As I have argued elsewhere, this milieu motivated more respectable currents like evolutionism to strive after spiritual or statistical—but equally parasensual—"super-visions" that could help conjectures of the occult causes of past, present, and future (Pels 1995:85-86). Thomas Huxley called this method "retrospective prophecy" (1881), and as we shall see, that was precisely what John Jackson made of it when he became an anthropologist.

Anthropological Authorities and the Kabbala of Race

After Davey's death, Jackson moved to Glasgow, where he presided over the Curative Mesmeric Association and helped to found the Glasgow Psychological Association (Jackson 1869b). Yet he kept his contacts with the Edinburgh plebeian scene by becoming a member of the Edinburgh Phrenological Association, which sided with Elliotson against the Edinburgh Phrenological Society under George Combe, and during 1867 he acted several times as a practical mediator between this Association and some critics of phrenology in the Anthropological Society. Jackson may have found his way into anthropology through Luke Burke, phrenological editor of several unsuccessful ethnological journals and other publications, to one of which, *The Future*, Jackson contributed in 1860. In Jackson's first anthropological work, his only references to living authorities are to Luke Burke and to the Frenchman M. Terres. In particular, Jackson supported Terres' idea that humanity was not just a different species of mammalia, but a whole new kingdom of nature on its own, a kingdom which carried in its present diversity of races the germs of the future development of a multitude of human species (1863:20–21).

This kind of prophetic polygenism pervaded Jackson's anthropology. His language was that of the most virulent racism, and phrenology may indeed have been one of the main vehicles by which racism became a popular doctrine (De Giustino 1975:70). Jackson distinguished three main human races: Negro, Mongol, and Caucasian. The Negro, he wrote, was "embryonic, . . . swallowed up in the Present. It is not that the basilar region of his brain, with its Alimentiveness and Amativeness, is so inordinately powerful, but that the counterpoising elements are so pitiably weak, that the poor child cannot help giving way to his passing appetites" (1863:37). Yet, if this "great rearguard of the human army" will march onward—and it will perish if it doesn't—it will yet reveal "the gorgeous splendour of Negro civilisation" and teach humanity "to what *external* life can be raised" (41–42). Whereas the Indo-Germanic nations may have scaled the heights of reason and fathomed the depths of thought, the true realization of the passions and emotions by those who dwell under the equatorial sun "will add another page to the tragic in Poetry and the sublime in Oratory. Nor will Art fully know how the canvass can speak, or what light and shadow and colour can accomplish, till the easel has been placed south of the Sahara . . ." (43).[6]

The condition of this evolution is the return of descendants of the slaves

6. As surprising as these prophecies about the future of the Negro is Jackson's critique of ethnocentrism where he accuses writers of history of taking a too exclusively "Caucasian" point of view—that is, relying on written records only (1863:53, 65, 1865:234).

from the Americas after having received an "intellectual baptism" by Caucasian blood. This statement is Jackson's doctrine of "cyclical repetition," which implied that every race gets a regular dose of what it constitutionally lacks from one of the neighboring races. Negro and Mongol would improve their coronal region by such "Caucasianization," while the Aryan or Caucasian, whenever his intellectual activities had made him too effete, would be restored by a "baptism of bone and muscle" from an invading Mongol horde (1863:31, 1872).

Jackson's racist prophecies—which he also applied to the Mongol or Turanian (Jackson 1863, 1868a)—were well received by the *Anthropological Review*, which recommended his "prophetic scientific penetration into the future," his flamboyant style, and his phrenology (Anonymous 1863). Jackson became a regular contributor to the journal, writing two or three sometimes lengthy articles or reviews a year until the death of its editor, James Hunt, in 1869. Indeed, some of Jackson's unsigned papers (1865 and 1866a in particular) have been attributed to Hunt himself (Biddiss 1979:113; wrong attributions by Rainger 1978: n. 56, n. 63; Weber 1974:283 n. 22). "Race" had been, of course, the central notion of British ethnology ever since its inception, although twentieth-century disciplinary history has either ignored or written around that fact (Stocking 1973:xxxiii; Weber 1974). Yet the polygenist form of racism was something one encountered in the pages of the *Phrenological Journal* (De Giustino 1975:70), rather than the *Journal of the Ethnological Society*. The word "anthropology," which was later so offensive to the ethnologists confronted with James Hunt's Anthropological Society of London, was common among phrenologists and medics in general. Actually, there had been an earlier, shortlived, and *phrenological* Anthropological Society of London, established in 1836 by John Epps, who worked with Luke Burke (Cooter 1989:13, 44). Leading phreno-mesmerist John Elliotson used "anthropology" in the common sense of "the study of man" (quoted in Barrow 1986:90; *Oxford English Dictionary*). George Stocking has suggested that the polygenist, materialist, and Tory Anthropological Society of London was regarded as vulgar by its monogenist, dissenting, and liberal—but also more professional and "intellectually aristocratic"—rival, the Ethnological Society of London (1987:252–3). I want to suggest that this perception of vulgarity was not only based on political, religious, and theoretical differences, but also on the Anthropological Society's relative proximity to plebeian science, something which made it more accessible to phrenologists.

Although many phrenologists were members of the Ethnological Society of London in its first decades (including a president, John Connoly, and a secretary, Richard Cull—Cooter 1989:263), its main ideologues, James Prichard and Robert Latham, tried to keep phrenology out of the society's deliberations. Prichard regularly attacked phrenology (see Combe 1825, 1834, 1838), while Latham refused to have it discussed at the British Association in 1847—this earned Latham a phrenological analysis, which explained his "tiresome verbose style" by "the organ of Language in excess ... particularly when associated with large Order, Caution and Self-esteem" (Prideaux 1847:475).[7] The attacks of the evangelical Prichard were occasioned by phrenology's potential materialism, which had no room for a doctrine of the soul, largely because phrenologists assumed they had proven the existence of mental functions and their organic location (Combe 1825). Moreover, Prichard's Christian preference for a single origin of mankind must have prejudiced him against phrenology's association with polygenism. Since then, many former phrenologists saw a chance of dissociating themselves from its increasingly plebeian rather than upper-middle-class aura after the open declaration of mesmerism and materialism by a friend of John Elliotson, William Engledue, at the meetings of the British Phrenological Association in 1842 (Cooter 1978:94ff.). Phrenology's demotion to "pseudo-scientific" status did not completely discredit it in the eyes of the "Anthropologicals," since they were committed to a more right-wing plebeian style, one more deterministic, illiberal, and anti-Darwinian than the "Ethnologicals," and more openly political in their misogynist and racist plea for a meritocratic Republic of Science (Biddiss 1979:14; Rainger 1978; Stocking 1987:249–54).

This situation gives an interesting view of the place of race in Victorian culture. The images of race held by "Anthropologicals" and "Ethnologicals" should not be too sharply contrasted (Biddiss 1979:14). Both subscribed to the idea that race was natural difference and that difference implied hierarchy. But whereas a majority among "Ethnologicals" adhered to humanitarian and utilitarian ideas about human equality—true to the missionary and civil rights movements from which they descended (Rainger 1980)—"Anthropologicals" like Jackson and Hunt were united in their disgust at what Hunt called "the religious mania, and the rights-of-man mania" (Hunt 1867:lix; Jackson 1865, 1866a, 1866b). Thus, while race, or the issue of human biological variability, was the source of ethnology's main questions (Stocking 1973:xlix) and continued to drive anthropology after the Ethnological Society and Anthropological Society had fused into the Anthropological Institute in 1871, and indeed, until well into the twentieth century (Haddon 1934; Lorimer 1988), among the intellectual aristocracy it simply was "not done" to openly declare race to be a primary cause or central category for explanation, prediction, and control of human behavior, as Jackson did (1866a). The declarations of Disraeli and Knox that "race was everything" (Biddiss

---

7. The founder of the Ethnological Society of Paris in 1842, William Edwards, was also a phrenologist (Cooter 1989:117). Luke Burke's own first *Ethnological Journal*, published in 1848, carried "phrenology" in its subtitle.

1979:12) were made in the 1840s and 1850s, when both were marginal figures. As also evidenced by Marx (Poliakov 1971:246), those who professed
humanitarian, utilitarian, or socialist ideas of human equality seem to have
thought that racist ideas, although pervading nearly every way of thinking,
were less publicly acceptable and better professed in private.

John Jackson, however, set his racism in opposition to the intellectual aristocracy, attacking prophets of human equality like Henry Buckle, John Stuart
Mill, and Auguste Comte as well as more moderate, and only privately racist,
comparative anatomists like Huxley (Jackson 1865, 1866b, 1867b:264). As
nearly all the titles of his publications show, Jackson thought race was the
"foundation of things," and phrenology the "master key" to unlock its mysteries (1863:68, 1864:131, 1865:241, 1866b:312, 1875:18). Jackson adhered
to a strong notion of aboriginality, the biologist discourse of descent on which
nineteenth-century classifications of race or tribe—by colonial or civil servants as well as scientists—were based (see Pels 1999). "Aboriginals" were
ascribed traits appropriate to the original "seat" or place of origin of their
specific species. Polygenism was "strong" aboriginality in the sense that it supposed that no individual of a race or species could shed these original characteristics; as Jackson said, aboriginality was "ineradicable" (1866a:126). Hence
the denial, by Jackson and others, that hybridity could be anything else but
degradation and monstrosity, a merger of the vices of both parents that nature
would soon annihilate (1866a:125). This commitment to "strong" aboriginality, therefore, implied that human variation could never depart from type,
and that every individual's growth replicated the growth of the race (which
explains Jackson's frequent shifts between history and biography: 1859, 1864,
1866b). Every individual was a racial type, and the only variation possible
was in a future direction, through the spread of the Aryan institution of caste
hierarchy, which in turn would produce the new species of the intellectual
kingdom (1868b:129).

But this stability of type created a problem: since variation was only possible as growth, the question arose how development could occur in human
beings whose genetic endowments were conceived as "aboriginal" and therefore static. As we have seen, Jackson did not join other polygenists in deny-
ing the possibility of Negro development (although he shared their misgiv-
ings about missionary work: 1869a:54). Instead, he introduced his theory of
"cyclical repetition, in each distinct family, of the forms existent among its
neighbours" (1863:31). By invasion or migration, aboriginal races would be
"baptized" with characteristics they lacked but needed: Yankees would have
to become more Indian to survive in North America, Europeans had regularly undergone a "baptism of bone and muscle" by invading Mongol hordes,
and Negroes, as we have seen, needed some intellectual infusion in order
to progress (32). All these varieties were related to each other and stood in

a hierarchy "adapted when complete, for the most harmonious interaction, like the several parts and functions of a healthy physical organism" (33). The hierarchy of caste—of "race within race" (1866b:315)—was therefore not an invasion of the natural rights of man, but a law of nature. Nature was not democratic but hierarchical (1868b:125).

Jackson's organic metaphor was, of course, standard for many nineteenth-century thinkers. What is particularly interesting, however, is his racialization of caste—occurring at more or less the same moment as it did in India (Pels 1999)—and the way in which it was based on a *functional* conception of social coherence. As we have already seen, Jackson played a game of plebeian scientific politics by privileging the mental functions identified by cerebral physiology over the material structures identified by anatomy. By positing function as cause and structure as effect, he also resolved his doubts about the relation between the spiritual—which became the world of causes—and the material—the world of effect (1867b:258). This concept was linked to Jackson's caste doctrine by the idea that the division of labor of caste—a division of labor that, at least since James Mill's *History of British India* (1818) had been discussed in relation to "Iran" or "Aryans"—was, in reality, a specialization of function, and to Jackson, function or occupation was passed on within the race by hereditary transmission (1868b:129). Phrenology had, of course, already set out this hierarchy of functions, and put the intellectual faculties (such as Veneration or Conscientiousness) above the affective (such as Alimentiveness or Amativeness). Since, according to Jackson, growth was "the condition of life" (1863:32), humanity, while diversifying, would come closer and closer to these higher, intellectual functions, and simultaneously become more intimately related to the "imponderable elements" (1867b:266), the "one Divine Idea" (260) underlying the conception of this hierarchy. "Future man" would be "radiant and magnetic" (263).

Before we go into the occult qualities of mesmerism that Jackson introduced at this stage, it is worthwhile to compare his natural eugenics to the more artificial and "intellectually aristocratic" variety put forward by his contemporary Francis Galton. Although he later became a member of the intellectual aristocracy, Galton was also close to the onetime president of the Anthropological Society of London and general *bête noire*, Sir Richard Burton, and he had toyed with phrenology just as Burton toyed with mesmerism (Brodie 1967:250–51; Fancher 1983:66; Forrest 1974:37). Like Jackson, Galton was interested in "hereditary genius," although he probably would have rejected Jackson's classification of it as "ecstatic." Moreover, given their preoccupation with the future possibilities of humanity, both thinkers were less interested in the normal constitution of human beings than in the abnormal deviation from it—not just the negatively valued deviations such as the Negro (Fancher 1983:74), but also, and more important, the superior abnormality of genius (Forrest 1974:90). Contrary to this interest in deviation, the idea of normality was derived from medicine and translated into statistics as the "average man," *l'homme type* of Adolphe Quetelet. As has been shown by Ian Hacking, Galton departed from this notion of the "normal" or "average," a departure resulting—in ways I cannot discuss here—in the idea of a statistical law, that is, a regularity independent of the "host of petty independent causes" at the basis of the calculation of Quetelet's average. This shift was one of the most crucial steps in the "taming of chance" (Hacking 1990:185–86).

The comparison between the two is crucial precisely because of their different ways of dealing with chance: unlike Galton, Jackson did not tame chance, but excluded it altogether. In his nonstatistical universe, notions of population and quantification did not arise, and when talking of the "character" of a race, his idea of human collectives was built on the model of the person just as "History . . . is the biography of the Universal Man" (1863:61). Jackson's "strong" aboriginality, by insisting on the stability of type, excluded variation and chance from the development of humanity. His insistence on the ordered hierarchy—the functionality—of any organism by "Divine Idea" made sure that no effect of human nature could be randomly distributed and all of them should be seen as effects of race. In fact, such a "law of correspondential representation" also made the vegetable kingdom into the vascular, the animal into the muscular, and the hominal into the nervous system of the earth, "all resting on the mineral or osseous" (1875:37). This kind of absolute organism bears a parallel to the Kabbala, which, in Jorge Luis Borges' argument, excludes chance by regarding the Bible as an absolute book, in which no single letter can be distributed randomly or exist without a planned meaning (Borges 1980). Jackson's philosophy is a Kabbala of race, with each physical effect acting as an "emblem" (Jackson 1875:51) or "hieroglyph" (54) for the original, divine, imponderable, and occult distribution of types.

One can thus interpret the difference between Jackson and Galton in terms of scientific progress, and indeed, Galton's invention of statistical law made possible a way of thinking about human variation that reduced the need to rely on notions of essential human types as accounting for social regularities. Looked at from the present, Jackson's form of typification may seem dated, a sign of a prestatistical era in which humans were identified as racial essences rather than as collections of variables. But the arrival of the language of statistics as a dominant feature of modern science and society is also a struggle arising from and resulting in changes in the execution and definition of power (Asad 1993; Hacking 1990). The comparison between Jackson and Galton, then, can also be read against such a background, not as indicating that qualitative typification is made obsolete by notions of statistical law, but as indicating that the former method had to retreat from certain scientific fields while continuing to hold sway in other, more marginal, forms of knowledge production (such as ethnography; see Asad 1993). Obviously this shift has everything to do with the growing class of professional scientists demarcating their expertise—by, among other techniques, statistics—from that of a larger group of autodidact, plebeian, and amateur scientists. Statistics, and the schooling and clinical experimentation it required, must also be regarded as a barrier to the democratization of science. At the same time, in the hands of anthropologists like Franz Boas and William Rivers, statistical consciousness produced a critique of race as an explanatory category (Kuklick 1998). Consequently, both the methods and the results of statistical thinking helped to further occultize race as a doctrine of human classification.

Anthropology and "Theosophy"

Jackson's interest in anthropology (he dropped the use of the term "ethnology" after his first publication in the *Anthropological Review*) had already attuned him to London intellectual circles. After marrying at the mature age of 59, he moved with his family to London in 1869, in the hope of another chance of earning his living as a writer. Jackson was well acquainted with James Burns, then the leading publicist in Bloomsbury's occult circles. He had already published regularly in Burns's *Human Nature* before coming to London, and they became close enough for Burns to provide much-needed support for Jackson's young wife and children after Jackson's death. Burns published *Human Nature* ("A Monthly Journal of Zoistic Science, Intelligence, & Popular Anthropology") as a kind of successor to Elliotson's *The Zoist*, but with a strong emphasis on spiritualism apart from "physiology, phrenology, psychology, . . . philosophy, the laws of health, and sociology" (as listed on the inside cover of the journal). Burns was a true plebeian, opposing his democratic epistemology to the Christian establishment as well as to entrenched medical authority. His journals were supposed to help turn his readers into responsible individuals, not into a set of blind devotees, and he urged them to help one another rather than surrender to the monopoly of the medical establishment (Barrow 1986:105, 178, 193). That Jackson had come to share Burns's preoccupation with the spirits of the deceased is clear from the report by his wife that Jackson's last publication, *Man*, supposedly was written at the request of the spirits who frequented a Mr. Slater's seances (E. B. Jackson 1875:xv).

Jackson had already been a leading figure in the Glasgow Association of Spiritualists. Like many others, the most famous being John Elliotson and Alfred Wallace, Jackson was converted, after a materialist phreno-mesmerist phase in which he ridiculed spiritualism (Jackson 1854), to the idea that spiritual forces were the guiding instances and moving causes of the world's phenomena. In Jackson's case, his spiritualism was centered on the notion of function or mental action causing modifications of material structure: a view of causes and effects perfectly congruent with the phrenological idea that character shapes the bumps on one's head. Jackson's move towards spiritualism started in the late 1850s, when he became more and more convinced of the superiority of certain prophets and dedicated his *Ecstatics of Genius* (1859) to them: Pythagoras, Mohammed, Shakespeare (see also Jackson 1864), Newton, Swedenborg, and lesser seers like Mrs. Buchan and Joseph Smith. His preoccupation with cyclical movements, which he associated with the regularity of natural law, led him to suppose another, grand cycle, one that turned his "ethnic baptisms" into "epicycles."

The story of this grand cycle was, of course, that of the Caucasian race, for "all history is but a reproduction of Caucasian annals" (1863:53). But within the framework of his theory of racial evolution, Jackson's accounts show a certain development. In 1859, he argued that "to the East we owe our lineage and language, our religion and our philosophy," and clearly found the "East" synonymous with the Brahmin and the Persian (1859:4). Later, however, he started to play on the ambiguity of the imaginary geography of orientalism, implying that it might mean "Semitic," that is, Middle Eastern rather than Indian or Persian. He invented another "epicycle," a conquest of India by the Northwestern Caucasians before the emergence of Vedic religion and Sanskrit, to retain the Northern European aboriginality of Aryans (1865:238, 1866b:303). History at this point becomes a battle between the Aryans, who are really Caucasians from a Turanian "root," and Semites, who are Caucasians from a Negroid "root" (1869c).[8] On the intellectual plane, this theory is best expressed by the former's talent for natural and pantheistic philosophy and the latter's "grand monotheism," its talent for theosophy (1866b:294).

Semitic talent for theosophy, however, was also a later arrival in Jackson's scheme. He started out describing an "oriental theosophy" that was clearly Brahminical and Buddhist and that set "Asian intuition" against European deduction (1854:424, 1858:1, 1859:5). Theosophy, as intuition, was an immediate communication with things (1859:132). The reference to Brahmanism and Buddhism as theosophy disappears from his later writings, for both religions have shifted camp, and are now subsumed under the pantheistic, analytical, and natural philosophy of the Aryans. Theosophy's highest emanation becomes Judaism (1866b:294). One would expect, from Jackson's predictable statement that the Semitic type is inferior to the "vigorous" Euro-

8. Thus Jackson avoided the fallacy of making linguistic criteria into the determinants of race (see F. M. Müller 1854) by subdividing "Caucasians" into Aryans and Semites, and providing, like Müller, for a possible superiority of Aryans over Semites (cf. Peskowitz 1998). Nevertheless, he continued to argue that the "Caucasian type" was linked to the "Aryan language" throughout history (1869a:57) and regularly committed the same fallacy later (see below).

pean Aryan (301), that he would also subsume theosophy under the Aryan's philosophy. On the contrary, he criticized Auguste Comte—according to Jackson, a "pantheistic Aryan" whose positive religion of science worshipped humanity through a female image—because the Comtean religion would be unacceptable to the patriarchal and monotheistic Semites, the highest known development of religion in the world (291–92, 309). Instead, a new creed and a new prophet would have to come from Britain, not France (306).

This new creed would have to be a Christianity of castes; one strongly suspects its prophet was to be John Jackson. In any case, the conclusion seems inescapable that theosophy, whether it came from inferior Eastern Aryans or inferior Semites, was eventually supposed to be a superior mode of knowledge. Encompassing intuition, prophecy, or seerdom—those superior deviations from normality that Jackson tried to label with mesmerism's occult qualities— theosophy came closer to the "Divine Idea" than anything else. The first announcement of the new synthesis in theosophy and philosophy was, according to Jackson, Platonism. This "oriental theosophy robed in the intellectual vestments of philosophy" (1866b:295) was based on the idea that the entire universe is a divine conception, or, as Jackson phrased it, that "all structure [is] …simply spiritual force ultimated into form on the material plane" (1875:53). This new synthesis could not develop, however, until after the force of the monotheistic waves of Catholic Christianity and Islam was spent, and the disintegrative, analytical, and democratic thinking of Protestantism and science had intervened.

Jackson was, of course, not the only Victorian to look to (Neo-) Platonism for an inspired synthesis of science and religion. Moreover, there were others who, like him, combined this interest with a preoccupation with Aryans, racism, historical cycles of repetition, and "theosophy." Although I do not want to suggest that their notions of theosophy were identical, I nevertheless find it useful to compare Jackson's work with that of Helena Petrovna Blavatsky (1877, 1888) and Friedrich Max Müller (1893a). This comparison is especially interesting because Madame Blavatsky unambiguously posited herself on the side of the occult, while Max Müller, an established if somewhat marginal scientist, turned as unambiguously against it.

The first point of note in this comparison is that both Blavatsky and Müller devised their respective notions of theosophy at a time when the social struggle between plebeian and professional science had been decided by the slow but increasingly undisputed assumption of hegemony by the latter. After 1870, the democratic ideology of the "humble and self-taught" scientist, whose heroes were Herschel, Priestley and Faraday, was in retreat (Shapin & Thackray 1974:6, 11). It seems no coincidence that Blavatsky formulated "Theosophy" as a "third way" between science and religion in this period, and fashioned herself into the prototype of its intellectual authority, the Western guru (Washington 1993). This can be compared to Max Müller's attempt to establish "theosophy" as a specifically "psychological" form of knowledge and authority in a wholly novel field: the "science of religion." Both Blavatsky and Müller, though, accepted that secular and materialist science had become as established and hegemonic as the Christian religion, and both sought out or invented a field for their own "spiritual" knowledge that was relatively autonomous from either science or religion.

But if both of these theosophists were looking for a new nest in which to nurse their spirituality to maturity, their strategies were opposed to each other. Blavatsky came from plebeian spiritualism: self-taught, she had moved much in radical North American spiritualist circles, and rarely missed a chance to poke at the authority of the living symbols of professionalized science, John Tyndall and Thomas Huxley. Blavatsky even used Müller against Tyndall (1877:I, 4), but her appreciation of Müller as "Mahatma" was not reciprocated, which roused her suspicions (F. M. Müller 1893b:769). Max Müller, on the contrary, was an established scientist, but one whose spiritual point of view derived not from a Nonconformist background (as was the case with many friends of Huxley and Tyndall), but from Broad Church deism, a position closely allied to the point of view of hereditary nobility like the duke of Argyll (Gillespie 1977). Müller thus saw, in his science of religion, a way to "discover the strong rock on which the Christian as well as every other religion must be founded" (F. M. Müller 1893a:24). Müller had taken an amused interest in Blavatsky in 1879 (Müller & Müller 1902:II, 5), urged his Indian friends to make use of the Theosophical Publication Fund to print sacred Indian texts in 1888 (II, 233), and seems to have had a pleasant relationship with Henry Olcott, who co-founded the Theosophical Society with Blavatsky (II, 234). But after Blavatsky's death, when Müller himself wanted to employ the notion of theosophy in a nonoccultist way (F. M. Müller 1893a), he wrote a scathing review of Theosophy in *The Nineteenth Century*, vehemently criticizing the idea of "esoteric" Brahmanism and Buddhism, saying there was nothing secret about those religions and that was as it should be (F. M. Müller 1893b, 1893c; Müller & Müller 1902:II, 297–98; Sinnett 1893).

Despite Müller's affinity with the political and religious, rather than the scientific, "aristocracy," the dispute shows many markers of a debate between autodidact and plebeian science *versus* establishment intellectual pursuits. Compared, however, to Jackson's times there is a significant difference: the invocation of *secrecy*. Müller stressed an authority based on the ordinary training of an orientalist: access to and knowledge of ancient texts, language learning, and translating skills (F. M. Müller 1893b:767). Sinnett's critique of Müller was based on fairly typical plebeian strategies: personal experience in India and a critique of the excessive reliance on textual knowledge (like

Jackson's critique, directed at orientalists as well as Christian thinkers—and
Müller was both; Sinnett 1893:1020, 1022). But Müller emphasized the necessity of openness in inquiry (Müller & Müller 1902:II, 295), while Sinnett
insisted on a secret message in Brahminical and Buddhist texts that such orientalist expertise could never fathom (Sinnett 1893:1022). This emphasis on
secrecy was a novel strategy of plebeian intellectuals, and one that, from Blavatsky's grand synthesis of 1877 onward, allied it far more tightly with the
Western occult tradition (see Luhrmann 1989b). Secrecy of procedure had
been stressed consistently in the critique of the obscurantism and fraudu-
lence of spiritualist mediums by established scientists, for whom secrecy itself
spelled unmerited and uncontrollable power (while this language was itself, of
course, inherited from the Protestant disgust with "Popery" and its perceived
ritual obscurantism [cf. Tylor 1873:I, 139]). John Jackson had a comparable
"anti-occult" stance, arguing that "esoteric" phreno-mesmerist knowledge
meant knowledge that was not secret, but not yet assimilated by established
science, which signified a regrettable divergence in audience (Jackson 1866b:
308; see also 1867a, 1868a). But Helena Blavatsky turned secrecy into the
mark of superiority of Theosophy over established science. By adopting the
banner of "occultism"—a term coined by Theosophists in the late 1870s or
early 1880s (Braude 1989:178; Oxford English Dictionary)—she gave up the
hope of being admitted into equal discussion with established science and
assumed a superior secret insight instead.

   As a result, the three seem radically opposed, Jackson exemplifying the
plebeian scientist who hoped to convince the scientific establishment of the
value of his divination of the occult qualities of human races and divine character, while Müller and Blavatsky belong to the opposite sides of a divide
between established and occult science that emerged after Jackson's plebeian
hopes had been given up. Yet all three employ a favored race as carrier of
human destiny: Müller, like Jackson, emphasizing a felicitous merger between Aryan and Semite while the former remains in the ascendant (F. M.
Müller 1893a:ix–x), while Blavatsky—who did not like Christianity that
much—adopted a more radical position by downplaying the role of the Semite and finding the "cradle" of both the "secret doctrine" and "the race" in
India (1877:I, 575ff.). Moreover, all three used the term "theosophy" to indicate a foundational merger of science and religion which professed the Neo-
platonic idea that the ideal forged the material (Blavatsky 1877:I, xi; F. M.
Müller 1893a:x, 424ff.), thus referring back to the foundation of most European occult and mystical traditions. And finally, this respect for the achievements of a past ideal led all three to question the exclusive validity of a linear
conception of time. Although Jackson, Müller, and Blavatsky all endorsed
linear progression, they did so with the addition of some kind of tempo-

ral repetition: Jackson's cycles and epicycles, Müller's Christian bias toward degenerationism and repetition of natural revelation (Schrempp 1983:97; Stocking 1987:61), and Blavatsky's cycles of anthropogenesis (1888:II). As another leader of Theosophy, Annie Besant, later would make clear, such repetition, correspondence, or "reflexion" is necessary for divination, in order to prophesy "the coming race" (Besant 1909:103ff.).

The divinations of the theosophies of all three are, in the end, fully grounded in the repetition of racial causality. Jackson saw the future as determined by the repeated impact of the "intellectual" race of Caucasians on human growth, although his scheme was ambiguous as to the role played by either Aryans or Semites within that broader categorization, and this ambiguity was itself caused by the fact that Aryans were a repetition of Turanian or Mongol, and Semites of Negroid "root men," in Caucasian form. This idea of "root men" is close to Blavatsky's notion of "root races" succeeding each other (Besant 1909:210; Blavatsky 1888:II; Leopold 1974:586–87), with each race achieving a higher level of existence according to the cosmic master plan. With Müller, the idea of a succession of races according to the Divine Idea is absent, but he argued that history can only be the unfolding of a "Divine Drama" or "plot" revealing the realization of a rational purpose (F. M. Müller 1893a:vi). Thus even Müller, who, when faced with the claims of the Theosophists, took so much trouble to deny that there could be a secret or allegorical reading of the Hindu *Sastras*, ultimately provided the pretext to turn them into an allegory of race and reason that identified an occult quality of the perceptible world: the Logos as the "exclusively Aryan life-blood" of both Christianity and the Vedas (x).

Conclusion: Zadig's Method and the Dis-covery of Race

The road back to science from allegories of race and reason, and the systems of correspondences of prophecy and divination, may well seem long. Yet science and prophecy are connected by the practice of conjecture. In 1880, Thomas Huxley told the Working Men's College of Great Ormond Street, London, that conjecture was a legitimate function of science. Naming the method after Voltaire's Babylonian sage Zadig, who decoded minute signs of footprints to identify the fugitive pets of King Moabdar, Huxley indicated that sciences like archeology, geology, physical astronomy, and paleontology employed similar "retrospective prophecies," based on the commonplace assumption that one may conclude from an effect the preexistence of a cause competent to produce it (1881:134). In the course of outlining the method of paleontology, he also referred to contemporary occult practitioners. He found it rather surprising, that among the people from whom the circle-squarers, perpetual-motioners, flat-earth men and the like are recruited, to say nothing of table-turners and spirit-rappers, somebody has not perceived the easy avenue to nonsensical notoriety open to any one who will take up the good old doctrine, that fossils are all *lusus naturae*.[9] The position would be impregnable, inasmuch as it is quite impossible to prove the contrary. (Huxley 1881:138)

Consequently, it may be even more surprising to us that Huxley, after showing how reasonable *both* scientists and occult practitioners were in using the conjectural method, nevertheless portrayed it as the way in which future Zadigs were to oust the Babylonian Magi from the field of knowledge (1881: 148). As Carlo Ginzburg has argued, conjecture—a hunch based on certain correspondences between effects that lead the observer to hypothesize their imponderable, occulted cause—departs from a "low intuition" rooted in the senses, much more accessible and democratic than any form of "superior" knowledge of an elite (1983:110). Conjecture's strengths and weaknesses are therefore characteristic of *both* science *and* magic, and it does not seem appropriate to presume, as Huxley did, that a development toward more science and less magic will result from its application.

The hunches of conjecture, of course, can be disciplined, and this is what Huxley meant when he sternly admonished his listeners to follow the generalizations about structure of zoological morphology and not to be distracted by physiology's notion of functions (1881:145–46). But as we have seen, these framing disciplines, which apart from theory could also include clinical nominalism or medical statistics (Foucault 1963), could be questioned by plebeian scientists like Jackson without any major modification in the operation of the conjectural method as such. Conjecture has no independent testing possibilities except some as yet unknown confirmation in the future. This goes against Huxley's idea that Zadig's method is only retrospective (133), and Huxley thus refutes himself by calling in the help of the astronomer's "prospective prophecies" later on (137). But the problem lies deeper than that: the conjectural method defines certain occult qualities as causes, which, *because* they are occult and imponderable, are impossible to refute by subsequent testings. Huxley can claim as little right to an "objective" scientific use of conjecture as his "table-turners and spirit-rappers."

One might easily object here that statistics provided a way to discipline the hunches of conjecture so that reasonable conclusions about, for instance, a pattern of symptoms belonging to a conjectured disease could be drawn. This is true enough, although it should be kept in mind that a "reasonable" conclusion is still far from a "verified" one and that much medical knowl-

---

9. "Freaks of nature," that is, simulations of forms of animal and vegetable life caused by something else such as divine or demonic intervention.

edge is still based on conjecture (even if statistically confirmed). More important for our purposes, however, is that this points us toward the history of
the assumptions of scientific authority that are behind the designation of an
intellectual practice as "pseudo-scientific." Statistics was a practice of qualitative taxonomy, executed in circumstances of extending social control in
both the colonies as well as internally, before it became a quantitative scientific discipline in its own right (Hacking 1990; Pels 1999). In fact, Francis
Galton's career testifies to this, since his statistical discoveries were all set in a
larger project of proving—and eugenetically breeding—the superiority of his
own upper-middle-class intellectual aristocracy (Cowan 1977:191). Statistics' later career as a powerful quantitative language has eclipsed the extent
to which its early-nineteenth-century version used to be based on ethnography, that is, on conjectures about human customs and traits that could serve
to identify "types" of cultural difference—race, caste, tribe, and, especially,
lower-class character (Asad 1993; Pels 1999).

One unquestioned assumption of authority behind the qualification of certain nineteenth-century intellectual practices as "pseudo-scientific," therefore, is the later career of statistics—an anachronistic assumption, for Jackson's nonstatistical universe of racial types was something he shared with
his contemporaries, to some extent even Galton. Moreover, the erasure of
racism from mid-Victorian anthropology by many twentieth-century disciplinary historians may, after World War II, have been caused by embarrass-
ment about the Holocaust (Poliakov 1971) or a refusal to engage directly with
the colonial color bar (see Stoler 1995:23). In any case, a utilitarian genealogy
of "social" anthropology, jumping from Scottish Enlightenment philosophers
through James Mill to Henry Maine, has been devised that skirts most historical points at which one might have to consider the conclusion that British
ethnology and anthropology emerged as racist science (Lorimer 1988; Stocking 1968:42; Weber 1974).[10] This may partly be explained by the fact that the
reputation of the British founder of racist ethnology, James Cowles Prichard,
had gone into decline by 1900 (Stocking 1973:xii), but it is clearly not suffi-
cient, given that founding fathers of British anthropology like Galton, Haddon, and Rivers—people who, apart from being occupied with eugenics and
racial classification, were also crucial in formulating anthropological methods—are still not given the position in anthropology's history that is occupied
by Tylor, Frazer, Radcliffe-Brown, and Malinowski.

Contrary to this still prevalent image of anthropological history, I have
tried to show that John Jackson attunes us to an intellectual context differ-

---

10. A Dutch colleague of mine who presented a paper on racial anthropology in the early
nineteenth century during a recent conference in Oxford was appalled at the vehemence with
which British social anthropologists denied this part of their legacy.

ent from the "social" anthropological one; one in which race was, to both plebeian and "aristocratic" scientists, the most frequent cause conjectured. (Even Tylor, despite his insistence on the homogeneity of mankind, explained cultural change mostly by the influence of superior races on inferior ones, thus accommodating to polygenism[1873:I, 7, 48ff; Stocking 1987:270].) Jackson exemplifies a period in which "race" did not just signify observable characteristics, but also, and more important, human types as well as spiritual essences. Being based on conjecture, "race" may not have been visible as cause (for its origins lay far back in the past) but it was at least intellectually accessible to both "low intuition" as well as "superior knowledge" (to use Ginzburg's words). The ingredients of what was later classified as "occult science" or "occultism" occupied a similar position in intellectual life: like racism, they were situated at the crossroads of plebeian and "aristocratic" interests, and also promised to conjecture spiritual essences from minute visible effects by means that did not lend themselves to elite appropriation through method, scientific institutionalization, or technical complication. Although this idea needs further research, I find it useful to think of race and the occult as parallel elements in the history of anthropology: both are, in a sense, "excluded ancestors." More important, however, both forms of knowledge have now become "popular" (rather than plebeian), that is, seemingly divorced from most criteria of established scientific authority. Nevertheless, both the occult (in the shape of, for instance, Carlos Castaneda and other sorcerers' apprentices) and race (in the form of, for instance, a book like *The Bell Curve*) tend to return to anthropological consciousness time and again, serving as reminders that they are an inalienable part of anthropology's contribution to modernity.

References Cited

Annan, N. G. 1955. The intellectual aristocracy. *Studies in social history*, ed. J. H. Plumb, 243–87. London.

Anonymous. 1863. Review of *Ethnology and phrenology as an aid to the historian*. *Anthropological Review* 1:118–29.

Asad, T. 1993. Ethnographic representation, statistics, and modern power. *Social Research* 61:55–88.

Barrow, L. 1986. *Independent spirits: Spiritualism and English plebeians, 1850–1910*. London.

Besant, A. 1909. *The changing world and lectures to theosophical students*. London.

Biddis, M. D., ed. 1979. *Images of race*. Leicester, England.

Blavatsky, H. P. 1877. *Isis unveiled: A master-key to the mysteries of ancient and modern science and theology*. 2 vols. Wheaton, Ill. (1972).

Blavatsky, H. P. 1888. *The secret doctrine*. 2 vols. Pasadena, Calif. (1997).

Borges, J. L. 1980. La cábala. In *Siete noches*, 123–39. Mexico City.

Braude, A. 1989. *Radical spirits: Spiritualism and women's rights in nineteenth-century America.* Boston.

Brodie, F. M. 1967. *The devil drives: A life of Sir Richard Burton.* Harmondsworth, England.

Castaneda, C. 1968. *The teachings of Don Juan.* New York.

Castaneda, C. 1971. *A separate reality.* New York.

Clark, S. 1984. The scientific status of demonology. In *Occult and scientific mentalities in the Renaissance,* ed. B. Vickers, 351–74. Cambridge.

Clifford, J. 1981. On ethnographic surrealism. *Comparative Studies of Society and History* 23:539–64.

Combe, A. 1825. Dr. Prichard and phrenology. *Phrenological Journal* 2:47–55.

Combe, A. 1834. Cyclopeadia of Practical Medicine—Dr. Prichard and Phrenology. *Phrenological Journal* 7:649–51.

Combe, A. 1838. Remarks on Dr. Prichard's third attack on phrenology. *Phrenological Journal* 11:345–58.

Combe, G. 1828. *The constitution of man.* Edinburgh.

Cooter, R. 1978. *The cultural meaning of popular science: Phrenology and the organization of consent in nineteenth-century Britain.* Cambridge.

Cooter, R. 1989. *Phrenology in the British Isles: An annotated, historical bibliography and index.* Metuchen, N.J., and London.

Cowan, R. S. 1977. Nature and nurture: The interplay of biology and politics in the work of Francis Galton. In *Studies in the History of Biology,* vol. 1, ed. W. C. Coleman & C. Limoges, 133–208. Baltimore, Md.

Curtin, P. 1964. *The image of Africa.* 2 vols. Madison, Wis.

Darnton, R. 1968. *Mesmerism and the end of the Enlightenment in France.* Cambridge, Mass.

De Giustino, D. 1975. *Conquest of mind: Phrenology and Victorian social thought.* London.

Dirks, N. B. 1993. Colonial histories and native informants: Biography of an archive. In *Orientalism and the postcolonial predicament,* ed. C. Breckenridge & P. van der Veer, 279–313. Philadelphia.

Dorson, R. M. 1968. *The British folklorists: A history.* London.

Evans-Wentz, E. 1911. *The fairy-faith in Celtic countries.* Oxford.

Fabian, J. 1983. *Time and the other: How anthropology makes its object.* New York.

Fancher, R. E. 1983. Francis Galton's African ethnography and its role in the development of his psychology. *British Journal of Historical Studies* 16:67–79.

Flaherty, G. 1992. *Shamanism and the eighteenth century.* Princeton, N.J.

Forrest, D. W. 1974. *Francis Galton: The life and work of a Victorian genius.* London.

Foucault, M. 1963. *Naissance de la clinique: Une archéologie du regard medical.* Paris.

Gillespie, N. C. 1977. The duke of Argyll, evolutionary anthropology, and the art of scientific controversy. *Isis* 68:40–54.

Ginzburg, C. 1983. Clues: Morelli, Freud, and Sherlock Holmes. In *The sign of three: Dupin, Holmes, Peirce,* ed. U. Eco & T. Sebeok, 81–118. Bloomington, Ind.

Gould, W. 1990. Frazer, Yeats, and the reconsecration of folklore. In *Sir James Frazer and the literary imagination: Essays in affinity and influence,* ed. R. Fraser, 121–53. Basingstoke and London.

Grant, K. 1972. *The magical revival*. London.

Hacking, I. 1990. *The taming of chance*. Cambridge.

Haddon, A. C. 1934. *History of anthropology*. London.

Hunt, J. 1867. President's address. *Journal of the Anthropological Society of London* 5: xliv–lxx.

Hutchinson, K. 1982. What happened to occult qualities in the scientific revolution? *Isis* 73:233–53.

Huxley, T. H. 1860. A lobster; or, the study of zoology. In *Man's place in nature and other essays*, 352–72. London (1906).

Huxley, T. H. 1881. On the method of Zadig: Retrospective prophecy as a function of science. In *Science and culture and other essays*, 128–48. London.

Jackson, E. B. 1875. Preface. In J. W. Jackson 1875:v–xv.

Jackson, J. W. 1851. *Lectures on mesmerism*. Dublin.

Jackson, J. W. 1854. Table-movings, rappings, and spiritual manifestations. *The Zoist* 11:412–29, 12:1–17.

Jackson, J. W. 1858. *Mesmerism in connection with popular superstitions*. London.

Jackson, J. W. 1859. *Ecstatics of genius*. London and Edinburgh.

Jackson, J. W. 1863. *Ethnology and phrenology as an aid to the historian*. London.

Jackson, J. W. 1864. Ethnology and phrenology as an aid to the biographer. *Anthropological Review* 2:126–41.

Jackson, J. W. 1865. Race in history. *Anthropological Review* 3:233–48.

Jackson, J. W. 1866a. Race in legislation and political economy. *Anthropological Review* 4:113–35.

Jackson, J. W. 1866b. Race in religion. *Anthropological Review* 4:289–320.

Jackson, J. W. 1867a. On the value of phrenology in anthropological investigations. *Anthropological Review* 5:71–78.

Jackson, J. W. 1867b. The theory of development, and its bearing on science and religion. *Anthropological Review* 5:257–76.

Jackson, J. W. 1868a. Address to Edinburgh Phrenological Association, in Physio-anthropology in Edinburgh. *Anthropological Review* 6:64–68.

Jackson, J. W. 1868b. Iran and Turan. *Anthropological Review* 6:121–37, 286–301.

Jackson, J. W. 1869a. The race question in Ireland. *Anthropological Review* 7:54–76.

Jackson, J. W. 1869b. Inaugural address to the Psychological Association of Glasgow. *Anthropological Review* 7:259–68.

Jackson, J. W. 1869c. The Aryan and the Semite. *Anthropological Review* 7:333–65.

Jackson, J. W. 1872. On the racial aspects of the Franco-Prussian war. *Journal of the Anthropological Institute* 1:30–43.

Jackson, J. W. 1875. *Man contemplated physically, morally, intellectually and spiritually*. London.

Kaplan, F. 1975. *Dickens and mesmerism: The hidden springs of fiction*. Princeton, N.J.

Kuklick, H. 1998. Speaking with the dead. Review essay. *Isis* 89:103–11.

Lang, A. 1895. Protest of a psycho-folklorist. *Folk-Lore* 6:236–48.

Leahey, T. H., & G. E. Leahey. 1983. *Psychology's occult doubles: Psychology and the problem of pseudoscience*. Chicago.

Leopold, J. 1974. British applications of the Aryan theory of race to India, 1850–1870. *English Historical Review* 89:578–603.

Lorimer, D. 1988. Theoretical racism in late Victorian anthropology, 1870–1900. *Victorian Studies* 31:405–30.

Ludden, D. 1993. Orientalist empiricism. In *Orientalism and the postcolonial predicament*, ed. C. Breckenridge & P. van der Veer, 250–78. Philadelphia.

Luhrmann, T. 1989a. *Persuasions of the witch's craft: Ritual magic in contemporary England*. London.

Luhrmann, T. 1989b. The magic of secrecy. *Ethos* 17:131–65.

Marty, M. 1970. The occult establishment. *Social Research* 37:212–30.

Mauskopf, S., & M. R. McVaugh, eds. 1980. *The elusive science: Origins of experimental psychical research*. Baltimore, Md., and London.

Mill, J. 1818. *The history of British India*, 5th enl. ed. by H. H. Wilson. London (1858).

Müller, F. Max. 1854. Letter on the Turanian languages. *Outlines of the philosophy of universal history, applied to language and religion*. 2 vols. London.

Müller, F. Max. 1893a. *Theosophy or psychological religion*. London.

Müller, F. Max. 1893b. Esoteric Buddhism. *The Nineteenth Century* 33:767–88.

Müller, F. Max. 1893c. Esoteric Buddhism, a rejoinder. *The Nineteenth Century* 34:296–303.

Müller, F. Max & G. A. Müller. 1902. *The life and letters of the right honourable Friedrich Max Müller*. 2 vols. London.

Owen, A. 1989. *The darkened room: Women, power and spiritualism in late Victorian England*. London.

Pels, P. 1995. Spiritual facts and super-visions: The "conversion" of Alfred Russel Wallace. *Etnofoor* 8(2):69–91.

Pels, P. 1999. The rise and fall of the Indian aborigines: Orientalism, Anglicism, and the making of an ethnology of India. In *Colonial subjects: Essays in the practical history of anthropology*, ed. P. Pels & O. Salemink, 82–116. Ann Arbor, Mich.

Pels, P., & O. Salemink. 1994. Introduction: Five theses on ethnography as colonial practice. *History and Anthropology* 8:1–34.

Peskowitz, M. 1998. Religion posed as a racial category: A reading of Emile Burnouf, Adolph Moses, and Eliza Sunderland. In *Religion in the making: The emergence of the sciences of religion*, ed. A. L. Molendijk & P. Pels, 231–51. Leiden, The Netherlands.

Poliakov, L. 1971. *The Aryan myth: A history of racist and nationalist ideas in Europe*. London.

Prideaux, Th. S. 1847. The British Association and cerebral physiology, letter to the editor. *The Zoist* 6:473–80.

Rainger, R. 1978. Race, politics, and science: The Anthropological Society of London in the 1860s. *Victorian Studies* 22:51–70.

Rainger, R. 1980. Philanthropy and science in the 1830s: The British and Foreign Aborigines' Protection Society. *Man* 15:702–17.

Rivers, W. H. R. 1912. Obituary of Andrew Lang. *Folk-Lore* 23:369–371.

Salmasi, A., & A. N. Nicolaides, eds. 1991. *Occult atherosclerotic disease: Diagnosis, assessment, and management*. Dordrecht, The Netherlands.

Schrempp, G. 1983. The re-education of Friedrich Max Müller: Intellectual appropriation and epistemological antinomy in mid-Victorian evolutionary thought. *Man* 18:90–110.

Shapin, S. 1979. Homo Phrenologicus: Anthropological perspectives on an historical problem. In *Natural Order*, ed. B. Barnes & S. Shapin, 41–71. Beverly Hills, Calif., and London.

Shapin, S., & A. Thackray. 1974. Prosopography as a research tool in history of science: The British scientific community, 1700–1900. *History of Science* 12:1–28.

Sinnett, A. P. 1893. Esoteric Buddhism. *The Nineteenth Century* 33:1015–27.

Stocking, G. W., Jr. 1968. *Race, culture, and evolution: Essays in the history of anthropology* (Phoenix edition). Chicago and London (1982).

Stocking, G. W., Jr. 1971. Animism in theory and in practice: E. B. Tylor's unpublished "Notes on Spiritualism." *Man* 6:88–104.

Stocking, G. W., Jr. 1973. From chronology to ethnology: James Cowles Prichard and British Anthropology, 1800–1850. In *Researches into the physical history of man*, J. C. Prichard, ix–lxxv. Chicago and London.

Stocking, G. W., Jr. 1987. *Victorian anthropology*. New York.

Stoler, A. L. 1995. *Race and the education of desire: Foucault's* History of Sexuality *and the colonial order of things*. Durham, N.C.

Stoller, P., & C. Olkes. 1987. *In sorcery's shadow: A memoir of apprenticeship among the Songhay of Niger*. Chicago.

Tiryakian, E. A. 1973. Toward the sociology of esoteric culture. *American Journal of Sociology* 78:491–512.

Truzzi, M. 1972. The occult revival as popular culture: Some random observations on the old and the nouveau witch. *Sociological Quarterly* 13:16–36.

Turner, E. (with W. Blodgett, S. Kahona, & F. Benwa). 1992. *Experiencing ritual: A new interpretation of African healing*. Philadelphia.

Tylor, E. B. 1873. *Primitive culture*, 2d ed. 2 vols. London.

Van Binsbergen, W. 1991. Becoming a Sangoma: Religious anthropological fieldwork in Francistown, Botswana. *Journal of Religion in Africa* 21:309–44.

Van Dijk, R., & P. Pels. 1996. Contested authorities and the politics of perception: Deconstructing the study of religion in Africa. In *Postcolonial identities in Africa*, ed. R. P. Werbner & T. O. Ranger, 245–70. London.

Waite, A. E. 1891. *The occult sciences*. London.

Washington, P. 1993. *Madame Blavatsky's baboon: Theosophy and the emergence of the western guru*. London.

Webb, J. 1974. *The occult underground*. La Salle, Ill.

Webb, J. 1976. *The occult establishment*. La Salle, Ill.

Weber, G. 1974. Science and society in nineteenth century anthropology. *History of Science* 12:260–83.

RESEARCH, REFORM, AND RACIAL UPLIFT

The Mission of the
Hampton Folk-Lore Society, 1893–1899

LEE D. BAKER

Playing Dead Twice in the Road
(version d)

Once a fox heard a rabbit had outwitted a wolf. He decided not to be friends to her any more. But Mis' Rabbit came and begged his pardon, and it was granted. Mr. Fox offered to go hunting with Mis' Rabbit; but the rabbit was lazy and played off sick, and staid at Mr. Fox's house till he was very near ready to come back. Then she ran way down the road, and curled up and played off dead. Brer Fox came 'long and looked at her; but he thought probably she had been dead too long, so he passed on. As soon as Brer Fox was out of sight, Mis' Rabbit jumped up and ran through the field and got ahead of him, and laid down again to fake Mr. Fox. This time he looked at her and looked into his bag. His bag was large enough to accommodate one or two more, so he put Mis' Rabbit in, and put his bag in the grass, and went back to get the other rabbit. Before he was around the corner Mis' Rabbit jumped up and ran home with Mr. Fox's game. So Mr. Fox found no game when he returned.

But one day Mis' Rabbit was walking along, and she asked Mr. Fox what he killed. He said he killed a lot of game, but he had learned a headful of Har'sense. She laughed and went on.

(Written by Andrew W. C. Bassette, reprinted in Waters 1983:398)

Lee D. Baker is Associate Professor of Cultural Anthropology at Duke University. He has written extensively on the history of anthropology, and is the author of *From Savage to Negro: Anthropology and the Construction of Race, 1896–1954* (University of California Press). He is currently working on a new book tentatively titled *Racial Politics of Culture: Anthropology and the Negro Problem*.

This folktale, with its distinctive pan-African trickster motif, was recorded by a member of the Hampton Folk-Lore Society (HFS), founded in 1893 by Alice M. Bacon. The educators and graduates of Hampton Normal and Agricultural Institute formed the society to record cultural practices of rural blacks to demonstrate that industrial education succeeded in fostering the so-called Christian civilization of its graduates—in part by using folklore to evaluate how much African heritage remained to be rooted out. "Playing Dead Twice in the Road" was one of hundreds of tales, jokes, and conundrums Bacon organized into the society's many notebooks of fieldwork during the last decade of the nineteenth century.

Bassette's tale was eventually published in 1922 in an article in the *Journal of American Folk-Lore* titled "Folk-Lore From Elizabeth City County, Virginia." Although Bacon had died in 1918, the authors of the 1922 article were noted as "A. M. Bacon and E. C. Parsons," and it was the last article in an issue devoted exclusively to Negro folklore.[1] In her preface, Parsons wrote that "two decades ago or more, Miss A. M. Bacon conducted a folk-lore society in Hampton Institute. Some of the material recorded was published in 'The Southern Workman'. Through the kindness of Miss Herron of the Institute the unpublished material was given to me to edit, and appears in the following" (Bacon & Parsons 1922:251). The following 77 pages of that article included the remaining unpublished notebooks of the HFS.[2]

Leonora Herron, librarian at the Hampton Institute, had been a member of the HFS, which from its inception to its end in 1899 had found in the American Folk-Lore Society (AFLS) its staunchest supporter. Herron thus had a personal connection with the society and its journal, and presumably that is why she turned over an old notebook of Negro folklore to a rich white lady who conducted ethnographic fieldwork in Zuñi (Waters 1983:3). Among her many initiatives, Elsie Clews Parsons underwrote, organized, and guest-edited, under *Journal of American Folk-Lore* editor Franz Boas, 14 single-theme issues on African and African American folk traditions between 1917 and 1937 (Deacon 1997:173, 282–83).

Along with nearly two dozen other articles on African folklore from the

1. Reproducing the belief that African folklore diffused across the diaspora north and west, the first two short collections came from south-central Cameroon and Malawi. Moving north and west, the next collection was from Nigeria, followed by a collection of "Negro Spirituals From the Far South," and finally one from the border state of Virginia. This article concluded with a collection of "Irish Stories" told by Negroes, which supposedly demonstrated "how hospitable Negro folk-lore is to new comers" (Bacon & Parsons 1922:251).

2. The story I used as an epigraph (originally published in Bacon & Parsons 1922:251) was written by Andrew W. C. Bassette, who probably recorded it as a class project during his sophomore year in 1899, the last year the society was functioning. According to Waters (1983:105), Bassette was a member of the class of 1903.

diaspora, Bacon and Parsons' 1922 article was cited in Alain Locke's 1925 *New Negro* (1925:444). Yet in that volume, such folklore was not, as it were, the same rabbit as the one collected by the HFS—for the purpose of Locke and his associates was to demonstrate that New Negro intellectuals were succeeding in empowering new understandings of black culture, in part by using folklore to embrace their African heritage. Thus the HFS rationale for collecting folklore in the 1890s was virtually the opposite of the New Negro rationale in the 1920s. The divergent ways these two groups of black and white intellectuals interpreted Negro folklore during two very different historic periods suggests that anthropology in the United States routinely played a part in a complex racial politics of culture.[3]

A Racial Project for Reconstruction

One must turn to the founder of the Hampton Institute, General Samuel Chapman Armstrong, to begin to understand the complicated racial project articulated at Hampton during the 1890s. It was in the Sandwich, or Hawaiian, Islands of the 1840s that Armstrong developed his philosophy of industrial education and used folklore as a yardstick to measure civilization.

The American Board of Commissioners for Foreign Missions was founded in 1810 and began its campaign in Hawaii in 1819. In 1831, General Armstrong's father, Dr. Richard Armstrong, a recent graduate of the Princeton Theological Seminary, married Clarissa Chapman, a recent graduate of Westfield Normal School and a teacher at the Pestalozzian Infant School in Brooklyn, New York. He decided to be a missionary in the Pacific and convinced his bride to do the same. The newlyweds took an arduous voyage to Honolulu, where they were stationed for less than a year before they assumed a difficult mission in the Marquessas Islands, which they soon abandoned. The Missionary Board then found a suitable mission for the Armstrongs and their growing family on the island of Maui, where they stayed for seven years until Dr. Armstrong was appointed to the First Native Church in Honolulu. During his years on Maui, Armstrong observed that the natives were in need of "steady industrial occupation."[4] Thus, as he ministered to the health of the

3. The young Franz Boas, Frederick Ward Putnam, William Wells Newell, and Daniel G. Brinton were all involved in one way or another with the HFS, which suggests that African American culture was a marginal but salient topic of inquiry during the 1890s—the formative period of academic anthropology in the United States.

4. He succeeded in having the indigenous Hawaiians build much of the island's infrastructure, although they probably engaged in various forms of resistance, as Mrs. Armstrong suggests: "The natives were awkward and very destructive, breaking their tools and ox-carts and always relying upon their 'kumu' to repair them" (M. F. Armstrong 1887:21).

populace, he also convinced the Hawaiians to build schools, churches, sugar plantations, and saw mills.

Dr. Armstrong quickly rose through the ranks of the missionary and government agencies. Closely associated with other powerful Protestant missionaries like Richard Williams and Gerritt P. Judd, he became the Islands' minister of education, a member of the House of Nobles, a member of the King's Privy Council, and a close advisor (both on spiritual and policy matters) to King Kamehameha III (Lindsey 1995:1–2; Talbot 1904:3–37; S. C. Armstrong 1909:1–4; *The Friend* 1860:76–77). Armstrong was perhaps best known for his creation and administration of the many missionary and government schools bearing his philosophy of moral and industrial education, which above all aimed to civilize the natives. He outlined his teaching philosophy in a letter responding to his appointment by King Kamehameha III as Minister of Public Education in 1847.

> No sphere of labor sir, would be more congenial to my feelings, than the department of public instruction, and I may add, no branch of the government, seems to me of more vital importance to the welfare, of the Hawaiian race than this. Education, intellectual, moral, and physical, is the great lever by which philanthropists of every land, are seeking to redeem and elevate the mass of people. *Here* it is of peculiar importance, where the glory and safety of the nation must depend in so great a degree upon the proper training of the young. If depopulation here is to be arrested; if the vices which are consuming the natives are to be eradicated; if an indolent and thriftless people are to become industrious and thrifty: if Christian institutions are to be perpetuated, the work must be occomplished [sic] mainly where it has been so prosperously begun, *in the education of the young.* (Quoted in M. F. Armstrong 1887:29–30)

Writing to his daughter in 1844, he explained why the "inhabitants" were in need of this type of education: "Had they skill and industry they might abound in every good thing. . . . But, poor creatures, they will not very soon shake off the low wretched habits of their former state. Their government, until recently, was one of the worst forms of despotism . . . and in those days *a character* was formed which will not soon be entirely reformed. When I look over this valley, I think what a little Yankee skill would do here." (LSCA: RA/CA 10/6/1844). Armstrong even complained that the "king himself is as near to being an animal as man can well be & most of the high chiefs are ignorant, lazy, and stupid." His remedy to help advance what he called "Christian civilization" among these near-animal heathens was to improve "the heart, the head & the body at once." As he surmised, "this is a lazy people & if they are ever to be made industrious the work must begin with the young. So I am making strenuous efforts to have some sort of manual labor connected with every school . . . without industry they cannot be moral" (RAP: RA/RCA 2/18/1844).

The combination of morality, industry, and church was not a novel philosophy of education. Mrs. Armstrong, for example, had been an instructor in a school modeled after the philosophies of Johann Heinrich Pestalozzi, who incorporated similar values in his curriculum. What made Dr. Armstrong so successful as an educator, missionary, and confidante to the king was his intimate knowledge of the traditional language, customs, and folklore of his charges. Using his genuine respect for Hawaiian language and culture, he was an important facilitator of the so-called Great Awakening during which thousands of Hawaiians converted to Christianity by the mid-nineteenth century. Even King Kamehameha IV, who detested the influence of missionaries, noted that Armstrong "was an eloquent preacher in the Hawaiian language" and commented on "his accurate knowledge of the Hawaiian language, and the facility with which he wielded the pen of a translator" (*The Friend* 1860:76; see also M. F. Armstrong 1887:57–58).

Armstrong often used cultural markers to demonstrate how far the Hawaiians had come, suggesting, for example, that the natives "have better clothes than they used to have" and explaining that "we rarely see a native now unclad or even wearing native kapa." But he also used such markers to show how much civilizing work remained to be done, lamenting that the natives "still live in small and filthy grass huts, destitute of every comfort, and herding together often a dozen sleeping on mats in one small house without even a partition, and some of them, as if to make bad worse, keep their dogs and ducks in the house during the night" (M. F. Armstrong 1887:63).

During their final year on Maui in 1839, Mrs. Armstrong gave birth to Samuel Chapman Armstrong, the sixth of their 10 children. Samuel grew up close to his father, and in a memoir titled "From the Beginning," explained how Richard Armstrong's philosophy of education shaped that of Hampton. Comparing the Lahaina-luna Seminary, which taught Greek and Latin, to the Hilo Boarding and Manual Labor School, Armstrong remarked that "as a rule the former turned out more brilliant, the latter less advanced but more solid men. In making the plan of Hampton Institute that of the Hilo School seemed the best to follow. . . . Hence came our policy of teaching only English and the system of industrial training at Hampton. Its graduates are not only to be good teachers but skilled workers, able to build homes and earn a living for themselves and encourage others to do the same" (S. C. Armstrong 1909:4–5).

In 1860 Samuel Armstrong left Hawaii to attend Williams College, where he came under the influence of its president, the philosopher and missionary Mark Hopkins. As the Civil War erupted, he answered Abraham Lincoln's call for Union Army volunteers. Accepting a commission as captain, he recruited and trained Company D of the 125th Regiment of New York. Promoted to major and then to colonel, Armstrong was put in command of the 9th Regiment of U.S. Colored Troops, and in March of 1865 Abraham Lincoln made the 26-year-old Hawaiian citizen a brevet brigadier general.

Although Chapman demonstrated great leadership and courage in battle to preserve the Union, he confessed to his mother that "the Union is to me little or nothing." He explained that he "was a foreigner, a Sandwich Islander, who had no local sympathies." He saw "the great issue to be that of freedom or slavery for 4,000,000 souls" (Talbot 1904:115–18), but as he told his Williams classmate, Archibald Hopkins: "I am sort of [an] abolitionist, but haven't yet learned to love the Negro." His most consistent reason to fight was rooted in his faith that God did not intend for the souls of people to be bought and sold: "I go in, then, for freeing them more on account of their souls than their bodies, I assure you" (Talbot 1904:86). In a less searching letter to Archibald Hopkins, he castigated those who fought for honor or God, saying, "That's all poppy cock." Armstrong provided a set of more quotidian reasons: "I say *strike*, in order that you may get $100 or so per month, see the country, wear soldiers' clothes, save the land from anarchy, rescue the Constitution and punish the rebels—long live the Republic!" (LSCA: SCA/AH 12/8/1862).

As the war ended, he searched for a mission in life, both personal and Christian. As a commander of Negro troops, he had been impressed by "their quick response to good treatment and to discipline" and he was convinced that African Americans yearned for education because he witnessed how his soldiers were "often studying their spelling books under fire" (S. C. Armstrong 1909:6). Immediately after the war, the commissioner of the Freedmen's Bureau, General Oliver Otis Howard, appointed Armstrong as the superintendent for the tidewater area of Virginia; its headquarters was the small town of Hampton. General Armstrong's jurisdiction was populated with a large number of formerly enslaved people, and his area quickly became a bellwether for radical Reconstruction experiments as missionaries, bureau agents, and the new freedmen and women negotiated competing agendas, policies, and plans.

After the war, the American Missionary Association took the lead in establishing schools for African Americans in the South. Armstrong used his access to both government and missionary resources to establish a coed industrial and normal school to train African American elementary school teachers, which soon became independent of both the missionary association and the government. It opened in 1868 with two teachers and 15 pupils but grew quickly. Armstrong often touted his brand of industrial and moral education, known as the Hampton Idea, as "the only way to make them good Christians" (S. C. Armstrong 1909:12). The Hampton Idea found powerful support among philanthropists, missionaries, and the nation's political and industrial leaders. Although interest was generated by Hampton's civilizing mission, white backers were also attracted to its political and economic components which, as they saw it, would foster regional stability by discouraging students from participating in party politics while encouraging the efficient exploitation of their labor (Spivey 1978:22). As George Frederickson explains, Hampton's financial backers "anticipated that blacks would make a more effective contribution to general prosperity and individual white profit making if they were taught useful skills" (Frederickson 1971:216). The method and message Armstrong used to teach African Americans how to become civilized and virtuous was simple and consistent: "Work, work, work" (*Southern Workman*, March 1874:2). The majority of black colleges followed Hampton's model, and when Hampton's own graduate, Booker T. Washington, reproduced Armstrong's model at Tuskegee Institute in the late nineteenth century, it became *the* most influential model for black schools (Fredrickson 1971:216).

Not only did Armstrong create the blueprint of Washington's popular industrial education with its concomitant policies of racial accommodation and cultural assimilation, he also helped to shape the federal government's policies regarding Native American assimilation through education. Between 1878 and 1893, Hampton "experimented" with Indian education, again employing the notion that industrial education helped to civilize the savages (Lindsey 1995; Robinson 1977; Adams 1995:28–59). In 1878, Captain R. H. Pratt, who, after the Civil War, had commanded black troops and Indian scouts on the Great Plains, searched without success for a school to continue the education of a group of Indians under his control. General Armstrong welcomed the opportunity to extend Hampton's civilizing mission to American Indians, and invited Pratt to bring them to Hampton. The experiment was seemingly so successful that President Rutherford B. Hayes announced in his State of the Union address the following year that the Department of Interior would reproduce Armstrong's Hampton Idea for Native Americans.

Initially, Hayes voiced his concerns about hostile Indians, but assured Congress and the nation that the "vast majority of our Indian population have fully justified the expectations of those who believe that by human and peaceful influences the Indian can be led to abandon the habits of savage life and to develop a capacity for useful and civilized occupations." He then extolled the virtues of "the experiment of sending a number of Indian children of both sexes to the Hampton Normal and Agricultural Institute, in Virginia, to receive an elementary English education and practical instruction in farming and other useful industries, [which] has led to results so promising that it was thought expedient to turn over the cavalry barracks at Carlisle in Pennsylvania to the Interior Department for the establishment of an Indian school on a larger scale" (Hayes 1879 [1966]:1390). That year, 1879, Captain Pratt along with some American Indian students from Hampton started the influential

A class in American history, ca. 1891. (Courtesy of Hampton University Archives.)

Carlisle Indian Industrial School. Like Tuskegee and Hampton for Negroes, Hampton and the Carlisle School became defining institutions for education policy to assimilate Indians (see also Adams 1995; Hampton Normal and Agricultural Institute 1893; Makofsky 1989; Robinson 1977).

Armstrong's gospel of industrial education was even spread to Africa. With close ties to the American Missionary Association, Hampton provided many recruits for the Association's work of converting and educating West Africans. In reports published in the *Southern Workman*, Hampton graduates who became missionaries routinely testified that the Hampton Idea in Africa was helping the Lord in the "upbuilding of his kingdom" (see, e.g., White 1878:54; Sharps 1991:121). Mary Francis Armstrong, Samuel Armstrong's wife, explained that the general's unparalleled success in establishing his school stemmed from the fact that he "brought from Hawaii to Virginia an idea, worked out by American brains in the heart of the Pacific, adequate to meet the demands of a race similar in its dawn of civilization to the people among whom this idea had first been successfully tested" (Armstrong & Ludlow 1874:22–23; see also Kaplan 1993:16). General Armstrong deployed a transnational and transracial discourse about civilization, assimilation, Christianity, and industrial education to build an institution that defined dominant approaches to the education of African Americans, Native Americans, and even Africans. And, like his father, General Armstrong realized that understanding the folklore and cultural practices of these peoples would facilitate his civilizing mission.

Bedeviling Christian Civilization

Armstrong explained the role of what he called "comparative ethnology" in an introduction to a series of reports published in the 1878 volume of the *Southern Workman*, which explored Negroes' "firm belief in witchcraft and conjuration" from Virginia to Florida. He compared the way Negroes and Sandwich Islanders practiced the "tangle of superstition, demonology, and fetish worship," which he described as "a combination of Salem and Central Africa." After discussing the parallels between the Hawaiian " 'kahuna' or native witch-doctor" and the Negro conjure doctor, he concluded that both groups had "the same love of the supernatural, and dense ignorance of the laws of living," and that the Negroes thus possessed the "elements which form the soil for a growth of superstition as rank and as fatal as that which is helping to depopulate Hawaii" (S. C. Armstrong 1878:26).

The reports on conjure doctors were intended "to throw light upon the mental condition of the masses of this people, and the kind of work that must be done among them if they are to be raised to civilization or even saved from extinction" (S. C. Armstrong 1878:30). They spawned a flurry of published responses. Orra Langhorne, a regular contributor to the *Southern Workman*, reminded readers that conjure doctors were "evidently a legacy handed down to [American Negroes] from their savage ancestors. I sometimes think such ideas are growing with them, in spite of their chances for education." She used these reports to articulate a common theme sounded during the Reconstruction period, that slavery provided a veneer of civilization that was therapeutic for the Negro but disappeared once slavery ended.

> My husband, who lived in what natives know as "Old Virginia," says there was always a great deal of superstition among the slaves of this section, but it was held in check by their owners, who always forbid the discussion of such subjects, and by the laws which prevented the assembling of negroes in large gatherings, except for religious worship, even that being restricted. Now there is no check of that kind and the belief of the more ignorant colored people in "conjuring, witches, &c," is astonishing. (Langhorne 1878:67)

As if to illustrate Langhorne's contentions, a member of Hampton's junior class offered compelling examples of the good and ill work of conjure doctors, and closed his letter to the editor "by saying that I believe in the conjure Drs. And all this that I have written I can vouch for my self" (quoted in S. C. Armstrong 1878:30). Armstrong's faith in the civilizing mission of Hampton Institute prompted him to comment, "Two years more in the school will change his ideas, it is to be hoped" (ibid.).

Other responses to the reports focused not on the practices described but on the utility of their publication. For example, W. I. Louis, a Hampton alumnus teaching in Spartansburg, South Carolina, was upset with the reports, stating: "I fail to see what is gained by your repeating this dark legend of a by-gone day." He wanted the *Southern Workman* to report "facts that are elevating, facts that will inspire even the humblest." Louis concluded by noting that "our days of childhood are (if not, they should be) fast taking their flight, and the advent of manhood is at hand" (quoted in S. C. Armstrong 1878:35).[5] This letter provoked perhaps the most spirited response from General Armstrong; he described why the *Southern Workman* frequently published missionary accounts and folklore from around the world.

> It is time for every man who loves his people to lay aside sensitive feeling and go to work with all the aid he can get. And the first step of all is to make known the true state of the case. When a general begins a campaign, the first point is to get a true map of the country, and spy out all the enemy's forces and know the strength of every battery. It is not the beauty of his banners and his martial music that will win the victory, but knowledge of the work before him, and hard fighting. . . . let us not be afraid to face our own faults and follies, to drag them into the light where they will show for what they really are. (S. C. Armstrong 1878:35)

Combining espionage with exorcism, folklore, and ethnology became a way of demonstrating how Hampton succeeded at civilizing students, and it also demonstrated the need for continual financial support of this institution that was so committed to uplifting the race. More important, the *Southern Workman* reports of the cultural practices of Native Americans, Hawaiians, and African Americans were used in the service of a complicated racial project that articulated a putatively progressive discourse about an individual's ability to rise to a state of civilization, during a period when many scholars argued that every member of these groups was doomed to eternal savagery.

The graduates and educators of Hampton, Fisk, Howard, and other black schools explicitly used the terms of this discourse in their programs of "racial uplift." These self-described Negro elites most often framed their pejorative descriptions of their less civilized neighbors in terms of class, but the Hampton Folk-Lore Society did so in terms of culture (see Gaines 1996). Virtue, chastity, and cleanliness were key signifiers of civilization that black elites

5. As with many of the letters to the editor in the *Southern Workman*, some are signed, some initialed, and some anonymous. For these letters addressing the papers on conjuring, I note them all under the editorship of Armstrong because he clearly chose which submissions to print and which to respond to.

embraced while chastising vice and sensuality. For example, Booker T. Washington was fond of remarking: "In all my teachings I have watched carefully
the influence of the tooth-brush, and I am convinced that there are few single
agencies of civilization that are more far reaching" (1901:75).

Uncivilized blacks were the ones who believed in conjure doctors, told
the animal stories, sang the work songs, and gyrated their bodies in the ring
shouts and jook joints. They were also the field hands, manual laborers, do-
mestics, and washer women who never had the opportunity to attend one of
the normal schools in which strict discipline and obsession with proper behavior convinced students they had become civilized. And it was the uneducated and less refined souls who were held responsible for the vice, promis-
cuity, and debauchery associated with all black Americans. Moreover, many
Negro elites found the main culprit of their neighbors' cultural degradation
in African cultural patterns. The notion that African culture underpinned
the behavior of uncouth black people was so routine that it provided a useful
shorthand for one Hampton graduate who complained about the rural school
district of his first teaching job. Displeased with all of the "drinking, swear-
ing and fighting," he reported, "when I came here I thought that there was as
much Africa here as I cared to witness" (*Southern Workman* 1876:46; see also
Hunter 1997:175).

During the 1870s and 1880s the boosters of the civilizing project combined ideas from many sources. They employed referents from the Bible that
resonated with the ideas of Adam Smith, Herbert Spencer, Jean Baptiste
Lamarck, Lewis Henry Morgan, and Louis Agassiz to foster the idea that individuals could work hard and attain civilization while unloading the cultural
baggage of African savagery. As General Armstrong explained, however, in
order to civilize the Negroes, reformers had first to "spy out" those African-
isms which bedeviled the civilizing project and debilitated the health and welfare of the poor. His approach influenced Alice Mabel Bacon and, through
her, the HFS.

Theory and Practice of the Hampton Folk-Lore Society

Alice Bacon, born in 1858, was the youngest daughter of Leonard Bacon, an
influential abolitionist, professor at Yale Divinity School, and long-standing
pastor of the First Church of New Haven. Her brother Francis was a professor of surgery at Yale, and married Georgeanna Woolsey, who was the cousin
of Yale's president, Theodore Dwight Woolsey. Georgeanna was the sister of
Jane Stuart Woolsey, who supervised nurses during the Civil War and established training schools for nurses in New York City and New Haven. Jane
was stationed in Virginia during the final campaigns of the Civil War, and

Alice Mabel Bacon (1858–1919), ca. 1893. (Courtesy of Hampton University Archives.)

General Armstrong persuaded her to come to Hampton Institute in 1868 to direct the Girls Industrial Department, where she stayed until 1872. She left Hampton to become the first resident-director of Presbyterian Hospital in New York City. Jane was accompanied by her sister-in-law, Rebecca Bacon, who became Armstrong's assistant principal (Waters 1983:5).

In 1870, just two years after Hampton was underway, Rebecca Bacon brought her youngest sister, Alice Mabel Bacon, for "a year at Hampton . . . among the pleasant, sweet-voiced, kindly faced Negro girls, whom even in her Northern home she had learned to know and trust" (Bacon 1909:75). During that year she earned the nickname "junior professor" because she instructed her peers. She also formed a lifelong commitment to Hampton, vowing to come back and teach at the school (Waters 1983:5). In 1882 her mother passed away, and she immediately applied for a post at Hampton, where she taught for five years. At the invitation of her friend Countess Oyama, she then left Hampton to spend a year in Japan, where she worked to help Westernize the schools for elite Japanese women (Waters 1983:6; Sharps 1991:32). Returning to Hampton in 1889, she worked to establish Hampton's Dixie Hospital to provide health care to the needy in the area and nursing training for students at Hampton Institute. Bacon conducted case studies of individual people in communities in the surrounding Elizabeth City County to assess the need for the hospital, and, in an effort to raise funds for the hospital, she wrote an essay for the *Southern Workman* that included graphic descriptions based on her case studies. Her essay reflects both her missionary sensibility and the type of language that was expected by her audience of philanthropists and "the better class of colored people" who were "anxious to co-operate" in establishing the hospital (Bacon 1890:124).

The essay was published under her occasional column titled "Silhouettes," and it opened by describing "the poorest and most ignorant of the colored people" who lived "in the little slab cabins with their mud chimneys, where father, mother, children of both sexes, and frequently adult lodgers of either sex, are thrown together at all times under all circumstances." She surmised that this "life must be more the life of the savage than that of civilization."

> That the Negroes are by degrees moving upward, that every year more and more of them lift themselves a little above the merely animal life of the roughest plantation hand, is a fact that none but the most pessimistic can doubt, but to those who are working among them the question often arises, what can we do that will help to relieve, on some measure, those who from years or by reason of infirmities can never lift themselves out of the squalor and misery about them? (Bacon 1890:124)

All they needed, she proposed, was basic medical attention and the "healing gift of Christian civilization."

One of the challenges she identified in offering health care was the difficulty of determining who was needy and who was not. According to her, the people seeking aid could "be roughly divided into two classes, those who suffer without complaint, and those who complain without suffering, for these people are like the lower animals in that a small ailment will often produce groans and cries, where a great one will be endured with pathetic dumbness" (Bacon 1890:124). After describing near miraculous recoveries from serious ailments that could have been cured at their outset with basic medical aid, she made her pitch: "This is the work that is already begun, and it is this work that we wish to establish on a permanent foundation, and to increase so that it may include within its scope not only the work in the cabins but also a hospital in which we can nurse the sick who can not be cared for in their own homes, and a training-school in which colored girls can be trained for either missionary or private nursing" (ibid.). She continued conducting interviews and writing case studies, but soon discovered that one of the chief obstacles to delivering medical care and Christian civilization to those she euphemistically called the cabin people was their tenacious belief in conjuring and superstitions. Thus, in her view, sociological and anthropological research ought to be used as an aid in missionary and health work (Waters 1983:36).

By 1893, Bacon's efforts were joined by some Hampton alumni, students, and faculty who began to see the need to salvage the songs, stories, and African survivals that made up Negro folklore. Combining Armstrong's commitment to espionage and exorcism with a desire for historical preservation, Bacon published a call to form the HFS in the form of a circular letter, reprinted in the December 1893 *Southern Workman*.

Dear Friends: The American Negroes are rising so rapidly from the condition of ignorance and poverty in which slavery left them, to a position among the cultivated and civilized people of the earth, that the time seems not far distant when they shall have cast off their past entirely, and stand as an anomaly among civilized races, as a people having no distinct traditions, beliefs or ideas from which a history of their growth may be traced. If within the next few years care is not taken to collect and preserve all traditions and customs peculiar to the Negroes, there will be little to reward the search of the future historian who would trace the history of the African continent through the years of slavery to the position which they will hold a few generations hence. Even now the children are growing up with little knowledge of what their ancestors have thought, or felt, or suffered. The common school system with its teachings is eradicating the old and planting the seeds of the new, and the transition period is likely to be a short one. The old people, however, still have their thoughts on the past, and believe and think and do much as they have for generations. From them and from the younger ones whose thoughts have been moulded by them in regions where the school is, as yet, imperfectly established, much may be gathered that

will, when put together and printed, be of great value as material for history
and ethnology.

But, if this material is to be obtained, it must be gathered soon and by many
intelligent observers stationed in different places. It must be done by observers
who enter into the homes and lives of the more ignorant colored people and
who see in their beliefs and customs no occasion for scorn, or contempt, or
laughter, but only the showing of the first child-like, but still reasoning philosophy of a race. . . . To such observers, every custom, belief or superstition, foolish
and empty to others, will be of value and will be worth careful preservation.
The work cannot be done by white people, much as many of them would enjoy
the opportunity of doing it, but must be done by the intelligent and educated
colored people who are at work all through the South among the more ignorant
of their own race, teaching, preaching, practising medicine, carrying on business of any kind that brings them into close contact with the simple, old-time
ways of their own people. (Bacon 1893:180–81)

Bacon's initial rationale for continued research on the so-called cabin
people was to make missionaries more efficient health care providers, and
she effectively articulated this rationale in her later work (*Southern Workman*
1895, 24:11, 193–94, 24:12, 209–11; Bacon & Herron 1896). But the emphasis on cultural preservation so evident in her 1893 statement spoke to
another, perhaps less obvious motivation: the urgency with which Bacon en-
joined the graduates to go out and salvage disappearing Negro lore stemmed
from the educators' need to demonstrate the success of the Hampton Idea.
One of the most effective publicity and fundraising tools of both Hampton
Institute and the Carlisle School were before and after photographs of Indian
students. Native Americans were routinely photographed fully adorned in
their religious regalia before they began school, and then later in a formal suit
and tie, to demonstrate the schools' success at civilizing their charges (Adams
1995:45). In her 1893 call, Bacon seems to suggest that her proposed folk-
lore society might be the last opportunity of Hampton educators to record
the "ignorant people," before the impact of common schools eclipsed the remaining folk culture. Armed with a record of African American folklore that
was no longer practiced, the educators at Hampton would be able to reproduce the popular before and after images used to raise money for their Indian
program.

Bacon's call for the formation of the Hampton Folk-Lore Society was
greeted with great enthusiasm. Letters of support came in from all corners of
the intellectual community. The popular Harvard geologist Nathan South-
gate Shaler supported the effort. Although Shaler routinely spoke about
Negroes' inherent inferiority, he chimed in to offer his "best wishes." On the
other side of the political spectrum was author, abolitionist and suffragist,
and former colonel of Negro troops, Thomas Wentworth Higginson, who sug-

gested that Hampton students would be acting as scientists, which would "enlarge their lives and dignify their position." Booker T. Washington "approved heartily" of the plan, as did T. Thomas Fortune, publisher of the *New York Age*. Even the venerable Southern historian and folklorist, George Washington Cable, supported the venture and offered his "service" (*Southern Workman* 1893, 22:179–80, 1894, 23:5).

Although the *Southern Workman* published only ringing endorsements, there is much evidence to suggest that African American supporters of the society held more nuanced views of its promise. For example, the missionary, educator, and early pan-Africanist Alexander Crummell strongly supported the formation of the society, but he warned that its members must offer a positive and not a negative interpretation of their African heritage. "The truth," he explained, has been "the dinning of the 'colonization' cause into the ears of the colored people—the iteration of the idle dogma that Africa is THE home of the black race in this land; has served to prejudice the race against the very name of Africa. And this is a double folly:—the folly of the colonizationists, and the folly of the black man; i.e. to forget family ties and his duty to his kin over the water" (*Southern Workman* 1894, 23:5). Another activist, educator, and author, Anna Julia Cooper, also commented on the philosophical foundation of the organization.

> What you say is true. The black man is readily assimilated to his surroundings and the original simple and distinct type is in danger of being lost or outgrown. To my mind, the worst possibility yet is that the so-called educated Negro, under the shadow of this over powering Anglo-Saxon civilization, may become ashamed of his own distinctive features and aspire only to be an imitator of that which can not but impress him as the climax of human greatness, and so all originality, all sincerity, all *self*-assertion would be lost to him. What he needs is the inspiration of knowing that his racial inheritance is of interest to others and that when they come to seek his homely songs and sayings and doings, it is not to scoff and sneer, but to study reverently, as an original type of the Creator's handiwork. (*Southern Workman* 1894, 23:5)

The comments by both Crummell and Cooper suggest that even with the formation of the first black folklore society, some African Americans understood that folklore could provide a positive interpretation of their African heritage or a scientific basis to identify and preserve their distinctive culture. Still, they did little to influence the 20 or so Hampton students, teachers, and alumni who made up the society. Most Hampton graduates did not question their desire to ascend to a civilized state, and even more perhaps loathed any association with Africa. However, two of the society's elected leaders, Robert R. Moton and Daniel Webster Davis, made a significant departure from the espionage and exorcism outlined by Armstrong and adapted by

Robert Russa Moton (1867–1940), ca. 1907. (Courtesy of Hampton University Archives.)

Bacon (Waters 1983:45). Moton used the folklore and the society to challenge the "contempt and derision" of the minstrelsy industry that transformed black folk-songs, stories, and sayings into laughing-stock buffoonery, which crystalized stereotypes for all African Americans (Lott 1993). Challenging those who made the "experience of the Negro a joke for white audiences," Moton reported to the 1895 annual meeting of the AFLS that all folklorists need to distinguish between "real folk-music" and those popular songs that were an "imitation by white 'nigger minstrels'" (Moton 1895:209).

Moreover, one can argue that the HFS's approach amounted to a form of "applied folklore" (Sharps 1991:65). The core of the HFS was a group of young men and women who graduated from Hampton and went on to work in business, education, or medicine. By better understanding the practices and lore of their clients, patients, and students, these young professionals believed they could contribute to racial uplift by developing more efficient ways to sell, heal, and teach. More generally, the society's work, as published in Hampton's *Southern Workman,* formed part of a missionary discourse integrated into a complicated racial project whose proponents engaged in a racial politics of culture that shaped communities from Hawaii to Hampton.

Although missionary efforts to civilize people of color made little distinction with regard to the savage state of Indians, Hawaiians, and Negroes, their methods and rhetoric served remarkably well at making distinctions between individuals within each group who had supposedly reached a state of civilization. Specifically, the putatively civilized people of color in the late nineteenth century used the discourse that homogenized difference between groups to mark the heterogeneity within their group—describing and inscribing a distinction between themselves, the civilized, and those others, the uncivilized.

As the next section shows, the AFLS participated in and scientifically validated this racial project by supporting and collaborating with the HFS. From its inception in 1893 until 1899, when Bacon left Hampton to return to Japan and it disbanded, the HFS found in the AFLS its chief supporter.

Theory and Practice of the American Folk-Lore Society

William Wells Newell (1839–1907) was born in Cambridge, Massachusetts. Son of a Unitarian minister, he graduated second in Harvard's class of 1859 and then enrolled in Harvard's Divinity School to pursue the ministry. Instead of serving a parish, he entered the Union Army during the Civil War as part of the Sanitary Service. After the war, he followed in his father's footsteps as a Unitarian minister but quickly learned that he was ill-suited as a man of the cloth and better suited as a man of letters. In 1871, he earned a master's degree and moved to New York City to open a private school. In New York,

Newell became fascinated with the games children played and began transcribing and recording them. His patient research and scrupulous attention to detail resulted in his most celebrated book, *Games and Songs of American Children* (1883). In 1884, he decided to leave his private school in New York and return to Cambridge to pursue his scholarly interests as a financially independent scholar, and help organize a national folklore society.

In the spring of 1887, Newell drafted a circular letter that outlined the scope of "a society for the study of Folk-Lore, of which the principal object shall be to establish a Journal, of scientific character." He organized prominent scholars in anthropology and literature to sign the letter and commit to participating in the society. On January 4, 1888, in Cambridge, Massachusetts, the AFLS was officially incorporated (Newell 1888:3); from the beginning, Newell was the central and most prominent figure in the organization. He served as permanent secretary of the society and the editor of its journal from 1888 to 1900. While other officers had university, museum, or other responsibilities, Newell was able to devote considerable time and money to the development of the fledgling society (Bell 1973:10).

In the first issue of the journal, Newell explained its various departments or divisions. The first division was Old English Lore, and he explained that old ballads, fairy tales, historical reminiscences, and beliefs in witchcraft were quickly disappearing. But with the advent of the folklore society, "there is reason to hope that some of these may be saved from oblivion" (Newell 1888:4). "The second division," he continued, "is that belonging to the American negroes." Newell explained that "the origin of these stories, many of which are common to a great part of the world, has not been determined." He believed that the animal stories should be "recorded as complete as possible" and he also directed the society to make thorough studies of "negro music and songs" because, as he put it, "such inquiries are becoming difficult, and in a few years will be impossible." He finally emphasized that the "beliefs and superstitions that exist among this people need attention, and present interesting and important psychological problems connected with the history of a race, who for good or ill are henceforth an indissoluble part of the body politic" (5). Another division that Newell discussed in terms of progress and the civilizing mission included the "traditions of the Indian tribes." "A great change is about to take place in the condition of the Indian tribes, and what is to be done must be done quickly. For the sake of the Indians themselves, it is necessary that they should be allowed opportunities for civilization; for our sake and for the future, it is desirable that a complete history should remain of what they have been, since their picturesque and wonderful life will soon be absorbed and lost in the uniformity of the modern world" (5).

Despite such predictions concerning the course of modern civilization and the fate of colonized peoples within it, Newell did not advocate that the AFLS make any political interventions, nor that its editors use the journal to pro-mote policy positions. In this, he was clearly less ambitious than Alice Bacon and the HFS; he was resigned to the fact that "all that a single journal can hope to accomplish is to print a few articles of limited extent, to stimulate inquiry, keep a record of progress, and furnish abstracts of investigations" (Newell 1888:6).

The first president of the AFLS was Francis J. Child, a professor of En-glish at Harvard University and an authority on English and Scottish ballads. He, however, retired from the organization within a year. Although none of the initial members of the governing council of the AFLS was affiliated with Harvard's Peabody Museum of American Archaeology and Ethnology, Newell wanted to make folklore a science and distinguish it from literature, so he turned to anthropology and established a link with Franz Boas, who, in the fall of 1889, had assumed a position at Clark University. As chair and secretary, respectively, of the council, Boas and Newell worked together to change the character of the organization from a literary society of wealthy enthusiasts and reformers into a scientific organization. Newell admired and deferred to the young academic from Germany, and "gave Boas virtually a free hand in publishing his own materials and those of his early students" (Darnell 1973:28). Boas took advantage of that opportunity to publish ma-terial he collected in the Pacific Northwest. Although Boas chose more presti-gious venues to articulate his theoretical and methodological positions (Boas 1887a, 1887b, 1888, 1889, 1894, 1896a), he used the *Journal of American Folk-Lore* to formulate his work on diffusion (1891, 1896b).

The concept of diffusion was also important to Newell (Newell 1888:7, 1895), but he had more pressing issues: he needed to recruit enough people to sustain the journal and the society. He explained to Boas that his "efforts to enlarge circulation" had taught him that "the general public is very indif-ferent" and that "vanity is the only spring of action which can be relied on."

If you write to ten men that the Council of the American Folk-Lore Society wishes their cooperation, one out of those ten will feel flattered, and join. I have got eight subscribers out of the 80 letters, one from you, and one from Prof. Crane! The other letters are to hear from. I think, if names of about thirty New Yorkers of prominence and fortune were sent to me, men identified with the geographical and historical societies, and I wrote them, some would unite with us. (BPP: WWN/FB 3/26/1889)

Newell needed the support of wealthy enthusiasts, but he was concerned that attempts to enlarge the society would inhibit its professionalism. Newell expressed this tension in another letter to Boas about "Dr. Mann of Brook-lyn" who wanted to join the society. Newell deemed it necessary to "exclude him from a learned society" and even felt that "it would be a nuisance to have him in a Brooklyn local society." He suggested that the prickly issue of membership "might be averted, should the need arise, by making such a society elective. However, as our society is pretty promiscuous, perhaps it would be harsh to keep him out" (BPP: WWN/FB 12/10/1890).

Newell only toyed with the idea of an elective society, focusing his efforts instead on securing wealthy and responsible collectors and professional anthropologists. As secretary and editor, he was able to set rigorous standards for the scholarship published in the society's organ. With well-attended annual meetings, a scholarly journal, and growing numbers of both amateur and professional scientists, Newell's launching of the society was perceived as a success. The AFLS also emerged as a formidable anthropological organization. Daniel Garrison Brinton, from Philadelphia's Academy of Natural Sciences, served as its president in 1889, followed in 1890 by F. W. Putnam from Harvard, in 1891 by Otis T. Mason from the the Smithsonian's National Museum and in 1892 by the director of the Bureau of American Ethnology, J. W. Powell (Darnell 1973:38). Newell used the presidency to gain the support of the various leaders in U.S. anthropology, which in turn gave the budding society increased visibility and validity. From the beginning, however, Newell structured the office of the president in a way that limited its power. The executive officer of the society was the secretary, and the editor of the *Journal of American Folk-Lore* controlled everything that was printed under the society's name. Those two offices were filled by Newell, who often deferred to the wishes of Boas, the chair of the society's governing council.

By 1893 Newell had distinguished himself as a skilled administrator and editor within the closely knit anthropological circles, but he also wanted to distinguish himself as a folklorist and folklore as its own discipline, not an adjunct to anthropology (Darnell 1973:28; Bell 1973:11–13). When Alice Bacon organized the Hampton society, Newell saw an opportunity to develop the Negro department of the journal, and thus to pursue a topic that few anthropologists were then exploring. He was "a personal friend" of one of Hampton's trustees, and there was considerable overlap between the founders of the AFLS from the Boston area and supporters of the Hampton idea, well before the HFS was even formed (Newell 1894:187). At the first annual meeting of the AFLS, the Boston-area members elected to its council included Mary Hemenway, Thomas Wentworth Higginson, and Alice C. Fletcher.

Mary Tileston Hemenway (1793–1894) was one of Hampton's chief benefactors. Her philanthropic support enabled Armstrong to launch the *Southern Workman*, buy more land, build Virginia Hall, and underwrite the popular Hampton Student Singers, who often performed in her Boston parlor, the same parlor where Boston-area members of the AFLS convened. She supported research on, and reform for, both Native and African Americans, and her philanthropic support of anthropology enabled Frank Hamilton Cushing to direct the Hemenway Exploring Expedition in Arizona (Lindsey 1995:50; Hinsley 1989:178–90; Armstrong & Ludlow 1874:139; Sharps 1991:31, 38; Ludlow 1909:122; Newell 1890:2, 9). Alice C. Fletcher (1845–1923) was also elected to the council. Although she could not, as a woman, attend Harvard, she was one of the first women to receive professional training in anthropology, studying with Frederic Ward Putnam at the Peabody Museum of American Archaeology and Ethnology. An enthusiastic supporter of the Hampton Idea, she worked to recruit Indian students to both the Hampton Institute and the Carlisle School. In addition, her longtime collaborator, Francis La Flesche, was a graduate of Hampton's Indian program (Fletcher & La Flesche 1911; Lindsey 1995:198; Adams 1995:303; Newell 1890:9). Thomas Wentworth Higginson (1823–1911), a Unitarian minister and Boston-based radical reformer, was also elected to the AFLS council. A champion of both racial uplift and women's suffrage, and a longtime supporter of Negro normal schools, he had written one of the initial letters of support for Hampton's folklore society.

Newell wasted no time incorporating the members of the HFS into the AFLS. On May 25, 1894, he traveled to Hampton to deliver the keynote address for Hampton's first folklore conference, which followed the spring commencement exercises. Speaking to "trustees, teachers, officers and graduates of the school," he gave a talk entitled "The Importance and Utility of the Collection of Negro Folk-Lore," which struck a note that resonated more with General Armstrong's notion of civilization than with Boas' ideas about diffusion. He began by explaining, "I came from Cambridge, in the hope of forwarding an undertaking which appears to me most meritorious, and of promoting the work of the Negro Folk-lore societies, a movement which is significant in regard to the present intelligence and rapid progress of Southern Negroes" (Newell 1894:186). He then asked, "What is Negro Folk-lore?"

> It is that body of songs, tales, old-fashioned religious beliefs, superstitions, customs, ways of expression, proverbs, and dialect, of American Negroes. Lore means learning; folk, as I shall here use the word, means race. The Folk-lore of Negroes in the United States then, is the learning or knowledge peculiar to the Negro race. It is that mass of information which they brought with them from Africa, and which has subsequently been increased, remodelled, and Anglicized by their contact with the whites. All this body of thought belongs to the past. It is vanishing in proportion to the progress of Negro education; it fades away before the light of such institutions as Hampton; it is superseded by more advanced ideas, habits, morals, and theology. (Newell 1894:186)

This notion of folklore was part of a larger theory of civilization. According to Newell, "each race has its distinctive customs, ideas, manners; civilization has but one set of customs and ideas for all races. The race is formed to be merged in the unity of races, as rivers flow to disappear in the ocean." Nevertheless, he believed that a race needed a record or memory of the past. Evoking the before-and-after pictures of the Indian students, Newell argued that Negroes should be able to demonstrate "the height to which they rose, the depth through which they have passed.... For the sake of the honor of his race, he should have a clear picture of the mental condition out of which he has emerged: this picture is not now complete, nor will [it] be made so without a record of songs, tales, beliefs, which belongs to the stage of culture through which he has passed" (1894:187–88).

Newell went on to describe various types of Negro folklore that needed to be collected, focusing on the value of the music. When he broached the subject of "spirits and demons," he argued, recalling Armstrong and Bacon, that "the best way to correct superstitious notions is to collect and study them. When all are gathered and made to elucidate each other, what is false and absurd is at once seen to be false and absurd. Thus, in order to get rid of a disgraceful custom, or of an ancient credulity, the best way is not to try to ignore its existence, but to face and find out what it is" (Newell 1894:189). Newell concluded, optimistically, that African Americans would be the ones to develop "Negro civilizations" on "the Dark Continent" (190).

Working with Alice Bacon, Newell arranged for a delegation from the HFS to participate the following December at the 1894 annual meeting of the AFLS in Washington, D.C. Bacon's call to form the society was printed in December of 1893, and exactly one year later members of the HFS were sailing up the Chesapeake to the nation's capital to deliver papers alongside Franz Boas, Frank Hamilton Cushing, J. Walter Fewkes, William Wells Newell, "and others equally well known along the lines of ethnological research" (*Southern Workman*, 1895, 24:30). Otis T. Mason chaired the meetings, hosted by the Anthropological Society of Washington and the Woman's Anthropological Society (*Journal of American Folk-Lore* 1895, 8:5).

The HFS delegation consisted of Robert Moton, F. D. Banks, William E. Daggs, and J. H. Wainwright. It was on this occasion that Robert R. Moton challenged the appropriation and distortion of Negro music by minstrels. His paper, "Negro Folk Songs," distinguished secular from spiritual music, and organized the secular music into two categories: "Corn-Songs" (a variety of "work songs") and "Dance Songs." As he delivered his paper, his HFS colleagues joined him to form a quartet that performed examples of the type of music he was describing. Commenting then on the Juba, next in their performance, Moton explained that "in some of these, the rhythmic expression is mainly through the beating of feet and patting of hands, while the vocal expression is simply a rude chant. The whole effect of this music, if music it can be called, is as barbarous as if rendered in African forests at some heathen festival" (1895:212).

The performance was such a success that Newell and Thomas Wilson proposed to record the music on phonographic cylinders, "which was found to reproduce the songs with considerable exactness." As Bacon reported in the *Southern Workman*, "it is to be hoped that [at] sometime the Hampton Folk-Lore Society will be able to secure a phonograph of its own" (Waters 1983:208). The HFS was off to a strong start, with powerful backing from the nation's leading folklore society. Each month the members convened to decide upon a topic, such as courting stories and hag stories, healing and medicine, jokes and proverbs, or work songs and dance songs. The next month they presented or performed the work done since the last meeting, and chose the topic for the upcoming month. Each month the society's collections were published in the "Folklore and Ethnology" department of the *Southern Workman*.

Almost every year between 1893 and 1899 the society held a major conference that coincided with commencement exercises, attracting such notable participants as William Scarborough, professor of classics at Wilberforce, and Anna Julia Cooper, author of *A Voice From the South* (1892), who earned a B.A. from Oberlin and a doctorate from the Sorbonne. The HFS also developed an elaborate network of corresponding members who taught in the small schools scattered throughout the rural south. Corresponding members submitted their collections to the HFS secretary, who read them during meetings and then published them in the *Southern Workman*.

Alice Bacon became an integral member of the AFLS and eventually was elected to its council. Bacon and delegates from the HFS participated in the meetings of the AFLS, and she and her colleagues published several collections in the *Journal of American Folk-Lore* (Banks 1894, 1895; Bacon 1898; Bacon & Herron 1896). Bacon's interaction with members of the AFLS did not sway her, however, from her commitment to use the study and description of cultures in the same way missionaries had used it for years—to learn how to civilize their charges (Mead & Bunzel 1960:59). In "Work and Methods of the Hampton Folklore Society," a paper presented in 1897 and published in the *Journal of American Folk-Lore* in 1898, she reiterated that the Folk-Lore Society was sustained by "a strong desire on the part of some of those connected with the Hampton work to bridge over, if possible, the great gulf fixed between the minds of the educated and the uneducated, the civilized and the uncivilized—to enter more deeply into the daily life of the common people, and to understand more thoroughly their ideas and motives" (Bacon 1898:17). "Our interest in folklore is used," she explained, "not so much to help us in interpreting the past as it is to aid us in understanding present conditions, and to make it easier for us to push forward the philanthropic work that Hampton is doing" (ibid.).

After a brief overview of the society and a quick discussion of the type of material the members collected, she described the difficulty of transcribing a "weird melody chanted at baptism" or a "complicated negro religious ritual" and appealed for help to the AFLS: "If we can only secure and preserve them by some other method than that of writing them down. . . . If we can obtain a graphophone, and thus make records not only of songs, but sermons, prayers, etc. and so gather, as we cannot now gather, some complete records of entire religious services, we are convinced that through this means we may add much to the common fund of knowledge of the negro music" (Bacon 1898:20).

Newell believed that providing Hampton Institute with the latest scientific technology would help to advance the science of folklore. Writing to Boas shortly before the 1898 AFLS meeting in New York City, Newell explained that he had "promised to procure a graphophone for . . . Miss Alice M. Bacon, of the Hampton Institute, [who,] as you know, takes a great interest in negro music." Since Boas would "be in a position to know the best recording instrument," Newell asked him to "order an instrument of this sort, if you think that form the best, to be shipped at once to Miss Bacon . . . with fifty cylinders, and send the bill to me." Bacon, Newell explained, "already has a great body of collections of tales, &c, and I hope will be able to prepare a volume suitable for publication in the series of Memoirs. If this instrument can be got to Hampton at once, Miss Bacon will send, or bring, a number of cylinders to our meeting. I think that would have an excellent effect toward exhibiting the scientific energy of our Society" (BPP: WWN/FB 12/9/1898).

Boas did not respond to the first request, and now with the meeting less than two weeks away, Newell wrote Boas again about the graphophone, reiterating the urgency: "I want them to get cylinders for the meeting" (BPP: WWN/FB 12/14/1898). Forty-eight hours later, and now just days before the meeting, a testy Newell pleaded with the man he had supported for so many years: "I should like to have the instrument sent to Hampton at once, and the bill to me. . . . Pray send the machine at once" (BPP: WWN/FB 12/16/1898).

During the month of December, Alice Bacon was eagerly awaiting the graphophone. By December 21 she realized that even if it came, she could not make the recordings. She wrote Newell that "I am afraid that it will be impossible for us to get up anything with its aid for the annual meeting." Instead, she proposed the real thing.

> A most delightful paper by Prof. D. W. Davis of Richmond, on "Echoes from a Plantation Party," which may be worth studying up on. Davis is a full blooded Negro, a teacher in Richmond and the authority of a number of dialect processes. He takes a real interest in the old customs of his own people, and has been at considerable pains to collect all he can. . . .
> I asked him if he would be willing to describe it [his paper] in New York at the annual meeting and he says that he can. . . . The songs are a great part of it. It is rather better than a phonographic reprint as he gives it. (BPP: AMB/WWN 12/20/1898; Davis 1899)

Newell did not give up on the graphophone, nor on Boas. Two months after the New York meeting, he again pestered Boas. "Pray let me know if you have been able to send the graphophone to Miss A. M. Bacon at Hampton Institute as directed by me. If you do not wish to take the responsibility of sending it, I will write direct to the Columbia Graphophone Company" (BPP: WWN/FB 2/21/1899). The correspondence between Newell and Boas is incomplete, but the tone of the preceding letter suggests Boas agreed to do it, but never followed through. Newell then turned to Frederic Ward Putnam for advice and counsel about the proper graphophone to send, but, as he explained to Boas in one final plea,

> Prof. Putnam says that it is not safe for me to order the instrument, as it is very easy to get instruments which are practically worthless. He thinks I had better leave it to you. But he also says that perhaps they will not forward the instrument without previous payment. If so, I will remit a check. . . . As you are interested in musical collection, I hope you will not think this too much trouble; it seems to me that here is an opportunity." (BPP: WWN/FB 3/8/1899)

It appears that the HFS never got its graphophone. One can only speculate as to why Boas ignored such a simple request. What we do know is that he began seriously engaging African American issues after 1905—before then it probably was not a high priority.

Alice Bacon left Hampton in 1899 to return to Japan to administer a school for young women, and the HFS was not sustained. Her major literary contributions remain those on Japanese women (Bacon 1891). Robert Moton left Hampton to be one of Washington's chief lieutenants at Tuskegee, and Leonora Herron remained as Hampton's librarian. Bacon died in 1918, but the notebooks of folklore she collected to articulate one racial project were republished in 1922 under her name and used to articulate a different one.

Lifting As We Climb

The HFS was operational as the so-called Progressive Era waxed and the Gilded Age waned. During that period, the tidewater region of Virginia was marked by increased lynchings and restrictions on black male suffrage, and the routinization and legalization of Jim Crow segregation. Under the leadership of Bacon, the work of the HFS can be seen as cut from the same cloth as Jane Addams and the settlement house movement—a tapestry of thrift, self-reliance, morality, and Christian faith. The HFS does not, however, fit neatly within the discursive practices of Progressive Era reformers, the black women's club movement, or the black men's self-help leagues. Although its members grappled with identical issues, and emulated many of these other groups' practices, they are distinguished from the others by the particular attention they paid to ideas about culture, as well as class, to articulate the ideology of racial uplift.

The former students of Hampton who made up the bulk of the membership of the society were part of a Negro elite who shared faith in Jesus and a moral obligation to uplift the race. Shouldering the responsibility of what would have amounted to a talented 2 percent, these "college-bred" Negroes (Du Bois & Dill 1910) of the late nineteenth century promulgated a complex ideology of racial uplift inflected with gender and class distinctions. Black ministers, educators, journalists, doctors, and social workers used rhetoric, research, and writing to combat egregious and dehumanizing claims that African Americans were inherently inferior, and not capable of assuming the rights and responsibilities of citizenship or civilization.

Imbued with the optimism and progressive spirit of the age, these black leaders enlisted the support of white political and business leaders to foster racial progress, primarily through a trickle-down theory of education. College graduates would fan out throughout the South, teaching students in small schools the Victorian and Yankee ideals learned from the missionaries, which would improve the material conditions of blacks and demonstrate that they were capable of citizenship and civilization, indeed humanity. The efforts to show racial progress, however, were largely predicated upon identifying distinctions between those blacks who rose to a civilized state and those not quite there, and such distinctions often turned on status or class distinctions.

The National Association of Colored Women, founded in 1896, struck the keynote of this ideology with their motto "Lifting as we climb," which had been something of a credo for years among educated black folks. The catchwords, however, signified a distinction between the lifters and lifted, the climbers and pulled. As Kevin K. Gaines has argued, "generally, black elites claimed class distinctions, indeed, the very existence of a 'better class' of blacks, as evidence of what they called race progress" (1996: xiv). Gaines further argues that "the attempt to rehabilitate the image of black people through class distinctions trafficked in claims of racial and gender hierarchy." These hierarchies created obvious tensions. "On the one hand, a broader vision of uplift signifying collective social aspiration, advancement, and struggle had been the legacy of the emancipation era. On the other hand, black elites made uplift the basis for a racialized elite identity claiming Negro improvement through class stratification as race progress, which entailed an attenuated conception of bourgeois qualifications for rights and citizenship" (Gaines 1996: xv). Although proponents of uplift did not advance unified themes about racial progress, the idea that the race would progress toward a civilized citizenry served as a unifying theme as people searched for various ways to create an authentic and positive black middle-class subjectivity. Through essays, pamphlets, newspaper articles, poetry, and books, people like Ida B.

Wells, Booker T. Washington, Anna Julia Cooper, Robert Moton, W. E. B. Du Bois, Francis Ellen Harper Watkins, James Corrothers, Paul Lawrence Dunbar, and a host of others announced to the world that "we are here!"—right here, in the Christian brotherhood of civilization (see Alexander 1997:67).

The HFS was also articulating racial uplift ideology. They, too, were propounding the notion that "we are here." But it was not the temporally static "we are here, right here." It was a "we are (up) here, not (down) there." Knowingly or not, HFS members used an anthropologically informed folklore to plot the perceived temporal distance between the college-bred Negroes and the cabin people. Although this folklore helped to demonstrate how far they had come in their racial progress, it was ultimately deployed to document how quickly they were closing the gap, and to measure the success of lifting as they climbed.[6]

The HFS provided an additional dimension to the idea of racial uplift by inserting notions about stages of culture. By explicitly distinguishing the low and savage African culture from the high and civilized Christian culture, they appropriated the comparative method of evolutionary anthropology to bolster a politics of culture that advanced the status of many individuals as citizens. After all, it was E. B. Tylor who suggested that based on customs and behavior, not race, "we may draw a picture where there shall be scarce a hand's breadth difference between an English ploughman and a negro of Central Africa" (1871:7).

Twenty years later, well after Boas' critique of the comparative method, members of the New Negro movement appropriated Boasian ideas of diffusion and the particularity of cultures to bolster a very different politics of culture that advanced the idea of a proud African heritage. Although the HFS no longer existed, the material they collected was recycled into this very different racial project during the Harlem Renaissance.

That Tricky Rabbit Again

World War I served as a fulcrum for events that galvanized the New Negro movement or the Harlem Renaissance. Before the United States sent troops to Europe, northern industrial cities absorbed the first waves of the northern migration, filling the labor demand caused by war-related production and immigration restriction. Although many whites migrated, floods and crop

---

6. The Hampton Folk-Lore Society was not the first group of nineteenth-century black Americans to find anthropology conducive to their progressive and explicitly modernist efforts for racial uplift. For example, Frederick Douglass wrote *The Claims of the Negro Ethnologically Considered* in 1854, and in 1879 Martin Delany put forth *Principia of Ethnology: The Origin of Races and Color, with an Archeological Compendium of Ethiopian and Egyptian Civilization, from Years of Careful Examination and Enquiry.*

failure, combined with lynching, segregation, and disfranchisement, significantly increased the push and pull of African Americans from south to north.
As African Americans began to relocate, residential segregation and racially
exclusive unions created conditions of overcrowding and cheap labor, which
intensified the rigid color line and sparked violence. After U.S. troops returned—returned from keeping the world safe for democracy—pogroms became routine in the North and lynching was sustained in the South. Artists
and intellectuals who followed on the heels of their less well-heeled neighbors
began to magnify the cruel irony that the United States was not safe for African Americans, let alone for democracy, fueling by their writing a militant
New Negro movement.

New Negro boosters used various venues to advance their agendas. W. E. B.
Du Bois' *Crisis* under the auspices of the NAACP, and Charles S. Johnson's
Opportunity under the auspices of the National Urban League were the most
notable, but the circulation of all types of publications kept rich and poor
alike informed. Politics and news were important, but publishers also exhibited the cultural production of the New Negro by sponsoring contests for
various categories of literature and social science, and then publishing winners' submissions.

The *Journal of American Folk-Lore* was one such organ, and it should be
viewed as playing the same role in the movement as the *Crisis*, *Opportunity*,
and the *Messenger*. Each outlet provided opportunities to carve out new interpretations of the African American experience and served as a forum to
challenge ideas about the racial inferiority and cultural degradation of African Americans. Specifically, the *Journal of American Folk-Lore* would be on
par with the *New Republic*, the *Nation*, the *American Mercury* and the *Survey
Graphic*. These periodicals targeted primarily white audiences, but delivered
the ideas, initiatives, and aesthetics of the intellectuals of the New Negro
movement across the color line (Hutchinson 1995:209–49).

The *Survey Graphic* was one of a handful of white periodicals that explicitly
crossed the color line. In 1925, Paul Kellogg, its editor, decided to devote a
single issue to the writers and intellectuals of the so-called New Negro movement. The issue's masthead read "Harlem: Mecca of the New Negro," and
when it came out in March, the *Survey*'s circulation nearly doubled. Adding
African-inspired images designed by Winold Reiss and Aaron Douglas, Alain
Locke (its editor and compiler) quickly expanded the collection of essays and
award-winning poetry into a book. Published as *The New Negro* in the final
months of 1925, the book would help Negroes, Locke suggested, in "finding
a new soul."[7]

---

7. There were 38 contributors to the book, all but four of whom were black. Of the four white
contributors, one was Herskovits.

At the conclusion of the text, there were several bibliographies document-ing the writing and research (past and present) that contributed to the New Negro movement. Arthur Fauset compiled one of them, which included 10 references to the work of Elsie Clews Parsons, and more than 30 citations of the *Journal of American Folk-Lore*. Fauset was articulating a specific theme or project of the Harlem Renaissance — to demonstrate that the New Negro was unique and had a distinct culture with a proud history and heritage. In this emergent discourse, scientists and artists identified African cultural conti-nuities within African American culture as a source of empowerment, beauty, inspiration, and authenticity (Fauset 1925a; Schomburg 1925).

Anthropology and the Heritage Project

Anthropologists at Columbia University who were involved with the *Journal of American Folk-Lore*'s Negro numbers served to validate Negro history and cultural specificity while authenticating cultural linkages between African Americans and West Africans.[8] Parsons' and Boas' attention to black folk-lore reflected their interest in cultural diffusion, yet there is evidence that they were aware they were party to the New Negroes' efforts to "find par-allels in Negro stories bearing indubitable traces of African origin" (Fauset 1925a:242). New Negro intellectuals identified these anthropologists with what I will call the "heritage project." Often it was articulated in opposition to the "assimilationist project" that became associated with sociologists at Chi-cago. Although everyone's motives were perhaps different, all camps became engaged in the volatile racial politics of culture.

Like the editors of the *Crisis* and *Opportunity* magazines, Boas and Parsons worked with Carter G. Woodson in 1923 to sponsor a contest for the best col-lection of black folklore. The award for the winner was to be $200, and adver-tisements were dispatched to all of the leading Negro newspapers. Circulars were also given to 60 African American organizations and the contest was publicized at 225 secondary schools and colleges (BPP: CGW/FB 2/15/23). But, as Fauset saw it, Boas and Parsons did more than sponsor contests. Fauset identified them in *The New Negro* as anthropologists who scientifically au-thenticated the New Negro heritage project. In the section of *The New Negro* titled "The Negro Digs Up His Past," Fauset explained that African Ameri-cans had to go beyond the "quaint and sentimental humor" of Negro folklore emphasized by Joel Chandler Harris's depictions of the Uncle Remus stories.

8. Arthur H. Fauset and Zora Neale Hurston were perhaps the two most notable contributors to both the New Negro literary movement and the *Journal of American Folk-Lore*'s black folk-lore issues (Fauset 1925a, 1925b, 1927a, 1927b, 1928, 1931, 1938, 1944; Fauset & Duckrey 1924; Hurston 1931a, 1931b, 1934a, 1934b, 1935, 1937, 1938).

He called for more sophisticated and "scientific" analysis of the stories, explaining that "it is not necessary to draw upon sentimènt in order to realize the masterful quality of some of the Negro tales: it is simply necessary to read them. Moralism, somber and almost grim, irony, shrewd and frequently subtle, are their fundamental tone and mood—as in the case of their African originals" (Fauset 1925a:241). Fauset went on to explain that "American folk-lorists are now recognizing this, and systematic scientific investigation has begun under the influence and auspices of the Society for American Folk Lore and such competent ethnologists as Franz Boas, Elsie Clews Parsons, and others" (242).

A decade later and well after the promoters of the heritage project produced a wide-spread discourse on the value and importance of Negroes' African roots, Boas wrote an introduction for Zora Neale Hurston's *Mules and Men*, where he reinforced the keystone of this project. Boas asserted that African American culture was a "peculiar amalgamation of African and European tradition which is so important for understanding historically the character of American Negro life, with its strong African background in the West Indies, the importance of which diminishes with increasing distance from the south" (1935:x).

Despite Boas' support of the science that validated the New Negroes' African heritage, he was "absolutely opposed to all kinds of attempts to foster racial solidarity" (BPP: FB/DSA 10/26/33). Furthermore, he favored cultural assimilation as an effective strategy to ameliorate the so-called Negro problem (Boas 1905:87). Boas went beyond supporting a strategy of assimilation to advocate phenotypic miscegenation, explaining that "the negro problem will not disappear in America until the negro blood has been so much diluted that it will no longer be recognized just as anti-Semitism will not disappear until the vestige of the Jew as a Jew has disappeared" (1921:395).

Although proponents of assimilation did not try to get Boas to support their position, his research on race was used increasingly by them. As the New Negro movement was eclipsed by the depression, sociologists like E. Franklin Frazier and Charles Johnson increasingly used Boas' research on race to assert that African Americans were not racially inferior. The same black scholars discarded his research on culture because it implied that Negroes could not easily assimilate (Baker 1998:178). Proponents of assimilation ignored the folklore published in the *Journal of American Folk-Lore*, and routinely denounced the fieldwork of Melville Herskovits, who identified African cultural patterns in the New World (see Johnson 1922, 1925; Frazier 1932, 1939: 125–45; Blackwell & Janowitz 1974:57–117; Scott 1997:19–40). Challenging Herskovits in a public forum, Frazier asserted that "if whites came to believe that the Negro's social behavior was rooted in African culture, they would lose whatever sense of guilt they had for keeping the Negro down. Negro crime, for example, could be explained away as an 'Africanism' rather than as due to inadequate police and court protection" (Myrdal 1944:1242).

Herskovits remained committed to his research on African cultural patterns in the Americas, but developed an understanding that the research could have both radical and conservative implications (Jackson 1986:100). Routinely attacked by African American proponents of the assimilation project, he resented the way his research was appropriated by the promoters of the heritage project. An example of this resentment is revealed in a letter he wrote to Parsons, trying to convince her to join him in resigning from W. E. B. Du Bois' advisory committee for a projected encyclopedia of the Negro. Herskovits feared that he would not have any substantive input and that he was being used.

> After talking with a number of people and going over the material that was sent us, I am more and more dubious about the project. I have the feeling that it must inevitably be loaded with propaganda. . . . I do not think that there is any chance of accomplishing anything by working from the inside, but perhaps a few resignations might bring about a realization that not everyone is in agreement with the rather high-handed manner in which the thing is being pushed through. (EPP: MH/ECP 6/8/36)

In any case, despite Herskovits' reluctance, members of the New Negro movement did not necessarily need the support of individual anthropologists because anthropology itself supported the movement with its concepts and research.

Part of the militancy of the New Negro movement was fueled by the fact that no matter how hard African Americans played by the rules, or tried to assimilate, they would be lynched and their communities segregated (and sometimes leveled). Artists and intellectuals turned to the blues and spirituals, holiness churches and ring shouts, as well as other traditional cultural practices to offer an empowering way to transform segregation into a form of congregation by challenging the derogatory assessments that the culture of rural Negroes was backward and inferior (Huggins 1971:72–75; Levine 1977:269). As evidenced by The New Negro, they also turned to anthropology for lexicon, concepts, and scientific validation. Cultural patterns, specific historical reconstructions, geographical diffusion of rites and rituals, evidence of African survivals and of ancient African civilizations—all became anthropological grist used to produce new interpretations of culture by those New Negroes articulating the heritage project.

But while Boas often engaged in a form of intellectual philanthropy with African American organizations and spoke in glowing terms about ancient African civilizations, he limited his work along these lines. Examining the possible reasons why Negro folklore studies at Columbia declined during the late 1930s, William Willis suggested that "perhaps Boas sensed the nationalistic strivings in black folklore" (1973:327). The most useful anthropologist for the heritage project was Melville Herskovits. People like Fauset and Woodson used Herskovits' research on African survivals and his philosophy of cultural relativism to embolden their racial project and validate cultural differences. Micaela di Leonardo notes, however, that his relativism was limited: "Herskovits explicitly confined this orientation to fieldwork, rejecting the 'moral relativism' his attackers, primarily [white] philosophers, accused him of espousing" (1998:341). Moreover, he confined his ethnographic research on the retention of African cultural patterns to sites outside the United States.

Boas also circumscribed his relativism. As George Stocking points out, "it could easily be shown that Boas was not a relativist in a consistent sense" (1968:231). And like Herskovits, Boas saw relativism as a methodological tool, not a way to foster cultural pride. In an early discussion of methodology, Boas explained how his relativist orientation was best used only in the field: "the student must endeavor to divest himself entirely of opinions and emotions based upon the peculiar social environment into which he is born. He must adapt his own mind, so far as feasible, to that of the people whom he is studying. The more successful he is in freeing himself from the bias based on the group of ideas that constituted the civilization in which he lives, the more successful he will be in interpreting the beliefs and actions of man" (1901:1).

Parsons, in contrast, did not limit her involvement to collecting stories in the field. She underwrote the research and writing of Fauset, supported the publication of Hurston's work in the *Journal of American Folk-Lore*, and facilitated the publication of many amateur folklorists in the journal during the New Negro movement. Even the doyen of the heritage project, historian Carter G. Woodson, knew he could turn to her for support. In 1934, he explained to her that he was "making a study of African survivals in America. Taking up the folk-lore, I am saying that many tales told by Negroes in the South were merely translations in modified form of stories handed down to them by the forebears who came from Africa. You have studied this for a number of years and I would like to know what you think?" (EPP: CGW/ECP 10/29/34). Schomburg, Fauset, Hurston, Woodson, and to a certain extent Locke pressed into service the liberal politics, relativistic orientation, and credentials of anthropologists who limited their exploration of African American culture to research and academic journals. Although the intellectuals of the movement were always careful scientists and historians or creative artists and performers, they were clear that scholarship and performance by and about black people involved political stakes that were entwined and woven into the very fabric of the movement to transform race relations and the meaning of being black in America.

Parsons obviously understood the value of feminist research, but it is not clear whether she believed that the study of Negro folklore could be explicitly empowering. The ambivalence and hesitation on the part of Herksovits and Boas, on the one hand, suggests a fear that essentialist renditions of the heritage project could spawn a black nationalism undistinguishable from the nationalisms raging in Europe. On the other hand, it suggests a naive understanding of U.S. racism—specifically, of the role that descriptions of African American culture as degraded, pathological, or backward played in the maintenance of white supremacy outside, and divisiveness within, black communities.

Of course Boasian anthropologists were consistently vocal in public forums when it came to challenging ideas about the racial inferiority of the Negro; on ideas about their cultural inferiority, they were conspicuously silent—limiting their discussion to research in the field. Moreover, they simply did not understand that careful exploration of the contours and specificity of African American culture, through history and folklore, could lead to a reflexive and critical study of cultural diversity within American society, and not the propaganda-peppered nationalism they seem to have feared (Herskovits 1946:92). The "classic relativism" of Boas and Herskovits, Michaela di Leonardo argues, was a "fascinating oxymoron" and an exercise in "powerful powerlessness": "In its heyday, it was a toothless liberalism that spoke judiciously, tolerantly of varying initiation rituals, bodily alterations and adornment, polygyny and polyandry, millenarian movements, crop rotation cycles, while remaining largely silent on both the role of Western power in the political economic settings of these shifting practices and the comfortable position of the Western (or non-Western) ethnographer evaluating them" (1998:342).

The New Negroes on the other hand began to understand the power relations involved in the racial politics of culture as they sought to engage in the cultural politics of race and racism. If one scrutinizes the bibliography Fauset compiled for *The New Negro,* one finds dozens of references to the *Journal of American Folk-Lore* during William Newell's editorship. There exists an equal number of pieces published in the *Southern Workman* and authored by members of the HFS. Parson's collection of folklore from Elizabeth City County in 1922 at the dawn of the New Negro movement, and Fauset's 1925 references to publications at the dusk of the nineteenth century, suture together two different time periods and two different interpretations of African American culture. Franz Boas and the American Folk-Lore Society form the common thread.

Acknowledgments

I would like to thank George Bond, James Ferguson, Bayo Holsley, Maureen Mahon, Moira Smith, Noenoe K. Silva, George Stocking, and my lovely wife Sabrina Thomas

Baker for their assistance, support, and ideas. Special thanks to David Rease and Bayo Holsley for providing research support and to Richard Handler who provided invaluable editorial support. He is doing a great job filling some big shoes. I have given versions of this paper at Wesleyan University, New York University, Columbia University, University of California, Irvine, and the University of Missouri, St. Louis, and each audience provided me valuable feedback. Funding for this research was provided by a Mellon Resident Fellowship at the American Philosophical Society Library and a Ford Foundation Post-Doctoral Fellowship for Minorities. Additional funding was provided by the Institute for Research in African American Studies, Columbia University.

References Cited

Adams, D. W. 1995. *Education for extinction: American Indians and the boarding school experience, 1875–1928.* Lawrence, Kans.

Alexander, E. 1997. "We must be about our father's business": Anna Julia Cooper and the incorporation of the nineteenth-century African American woman intellectual. In *In her own voice: Nineteenth-century American women essayists,* ed. S. L. Linkon, 61–80. New York.

Armstrong, M. F. 1887. *Richard Armstrong: America, Hawaii.* Hampton, Va.

Armstrong, M. F., & H. W. Ludlow. 1874. *Hampton and its students, with fifty cabin and plantation songs.* New York.

Armstrong, S. C. 1878. Editorials about papers on conjuring. *Southern Workman* 7:26–35.

Armstrong, S. C. 1909. From the beginning. In *Memories of old Hampton,* ed. Armstrong League of Hampton Workers, 1–15. Hampton, Va.

Bacon, A. M. 1890. Silhouettes. *Southern Workman* 19:124–25.

Bacon, A. M. 1891. *Japanese girls and women.* Boston.

Bacon, A. M. 1893. Folk-lore and ethnology. *Southern Workman* 22:180–81.

Bacon, A. M. 1898. Work and methods of the Hampton Folk-Lore Society. *Journal of American Folk-Lore* 11:17–21.

Bacon, A. M. 1909. A child's impressions of early Hampton. In *Memories of Old Hampton,* ed. Armstrong League of Hampton Workers, 17–21. Hampton, Va.

Bacon, A. M., & L. Herron. 1896. Conjuring and conjure doctors in the southern United States. *Journal of American Folk-Lore* 9:143–47, 224–26.

Bacon, A. M., & E. C. Parsons. 1922. Folk-lore from Elizabeth City County, Virginia. *Journal of American Folk-Lore* 35:250–327.

Baker, L. D. 1998. *From savage to negro: Anthropology and the construction of race, 1896–1954.* Berkeley, Calif.

Banks, F. D. 1894. Plantation courtship. *Journal of American Folk-Lore* 7:147–49.

Banks, F. D. 1895. Plantation courtship. *Journal of American Folk-Lore* 8:106.

Bell, M. J. 1973. William W. Newell and American folklore scholarship. *Journal of the Folklore Institute* 10:7–21.

Blackwell, J. E., & M. Janowitz, eds. 1974. *Black sociologists: Historical and contemporary perspectives.* Chicago.

Boas, F. 1887a. Museums of ethnology and their classifications. *Science* 9:587–89.

Boas, F. 1887b. The occurrence of similar inventions in areas widely apart. *Science* 9:485–86.

Boas, F. 1888. *The Central Eskimo.* Lincoln, Neb. (1964).

Boas, F. 1889. On alternating sounds. *American Anthropologist* 2:47–53.

Boas, F. 1891. Dissemination of tales among the natives of North America. *Journal of American Folk-Lore* 4:13–20.

Boas, F. 1894. Human faculty as determined by race. *Proceedings of the American Association for the Advancement of Science* 43:301–27.

Boas, F. 1896a. The limitations of the comparative method of anthropology. *Science* 4:901–9.

Boas, F. 1896b. The growth of Indian mythologies. *Journal of American Folk-Lore* 9:1–11.

Boas, F. 1901. The mind of primitive man. *Journal of American Folk-Lore* 14:1–11.

Boas, F. 1905. The Negro and the demands of modern life. *Charities* 15:85–88.

Boas, F. 1921. The problem of the American Negro. *Yale Quarterly Review* 10:384–95.

Boas, F. 1935. Preface. In Hurston 1935 (1990): xiii–xiv.

Cooper, A. J. 1892. *A voice from the South by a black woman of the South.* Xenia, Ohio.

Darnell, R. 1973. American anthropology and the development of folklore scholarship. *Journal of the Folklore Institute* 10:23–39.

Davis, D. W. 1899. Echoes from a plantation party. *Southern Workman* 28(2):54–59. Reprinted in Waters 1983:316–23.

Deacon, D. 1997. *Elsie Clews Parsons: Inventing modern life.* Chicago.

Delany, M. R. 1879. *Principia of ethnology: The origin of races and color, with an archeological compendium of Ethiopian and Egyptian civilization, from years of careful examination and enquiry.* Philadelphia.

di Leonardo, M. 1998. *Exotics at home: Anthropologies, others, American modernity.* Chicago.

Douglass, F. The claims of the Negro ethnologically considered: An address delivered in Hudson, Ohio, 12 July 1854.

Du Bois, W. E. B., & A. G. Dill. 1910. The college-bred Negro American: Report of a social study made by Atlanta University under the patronage of the trustees of the John F. Slater fund; with proceedings of the 15th annual conference for the study of Negro problems, held at Atlanta University, on Tuesday, May 24th, 1910. In *The Atlanta University Publications,* ed. W. L. Katz, 1–112. New York, 1968.

Fauset, A. H. 1925a. American Negro folk literature. In Locke 1925 (1968):238–44.

Fauset, A. H. 1925b. Folk-lore from the half-breeds of Nova Scotia. *Journal of American Folk-Lore* 38:300–15.

Fauset, A. H. 1927a. *For freedom: A biographical story of the American Negro.* Philadelphia.

Fauset, A. H. 1927b. Negro folk-lore from the south (Alabama, Mississippi, and Louisiana). *Journal of American Folk-Lore* 40:213–303.

Fauset, A. H. 1928. Tales and riddles collected in Philadelphia. *Journal of American Folk-Lore* 41:529–57.

Fauset, A. H. 1931. Folklore from Nova Scotia. Memoirs of the American Folklore Society, Vol. 24. New York.

Fauset, A. H. 1938. *Sojourner Truth: God's faithful pilgrim.* Chapel Hill, N.C.

Fauset, A. H. 1944. *Black gods of the metropolis: Negro religious cults of the urban North.* Philadelphia.

Fauset, A. H., & T. G. Duckrey. 1924. *Booker T. Washington.* Philadelphia.

Fletcher, A. C., & F. La Flesche. 1911. *The Omaha tribe.* Washington, D.C.

Frazier, E. F. 1932. *The Negro family in Chicago.* Chicago.

Frazier, E. F. 1939. *The Negro family in the United States.* Chicago.

Fredrickson, G. M. 1971. *The black image in the white mind.* Hanover, N.H.

The Friend. 1860. Death of Rev. Richard Armstrong, 9(10 n.s.):76–77.

Gaines, K. K. 1996. *Uplifting the race: Black leadership, politics, and culture in the twentieth century.* Chapel Hill, N.C.

Hampton Normal and Agricultural Institute. 1893. Twenty-two years' work of the Hampton Normal and Agricultural Institute at Hampton, Virginia: Records of Negro and Indian graduates and ex-students. Hampton, Va.

Hayes, R. B. 1879. Third annual message (State of the Union address to the 46th Congress). In *The State of the Union messages of the presidents,* ed. F. L. Israel, 1371–95. New York (1966).

Herskovits, M. J. 1946. Folklore after a hundred years: A problem in redefinition. *Journal of American Folklore* 59:89–100.

Hinsley, C. M. 1989. Zunis and Brahmins: Cultural ambivalence in the Gilded Age. In *Romantic motives: Essays on anthropological sensibility,* ed. G. W. Stocking, Jr. HOA 6:169–207.

Huggins, N. 1971. *Harlem renaissance.* New York.

Hunter, T. W. 1997. *To 'joy my freedom: Southern black women's lives and labors after the Civil War.* Cambridge.

Hurston, Z. N. 1931a. Dance songs from the Bahamas. *Journal of American Folk-Lore* 43:294–312.

Hurston, Z. N. 1931b. Hoodoo in America. *Journal of American Folk-Lore* 44:317–417.

Hurston, Z. N. 1934a. Characteristics of Negro expression. In *The Negro: An anthology made by Nancy Cunard,* ed. N. Cunard, 24–31. London.

Hurston, Z. N. 1934b. *Jonah's gourd vine.* London.

Hurston, Z. N. 1935. *Mules and men.* New York (1990).

Hurston, Z. N. 1937. *Their eyes were watching God: A novel.* Philadelphia.

Hurston, Z. N. 1938. *Tell my horse.* Philadelphia.

Hutchinson, G. 1995. *The Harlem renaissance in black and white.* Cambridge.

Jackson, W. A. 1986. Melville Herskovits and the search for Afro-American culture. In *Malinowski, Rivers, Benedict and others: Essays on culture and personality,* ed. G. W. Stocking, Jr. HOA 4:95–126.

Johnson, C. 1922. Black housing in Chicago. In *The Negro in Chicago: A study of race relations and a race riot,* ed. The Chicago Commission on Race Relations, 152–86. Chicago.

Johnson, C. 1925. New frontage on American Life. In Locke 1925 (1968): 278–98. Boston.

Kaplan, A. 1993. Left alone with America: The absence of empire in the study of American culture. In *Cultures of United States imperialism*, ed. A. Kaplan & D. E. Pease, 3–20. Durham, N.C.

Langhorne, O. 1878. Correspondence. *Southern Workman* 7(9):67.

Levine, L. W. 1977. *Black culture and black consciousness: Afro-American folk-thought from slavery to freedom*. New York.

Lindsey, D. 1995. *Indians at Hampton Institute, 1877–1923*. Urbana, Ill.

Locke, A., ed. 1925. *The New Negro*. Boston (1968).

Lott, E. 1993. *Love and theft: Blackface minstrelsy and the American working class*. New York.

Ludlow, H. W. 1909. The Hampton student singers. In *Memories of Old Hampton*, ed. The Armstrong League of Hampton Workers, 105–28. Hampton, Va.

Makofsky, A. 1989. Experience of Native Americans at a black college: Indian students at Hampton Institute, 1878–1912. *Ethnic Studies* 17:31–46.

Mead, M., & R. L. Bunzel. 1960. *The golden age of American anthropology*. New York.

Moton, R. R. 1895. Negro folk-songs. *Southern Workman* 24:30–32. Reprinted in Waters 1983:209–15.

Myrdal, G. 1944. *An American dilemma*. New York (1964).

Newell, W. W. 1883. *Games and songs of American children*. New York.

Newell, W. W. 1888. On the field and work of a journal of American folk-lore. *Journal of American Folk-Lore* 1:3–7.

Newell, W. W. 1890. First annual meeting of the American Folk-Lore Society. *Journal of American Folk-Lore* 3:1–16.

Newell, W. W. 1894. The importance and utility of the collection of Negro folklore. *Southern Workman* 23(7):131–33. Reprinted in Waters 1983:186–90.

Newell, W. W. 1895. Theories of diffusion of folk-lore. *Journal of American Folk-Lore* 8:7–19.

Robinson, W. H. 1977. Indian education at Hampton Institute. In *Stony the road: Chapters in the history of Hampton Institute*, ed. K. L. Schall, 1–33. Charlottesville, Va.

Schomburg, A. 1925. The Negro digs up his past. In Locke 1925 (1968):231–37.

Scott, D. M. 1997. *Contempt and pity: Social policy and the image of the damaged black psyche, 1880–1996*. Chapel Hill, N.C.

Sharps, R. L. 1991. Happy days and sorrow songs: Interpretations of Negro folklore by black intellectuals, 1893–1928. Doct. diss., George Washington Univ.,

Southern Workman. Newsletter for the Hampton Institute. Hampton, Va.

Spivey, D. 1978. *Schooling for the new slavery: Black industrial education, 1868–1915*. Westport, Conn.

Stocking, G. W., Jr. 1968. *Race, culture, and evolution: Essays in the history of anthropology*. New York.

Talbot, E. A. 1904. *Samuel Chapman Armstrong*. New York (1969).

Tylor, E. B. 1871. *Primitive culture: Researches into the development of mythology, philosophy, religion, art, and custom*. London (1920).

Washington, B. T. 1901. *Up from slavery: An autobiography*. New York.

Waters, D. J. 1983. *Strange ways and sweet dreams: Afro-American folklore from the Hampton Institute*. Boston.

White, A. E. 1878. To the Hampton Alumni Association. *Southern Workman* 7:54.
Willis, W. S., Jr. 1973. Franz Boas and the study of black folklore. *Proceedings of the American Ethnological Society* 1973:307–34.

Manuscript Sources

LSCA   Personal Memories and Letters of S. C. Armstrong, compiled by Helen Ludlow, Williams College Archives and Special Collections, Williamstown, Mass.

RAP   Richard Armstrong Papers, Manuscript Division, Library of Congress, Washington, D.C.

BPP   Franz Boas Papers, Professional Correspondence, American Philosophical Society Library, Philadelphia.

EPP   Elsie Clews Parsons Papers, Collection 29, American Philosophical Society Library, Philadelphia.

WORKING FOR A CANADIAN SENSE OF PLACE(S)

The Role of Landscape Painters in Marius Barbeau's Ethnology

FRANCES M. SLANEY

Our consideration leads us to the conclusion that geography is part of cosmography, and has its source in the affective impulse, in the desire to understand the phenomena and history of a country or of the whole earth, the home of mankind.

(Boas 1887:647)

. . . while the collapse of spatial barriers has undermined older material and territorial definitions of place, the very fact of that collapse (the threat of "time-space compression" as I called it in The Condition of Postmodernity*) has put renewed emphasis upon the interrogation of metaphorical and psychological meanings which, in turn, give new material definitions of place by way of exclusionary territorial behaviour. Explorations of this sort should help clarify the thorny problem of "otherness" and "difference" (made so much of in postmodern rhetoric) because territorial place-based identity, particularly when conflated with race, ethnic, gender, religious and class differentiation, is one of the most pervasive bases for both progressive political mobilization and reactionary exclusionary politics.*

(Harvey 1993:4)

In the 1990s anthropologists have become increasingly preoccupied with geography, with issues of place and space (e.g. Hirsch & O'Hanlon 1995).

Frances M. Slaney is Assistant Professor of Anthropology at the University of Regina. She has done ethnographic research in the Sierra Tarahumara of northern Mexico and has published articles on this work, including pieces in American Ethnologist 24 (2), 1997, and Anthropologie et Sociétés 18(1), 1994. She is currently writing about the history of anthropology and the anthropology of art in Canada.

Along with a postmodern focus on space through globalization and diaspo-
ras (e.g. Gupta & Ferguson 1997; Lavie & Swedenburg 1996), local notions
of place have come to the fore (e.g. Feld & Basso 1996). Like most trends in
anthropology, both tendencies have been pursued as if they mark "the beginning of something that will reach far beyond the matters under immediate
consideration" (Geertz 1996:262). In this regard, Geertz has identified the anthropology of place as having recently acquired a peculiar relevance, a sense
of "promise" (ibid.). I do not contest Geertz's observation. Rather, I intend to
explore this sense of relevance by contextualizing current research within social and political conditions and in relation to an earlier comparable period in
the discipline's history. Through this process I propose to address the following questions: Why might anthropologists find the location of culture relevant now? Are we launching into an entirely new set of research concerns, or
can we build on an earlier phase of anthropological investigations? Instead
of directly reinterpreting present conditions, therefore, I will look back at a
similar conjuncture in the history of anthropology: Marius Barbeau's treatment of space and place in Canada during the 1920s and 1930s. I have not
selected Barbeau as an ethnological renegade or paragon. His case is more in-
formative if we regard him as neither a hero nor an antihero. What makes him
worthy of study is that he was an influential and active ethnographer who
worked with the urgency of someone convinced that what he called "human
geography" held "promise" (in Geertz's terminology) for reconciling diverse
cultures within a shifting geopolitical order.

Under the supervision of Edward Sapir, and through collaborations with
Franz Boas, Barbeau modified their concerns with aesthetics and nation
building to suit his own diffusionist agenda. Somewhat discredited among
anthropologists and in academic circles (Beals 1945; Duff 1964), Barbeau remains an important historical figure because of his role as a popularizer of
Quebec folklore, native art and ethnography, and Canadian art history. His
lengthy appointment at the National Museum of Canada (1911–48), and his
continued work there after retirement, gave him influence far beyond his
circle of contemporary colleagues, much as Margaret Mead's influence radi-
ated beyond the American Museum of Natural History and university cam-
puses during a later phase of modernity in North America. Barbeau's career
can thus be summarized, I believe, as a grand project: to reconfigure and promote a multicultural sense of space and place for North Americans, and to
foster an ethnically and historically rich, modernist sense of place for Canadians through modern landscape aesthetics.

The Geopolitics of Culture
in Early- and Late-Twentieth-Century Anthropology

As a turn-of-the-century diffusionist, Marius Barbeau saw ethnology as an historical task comparable to beachcombing. He collected as many specimens as possible, and understood culture largely as a site-specific result of diverse accumulations delivered from other sites. He found it highly significant that his recordings of Tsimshian funerary songs sounded like Chinese dirges (suggesting recent native migrations from Asia); that Quebec wood carving, folk songs, and folk tales he collected had washed over from France (to perpetuate the European Renaissance in twentieth-century North America); and that various North American indigenous groups had become distinguished by art forms either learned from French nuns or inspired by other types of contact with Europeans (Barbeau 1930a; Saint-Martin 1976). Barbeau, then, was particularly attuned to the spatial distribution and redistribution of cultural forms through time. Perhaps for this reason, he expanded his job as museum anthropologist to give university courses on "Human Geography" and to become director, then lifetime member, of the Canadian Geographical Society. His emphasis on geography, however, became a response to pressing social conditions of his era, as Barbeau devoted himself to the problem of reconciling cultural landscapes with political boundaries.

Like Spencer (1876), Barbeau assumed that political units become ever larger and more heterogeneous according to natural law, but unlike many evolutionists he lamented the loss of cultural traditions through modernization. Despite his view of cultures as layers of diffusions and adaptations, he did not accept the obliteration of older traditions by modern life. How could his field-work sites retain their ethnographic specificity—their unique syntheses of cultural deposits—within the territorial boundaries of large, modern nation-states? Apparently in response to this question, Barbeau developed an early multicultural form of territorial aesthetics. He encouraged landscape painters to construct images of landscapes specific to various cultural communities within Canadian state boundaries. Little interested in political action, rhetoric, or theorizing, Barbeau promoted the production and popularization of a vast array of such images as part of a multicultural prototype and an aesthetic imperative for "New World" nation-states. He was not particularly dedicated to the boundaries of Canada per se. Not only did they change a great deal during his lifetime, but he thought it might be better if Canada joined the United States (Art Price, pers. comm. 7/92). Rather, his point was that large, modern nation-states would inevitably be formed in North America, and that the various ethnic groups he was familiar with would have to find a place within whatever larger political bodies arose.

Through the development of ethnographic and aesthetic consciousness among the citizenry of "new world" countries, he expected the ethnic minorities from which they were formed would be valued and conserved. Rather than assume that all citizens would be equal and the same within a uniform state, Barbeau wanted to promote an appreciation of diversified local "colour" that would connect each citizen to numerous regional histories and culturally charged places. To this end, he included various artists in his fieldwork entourage and illustrated his publications with their work. He also diversified his professional activities to include those of art critic, evaluator, curator, historian, and broker. His collaboration with landscape painters, however, best illustrates Barbeau's almost mystical vision for connecting specific local topographies and cultural areas to a larger Canadian territory and community. He considered the cultural composition of Canada too diversified for modern Canadian aesthetics to be based on any one cultural community and sought to remedy this by turning to landscape as the basis of multicultural aesthetics. The land itself was to provide a common ground for preserving and integrating diverse local cultural traditions.

Issues of cultural hybridity, identity, and disjunctured locality arising from Barbeau's project are comparable, yet contradictory, to postmodernism. He celebrated cultural hybridity and global mobility like postmodernism, but he did so to salvage and romanticize traditional cultures rather than to criticize the ways they have been exoticized or essentialized. Similarly, Barbeau worked to prevent a "melting pot" ideology from silencing minority voices, yet he was not concerned with issues of "cultural appropriation." On the contrary, he actively encouraged "primitivism" (Goldwater 1938; Hiller 1991; Price 1989; Torgovnick 1990). He took a classically liberal view that Canadian ethnological collections should be a national resource available to all artists. On the one hand, he encouraged non-native artists to sculpt totem poles or hook rugs and make pottery bearing native West Coast crest motifs. He approved of Florence Wyle's totemic book ends (MBP: MB/FW 11/30/27) and of Art Price's totem poles for the Royal York Hotel in Toronto. When Emily Carr came to Ottawa for a show organized by Barbeau, he not only exhibited her pottery and hooked rugs decorated with West Coast native designs, he also promoted and sold them. Barbeau judged all these art forms to be laudable revitalizations, not desecrations, of native arts, and he was critical of other museologists' reticence to acquire such hybrid constructions. On the other hand, he expected local artists to profit from metropolitan art practices. A Group of Seven painter in Barbeau's fieldwork entourage on the Ile d'Orléans furnished one of his informants with designs for her fabric arts (Jackson Groves 1988:32 [Figure 1]). Barbeau himself gave compositional "advice" to the Quebec folkcarver, Médard Bourgault, who became renowned under the ethnographer's patronage (MBP: MB/M. Bourgault 4/11/35). He clearly expected such diffusionist activism to revitalize

Figure 1. A. Y. Jackson 1882–1974, Horse and Carriage: *Design for Mad. Cimon*, 1925. Watercolor; ink; graphite on paper 14.2 × 22.9 cm. (Gift of Dr. Naomi Jackson Groves. McMichael Canadian Art Collection 1985.51.18.)

French Canadian culture and promote its recognition. In all these acts, Barbeau's aesthetic project was motivated by a sense that relations within and between cultural groups were being, and perhaps needed to be, *re*territorialized and *re*historicized. In that regard his aesthetic project was consistent with the work of some contemporary anthropologists.

Gupta and Ferguson have asserted that deterritorialization and dehistoricization are not evidence of confronting a void, but of undergoing *re*territorialization, and that in contemporary anthropology a sense of this transition has increased awareness of the importance of space. "In the pulverized space of postmodernity, space has not become irrelevant: it has been *re*territorialized in a way that does not conform to the experience of space that characterized the era of high modernity. It is this that forces us to reconceptualize fundamentally the politics of community solidarity, identity, and cultural difference" (Gupta & Ferguson 1992:9). If Barbeau's projects also raise spatial issues, then it is presumably because he helped establish the modernist cultural landscape that is currently being transformed even as it is being reexamined. In other words, Barbeau, like contemporary anthropologists, identified a moment of cultural fluidity; and such periods characterize transition into and out of modernity (García Canclini 1990). At these times, issues of cultural history and geography, questions of how we are situated in space and through places, come to the forefront.

To recognize this is to shift away from regarding culture as independent of geography, a stance once required to oppose nineteenth-century geographical determinism as well as to limit extreme diffusionist perspectives in anthropology. Regarding geography as an arbitrary background separable from culture was also, however, a vision that assumed a fixed geopolitical world order. Because this sense of order is now being questioned (or abandoned), heterogeneity and interconnectedness between local communities has become increasingly visible to us again. Academic references to cultural or ethnic groups cautiously qualify local communities as porous and mobile, while fixed "culture areas" are reconfigured as shifting global "ethnoscapes" (Appadurai 1991).

This return to emphasis on geography and history was partly initiated by anthropological critiques of nationalist ideologies. Nation-state boundaries, it was pointed out, are no less homogenizing and arbitrary constructions than ethnography's insistence that cultural groups be neatly bounded isolates (Anderson 1983; Handler 1988; Herzfeld 1987). National "traditions" were shown to be "inventions" (Hobsbawm & Ranger 1983) devised to authenticate the boundaries of nation-states. On a global scale, it was revealed that maintaining a Eurocentric sense of history, and attributing a lack of history to other societies, is a geopolitical stance initiated by colonialism (Fabian 1983; Wolf 1982). Thus, contrary to Soja's impression of moving from history-focused to geography-focused ideologies (1989), anthropologists recently rediscovered history and geography more or less in tandem.

Nevertheless, despite all these reevaluations of time, space, and community, unease continues to surround these topics. Marc Abélès, for example, writes that the European Union is precipitating a tragic denial of national history and tradition. He thinks it is imposing both "*déterritorialisation*" and "*déshistoricisation*" upon citizens. Although he sees certain common interests among European nations, he expresses concern that there is no emergence of a "European identity," but only a "vast multicultural *bricolage*" (Abélès 1996:44; my trans.). By documenting and examining this contemporary process towards geopolitical redefinition, he claims he is developing a field of study that departs from classical anthropology's focus on homogeneous cultural groups (ibid.). He apparently sees this as a question of unprecedented social amalgamations forcing anthropologists to consider entirely new objects of study. But was that an accurate assessment of anthropology's history?

Barbeau and other early North American anthropologists responded to comparable conditions in the Americas more than seventy years ago. Here, as in contemporary Europe, numerous cultural communities were engulfed by new political bodies: the emerging nation-states of Mexico, the United States, and Canada. Boas, and many of his early collaborators, were dedicated to charting, analyzing, and facilitating the amalgamation of immigrant, self-governed indigenous, and established European settlements, all into these vast new nation-states (Boas 1940). Boas himself regarded the American "melting pot" as a process comparable to the earlier and slower formation of Europe "during the centuries when the people of northern Europe were not yet firmly attached to the soil" (1931:6). He calculated that if cultural nonconformity was treated with tolerance during a "period of adjustment," "assimilation" would occur in the United States even quicker than it had in medieval Europe (Boas 1921). From reallocations of space, reformulated notions of place would emerge. Marius Barbeau engaged directly in a comparable integrative process, practicing a form of applied anthropology to mitigate against the sort of sentiments poignantly described by Abélès as "a current of uncertainty and even anguish" experienced by people unable to "situate themselves" (Abélès 1996:44; my trans.).

The goal of this paper is to advance a less "dehistoricized" perspective on the production of place, relocating anthropology's changing theories and methods within shifting social histories. Now that we are freshly aware of how images of the landscape are both cultural constructions and conditions of modern social life, we can examine how such images were reconfigured in the past, with the help of an ethnologist.

Boas, Barbeau, and Canadian Folklore

Under R. R. Marett's tutelage at Oxford University, Barbeau studied folklore and wrote a library thesis about native populations in western Canada he had never seen. Thus educated in the nineteenth-century armchair tradition of textual interpretation and folklore, he had to acquire fieldwork techniques upon his return to Canada in 1911. Marett considered this a fortuitous opportunity to learn from the "clever" Edward Sapir (MBP: RM/MB 1/16/11), who was Barbeau's boss at Ottawa's National Museum. Yet Barbeau always resisted acknowledging Sapir's influence, seldom citing or crediting him. Despite their common interests in art and ethnology, each man linked these interests differently to history and geography. Unlike Sapir, Barbeau became passionately engaged in salvaging each cultural community he ventured into, and to that end he voraciously collected ethnographic data, incurring great budget overruns to stockpile material culture for the future enrichment of modern nations in North America. Feeling isolated and unhappy in Ottawa, Sapir took to composing music and writing poetry. He developed theories of art that departed from Boas' perspective by drawing more heavily on German philology and romantic philosophy, particularly Herder. For a while this meant interpreting art in terms of individual artistic "geniuses" (with himself as a potential candidate) who express the collective *Geist* of their national groups (1922a, 1922b). Perhaps to resolve his personal incertitude,

Sapir questioned whether the "conscious knowledge of the ethnologist [can] be fused with the intuitions of the artist?" (1922a:570; Handler 1983:224). As we shall see, Barbeau devoted much of his life to answering this question in the affirmative. He developed field techniques and interpretive methods through professional collaborations with artists, fusing his own ethnology with their insights in ways that Sapir had never envisioned. Thus, while Sapir dabbled in the arts during the early 1920s because he felt intellectually and culturally isolated from the stimulation of big city life in the United States to which he was accustomed (Darnell 1990; Handler 1983), Barbeau became enthusiastically engaged in preserving, through art, the very landscape Sapir found wanting.

Boas, on the other hand, justified, institutionally supported, and considerably expanded Barbeau's salvage operations. Although Boas emphatically argued that geography could not be a creative force on culture, but only an influence upon existent cultures (1932:256), his intercontinental and pan-American examination of the "complex historical growth" of individual cultural groups through borrowing and migrations lent his work a highly geographical flavor (1910:340). In keeping with both this perspective and his previous work in geography, he was greatly interested in issues of diffusion and intercultural relations in the Americas. During the Jesup North Pacific Expedition, Boas explored Asian influences on "New World" cultures. His Mexican studies evaluated how Spanish folklore influenced the cultural life of indigenous groups in Latin America. When the Mexican Revolution cut short those investigations, Boas turned to an assessment of other intercontinental diffusions affecting the Americas. For his investigation of French influences on North American Indians, he chose Barbeau as a collaborator, inviting him to investigate Quebec folklore and to join him as an editor of the *Journal of American Folk-Lore* (CMC: FB/RB 1/14/14). Thus Boas pushed Canadian government research further into diffusionist studies and toward folklore. Barbeau became so devoted to these themes that his work became the basis of two folklore centers in Canada (at the Canadian Museum of Civilization in Ottawa and at Laval University in Quebec City). He also wrote numerous articles supporting cultural diffusion long after it had fallen out of academic fashion (Duff 1964), leaving a three-volume migration analysis unpublished at his death (Nowry 1995:251). One must remember, however, that he studied anthropology when more data was drawn from folklore than from ethnography, and when history and geography were central themes in ethnology. One of the latest publications at the time of Barbeau's graduation was A. C. Haddon's *The Wanderings of Peoples* (1911), which states, "The study of human migrations emphasises the fact that ethnology and history can be satisfactorily elucidated only from the geographical standpoint" (v). Such was Barbeau's point of departure.

Yet Boas' folklore plans for Barbeau met resistance from Sapir, who apparently thought the "proper work" of Canada's national museum should be "the study of the aborigines of the Dominion" (BP: ES/MB 10/7/18; cf. Preston 1976; Nowry 1995), and Sapir's opposition obliged Barbeau to justify his folklore studies as a device to examine more thoroughly how native groups had been influenced by European folklore (MBP: ES/MB 9/24/20). Relations between these three men are probably too complex to recover here. For their research programs, Boas and Sapir drew from the same labor pool of anthropologists, shunting Radin, Mason, and Mechling between Mexico, the United States, and Canada. Barbeau expressed irritation that Sapir kept the West Coast "more or less reserved to him" until 1915 (Nowry 1965). That is, he withheld it until just after Boas wrote to Sapir's superior at the Canadian Museum of Man for Barbeau's assignment to French Canadian Folklore. Boas expressed dismay that he was not told about Barbeau's entry into Tsimshian work (CMC: FB/ES 1/5/15), and perhaps he was shocked by Barbeau's stinging attack on *Tsimshian Mythology* (Boas 1916), printed in *American Anthropologist* under Lowie's editorship (Barbeau 1917). Barbeau's eventual independence in Quebec folklore studies must have come not only from Boas' greater authority in the discipline, but may have been influenced by Barbeau's financial backing for Sapir's relatives emigrating from Europe (Asen Balikci, pers. comm. 5/31/96; cf. MBP: MB/ES 11/11/20). Barbeau may also have appealed to Sapir's vanity as a musician and poet. For within a short time, Sapir was publishing English translations of French Canadian songs (Sapir 1917, 1919), and he became enthusiastic enough to propose co-authoring an entire volume of them with their collector, Barbeau (Barbeau & Sapir 1925), who corrected the French (MBP: MB/ES 4/15/21, 6/20/22, 6/27/22, 8/24/24). Still, although Sapir joined Canadian folklore societies that Boas had pressured Barbeau to organize for *Journal of American Folk-Lore* fundraising, folklore never became important to Sapir's work. The field was left to Barbeau. This difference contributed, as we shall see below, to rather divergent visions of "New World" nation building among Boas, Barbeau, and Sapir.

Once recruited by Boas, Barbeau plunged enthusiastically into Quebec folklore studies. He recorded songs from his father in the Beauce region, and returned to his Huron informants for French folklore he had earlier refused in favour of "pure" Indian material. Barbeau's fieldwork was key to realizing Boas' plan for publishing "French numbers" of the *Journal of American Folk-Lore*, and Barbeau seized the opportunity to publish his voluminous data. In a regular issue of the journal we see an interesting illustration of Barbeau's emerging ethnological technique and aesthetic aspirations (1920b:33). Barbeau presented a geographical distribution survey of family names and nicknames in Quebec which was conventionally modeled after a similar folklore study in France (1920a). As a sequel, he attempted to illustrate a link between

Quebec folklore and the land by presenting a selection of his own photographs (supplemented by one or two he did not take) titled, "Photographies de gens et de choses du terroir canadien" ("Photographs of people and things of the Canadian soil").

The apparently jumbled assortment of 46 photographs was accompanied by little commentary. Each one was labeled by location and the culturally significant features Barbeau wished to connect to that site. These features included architectural styles of barns, windmills, churches, and houses ("construite en pierre des champs" or "à encorbellement"). He also highlighted items from the material culture of rural Quebec, such as beds, rocking chairs, and homemade fabrics ("Lit à rideaux avec 'courte-pointe' en 'flanelle du pays,' à Saint-Joachim"). Photos of the landscape itself depicted unusual land formations ("Le Cap Chat (Gaspé)") or settings for architectural features and towns ("Château-Richer; partie nord-est," and "La 'Petite-ferme,' à Saint-Joachim (Montmorency)"). Finally, he included portraits, often of his informants ("Prudent Sioni, conteur, métis de la tribu des Hurons de Lorette (Quebec)"), including his father. These people, too, were labeled by location. Occasionally, they were singled out for special ethnographic qualities ("Jeune paysanne, en 'bottes sauvages,' à Saint-Ferréol") and, more often, were given occupational markers ("pêcheur," "cultivateur"). The overall discursive thrust of this indexical project, framed consistently by locative markers, is to render people into local "types" comparable to architectural or furniture styles. As such, they help define the local character of their landscape (on folkloric labeling, see Handler 1988:78–79). This gallery, then, was an attempt to record and disseminate images of a culturally charged "soil," which the journal's subscribers were expected to find visually apprehendable, or readable, from photographs.

Barbeau took comparable photographs at his ethnographic sites among native groups in British Columbia (Riley 1988). Unconcerned with the "authenticity" of posed portraits, he encouraged informants to wear ceremonial clothing or to demonstrate curing and dancing techniques for his camera. He then used some of his photographs in a profusely illustrated article for the *Canadian Geographical Journal* (Barbeau 1930b), with the intention of luring tourists into the Skeena area. (For his earlier thoughts on Skeena tourism, see MBP: Jenness correspondence, 1923.) Recounting fragments of a native legend about a land called Temlaham, Barbeau suggested that the native image of a "paradise lost" was a contemporary reality for visitors: "Most of this country has now passed into the hands of the white man. Yet it retains unmistakable traces of its earlier occupation and colourful memories of old. Its scenic grandeur and beauty evoke reminiscences of Temlaham, of an earthly paradise, where enchantment belongs not only to the past, but pervades the air on every side" (1930b:141). Trying to capture how this mystical presence of cultural history "pervades" the local landscape proved too great a representational challenge for the camera, however, and Barbeau later admitted that he became unsatisfied with his photographic documentation. His problem was that photographs only reproduced outside surfaces, without being able to "recreate things" from the inside (Barbeau 1955). This view of representation characterized modernist theories of aesthetic expression which gained force among Canadian artists during the 1920s.

Fieldwork with Artists

Barbeau became convinced that artists could transcend the representational obstacles he encountered with his camera. The Canadian Pacific Railway commissioned him to work with an American painter, Langdon Kihn, on tourist propaganda about Plains Indians (Barbeau 1923a). Although Kihn did mostly Indian portraits, Barbeau considered him "among the first to interpret" the country, and to open up the field for other artists. Sapir was enthusiastic about Kihn's work and attempted to purchase a series of his paintings for the museum "to beautify our exhibits . . . They would give a wonderful touch of life to our West Coast exhibits" (CMC: ES/W. McInnes 2/26/25). Barbeau, however, believed that Kihn's "collaboration . . . made it possible to resurrect many things now passing, which otherwise would have gone to complete oblivion" (1932a:331). "Though an outsider himself [i.e. a non-Canadian], he has contributed to open up a new field, so far neglected, and thus to enrich national consciousness" (Barbeau 1932a:331, 1932b:198).

Building on the skills he saw in Langdon Kihn, Barbeau then tried to extend his ethnological grasp by collaborating with Canadian painters. He ran virtual field schools for prominent and concertedly nationalist landscape painters of the Group of Seven, such as A. Y. Jackson and Arthur Lismer, on the Ile d'Orléans (Jackson 1958; Jackson Groves 1988). Through correspondence, he also assisted them with ethnographic and practical information for independent sketching trips. Several of these artists became part of Barbeau's entourage during his 1920s field trips to the Tsimshian area of northern British Columbia or consulted with him about visiting the area.[1]

Barbeau was tremendously excited about the contribution those artists made to ethnography. In a popular magazine, he described their fieldwork. "Scenery, totem poles, native graveyards and Indian physiognomies all went

---

1. The Group of Seven painters Lawren Harris, A. Y. Jackson, and J. E. H. MacDonald, as well as Edwin Holgate, Pegi Nichol, George Pepper, W. J. Phillips, Anne Savage, and sculptor Florence Wyle all collaborated with Barbeau (cf. Hill 1995), as did John Byers of Toronto and Paul Loze of France. He also collaborated with composers and musicians (Barbeau 1929a:30).

down upon canvas or into plastic clay at a terrific pace . . . When the time came for the visitors to depart, they buckled up their fat portfolios with a light heart. Their search for truth and beauty had not been idle. They carried off with them new riches that had become their own" (1929a:13). Because this "search for truth and beauty" was one that Barbeau felt himself unable to satisfy through standard ethnographic and photographic techniques, he wrote rather bitterly, "The ethnologist is a fool who so far deceives himself as to believe that his field notes and specimens, gathered in the raw from half-breeds or decrepit survivors of a past age, still represent the unadulterated knowledge or crafts of the prehistoric races of America" (1927a:52). The very history he so fondly set out to represent in his photographs of the "terroir" (soil) imposed a veil over what he was trying to observe empirically. The Indians had "changed as radically as have their surroundings." He found, though, that if he took artists into the field (or lent them ceremonial regalia from museum collections with which to deck out their portrait subjects), they could "penetrate under the surface" of this confused ethnographic condition. With the help of a "gifted" artist of "ample imagination" one could achieve "a clear, individual reading of human souls even at a time when they seem about to fade away from this materialistic world" (1923b:95; cf. 1932a:337, 1932b:202). To Barbeau, the artist was the one who could record human and cultural "truths" when categories in the physical world were too confused for empirical observation by the ethnographer. In response to Sapir's question of whether the ethnologist's knowledge could ever be fused with the artist's intuition, then, Barbeau found that the "intuitions of the artist" often surpassed and extended "the conscious knowledge of the ethnologist."

Barbeau's modernist diffusionism required trained seers to discern cultural "riches" buried in local peoples and their landscapes. For West Coast and Skeena cultures, Barbeau was pleased with Kihn and Holgate's ability to "characterize their Mongolian features in forceful portraits, and their country in landscapes which . . . provide a background as decorative as they are exotic" (Barbeau 1932b:332). These features are depicted, for example, in Kihn's portrait of a Gitksan Fireweed Chief (photographed by Barbeau ca. 1924 [Figure 2]), who, Barbeau thought, bore features that revealed his Asian ancestry. The chief's ceremonial clothing was later donned by Kihn himself, who was in turn also photographed by Barbeau (Figure 3). The artist's ability to penetrate the "truths" of Gitksan culture apparently rendered him honorary Gitksan "identity" in the sense that he had a primitivist "affinity" with it (Rubin 1984).

Barbeau similarly wrote that the landscape vistas inhabited by "Mongolian" people of the West Coast "bespeak the Orient" (1930b:147). He described panoramas at Port Essington as "Japanese-like" (an assessment he tried to capture in a photograph, 1930b:138). When Kihn adapted an oriental printmaking style for rendering mountains to execute his *Nootka Indian Fishing Village, North-west Coast of Vancouver Island* ([Figure 4]; Richmond 1925:346), Barbeau presumably saw this style as a fitting reflection of how the cultural (and "racial") diffusions embodied by village inhabitants spilled into their landscape. In other words, Barbeau reasoned that as cultural groups migrate, or cultural practices are borrowed, the landscape in which those groups live must accordingly transmute to reflect those cultural changes. "Racial" features, topographical qualities, and cultural practices were all partible traits that diffused and recombined to form distinctive cultural places whose qualities could be visually apprehended and appreciated.

As a corollary, Barbeau suggested that when cultural communities resist changes being imposed on them, this too, is expressed by the local landscape. "Even now that they [Stonies, Crees and Blackfeet] are barb-wired on reserves, their Indian agencies and missions stand in isolation, like symbols of the restrictions which have not yet won full recognition in the land" (1932a:332). Thus Barbeau's devotedly diffusionist viewpoint evoked conflicting messages of glory and despair. Janus-like, his vision was oriented forward and backward with equal measures of Romantic nostalgia and modernist acceptance or "realism," even optimism.

This partly explains why his attitude toward native arts and artists now appears so confused. On the one hand, he deplored the lack of interest young native people showed in their own traditions and skills, and he blamed European missionaries for forcing Indians to adopt Christianity: "Creative art among the British Columbia Indians has largely passed out, as they have abandoned paganism and adopted Christianity. Carving of marvellous totem poles, as insignia of tribal power and social rank, rose to its height . . . and today the art is dead . . . . They do not believe in traditions any longer . . . they do not, indeed, believe in themselves" (*Colonist*, Victoria B.C. 1/25/28). He was disturbed to see that "the owners themselves in the course of hysterical revivals under the spurious banner of Christianity" had destroyed totem poles on the upper Nass, and concluded that the "art now belongs to the past" (1929b:1). On the other hand, Barbeau hoped to mitigate against these conditions through a native arts revival (1957a:142). He never completely counted on revivalism, however, and interpreted the broken fabric of native social order as a sign that salvage operations were required and that a new wave of diffusions had irreversibly been set into motion.

He also assumed that modern non-native artists must take over where native ones left off. Thus his position towards native disarray was like that of Emily Carr, the painter whose career he greatly promoted. Carr proclaimed that if Indians were threatening to burn down totem poles and were ashamed of them, then non-native Canadians should treasure such native works as their own. They must become "to us Canadians what the ancient Briton's

Figure 2. W. Langdon Kihn, *Tsyebasa or Grouse with Closed Eyes* (Stephen Morgan), 1924. Photographed by Marius Barbeau ca. 1924. (Canadian Museum of Civilization Photo # 63002.)

Figure 3. Langdon Kihn in Gitksan chief's ceremonial robe and head-dress. Photographed by Marius Barbeau ca. 1924. (Canadian Museum of Civilization Photo #62544.)

Figure 4. Langdon Kihn, *Nootka Indian Fishing Village, North-west Coast of Vancouver Island*. Location unknown. (Published in Richmond 1925.)

relics are to the English" (Shadbolt 1979:38), cultural treasures for the modern nation-state and all its citizens. Barbeau made it clear he shared this view when he wrote:

> Even after their disappearance, they have left deep traces of their occupation and their prehistoric culture. The Red Skin will stay, in literature and the arts as well as in the country records, an effective force in the collective soul of the nations of the Americas. The great totems of the northwest coast, the cosmogonic myths of the *Raven* and the *Woman who fell from the sky*, the tales of worldwide diffusion, the poetic chants of Siberian and Mongolian inspiration, the words on the entire map, the thousand voices of prehistoric men in the forests, along the rivers, on the mountains, in the tundras of the great north and on the edges of glacial arctic seas, will never cease to confer on all of Canada distinctive traits that come from its own habitat. (1950a:217; my trans.)

Poignant regrets of a passing era are linked here to a recuperation scheme that draws upon an image of the land, of the state's territory, as a repository of all past and present cultures. Through the medium of the land, new occupants would absorb the cultures of previous occupants. New states in the Americas could be great because of all the cultural histories included within their territorial boundaries, and not *in spite of* all the other possible cultural hegemonies they might have crushed in attaining that land. Although vulnerable to the accusation that he too easily assumed the disappearance of indigenous cultures (Beaucage in Barbeau 1915:31), this schema was also an attempt at inclusion, at convincing nonindigenous people to view their Canadian locations as inalienable from the lives that previously animated those spaces.

This vision also presupposed a psychological connection to geography. Land was considered both a memory bank and the basis for contemporary knowledge and action. As such, a component of every citizen's personal memory was invested in the landmass of the nation-state. Land contributed to, and drew upon, the collective resource for expression and communication among citizens past and present. This territorial psychology was expressed in spiritual terms by some of Barbeau's closest painter-collaborators, particularly members of Canada's Group of Seven and Emily Carr. They drew inspiration from the American poet Walt Whitman, apparently accepting his definition of the artist's connection to "his" nation-state's slice of geography: "His spirit responds to his country's spirit . . . he incarnates its geography and natural life . . . To him enter the essences of the real things and past and present events . . . the tribes of red aborigines . . . He is the equalizer of his age and land" (Whitman:1855:7–9). In short, all of nature within territorial boundaries could be treated like a personal and political body, and doing portraits of it was a means of (re)capturing its "spirit" or soul. This assumed a dualist model of nationalism in which the nation's land is seen as a body and the people its soul (cf. Dumont 1970: 108). Passing cultural "essences" buried in geological layers of the land became accessible to citizens through artists' representations. Landscape painters functioned as spirit mediums or psycho-therapists. What they communicated was supposed to increase public con-sciousness, to expose each citizen to truths about their landscape and thereby themselves and their communities.

Although Barbeau collaborated with spiritualist artists and with art dealers who espoused psychoanalytic theories of the unconscious (cf. MBP: MB/W. Watson correspondence), I have found no evidence that he gave credence to either spiritualism or psychoanalytic theory. I speculate, however, that he may have taken a theoretical cue from Boas, who described linguistic work as a process of charting unconscious mediums of communication (Boas 1911 [1966]). To this, Barbeau seems to have proposed a geographical counterpoint in which national territories are unconscious repositories that are "spoken" by citizens who are not aware of how this works until it is illustrated by artists and ethnologists. Thus Barbeau's understanding of landscape aesthetics was effectively a counterpoint to Sapir's vision of language as a collective art form (Sapir 1921). Invisible forces that shape collective life were made visible by the expert who could perceive them—whether linguist, ethnologist, or land-scape painter.

Furthermore, if Canada's land base is a locus of cultural resources and com-munication, then living close to the land should logically give native artists and art forms a singular advantage. Thus, in a 1955 interview, when Bar-beau was asked about the "creativity" of native people as compared to non-native Canadians, he replied, "The reason why they are creative, is that they are close to the ground. They know their rivers . . . They are versed into their *terroir* [soil] and it's what every one of the white people should be. They should know their country in the first place" (Barbeau 1955). To a contem-porary observer, it might appear that Barbeau wishes to capture the inter-active and embodied local sense of place theorized by Bourdieu (1980) and Hanks (1996). But this was not enough for two reasons. First, Barbeau saw local landscapes as historically sedimented constructions, to which contem-porary native people had made only the most recent deposition. Although pivotal, their contribution was only one of many, and not definitive. Simi-larly, for Barbeau, ethnographic observation is impoverished because it can-not access the full historical content of the landscape. Second, native artists needed to be a conscious part of the national and international society that would give their art forms modern social currency. They had to be educated, so that they could make their sense of locality accessible to the national and international imaginary. Barbeau stipulated that although Indians know their *terroir* they must be "given a chance" (1955). By "chance," though, he said he meant the sort of program James Houston gave Inuits by introducing them to printmaking and sculpting techniques along with international marketing. Houston is now renowned for having influenced the media, style, and marketing of Inuit art forms. Against the Inuit interest in visual detail, for example, he advised simplified forms conforming with the European primitivist sculpture of Henry Moore (Graburn 1976; Houston 1995), an aesthetic directive conforming to Barbeau's advice for folk carvers in Quebec. Barbeau's multiculturalism, then, was an attempt to push both towards primitivism and modernism, a celebration of the local according to an internationally recognizable style. Just as he expected nonindigenous Canadians trained in European art schools to develop local forms of expression, he accepted that modernist revisions would be the criteria by which diverse indigenous and folkloric cultural traditions could become included in modern art forms. His Oxford professor expressed this in British class-bound terminology: "it is certain that the unconscious art of the folk can develop into art of the conscious and refined order, and must do so if the latter is to be truly national in type. Of course such a process of devulgarization is bound to involve innovation in no small degree" (Marett 1920:116–17; cf. Kemp 1948:59).

Whereas Barbeau advocated that native artists be trained in "conscious" art making, he also worked hard to introduce urban-schooled artists (particularly members of the explicitly nationalist Group of Seven) to ethnic communities where they typically painted landscape. Barbeau saw not only the land, but also all the cultural traditions it supported, as resources from the *terroir*. When he said that "white" artists should "know their country" topographically, he added without pause: "They should know its sources—its art, the folk songs, the folk art—so as to be able to create from this, instead of seeing it abolished from childhood on" (Barbeau 1955). This statement could be seen as a paradoxical, geographical reductionism of minority cultures that severely limited the multicultural and salvage aims of Barbeau's entire aesthetic vision. If folk cultures were already recorded in the land, then why collect specimens of their art to house separately in museums? And once their cultures were buried, how could the revitalization of any particular ethnic group be assured through contemporary art practices? Barbeau's tendency towards telluric reductionism, however, reinforced the institutional basis of the National Museum in which he worked. The museum was founded by a geologist, George Mercer Dawson, who collected ethnological specimens as part of his Geological Survey of Canada (Cole 1973). During most of Barbeau's career, the museum was administered as part of the Department of Mines or the Department of Northern Affairs and National Resources, and his stratigraphic vision of culture as diffusionist deposits conformed to geological perspectives as much as geographical ones. Thus Barbeau's ethnological work in aesthetics conformed to the broader institutional context of his

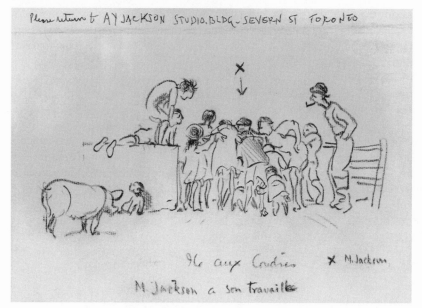

Figure 5. Arthur Lismer, M. *Jackson a Son Travaille* [sic], 1925. Pencil on paper 18.4 × 25.0 cm. (Gift of Dr. Naomi Jackson Groves. McMichael Canadian Art Collection 1985.32.)

work, focusing on the land as a resource through which Canada would gain definition and recognition as a nation-state.

Certainly Barbeau's nonfrancophone artist collaborators who worked in Charlevoix have been criticized for constructing images with an exoticizing, rather than indigenous, gaze (Gendreau 1982; Trépanier 1991). What I want to examine here, however, is less the cultural authenticity of the authors and their representations of the landscape than the observable fact that artists moved from ethnography to topography in their work processes. When artists went into the field with Barbeau, they produced innumerable portraits and sketches of material culture or social gatherings. Some of these were later used to illustrate Barbeau's ethnographic texts or his more popularized Quebec folktales and folksongs. Naomi Jackson Groves thinks that Barbeau may even have corrected (with a ruler) some of Jackson's Ile d'Orléans sketches in the interests of accuracy (1988:17). She has published numerous other sketches that demonstrate Jackson's interest in architectural structures, horse carts, plough mechanics, interior decoration, furniture, and family scenes. Indeed, the artists were often surrounded by interested bystanders while they worked (Figure 5). A. Y. Jackson and Arthur Lismer's finished oil paintings, however, toward which they ultimately worked, were usually unpopulated stretches of land, with only occasional architectural structures and figures

Figure 6. A. Y. Jackson, *Saint-Jean, Ile d'Orléans*, 1925. Oil on wood 21.2 × 26.6 cm. (National Gallery of Canada, Ottawa 6945.)

(Figure 6). Such lack of ethnographic detail seems an incongruous outcome of their wide-ranging fieldwork engagement, as if the ethnographic present is melted into the landscape. Apparently, though, they were regarded as evocative records of past and present inhabitants.[2]

Emily Carr's painting career followed a comparable trajectory from the ethnographically particular to "pure" landscapes (Moray 1993; Shadbolt 1979; Tippett 1979). At first she dedicated herself to salvaging native populations by painting meticulous records of totem pole carvings, human figures, and village landscapes (Figure 7). Like Barbeau, she used photography to improve her documentary accuracy (Tippett 1979:75, 108). Barbeau recognized the ethnographic value of Carr's 1912 and 1913 Haida paintings,

---

2. This emphasis on landscape as that which "possesses an inner coherence" was borrowed directly from Scandinavian symbolist landscape painting, a style first seen by Group of Seven members at a 1913 exhibition in Buffalo, N.Y. "The special quest of symbolic art" was "to re-establish contact with the primal sources of experience," and northern European nationalist painters used landscape as a vehicle for expressing connections to historic folk heroes and mythical pre-Christian figures (Nasgaard 1984:8).

Figure 7. Emily Carr, *Old Indian House, Northern British Columbia, Indians Returning from Canneries to Guyasdums Village*, 1912. Oil on card 96.2 × 65.1 cm, signed M. Emily Carr. (Courtesy Vancouver Art Gallery VAG 42.3.51; photo Trevor Mills.) This painting was exhibited in the 1927 show (see installation photograph, Figure 10), and used to illustrate Barbeau's *Totem Poles* Vol. 2, 1950 (1990):713.

Figure 8. Emily Carr, *Big Raven*, 1931. Oil on canvas 86.7 × 113.8 cm, signed M. Emily Carr. (Courtesy Vancouver Art Gallery VAG 42.3.11; photo Trevor Mills.)

and wrote of them as a vehicle for becoming familiar with Haida poles (Barbeau 1929b:25). Her primitivist project, however, was undoubtedly strengthened by studying in Brittany, France, where many painters worked according to Gauguin's example, and where Barbeau also studied painting briefly (see MBP: MB/A. Patterson correspondence). As Carr's career progressed, and particularly after her Barbeau-sponsored meeting with the Group of Seven, she dropped her conservationist ethnographic program in favor of "pure" landscapes. Through popular books, she explained how to read her "pure" landscape paintings as enveloping, but still containing, ethnographic detail. For her, "the Indian" was part of "Nature." Like Barbeau, then, she saw the landscape itself as resonating with native cultures that had once flourished in it. In this sense, her landscapes were, and remain for much of the Canadian public, imbued with an awareness of previously strong native cultures that once inhabited the land portrayed. Work from her transitional period shows how she moved from painting totem poles and villages to painting totem poles and trees as equally sculpted forms, a deliberate polysemy facilitated by modified cubism, which eventually led to the substitution of totem poles with trees (Figure 8). At the end of her life she painted relatively "pure" landscapes that de-emphasized sculptural qualities in favor of swirling delineations of forest

"spirit" and rhythms (Figure 9). Interestingly, Barbeau declared Carr's transitional and late paintings the most successful. In a CBC radio program, he
described how a friend from his own jaunt in Brittany, Ambrose Patterson,
along with American painter Mark Toby, convinced Emily Carr to leave poles
and Indians out of her canvases. He declared he was impressed with the results
during his 1929 visit to Victoria and Carr's studio. He saw that the advice he
had given her to go to the Nass in 1928 had been "not fruitful. She no longer
needed totems. Enthusiastic, I bought two canvases in her new style" (Barbeau 1957b:4; cf. Shadbolt 1979:206). Apparently, rather than documenting
ethnographic sites she had managed to represent a sense of place that included
and revered indigenous inhabitants even while assimilating them into nature.

In many ways the turning point of both Barbeau's and Carr's careers in aesthetic reterritorialization was a 1927 art show called "Canadian West Coast
Art: Native and Modern" that Barbeau co-curated with the director of the
National Gallery. This show was intended to draw together western and eastern as well as native and non-native art forms (Figures 10 and 11). Quibbles
about whether Barbeau "discovered" Carr in the course of organizing this
show (Tippett 1974) miss the important point that he saw her work as more
than regionally significant and actively promoted it (Hembroff-Schleicher
1978). Along with Emily Carr, other modern Canadian landscape painters
such as the Group of Seven participated in the exhibition to "provide back-
grounds to Northwest Indian Art" (Barbeau 1957b:3). Thus contextualized,
native artifacts and contemporary work by all people were all identified as
"art" and claimed as part of Canadian territory. "A commendable feature
of this aboriginal art for us is that it is truly Canadian in its inspiration. It
has sprung up wholly from the soil and the sea within our national boundaries," explained Barbeau in the exhibition catalogue (1927b:4). He apparently hoped that visitors to the exhibit would contemplate possible aesthetic
correspondences arising out of this geopolitical conjuncture of diverse cultural traditions. "The interrelation of totem poles and modern paintings displayed in close proximity made it clear that the inspiration for both kinds
of art expression sprang from the same fundamental background" (Barbeau
1932a:337–38). Despite separate histories and traditions, "the moderns responded to the same exotic themes." "One enhanced the beauty of the other
and made it more significant" (338). Historically distinct cultural aesthetics, then, could be linked through common territory. What is more, state
regionalism could be bridged through cross-regional aesthetic appreciation
of a continuous landscape. "At last the East and West have joined hands in
a common appreciation of one of America's most inspiring pictorial back-
grounds—the Rockies and the Northwest Coast" (ibid.). This show began an
exhibition formula for Barbeau, of landscape paintings juxtapositioned with
three-dimensional ethnic arts, which he considered appropriate for repre-

Figure 9. Emily Carr, *Roots*, ca. 1937–39. Oil on canvas 112 × 69 cm, signed Emily Carr. (The province of British Columbia Provincial Archives.)

Figure 10. Installation view of the Canadian West Coast Art: Native and Modern exhibition, 1927. On the left side is a rug hooked by Emily Carr using Westcoast native whale designs (now in the Folklore Division of CMC). The painting on the right is the Guyasdums one reproduced here (Figure 7). (National Gallery of Canada Archives, Ottawa.)

senting Canada a decade later at the World Fair in Paris (BP: MB/C. Comfort 3/22/37).

Barbeau, Sapir, and Boas: Theories of Art and Nation Building

The 1927 show, which Barbeau rightfully regarded as a highpoint in his aesthetic project, opened two years after Sapir's departure from Canada and the same year that Boas published his highly acclaimed *Primitive Art*. Given Barbeau's close association with these men in the years preceding this event, let us consider the possible influences of Sapir and Boas on this extraordinary ethnological statement about art and the Canadian landscape.

When Abélès refers to the European Union as a "vast multicultural *bricolage*" suffering from a "symbolic and ritual deficit" (Abélès 1996:44), he is echoing quite precisely the aesthetic dilemma Boas saw as the condition for all

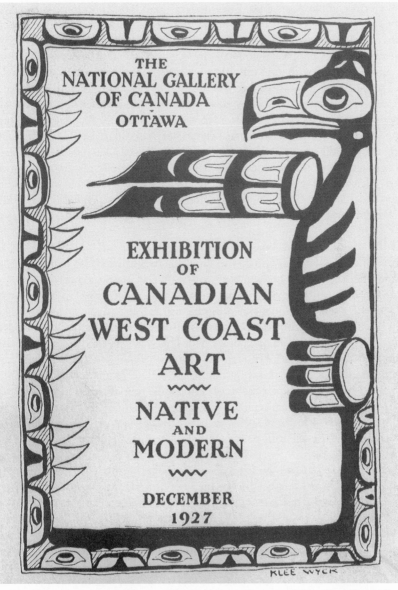

Figure 11. Emily Carr, catalogue cover design for the 1927 show, signed "Klee Wyck," an Indian name Carr used to sign her interpretations of West Coast native designs, reserving (variations on) her European name for other work belonging to the landscape tradition. This alternate identification is perhaps comparable to Kihn's adoption of Gitksan chiefly garb. (National Gallery of Canada Archives, Ottawa.)

modern "complex" societies. This modern quandary is succinctly expressed by Boas in *Primitive Art* (1927) when he states that collective responses to aesthetics require "a very firm and uniform cultural background, such as is possessed by many peoples of simple social structure, but that cannot exist in our complex society with its manifold, intercrossing interests and its great variety of situations that create different emotional centers for each of its numerous strata" (103). In modern society, Boas writes, "It is possible for an artist to train a group of followers and admirers in the symbolism that he cultivates, but it is exceedingly unlikely that such symbolism should develop in such a way that it would be felt automatically by all of us" (102). He regarded national flags as coming closest to evoking widespread symbolic responses in modern societies. Ever skeptical of nationalist ideology, though, he reminds his readers that the "strong emotional value" of flags is also a symbolic operation of exclusivity that operates within as well as between groups they represent (100–102).

On the other hand, Boas regarded the role of the artist in all societies as that of a singular individual who breaks through the constraints of traditions. Best known for his formalist work on West Coast totemic iconography (1897), Boas' anthropology of art later became an attempt "to break away from the formal treatment of primitive art . . . and to show the influence of the individual in the development of art style" (BP: FB/PJE Woodbridge 12/7/18; cf. Jacknis 1992; Jonaitis 1995). This was really an expansion of the notion of the "genius." Through that concept, Boas attempted to link cultural traditions to the possibility of progress. The genius was an ideal individual, and individual*ist*, capable of periodically reorienting an entire society. Thus the artist-hero figure, like the scientist-hero figure, became a key concept in Boasian anthropology because it upheld Boas' particular liberal aim of "establishing the scientific basis of individualism" and working for "progress" (Bunzel 1962:8).

Boas handed this aesthetic project over to Haeberlin, who published only one article on the subject before his premature death (1918). Thereafter, Sapir adopted the task, strongly promoting the image of the artist-genius in his own writings on aesthetics. While in Ottawa, he defended the romantic genius concept against Kroeber's proposed "superorganic" theory of scientific and artistic inventions, according to which great scientific inventions and art works are products of cultural areas and eras rather than exceptional individuals (Darnell 1990; Kroeber 1917; Sapir 1917). In Sapir's many versions of "Culture, Genuine and Spurious," he outlines a link between history and cultural "authenticity" that is operated by the artistic genius. That figure both guides social bodies through history and ensures their cultural vitality. Having been a Herderian scholar at a young age, Sapir thus returned to a simplified Herderian model of history and nationhood. He appears to have abandoned Boas' more pluralist interpretation of Herder (cf. Barnard 1968) for a return to earlier German romanticism. In these articles, Sapir assumes cultural homogeneity within national groups through a notion of *Volksgeist* embodied by the artist, and does little to address cultural heterogeneity in North America's emerging nation-states.

In "Culture in New Countries" (1922b),[3] Sapir applies his model of genius-driven history to "New World" nation building. He focuses on connecting normative individuals to societies through art, which allows the "welding of one's individuality with the spirit of one's civilization" (1922b:364). If art is not constantly renewed it degenerates to "the dross of conventionality" (cf. Handler 1986:147–48). At its best, though, art is the key to building from individuals to "culture," to "nations," and finally to "civilizations." As he put it, "the highest manifestations of culture, the very quintessence of the genius of a civilization, necessarily rest in art, for the reason that art is the authentic expression, in satisfying form, of experience . . . and art . . . is above all other undertakings of the human spirit bound to reflect culture" (ibid.). The problem he saw with "new countries" in the Americas was that they were concerned with the satisfaction of economic and material needs, while abandoning aesthetic and cultural ones. Their size and population distribution meant that they were "too small for the intelligent solution of the large problems in the sphere of direct ends [economics]; . . . too large for the fruitful enrichment of the remoter ends, for culture" (367).

Although Sapir thus seemed to take on nation building as a culturally homogenous project in these articles, such efforts to theorize national art forms were written at about the same time that he expressed doubts about the colloquial notion of "nations" (1921:208) and the assumed cultural unity of such social bodies (213). He suggested, for instance, that when it comes to "nationality," "at best . . . the linguistic unification is never absolute, while the cultural unity is apt to be superficial, of a quasi-political nature, rather than deep and far-reaching" (ibid.). This claim appears more Boasian because it insists upon variability within all human societies, and presents nationalism as an ideology that promotes closed and "pure" societies artificially (Boas 1931). Pitting what is "deep and far-reaching" against "superficial" politics, however, can be seen as a measure of "genuine" and "spurious" cultures.

In a "Prefatory Note" to "An Album of Prehistoric Canadian Art" written by Harlan Smith, Sapir endorsed a means of strengthening new nation-states by combining "direct" economic and "remoter" aesthetic ends through the

3. While in Canada, Sapir published three papers that were eventually all incorporated into his 1924 "Culture, Genuine and Spurious," published in the *American Journal of Sociology* (29: 401–29) and reprinted in David Mandelbaum's *Selected Writings of Edward Sapir in Language, Culture, and Personality* (1949:308–31). The three precursors were Sapir 1919, 1922a, and 1922b (cf. Darnell 1990:461, 463, 465).

use of primitive art for industrial design (1923). Echoing Haeberlin (1918: 263), he scolded "scientific students of primitive culture" for having "forgotten that primitive art is art as well as ethnological material," and suggested that "primitive" art could have an "invigorating influence" "on our own decorative art" (Sapir 1923:111). Modern designers could gain vitality from "primitive" ones, exploiting a resource for renewed symbolism, meaning, and value in modern societies. In other words, they could restore the "spirit" to overly economistic states where uniquely material interests were maintaining "tyrannical sway in the ordering of our lives" (1922a:177–78). Barbeau was to articulate this theme frequently during his career (Barbeau 1932a, 1932b, 1932c, 1933a, 1933b; Barbeau & Price 1956). Here, then, we see a primitivist program for New World art forms that acknowledges cultural heterogeneity while continuing to push for "genuine" cultures in "new countries."

Shortly after he left Canada, Sapir further sanctified his model of personhood, artistic creativity, and nation building, by suggesting that art could substitute for religion in modern societies. Art, he wrote, promotes "sensuous harmony" and "a feeling of wholeness precipitating the flux of things into tangible forms . . . religion gathers up all the threads and meaninglessnesses of life into a wholeness that is not manifest and can only be experienced in the form of a passionate desire" that is interested in "the impulsive conquest of reality" (1928:123–24). This is perhaps the closest Sapir came to dealing with art as a means of culturally representing social geographies, of imaging senses of place. His primary concern, in the terms evoked by Abélès, was with "historicization" as a vehicle for the cultural integration of individuals into vital political bodies. He saw nationalist groups primarily as "sentimentally unified" through art and history (Sapir 1921:213). Territorialization, except in regard to his remarks about the size of new countries in the Americas, was not a major consideration in his exploration of aesthetics.

Sapir's dualist view that art is a spiritual counterpart for materialist concerns, and art's role is to act as a connection between national traditions and modern progress, were two themes Barbeau explored and developed after Sapir's departure from Ottawa. Yet Barbeau deviated from Sapir's work on two major accounts. First, Barbeau's anthropology of art more clearly emphasized Boas' recognition that modern societies are culturally fragmented. This viewpoint was supported not only from his work with indigenous groups in the Americas, but from his involvement in folklore. The second major theoretical difference is that whereas Barbeau and Boas linked cultural history to geography, Sapir became less interested in diffusionism and the cultural significance of geography after his first years in Ottawa, at the same moment he was becoming more interested in art. Barbeau demonstrates these distinctions in an article he wrote after retirement, called "L'âme d'une grande nation moderne":

Certainly, the soul of a nation is above all not contained in the expanse of its territories, in its natural resources, in its industries, or even in its official history. If it were, Canada could be called . . . a soulless-body. But it also possesses its own soul. This soul, still young but overflowing with diverse aspirations, is of a double—even multiple—origin. It cannot fail to change while growing, through contact with elements that are at first foreign, but through time assimilated in a geographic milieu that is varied and irresistible. (1950a:216; my trans.)

Assimilation was not just an intercultural dynamic, but one of absorption into the landscape. In this landscape ontology, the state territory became a space so diversified that it contained multiple souls, expressed by localized places. Thus Barbeau continued: "Once conscious of itself, this vigorous soul will not be weakened by its persistent complexity" (1950a:218). In other words, neither cultural complexity or size of land mass were weaknesses in forging state-wide aesthetic sentiments, once citizens had acquired consciousness of how their landscape was permeated with traces of human experiences.

Nearing retirement, Barbeau wrote a paper that resolves the work he first attempted with his early photographs in the *Journal of American Folk-Lore*. He began the later paper with an assertion: "To whomever asks if painters have contributed to geographical knowledge of our country, one can answer yes, and give pointblank examples" (1942:33; my trans.). He then listed a number of Canadian painters for their ability to represent "a strong flavour of *terroir*" through portraits of ethnic "types," or for their depictions of "topography," and concluded that a wide variety of visual artists have contributed to Canadian geographical "data" (44).

Conclusions

Boas and Sapir each contributed to the latent theory behind Barbeau's collaboration with landscape painters. The peculiarly mystical quality of Barbeau's cultural stratigraphy, however, was a hybrid that emerged from his particular form of applied anthropology tailored to early twentieth-century Canadian social conditions. Tracing the precise theoretical roots of Barbeau's work is difficult because he was little given to theoretical statements or referencing (Preston 1976). His extensive activities and energetic ethnographic collecting did not lead to scientific generalization, and his collaboration with artists was focused on affective, aesthetic, and popularizing goals. Such refusal to draw "scientific" conclusions while elaborating on the historicity of peoples' connections to geography conforms to Boas' description of the "cosmographer." Cosmography, Boas wrote, "has its source in the personal feeling of man towards the world, towards the phenomena surrounding him. We may call this an 'affective' impulse" (1887:644), and it is "closely related to the arts"

(646). Written before Boas had completely rejected geographical determinism, his article speaks nonetheless to lingering themes in his anthropological work (Bunzl 1996; Liss 1996), and that of Barbeau. In particular, Boas' description of geography is applicable to Barbeau's work when Boas writes of the study as "gratifying the love for the country we inhabit, and the nature that surrounds us" (1940:647). Cosmography helps situate people in their geopolitical boundaries and natural environments, making them feel comfortable. Less about physical topography than about cultural investments in particular landscapes to produce aesthetic and affective responses, cosmography valorizes topographies and renders them familiar.

In regard to modern nation building, then, we can connect Barbeau's work to Anderson's query about how nationalist emotions can become so strong that people willingly die for them (Anderson 1983). Surely part of this sentiment springs from aestheticized ties to local landscapes. I am not referring here to the fact that each nation-state has acquired a cartographical shape that can be visualized in relation to the shapes of all other countries on the global map (Anderson 1983). Cartography undoubtedly did influence the formation of modern national "identities." However, each map's shape is only a territorial form that is invested with local "character" and aesthetic values not shown on the map. What Barbeau strove to develop through his particular form of applied anthropology were those more intimate, local geographical features. Rather than imagining Canada's territory as a featureless jigsaw puzzle piece belonging to a world map of similar puzzle pieces, he strove to have it consciously appreciated as a patchwork of local landscapes imbued with cultural and historical significance. Barbeau regarded political territories (and their map shapes) as relatively arbitrary political entities: but the local soil, or "terroirs," he considered "souls." These "souls" were supposed to animate emotive attachment to local geography and were the cultural foundation of landscape aesthetics. From Abélès' remarks about the future European Union, one can conclude that such aesthetics are more than trivial fantasies. They are orientations in the world that help create and communicate ontologies we live by. Landscape aesthetics are thus comparable to any other technology we have unquestioningly relied on to feel secure in the modern world (Giddens 1990). Barbeau's applied anthropology contributed to the formation of such an aesthetic technology.

The primitivist territorial aesthetics that Barbeau helped develop has lost its hold on Canadians by becoming an institutionalized cliché of contested force: yet it retains a certain currency even as it is criticized, modified, and expanded. Canada now encompasses such a broad repertoire of orientational ideologies and corresponding images of the landscape that it sometimes seems to have reentered a phase in which it is not entirely clear how "ontological security" might be constructed collectively. Accordingly, the cultural politics of landscapes by Carr and the Group of Seven lost ground after World War II even as it became a trite hallmark of Canadianness, and recently it has been directly confronted in art criticism and exhibitions (Mastai 1992; Nemiroff et al. 1992; Fulford 1993; Moray 1993; Townsend-Gault et al. 1995; Arnold et al. 1996; Vancouver Art Gallery 1996).

Following the war, artists turned toward internationalist imagery through abstract expressionism and hard-line abstraction, yet parallel assertions of ethnic revival arts also emerged. As Handler (1988) has noted, Barbeau's work on Québec folklore became a resource for Québec nationalists and separatists after the "Quiet Revolution" of the 1960s. By the end of the 1980s, however, interest in collecting armoires or decorating with Jean-Paul Lemieux's folkloric paintings and other tokens of Québec's preindustrial "authenticity" had dwindled. Similarly, the generation of anthropologists following Barbeau did their utmost to support a native arts revival movement on the West Coast, and their efforts met with popular support. By the end of the 1980s, though, many "native artists" had stopped focusing on purist reproductions of earlier West Coast styles or subject matter to develop syncretic landscapes that incorporate the European technique of perspective for representing topographies. These landscapes are usually produced by the sort of native artists Barbeau advocated: individuals from native communities who value native history and traditions and have attended art schools. Most of these artists are commonly assumed to be doing something new, taking a politically critical stance toward the work of Barbeau and his landscape artists. Yet one could easily argue that the direct juxtaposition of Emily Carr and Paul Yuxweluptun landscapes in a 1997 Vancouver Art Gallery show reinforced and built upon Carr's vision as much as discredited it. Nature is even more clearly marked as native in Yuxweluptun's work than it was in Carr's (Figure 12). Both his iconographic elements and the titles of his work articulate abuse suffered by natives and nature at the hands of "whites," and suggest that land claims present the solution for this social injustice. No longer concerned mostly with asserting the survival of indigenous cultures as were earlier native artists who reproduced museum pieces, Yuxweluptan focuses on themes of (re)territorialization and land claims (Townsend-Gault 1993, 1995). His political rhetoric gains strength and pictorial efficacity, however, largely by building upon the God-fearing and Romantic stance Carr established, for that is the moral ground upon which these later syncretisms are built and received. Similar West Coast syncretic landscapes also express continuity between earlier and recent landscape forms, but with less confrontational stances. Roy Vickers, for example, declares himself proud of both his "English" and Tsimshian family histories, as he too places native crest elements within his landscape imagery to continue Carr's message that nature is native and constantly present in the contemporary lives of all who dwell in it (Vickers n.d., 1988). Thus

Figure 12. Lawrence Paul Yuxweluptun, *Scorched Earth, Clear-cut Logging on Native Sovereign Land. Shaman Coming to Fix,* 1991. Acrylic on canvas 195.6 × 275.0 cm. (National Gallery of Canada, Ottawa 36950.)

recent syncretic and primitivist landscapes are both critiques and continuations of Barbeau's landscape aesthetics, demonstrating a homonymic quality between and within phases of syncretic Canadian landscape painting.

Immigrant populations are also part of the recent reevaluation of the landscape aesthetic Barbeau helped establish. We see this in the work of Jin-Me Yoon, who "arranged for sixty-seven members from Vancouver's Korean community to be individually photographed" in front of Emily Carr's painting *Old Time Coast Village* (1930) and Group of Seven member Lawren Harris's *Malign Lake, Jasper Park* (1924) (Arnold 1996). Arguably, these juxtapositions do not so much question Canadian landscape aesthetics from Barbeau's era as insert Koreans into an established landscape, art history, and popular aesthetics. Whether this representational strategy is about incompatibility or accommodation (Figures 13 and 14), it is certainly a revitalization of Barbeau's project.

As with Barbeau's pivotal show of primitive and modern art in 1927, these recent landscape forms have been institutionally promoted through major exhibitions organized by a combination of government anthropologists, art historians, and curators. In 1992 the National Gallery of Canada and the Canadian Museum of Civilization each mounted major shows of recent native art (McMaster & Martin 1992; Nemiroff et al. 1992). Whereas these two institu-

Figures 13 and 14. Jin-Me Yoon, *A Group of Sixty-Seven* (details), 1996. Cibachrome photograph on paper 40.0 × 50.0 cm each. (Vancouver Art Gallery VAG 97.2 a-g̲g̲g̲g̲g̲g̲; Courtesy Vancouver Art Gallery; photo Trevor Mills.)

tions shared a building in 1927, when Barbeau co-curated with the National Gallery director, Eric Brown, these recent shows were simultaneous but separately housed, suggesting competition over the institutional categorization of "native art." Each exhibit included recent syncretic landscapes (such as Yuxweluptun's) as a response to, and critique of, modernist primitivism that nonetheless oddly colluded with it (e.g. Young Man 1992). Was this "post" modernity, or more modernity? In 1996, the Vancouver Art Gallery mounted a show titled *Topographies: Aspects of Recent B.C. Art* that included artists of marked and unmarked ethnic affiliations. While it was not suggested that all the works presented had "sprung from the soil" within British Columbia's borders, there was an implicit curatorial suggestion that the accommodation of a diversity of British Columbian artists within an exhibit would directly represent diverse senses of place contributing to lives led on British Columbia land.

From this recent vantage point, therefore, as well as from that of Europeans anticipating the European Union, Barbeau's work to reconcile fractured ontologies within state boundaries appears newly pertinent. Our move toward senses of place as opposed to what we consider universalist space is also, however, a continuation of Barbeau's modern dualist vision of geography, and his primitivism is strikingly congruent with the inspiration Casey holds out to anthropologists when he admonishes us to seek and preserve "ontological wildness" and "alterity" in our local senses of place (Casey 1996: 35). Hardly a critical revision of modernity, our current return to landscape discourse feeds into continuous revitalizations of earlier localizing aesthetics. Our discipline goes through periodic phases of re-historicization and re-territorialization no less than the groups we study. Anthropology itself is shaped by the shifting social and political contexts in which it is practiced. Barbeau's work is thus not a "solution" for current conditions, but it does illuminate a formative point in a continually transforming Canadian primitivism. Although Barbeau tried to formulate an inclusive aesthetics (which can also be seen as hegemonic), after World War II his vision gave way to separatist nationalism. Current aesthetic trends in Canada include both of these tendencies; there has been a return to landscape imagery and promotion of ethnic "rights." Curiously outmoded, Barbeau's work nonetheless persistently offers a glimpse of ourselves—as citizens, and as anthropologists, reconsidering geography and our ties to local landscapes.

Acknowledgments

This article, written in 1996, draws upon support generously offered by people from a variety of positions and viewpoints. I am grateful to Marion Lake at the University of Regina for her dauntless approach to interlibrary loans. Archivist Peter Trepanier and curator Charles Hill assisted me at the National Gallery of Canada. Archivists Geneviève Eustache, Nicole Chamberlain, and particularly Benoît Thériault, guided me through the voluminous Marius Barbeau Papers at the Museum of Civilization in Ottawa, where I was also assisted by Denis Fletcher, Claudette Proulx, and Margot Reid. I am indebted to them all for their patience. I thank the British Columbia Archives, the McMichael Canadian Art Collection, the Museum of Civilization, the National Gallery of Canada, and the Vancouver Art Gallery for permission to reproduce works from their collections. I am particularly grateful to the artists Jin-Me Yoon and Lawrence Paul Yuxweluptan, and to Naomi Jackson Groves and Phyllis Kihn. The Rioux family graciously recounted to me their family reminiscences of Marius Barbeau. Asen Balikci, Ernest Côté, Renée Landry, George MacDonald, Art Price, Jori Smith, and Marc-Adélard Tremblay provided me with first-hand observations of Barbeau's work relations, habits, and contexts. Lucie Côté's hospitality was an important support for this project. I thank Peter Gose and anonymous reviewers for reading and commenting on my work. Richard Handler's encouragement and keen editorial judgment were also invaluable. These people contributed to an interpretive process beyond their control or responsibility, a condition that makes their assistance all the more generous and appreciated. This research was funded by the Social Sciences and Humanities Research Council of Canada Fellowships Division, No. 756–94–0536.

References Cited

Abélès, M. 1996. La Communauté européenne: une perspective anthropologique. *Social Anthropology* 4(1):33–45.

Anderson, B. 1983. *Imagined communities: Reflections on the origin and spread of nationalism.* London.

Appadurai, A. 1991. Global ethnoscapes: Notes and queries for a transnational anthropology. In *Recapturing anthropology: Working in the present,* ed. R. Fox, 191–210. Santa Fe, N.Mex.

Arnold, G. 1996. Shared terrain/contested spaces: New work by fifteen B.C. artists. In Arnold et al., 1–45. Vancouver, Canada.

Arnold G., M. Kin Gagnon, & D. Jensen, eds. 1996. *Topographies: Aspects of recent B.C. art.* Vancouver, Canada.

Barbeau, M. 1915. *Mythologie huronne et wyandotte,* trans. S. Dupont, ed. P. Beaucage. Montreal (1994).

Barbeau, M. 1917. Review of Tsimshian Mythology by Franz Boas. *American Anthropologist* n.s., 548–63.

Barbeau, M. 1920a. Blason, géographie et généalogie populaires de Quebec. *Journal of American Folk-Lore* 33(Jan–Mar):346–66.

Barbeau, M. 1920b. Photographies de gens et de choses du terroir canadien. *Journal of American Folk-Lore* 33(Jan–Mar):Plates 1–15.

Barbeau, M. 1923a. *Indian days in the Canadian Rockies.* Illus. Langdon Kihn. Toronto.

Barbeau, M. 1923b. An artist among the northwest Indians: Langdon Kihn has pictorially recorded some types of a little-known race. *Arts and decoration* 19(May):26–27, 95.

Barbeau, M. 1927a. The native races of Canada. *Proceedings of the Royal Society of Canada* Section 2:41–53.

Barbeau, M. 1927b. West Coast Indian art. *Exhibition of Canadian West Coast art: Native and modern.* National Gallery of Canada.

Barbeau, M. 1929a. Ancient culture vignettes past. *Canadian National Railways Magazine* 15(7):13, 30–33.

Barbeau, M. 1929b. *Totem poles of the Gitksan, Upper Skeena River, British Columbia.* Bulletin 61, Anthropological Ser. 12. National Museum of Canada. Ottawa.

Barbeau, M. 1930a. The origin of floral and other designs among the Canadian and neighboring Indians. *Proceedings of the 23d International Congress of Americanists* (1928):512.

Barbeau, M. 1930b. An Indian Paradise Lost. *Canadian Geographical Journal* 1(2):132–48.

Barbeau, M. 1932a. The Canadian Northwest: Theme for modern painters. *American Magazine of Art* 24:5(May):331–38.

Barbeau, M. 1932b. Indians of the Prairies and Rockies: A theme for modern painters. *University of Toronto Quarterly* 1(2):197–206.

Barbeau, M. 1932c. More profits from Canadiana. *Commerce of the Nation* 5(4):20, 27–28.

Barbeau, M. 1933a. Canadian souvenirs for tourist centres. *New Outlook* 9(24):457.

Barbeau, M. 1933b. A quoi bon les arts? *La Presse,* 8 April.

Barbeau, M. 1942. Notre géographie en peinture. *Bulletin de la Société de Géographie de Québec et de Montréal,* Nouvelle série, 1:5, 33–44.

Barbeau, M. 1950a. L'âme d'une grande nation moderne. *La Revue de l'Université Laval.* 5(3):215–18.

Barbeau, M. 1950b. *Totem poles according to location,* Vol. 2, Bulletin 119, Anthropological Ser. 30. Ottawa. Reprinted in Hull (1990).

Barbeau, M. 1955. Interview by J. Crawley. *Profile.* Canadian Broadcasting Corporation, 25 August.

Barbeau, M. 1957a. *Haida Carvers in Argillite.* Bulletin 139, Anthropological Ser. 38. National Museum of Canada. Ottawa.

Barbeau, M. 1957b. Emily Carr: Painter and writer. Canadian Broadcasting Corporation. Ottawa. 3 December.

Barbeau, M., & A. Price. 1956. *National asset: Native design.* Montreal.

Barbeau, M., & E. Sapir. 1925. *Folk songs of French Canada.* New Haven, Conn.

Barnard, F. M. 1968. Introduction. In J. G. *Herder on social and political culture,* trans. and ed. F. M. Barnard, 3–60. Cambridge.

Beals, R. 1945. Totemism, a modern growth on the North Pacific coast. *California Folk Culture Quarterly* 4:301.

Boas, F. 1887. The study of geography. In *Race, language, and culture,* F. Boas, 1940 (1982):639–47. Chicago.

Boas, F. 1897. The decorative art of the Indians of the North Pacific Coast. *Bulletin of the American Museum of Natural History,* Vol. 9: Article 10. New York.

Boas, F. 1910. Ethnological problems in Canada. In *Race, language, and culture*, F. Boas 1940 (1982):331–43. Chicago.

Boas, F. 1911. Introduction. In *Handbook of American Indian languages*, ed. P. Holder, 1966: 1–79. Lincoln, Nebr.

Boas, F. 1916. *Tsimshian Mythology*. 31st Annual Report of the Bureau of American Ethnology. Washington, D.C.

Boas, F. 1921. The great melting pot and its problem. *The New York Times Book Review and Magazine*. 6 February.

Boas, F. 1927. *Primitive art*. New York.

Boas, F. 1931. Race and progress. In *Race, language, and culture*, F. Boas, 1940 (1982):3–17. Chicago.

Boas, F. 1932. The aims of anthropological research. In *Race, language, and culture*, F. Boas, 1940 (1982):243–59. Chicago.

Boas, F. 1940. *Race, language, and culture*. Chicago (1982).

Bourdieu, P. 1980. *Le sens pratique*. Paris.

Bunzel, R. 1962. Introduction. In *Anthropology and modern life*, F. Boas, 4–10. New York.

Bunzl, M. 1996. Franz Boas and the Humboldtian tradition: From *Volksgeist* and *Nationalcharakter* to an anthropological concept of culture. In *Volksgeist as method and ethic: Essays on Boasian ethnography and the German anthropological tradition*, ed. G. W. Stocking, Jr. HOA 8:17–78.

Casey, E. S. 1996. How to get from space to place in a fairly short stretch of time: Phenomenological prolegomena. In Feld & Basso, 1996:13–52. Santa Fe, N.Mex.

Cole, D. 1973. The origins of Canadian anthropology, 1850–1910. *Journal of Canadian Studies* 8(Feb):33–45.

Darnell, R. 1990. *Edward Sapir: Linguist, anthropologist, humanist*. Berkeley, Calif.

Duff, W. 1964. Contributions of Marius Barbeau to West Coast ethnology. *Anthropologica* 6(1):63–96.

Dumont, L. 1970. *Religion, politics and history in India: Collected papers in Indian sociology*. The Hague.

Fabian, J. 1983. *Time and the other: How anthropology makes its object*. New York.

Feld, S., & K. H. Basso, eds. 1996. *Senses of place*. Santa Fe, N.Mex.

Fulford, R. 1993. The trouble with Emily. *Canadian Art* 10(4):32–39.

García Canclini, N. 1990. *Culturas híbridas. Estrategias para entrar y salir de la modernidad*. Mexico.

Gendreau, A. 1982. *Charlevoix, terre d'origine, lieu de l'autre*. Doct. diss., Laval Univ.

Geertz, C. 1996. Afterword. In Feld & Basso, 1996:259–62. Santa Fe, N.Mex.

Giddens, A. 1990. *The consequences of modernity*. Stanford, Calif.

Goldwater, R. 1938. *Primitivism in modern art*. New York (1967).

Graburn, N. 1976. Eskimo art: The Eastern Canadian Arctic. In *Ethnic and tourist arts: Cultural expressions from the Fourth World*, ed. N. Graburn, 39–55. Berkeley, Calif.

Gupta, A., & J. Ferguson. 1992. Beyond "culture": Space, identity, and the politics of difference. *Cultural Anthropology* 7(1):6–23.

Gupta, A. & J. Ferguson. 1997. *Culture, power, place: Explorations in critical anthropology*. Durham, N.C.

Haddon, A. C. 1911 The wanderings of peoples. Cambridge (1927).

Haeberlin, H. K. 1918. Principles of esthetic form in the art of the North Pacific Coast. American Anthropologist n.s., 20:258–64.

Handler, R. 1983. The dainty and the hungry man: Literature and anthropology in the work of Edward Sapir. In Observers observed: Essays on ethnographic fieldwork, ed. G. W. Stocking, Jr. HOA 1:208–31.

Handler, R. 1986. Vigorous male and aspiring female: Poetry, personality, and culture in Edward Sapir and Ruth Benedict. In Malinowski, Benedict, Rivers and others: Essays on culture and personality, ed. G. W. Stocking, Jr. HOA 4:127–55.

Handler, R. 1988. Nationalism and the politics of culture in Quebec. Madison, Wis.

Hanks, W. 1996. Language and communicative practices. Chicago.

Harvey, D. 1993. From space to place and back again: Reflections on the condition of postmodernity. In Mapping the futures: Local cultures, global change, ed. J. Bird et al., 3–29. London.

Hembroff-Schleicher, E. 1978. Emily Carr: The untold story. Saanichton, Canada.

Herzfeld, M. 1987. Anthropology through the looking-glass: Critical ethnography in the margins of Europe. Cambridge.

Hill, C. 1995. The Group of Seven: Art for a nation. Ottawa.

Hiller, S., ed. 1991. The myth of primitivism: Perspectives on art. London.

Hirsch, E., & M. O'Hanlon. 1995. The anthropology of landscape: Perspectives on place and space. Oxford.

Hobsbawm, E., & T. Ranger, eds. 1983. The invention of tradition. Cambridge.

Houston, J. 1995. Confessions of an igloo dweller: The story of the man who brought Inuit art to the outside world. Toronto.

Jacknis, I. 1992. "The artist himself": The Salish basketry monograph and the beginnings of a Boasian paradigm. In The early years of Native American art history, ed. J. Berlo, 134–61. Seattle.

Jackson, A. Y. 1958. A painter's country. Toronto (1964).

Jackson Groves, N. 1988. One summer in Quebec. Kapuskasing, Canada.

Jonaitis, A. 1995. A wealth of thought: Franz Boas on Native American art. Seattle.

Kemp, H. 1948. Top man in totem poles. Maclean's Magazine, 1 May.

Kroeber, A. L. 1917. The superorganic. American Anthropologist 19(2):163–213.

Lavie, S., & T. Swedenburg. 1996. Displacement, diaspora, and geographies of identity. Durham, N.C.

Liss, J. E. 1996. German culture and German science in the Bildung of Franz Boas. In Volksgeist as method and ethic: Essays on Boasian ethnography and the German anthropological tradition, ed. G. W. Stocking, Jr. HOA 8:155–84.

Mandelbaum, D. 1949. Selected writings of Edward Sapir in language, culture, and personality. Berkeley, Calif.

Marett, R. R. 1920. Psychology and folk-lore. London.

Mastai, J., ed. 1992. Emily Carr. Vancouver.

McMaster, G., & L-A. Martin, eds. 1992. Indigena: Contemporary native perspectives. Hull, Canada.

Moray, G. 1993. Northwest Coast native culture and the early Indian paintings of Emily Carr, 1899–1913. Doct. diss., Univ. Guelph.

Nasgaard, R. 1984. *The mystic north: Symbolist landscape painting in Northern Europe and North America, 1890–1940.* Toronto.

Nemiroff, D., et al. 1992. *Land, spirit, power: First nations at the National Gallery of Canada.* Ottawa.

Nowry, L. 1965. Nowry tapes. Marius Barbeau interviews. CMC Archives. Collection RC 166–68.

Nowry, L. 1995. *Man of mana: Marius Barbeau.* Toronto.

Preston, R. C. 1976. Marius Barbeau and the history of Canadian anthropology. In *The history of Canadian anthropology. Proceedings of the Canadian Ethnological Society,* No. 3, ed. J. Freedman.

Price, S. 1989. *Primitive art in civilized places.* Chicago.

Richmond, L. 1925. Indian portraits of W. Langdon Kihn. *Studio* 90:339–46.

Riley, L., ed. 1988. *Marius Barbeau's photographic collection: The Nass River.* Canadian Ethnology Service Paper No. 109. Ottawa.

Rubin, W. 1984. Modernist primitivism: An introduction. In *"Primitivism" in 20th century art: Affinity of the tribal and the modern,* vol. 1, ed., W. Rubin, 1–81. New York.

Saint-Martin, F. 1976. Origines et destin des cultures dans l'oeuvre de Marius Barbeau. *Voix et Images* 11(2):240–54.

Sapir, E. 1917. Do we need a "superorganic"? *American Anthropologist* 19:441–47.

Sapir, E. 1919. Civilization and culture. *Dial* 67:233–36.

Sapir, E. 1921. *Language: An introduction to the study of speech.* New York (1949).

Sapir, E. 1922a. Culture, genuine and spurious. *Dalhousie Review* 2(23):165–78.

Sapir, E. 1922b. Culture in new countries. *Dalhousie Review* 2(23):358–68.

Sapir, E. 1923. Prefatory note. In *An album of prehistoric Canadian art,* H. Smith, Victoria Memorial Museum Bulletin 37, Anthropology Ser. 8. Ottawa.

Sapir, E. 1928. The meaning of religion. Reprinted in *Culture, language, and personality: Selected essays,* ed. D. Mandelbaum, 1956:346–56. Berkeley, Calif.

Shadbolt, D. 1979. *The art of Emily Carr.* Toronto.

Soja, E. 1989. *Postmodern geographies: The reassertion of space in critical social theory.* London.

Spencer, H. 1876 *The principles of sociology,* ed. S. Andreski. London (1969).

Tippett, M. 1974. Who "discovered" Emily Carr? *Journal of Canadian Art History* 1:2 (Fall):30–34.

Tippett, M. 1979. *Emily Carr: A biography.* Markham, Canada.

Torgovnick, M. 1990. *Gone primitive: Savage intellects, modern lives.* Chicago.

Townsend-Gault, C. 1993. Impurity and danger. *Current Anthropology* 34(1):93–100.

Townsend-Gault, C. 1995. The salvation art of Yuxweluptun. In C. Townsend-Gault et. al., 1995:6–22. Vancouver, Canada.

Townsend-Gault, C., et al., eds. 1995. *Lawrence Paul Yuxweluptun: Born to live and die on your colonialist reservations.* Vancouver, Canada.

Trépanier, E. 1991. The expression of a difference: The milieu of Quebec art and the Group of Seven. In *The true north: Canadian landscape painting, 1896–1939,* ed. M. Tooby, 98–116. London.

Vancouver Art Gallery. 1996. Excerpts from an invitational seminar on the life and work of Emily Carr. *Collapse* 2 (Dec):78–121.

Vickers, R. H. 1988. *Solstice: The art of Roy Henry Vickers.* Tofino, Canada.

Vickers, R. H. n.d. *Return to Eagle Rock.* Video Lynx Images Releasing. Toronto.

Whitman, W. 1855. Preface to *Leaves of Grass.* In *The portable Walt Whitman,* ed. M. Van Doren, 1973:5–27. New York.

Wolf, E. 1982. *Europe and the people without history.* Berkeley, Calif.

Young Man, A. 1992. The metaphysics of North American Indian art. In McMaster & Martin, 1992:80–99. Hull, Canada.

Manuscript Sources

CMC   Canadian Museum of Civilization Archives, Ottawa.

MBP   Marius Barbeau Papers, Canadian Museum of Civilization Archives, Ottawa.

BP   Franz Boas Papers, Correspondence, American Philosophical Society Library, Philadelphia.

BCARS   British Columbia Archives, Victoria.

CHARLOTTE GOWER AND THE SUBTERRANEAN HISTORY OF ANTHROPOLOGY

MARIA LEPOWSKY

In 1988 I first taught a course at the University of Wisconsin–Madison called Anthropology by Women, a history of women in anthropology from the nineteenth century to the present. While preparing lectures, I read Margaret Rossiter's comprehensive study, *Women Scientists in America: Struggles and Strategies to 1940* (1982). Her tables, based on biographical listings in *American Men of Science* (Cattell 1933; Cattell & Cattell 1938), showed that in 1938 there were only 10 women anthropology faculty members at the rank of instructor or above in the United States (Rossiter 1982:170–71). Given the number of talented women already trained by Boas, Kroeber, Malinowski, and others by that point, this seemed a remarkably poor showing. Four were at elite Eastern women's colleges: Vassar, Mount Holyoke, Barnard, and Hunter. At the top 20 research universities, there were only three women anthropologists employed at faculty rank (Rossiter 1982:182–83). Listed by last name, they were all assistant professors: (Isabel) Carter in the Department of Social Relations at the University of Pennsylvania, and, in anthropology departments, (Ruth) Benedict at Columbia University, and someone named Gower at the University of Wisconsin.

I too was a female assistant professor at Wisconsin (one of three women in a faculty of 23), teaching on the history of women in the discipline, and I had never heard of Gower. When I began inquiring, senior colleagues did not know her name, nor did departmental oral histories record it. Troubled by this erasure, I reported my discovery to my Anthropology by Women class.

Maria Lepowsky is Professor of Anthropology at the University of Wisconsin–Madison. The author of *Fruit of the Motherland: Gender in an Egalitarian Society*, she is currently working on a cultural history of the Coral Sea islands and a study of frontier cultures and interethnic relations in nineteenth-century Southern California.

The following year, at a departmental memorial dinner, I asked distinguished physical anthropologist W. W. Howells about Gower. Howells joined the University of Wisconsin Department of Sociology and Anthropology in 1939 and went to Harvard in the 1950s.

"Oh yes, Charlotte," he said immediately. She was an archeologist, he recalled, with a Chicago Ph.D., and she had died in a Japanese prison camp in China during World War II, though he could not remember what she was doing in China. This oral version turned out to be not quite accurate: Howells corrected himself the following week, I discovered later, and added some intriguing details in a written memoir of Wisconsin anthropology (UWA: Howells 1989).

I continued to be troubled by the lack of institutional and disciplinary memory of Charlotte Gower. She disappeared, I later found, from the University of Wisconsin in her eighth year, 1938, just when she was listed in *American Men of Science* as an assistant professor. Was she fired, or denied tenure? Or did she quit a nonpermanent job to go off to China? What kind of research did she do? She came to symbolize to me all the women anthropologists whose traces I occasionally found in my readings: women whose works and lives had been forgotten or overlooked, in spite of their intellectual achievements and obvious personal sacrifices. I made a private promise to Charlotte Gower, and a public one to yet another cohort of Anthropology by Women students, that one day I would do the research necessary to find her and re-place her in the history of the discipline. This essay recounts some results of my search.

Charlotte Gower's life and career give us, I believe, at the close of the millennium, an enlightening perspective on the history of American anthropology. It is a view from the bottom up: not the one offered in standard survey courses on the history of the field, with their patrilineages of intellectual descent. Nor is it the view we derive from the stories of successful women pioneers like Ruth Benedict, Margaret Mead, and Hortense Powdermaker, who overcame barriers to become famous for their writings or teaching. Gower's story gives us a perspective on our disciplinary history from the point of view of the dozens of women—and quite a few men as well—who in the first four decades of this century got the training, did the fieldwork, wrote the book manuscripts and field reports, but who never secured permanent teaching positions, won recognition from their peers, or were remembered as part of the cultural and intellectual traditions of anthropology.

The Return of Charlotte Gower

Charlotte Gower was indeed taken prisoner by the Japanese in China, but she did not die in a prison camp. My first major breakthrough in terms of written

Charlotte Day Gower in 1935, during the term she spent on leave from the University of Wisconsin as Visiting Assistant Professor of Anthropology at the University of Chicago. (Photograph by Moffett Studios, Chicago. Courtesy of the Department of Special Collections, University of Chicago Library.)

information about her came from a source that was hard to dispute: the cover of her book, *Milocca: A Sicilian Village*. The book (which the university had to order for me through Interlibrary Loan and which is not at all archeological) has a startling publication date, 1971, considering that its author, Charlotte Gower Chapman, was born in 1902. *Milocca*'s cover and foreword tell a bizarre story. As the description on the back cover of the paperback edition puts it, "Written in 1935 by Dr. Charlotte Gower, *Milocca: A Sicilian Village* was the outcome of one of the first in-depth studies of underdeveloped communities. But publication was long delayed as the manuscript became lost in the confusion of the Depression and the Second World War. More than thirty-five years after it was written the brittle and yellowed pages of a carbon copy were discovered in the files of the Anthropology Department at the University of Chicago." The very last line, after a three-sentence biography, reads, "Mrs. Savilion H. Chapman currently resides in Washington, D.C."

Two people rediscovered the manuscript and caused it to be published: Fred Eggan of the University of Chicago, who joined the faculty in 1935 (Stocking 1979:25) but who had, he writes, known Charlotte Gower since her graduate student days, actually found the long-missing carbon copy. The other person was Constance Cronin, then an advanced graduate student just returned from Sicily herself, who, as Eggan says, "found the Gower manuscript to be so valuable that she urged its immediate publication" (1971:xi). Cronin called Gower's manuscript "an excellent and important study since it is the only full-scale Italian village study in existence which was carried out before World War II" (1970:18, 298). Cronin also noted that due to the paucity of scholarly studies, it was still necessary to rely on Italian fiction and realist films for insights into Sicilian social life (see Eggan 1971).

Milocca was only the second long-term community study of a "semi-literate" or "peasant" society ever carried out anywhere by an anthropologist (Chapman 1971:xiii), or by anyone else. The first, as many of us learned in freshman anthropology and again in graduate school, was *Tepoztlan: A Mexican Village*, by Robert Redfield (1930). But being second, and having her book manuscript lost for 35 years, did not help find Charlotte Gower a place in the history of anthropology.

Charlotte Gower and the Chicago School

Charlotte Day Gower was born in Kankakee, Illinois, a small city about 60 miles south of Chicago. Her family, which had New England origins, was locally prominent. Eben B. Gower, her father, was the senior partner in the downtown Kankakee law firm of Gower, Gray, and Gower; by 1940, he was Judge Gower (UCRLA). Charlotte Gower majored in psychology and received a bachelor's degree in 1922 from Smith College at the age of 20, an unusual accomplishment for a midwestern woman of her time. She was an assistant (a rank below instructor) in psychology at Smith in 1922–23 and an instructor in education at the University of Texas in 1923–24 (Cattell 1933; Cattell & Cattell 1938).

Gower responded to a 1977 survey conducted by George Stocking on the history of the University of Chicago Department of Anthropology (signing herself "Charlotte Gower Chapman [Mrs. S. H.]") and sent Stocking two follow-up letters, testifying about her undergraduate and graduate experiences. Listing her year as "instructor in Education at Texas," she typed, "The salary was good and I wanted money for study in Europe." Under "Comments on the Development of Your Intellectual Orientation," she elaborated,

> At Smith I regarded myself as a pre-Med student, and majored in Psychology because that major allowed me latitude to take pre-Med subjects; one of these was anthropology, with Harris Hawthorne Wilder, under whose guidance I prepared a paper that appeared in the *Journal of Physical Anthropology* [1923]. This gave me the idea of studying anthropology in Europe, so I joined the American School for Prehistoric Research in Europe, led by G. G. MacCurdy. While in Europe I met Alonzo Pond, who recommended the University of Chicago's new department, which was conveniently close to my parents. (Chapman 1977a)

Gower began graduate work in 1924 in what was then the Department of Sociology and Anthropology at the University of Chicago. Her arrival coincided with a major turning point, as the university's first anthropology professor, Frederick Starr, had retired in 1923 after 31 years (Stocking 1979:11–15). Starr, whom many colleagues and students recalled as ineffectual, had failed to build anthropology within the department; apparently he sometimes even failed to appear at his own classes (e.g. McMillan 1986). He was replaced the next year by Fay-Cooper Cole, a former student of Franz Boas who had done research in the Philippines, the Netherlands Indies, and Malaya.

In 1924, there were "twenty-four senior college and ten graduate students" in the anthropology emphasis of the Chicago joint department (Cole to Franz Boas, quoted in McMillan 1986:92–93). A year later Cole used Laura Spelman Rockefeller Memorial funds in 1925 to hire Edward Sapir. Cole apparently understood from the beginning that anthropology and sociology would separate and that he would chair the new department, which is what happened in 1929 (Stocking 1979:16–17; Darnell 1990:225–26; see also McMillan 1986).

"Dr. Cole," Gower wrote Stocking, "was one of the most self-effacing, noncompetitive men I have ever met, and among the most likable. When I was studying Anthropology at Chicago, it was generally recognized that Sapir was the star of the department, a fact clearly accepted and supported by Dr. Cole. Later, when I was in Wisconsin but still in touch with the University of Chicago, Radcliffe-Brown was taken on—also a star. Dr. Cole was the first to extol his colleagues, and was rather prone to give his students unstinted praise and support" (Chapman 1977b).

Gower's graduate training, and her M.A. and Ph.D. research, were an amalgam of Boasian four-fields anthropology and Chicago School sociology, with its emphases on "empirical sociology" and community studies—a par-

Professor and Mrs. Fay-Cooper Cole, apparently taken in 1948 at Professor Cole's University of Chicago retirement party. Mabel Cook Cole and Charlotte Gower, who were friends, were both members of the Society of Women Geographers. Mrs. Cole assisted her husband during his Field Museum–sponsored research in the Philippines, among the Tinguian of northwest Luzon from 1906 to 1908, and in Mindanao from 1910 to 1912. The Coles also co-authored a popular book on human prehistory in 1938. (Courtesy of the Department of Special Collections, University of Chicago Library.)

ticular University of Chicago blend that was to prove influential in the subsequent development of American anthropology. It was Cole, of the two anthropology professors, who transmitted to his students the influences of his sociology colleagues, as well as his own Boasian orientations. Gower listed both "Edward Sapir & F-C Cole" in the space for dissertation supervisor's name on Stocking's questionnaire (Chapman 1977a). "Sapir was the Linguist/Scholar/Genius in the department," she explained. "Cole was everything else. It was in his office that graduate students congregated informally. Sapir met us individually in his smaller and more remote office. I suspect that we may have consulted Sapir on more personal topics, Cole on ordinary things" (Chapman 1978). Gower took four courses from Sapir (Murray 1986:269), and Sapir's focus on the individual and culture, the main reason Chicago hired him (Darnell 1990:213–14), showed up later in Gower's teaching at the University of Wisconsin. By contrast, she reported having taken only one sociology course—which was required—in Chicago's joint department (Chapman 1977a), and she thanks both Cole and Sapir (and no other faculty members) in her dissertation acknowledgments.

At Chicago, Cole turned toward archeology, emphasizing the prehistory of Illinois for his own research, to set up a relatively inexpensive field program for his graduate students, and to tap wealthy Chicago businessmen for contributions to the department. "While I do now [sic] know why [Dr. Cole] started to build anthropology at Chicago around archeology, I suspect that he recognized that Columbia and California had pretty well staked out most of the available areas for ethnology in the United States" (Chapman 1978). Beginning in 1926, Cole's students went on summer excavations at nearby Indian mounds (Stocking 1979:17; cf. McMillan 1986), and Gower spent two summers as "a member of our archaeological field party," as Cole put it (UCRLA: FC/Olin Wannamaker, 4/12/38). This summer research was the subject of Gower's first participation at a professional meeting, the Central Section of the American Anthropological Association's Chicago meeting in 1927, where she presented the results of the field survey on behalf of the whole research party. "With maps and slides [Miss Charlotte D. Gower] detailed what had been accomplished the previous season. Three hundred and seventy-two mounds were found, of which 254 were previously unrecorded" (Fox 1928:526–28).

Gower's master's degree, awarded in 1926, was based on a thesis called "The Northern and Southern Affiliations of Antillean Culture." "In connection with my MA thesis, I made a tour of museums in the East, introduced by Dr. Cole, and I am sure that I owe to him the warm reception I received from scholars (whose names escape me) at Philadelphia, the Heye Museum, and the Smithsonian" (Chapman 1978). Published in 1927 as Memoir Number 35 of the American Anthropological Association, Gower's thesis was a classic piece of historical ethnology, discussing the possible origins, diffusion, and trading and other contacts of aboriginal West Indian cultures. Thirty-one of its 50 pages of text cover "Archaeology and material culture"—marking both Cole's influence and her initial intellectual focus on prehistory. The balance is devoted to brief sketches of social organization, religion, and language.

Her Ph.D. dissertation was another matter entirely. Its research topic and methods place Gower squarely within the Chicago School of sociology. In fact, her research design seems to be drawn directly from W. I. Thomas himself. Speaking in 1938 for a retrospective on his classic study of the Polish peasant (Thomas & Znaniecki 1918–1920), Thomas explains, "Immigration was a burning question. About a million immigrants were coming here annually . . . The larger groups were Poles, Italians, and Jews . . . eventually I decided to study an immigrant group in Europe and America to determine as far as possible what relation their home mores and norms had to their adjustment and maladjustment in America" (quoted in Bulmer 1984:46). Thomas, of course, chose the Poles. Gower took the Italians, or, more specifically, the Sicilians. She studied the Sicilian dialect for a year with three Chicago-area tutors (Chapman 1971:vii) and, with funding from Chicago's Institute for Juvenile Research, used "the methods of the ethnologist," particularly "informal interviews," to collect legends from Sicilian immigrants: 15 men and 7 women. (She interviewed no juveniles, despite her funding source.) Under the heading of "Field Work" on Stocking's questionnaire (Chapman 1977a), she recalled spending "10 Mos, Chicago, getting information for thesis from 3 Sicilian informants," likely her language tutors and principal informants.

Gower worked with Sicilians living all over the city, rather than in specific neighborhoods, disguising their identities and places of residence. This was not a community study. Her research focus was on Sicilian religion and the "reconstruction" of Sicilian culture, rather than on the immigrants' adaptations to life in the United States. The late 1920s was the middle of Prohibition and the peak of control by the Sicilian-dominated Chicago Mafia of the bootlegging trade and other rackets. Gower may have been following her intellectual interests and those of her professors and at the same time exercising prudence in steering clear of what her sociology colleagues referred to as Sicilian immigrants' "problems of adjustment."

Nor was Gower's dissertation, "The Supernatural Patron in Sicilian Life," a modernist ethnographic work based on participant observation. It was a work of Sicilian memory culture. As she explained, her "ethnological research" was "a preliminary study of the cultural background of the Sicilian immigrants to America . . . The proposed continuation of the study in Sicily will provide an interesting check on the validity of the method" (1928:1–2).

By the time her degree was awarded, in October of 1928, Gower was indeed already in Sicily. Supported by a Social Science Research Council fellowship, she began 18 months of field research in the remote mountain village of Milocca, recommended to her by one of her Chicago language tutors (Chapman 1971:xiii). The fellowship was a prestigious award. A report by the SSRC in the American Anthropologist shows that in 1928–29 there were only three Fellows in Anthropology, all women: Ruth Bunzel, Margaret Mead, and Charlotte Gower (Social Science Research Council 1928:553–54). Gower's award, like the publication of her master's thesis, is evidence that her work was regarded highly by the well-connected Cole.

In spite of Gower's generally positive experiences, the Chicago department was among the least hospitable to women. The anthropology department at Columbia University, led by Boas with the assistance of Benedict, had by 1940 awarded the Ph.D. to 22 women and 29 men (Yearbook of Anthropology 1955:703–5). At the University of California, Alfred Kroeber and Robert Lowie had trained quite a few women scholars, 9 of whom had completed the Ph.D. by 1940, along with 18 men (Yearbook of Anthropology 1955:737–

9).[1] And at the London School of Economics, Malinowski admitted and supervised several influential women anthropologists, beginning in 1926; 4 women and 20 men had attained the Ph.D. by 1940 (*Yearbook of Anthropology* 1955:744–45).

In contrast, Chicago's joint department in the 1920s and the separate Chicago Department of Anthropology from 1929 through World War II and beyond included few women in the Ph.D. program (Rossiter 1982; McMillan 1986; Stocking 1995). Gower was the first woman to receive a Ph.D. in anthropology at the University of Chicago. By 1940 there was only one other woman anthropologist, Florence Hawley Senter, with a Chicago Ph.D., and 27 men (*Yearbook of Anthropology* 1955:740–42). In the 1920s and 1930s, not only did few women study anthropology at the graduate level at Chicago, these few often did not pass beyond the M.A. stage. "Women, by and large, played the very slightest of roles in Chicago anthropology—beyond occasionally contracting in marriage for the needs of a male anthropologist" (McMillan 1986:239–41).[2]

Gower, the first woman and the exception, testified to her good treatment.

> On entering the University of Chicago, I applied for a fellowship, but none was available. However, on the basis of my year studying prehistory in Europe, Dr. Cole invited me to lecture on that subject to the beginning class. One thing led to another, and fellowships were forthcoming, as well as the kindest of treatment. People have often said that as a woman I must have had a bad time in my graduate work. Nonsense, for I suspect that things were made easier for me on that account. However, when I had finished, and would be needing a job, the alternative of two years of research in Sicily on a Social Science Research fellowship seemed a good solution. Thanks to Dr. Cole's efforts, I was promised the fellowship before I had my Ph.D.! So I have no negative reactions at all to my Chicago experience. (Chapman 1977b)

Her remark, "when I had finished, and would be needing a job..." points to a nationwide issue in American universities and colleges of the 1920s and 1930s (and in some cases well beyond). Discrimination against women (and Jews

1. Kroeber was reluctant to admit women to Berkeley's Ph.D. Program or to offer them fellowships on the grounds that they were unlikely to find jobs. Isabel Kelly and Lila O'Neale, for example, had to overcome Kroeber's objections (Buzaljko 1993:41; Scheville 1993:68). Kroeber also opposed including women students in summer research parties, particularly archeological digs, because "he felt they were not interested in archaeology, but only in male archaeologists" (Ralph Beals oral history, 1977, cited in Buzaljko 1993:41, 44). Fewer of Kroeber's women students than Boas' found permanent professional employment (see *Yearbook of Anthropology* 1955).

2. Women who did not complete a Ph.D. in the 1930s at Chicago include Edith Rosenfels, who did research with Apache and Klamath peoples and married fellow student Philleo Nash; and Malcolm Carr, who studied the Navajo and married graduate student Donald Collier. Rachel Commons, like Philleo Nash an undergraduate student of Charlotte Gower's, did research among the Wisconsin Winnebago but died shortly before finishing her dissertation (McMillan 1986:136–38, 239–41).

and nonwhites) for faculty positions was not merely present but open and explicit. Anthropology department chairmen routinely warned female students of their especially poor job prospects, and in some cases used this reality to justify awarding fellowships to male students only, or limiting awards to women students. For example, a 1929 report in the *American Anthropologist* on summer field-training scholarships, through the Laboratory of Anthropology at Santa Fe, listed three women recipients (Isabel Kelly of the University of California, Eva Horner of the University of Chicago, and Frances Watkins of the University of Denver) in the archeology program, but none in ethnology and linguistics. Committee members Fay-Cooper Cole, Roland Dixon, and A. V. Kidder justified their decision:

> That as there are at present open to women relatively few professional positions in anthropology, the number of scholarships granted to women should be limited. Furthermore, the conditions under which the investigations are being carried on during the summer of 1929 preclude the assignment of women to the ethnological and linguistic parties. Women therefore, were assigned only to the archaeological party, but it is hoped to arrange the field work in future years in such a way as to permit all properly qualified women students to have a least one season as a scholarship holder during the course of their graduate school work.[3]

Robert Redfield, Charlotte Gower, and University of Chicago Anthropology

Charlotte Gower's Ph.D. was awarded in 1928. In the four years she studied at Chicago (1924–28), 27 men and only one other woman[4] received a Ph.D. from the joint Department of Sociology and Anthropology. Leslie White, for his comparative dissertation titled "Medicine Societies in the Southwest,"

3. These prestigious scholarships in 1929 enabled the ethnological party to study the Walapai with Kroeber and linguists to study the Navaho with Sapir (Cole et al. 1929:571–72). Twenty years earlier, women students, including Barbara Freire-Marreco of Oxford—later editor of *Notes and Queries on Anthropology* (1912)—complained of being barred from a summer ethnology field stint in New Mexico and steered into the archeology group on the grounds that there were no suitable accommodations for women in the ethnology party (see also Babcock & Parezo 1988; Gacs 1989). Conversely, Franz Boas wrote Edward Day, Rockefeller Foundation president, in 1932 to defend his recommendations of women students for fellowships: "By way of a general statement let me say that I try to impress every student, and particularly women, with the difficulties of finding a career in anthropology." If they persist, "there is nothing to do but give them the best preparation possible." By 1941 he wrote, "The discrimination against Jews is hitting us hard. For the first time, official letters from universities have specified 'male gentile' in their letters about job possibilities" (quoted in McMillan 1986:265).

4. Sociologist Ruth Shonle Cavan's dissertation on "business girls" was published in 1929.

received the only anthropology Ph.D. awarded in 1927, while Robert Redfield, with a dissertation entitled "A Plan for the Study of Tepotzlan, Mexico" (Faris 1967:138–39), earned his degree in the same year that Gower did. Redfield carried out eight months of ethnographic research in Mexico in 1926–27 (1930:vii) with SSRC support, writing his dissertation under the supervision of Cole, who considered Redfield's Mexico research to be a background study of an American immigration source. Background studies elucidated W. I. Thomas's theoretical concerns with social disorganization among immigrants to the United States (Thomas & Znaniecki 1918–1920; Bulmer 1984:59–63). They were also designed to provide data to social reformers—closely allied to the formation of early-twentieth-century American academic sociology at Chicago and elsewhere—regarding immigrant "problems" in adjusting to life in the United States (Faris 1967; Bulmer 1984). This was undoubtedly why Gower's dissertation research in Chicago with Sicilian immigrants was funded by the Institute of Juvenile Research, even though she ended up writing mostly about village patron saints in the Old Country.

Redfield stressed in his 1925 SSRC grant applications and in his dissertation that his research in Mexico was a "background study" of immigrants to Chicago which would ameliorate the "lack of knowledge of the conditions under which the Mexican has been raised" (quoted in Godoy 1978:54). In the introduction to his 1928 dissertation, he explained, "Impetus to the project was given by the current practical interest in Mexican immigrants in the United States . . . [to] indicate the amount of adjustment they would have to undergo in accommodating themselves in the new milieu." Redfield omitted this language in his published monograph (Redfield 1930; Godoy 1978:47). Gower used similar language in the introduction to her own Chicago-based anthropology dissertation. It seems clear that Cole, in the mid-to-late 1920s, was directly influenced by his sociology colleagues in the joint department, advocating background studies of Chicago immigrant populations as priority sites of anthropological research by his advanced graduate students: ones for which, crucially, he could secure funding through Chicago and New York foundations.

In his foreword to Milocca, Fred Eggan noted that "Robert Redfield's pioneer study of Tepotzlan, a Mexican Village (1930) was being written when Charlotte Gower prepared for her field research by spending a year in the Sicilian community in Chicago" (1971:xi). The community study Gower carried out in Sicily for 18 months from 1928 to 1930, and later wrote about in the ill-fated Milocca book manuscript, most closely resembled in research design, method, and ethnographic content her classmate Redfield's soon-to-be-famous Tepotzlan peasant community study, rather than Thomas and Znaniecki's treatise on the Poles in America and Europe.

Gower spent 18 months, unaccompanied by spouse or family, in a remote mountain village, becoming fluent in the Sicilian dialect and in standard Italian. Redfield in 1920, before switching from law and biology to anthropology, had married sociology professor Robert Park's daughter, a career advantage not open to women Ph.D. candidates. His wife, Margaret, and their two young children accompanied him for three of his eight months of dissertation research in Tepotzlan, which he began in November of 1926. Redfield joined the Chicago faculty on receiving his Ph.D. and five years later became dean of the Social Sciences Division (Godoy 1978; Stocking 1979:23–25). In contrast to Gower, he not only had the comfort and counsel of his wife in the field but an active co-researcher. Margaret Park Redfield collected ethnographic information on "native cookery," childbirth, disease and healing, fiestas, ballads, and other topics. After three months, she reluctantly moved with her children to Mexico City as revolutionary partisans became more active in Morelos, and her husband began to make an arduous periodic commute from the capital to the pueblo. Robert Redfield's writings and private correspondence show that he was defensive and apologetic about his relatively brief stint of fieldwork—cut short by civil unrest, poor health, and family considerations—and particularly concerned about problems of communication in this Nahuatl- and Spanish-speaking community (1928, 1930; Godoy 1978). But as he wrote in a popular article (enlivened by a photograph of the author in profile wearing a striped serape and a large sombrero),

> The anthropologists of the University of Chicago are among those who are developing plans for the study of contemporary peoples. They hope that they may collaborate with the sociologists in scientific studies of foreign populations who do now and who promise even more to present practical problems to the people of the United States . . . I am much encouraged in the feeling that a technique for the study of these intermediate folk peoples can be developed which will warrant intensive work by many ethnologists. (Redfield 1928:243, 246)

Milocca: A Sicilian Village

In a 1970 preface to *Milocca*, Gower acknowledged her debt to Redfield's Tepotzlan research, listing two goals of her postdoctoral "study of the social organization and customs of a Sicilian village."

> This was to be the second application of anthropological methods, in imitation of Robert Redfield's work in Mexico, to the investigation of a semi-literate society. Sicily was chosen as the area of study partly because it was hoped that a knowledge of the background of the Sicilian immigrants to the United States might prove useful in understanding their problems in and reactions to their new environment. (Chapman 1971:xii)

"Sicily was chosen for post-doctoral research," Gower explained to Stocking 50 years later, "as being reasonably lady-like, and suitable for a sequel to Redfield's village study in Mexico" (Chapman 1977b). Her passive construction "was chosen" raises the question of who did the choosing. The issue of a "lady-like" location for field research was a vexing one for women anthropologists in training in the 1920s and 1930s. Indian reservations were considered relatively safe and accessible for unescorted young women until the murder of Boas' student Henrietta Schmerler on the White Mountain Apache Reservation in 1931 (McMillan 1986). But going abroad often engendered opposition, as the examples of Mead and Powdermaker show.[5]

Gower recalled that her opportunities in Sicily for "full participation" and "direct observation" were complicated by her sex and class position. "I could not avoid being ranged in the upper stratum of society where unmarried women are strictly guarded. As it was I could not escape affiliation with one of the two factions that divided the town, an affiliation that considerably limited my range of contacts among the leaders of the community" (Chapman 1971:xiv).

The two factions in Milocca in the late 1920s were the socialists — including agricultural workers, the midwife, the mayor, and a man from a prominent merchant family — and the fascists, led by the landowning families, who held enormous estates and were allied with the Catholic church. Gower's book thus contradicts the present-day stereotype that early- to mid-twentieth-century modernist anthropology ahistorically depicts the timeless, unchanging lives of "natives" or peasants. After brief accounts of her journey to the mountain village, its settlement and history, and how she came to move in with the local midwife, we learn about large estates, "latifondi, known locally as feudi" and about a 1920 uprising in which "the laborers armed and took by force" six of these estates.

5. Mead, who wanted to do research in the remote Tuamotus, was pressured by Boas and her father (who controlled degree-granting and fieldwork funds between them) to go to American Samoa and live with an American naval family (Mead 1972:126–30). Hortense Powdermaker, one of Malinowski's students and the first woman anthropologist to work alone, without a husband, in New Guinea, was prevented from going to Mafulu, in the interior, by Australian colonial government anthropologist E. W. Chinnery on grounds of the alleged risk of attack by "native men" on an unescorted white woman. She had little choice but to go instead to the site Chinnery selected, the New Ireland coast, which was under closer colonial control (Powdermaker 1966; Stocking 1982). Similarly, Chinnery told Alfred Cort Haddon in 1929, "Have written to Miss [Beatrice] Blackwood as you suggested. It isn't really safe for women to work alone in this country but you may rest assured that I shall assist as far as I can anyone sent up." (Blackwood eventually did landmark research on Buka in the Solomon Islands.) "If any more lady anthropologists are thinking of coming out here," Chinnery advised, "you had better suggest that they bring a husband with them. I know of no place where a woman can work without fear of molestation from the natives" (quoted in Stocking 1982:8).

This local socialist movement was only moderately successful. For forty-five stirring days they held the feudi, maintaining a force of a hundred men in each to defend the place from counterattack and to keep it going . . . the women of Milocca went into battle and helped their men keep what they had taken. The whole matter was finally settled, with the Milocchese allowed to rent half the land they had conquered, pending legislation. At present two of the estates are managed by the local cooperative bank and two more are rented by wealthy local men. The 1920 uprising was part of the post-war unrest which manifested itself all over Italy, with workers seizing factories in the north and land in the south. (Chapman 1971:3–5)

The fascists rose to power in Italy a few years before Gower's fieldwork, and the larger political situation frames her community study in Milocca: "Of course the leading citizens all joined the fascist party, and their wives made up the Fascio femminile" (Chapman 1971:6). The conflict between socialists and fascists, Gower explained, played out in the fascist government's war on the Sicilian Mafia, including the widespread imprisonment of suspected mafiosi and the confiscation of their livestock. After a two-year campaign, Milocca, the Mafia's last mountain stronghold, was the scene of mass arrests. "The little square in Milocca must have presented a strange spectacle that January [1928] morning, filled with bleating sheep, goats, horses and mules, while the police station was full of weeping women . . . In the fall of 1928, there were about one hundred Milocchese men in prison awaiting trial. In the early part of 1930 a few were released for lack of evidence against them" (1971:8).

Gower stressed further that class position and status did not predict the affiliation of a particular family with the mafiosi, and explained how current tensions affected her own position and the rounds of life in Milocca.

On my arrival, a rumor got about that I was carrying on investigations in regard to the prisoners, and so might be influential in getting them released. As long as this rumor was current, everyone sought to please the stranger. The belief may never have died completely, for no arrested man was ever described to me as anything but entirely innocent and a true saint. At the same time, the action of the government in making the arrests and destroying crime was always praised . . . it had put the entire community into a sort of mourning. Religious occasions were not celebrated with the usual splendor, for most of the men who had been active in such affairs were behind the bars. Prison-widows were numerous, and some were in serious financial difficulties so that for a time relief was administered to them in the form of free meals and condensed milk and flour for nursing mothers. The funds for this relief were soon exhausted. One woman had deviated from the path of virtue in the absence of her husband, and was condemned as much for her levity in a time of bereavement as for her unchastity. (Chapman 1971:8–9)

Following hard upon the more classically Boasian records of the ballad of "The Quarrel of the Mother and Daughter" and translated texts of village love songs, in an appendix entitled "Mussolini in Popular Literature," Gower analyzed two celebratory poems "in circulation in Milocca." "Finished are the times of the sweet repasts, Of anarchists, proletarians, and communists . . ." (Chapman 1971:239–51). Milocca's ethnographic descriptions were interwoven with accounts of ongoing factional and political tensions. "The procession [of Saint Joseph, Milocca's patron] in 1929 was as usual, save that the Fascist organization of small girls marched in uniform behind the *immaculatini* [young virgins wearing light blue mantles] . . ." (Chapman 1971:161, 177–78).

The book is a comprehensive community study, befitting the Chicago School sociology tradition, with a clear delineation of statuses and roles related to "Sex and Age" (see below), and of social stratification—including "class consciousness" and its limits in "intraclass antagonism." It is also, simultaneously, a modernist anthropological account of kinship, marriage, godparenthood, politics, and "spirits and witches." Indeed, the second half of *Milocca* is largely devoted to various aspects of religious belief and practice, with lengthy texts of prayers and charms and detailed accounts of saints, including their annual processions or *festas*—like the ones Gower left undescribed in her dissertation on Chicago Sicilians and their memories of village life and religion. "In Chicago, Sicilian colonies have established their former town patrons in their parish churches and celebrate the annual festa in much the same way that it is observed in the home village" (Chapman 1971:163; these festas continue today in Chicago's historically Italian neighborhoods).

Fred Eggan's foreword to *Milocca* (1971) suggests why Gower's long-vanished prewar manuscript was finally published. "*Milocca* is the only anthropological field study of a Sicilian *village* currently available. As such it has a special significance with regard to the contemporary controversies as to the nature of the Italian family system, and to the renewed interest in the persistence of ethnic identity in the face of strong forces for change." Eggan's "contemporary controversies" refers to the angry debate around 1970 in the anthropology of "peasant societies" regarding Edward Banfield's concept of the "amoral familism" of southern Italian peasants, which some later scholars extrapolated to all, or most, peasant societies. In *The Moral Basis of a Backward Society* (1958), Banfield, a political scientist, asserted that the "inability of the villagers to act together for the common good" kept them "prisoners of their [nuclear] family-centered ethos," trapped in misery and responsible for their own dire poverty (Banfield 1958:10, 15, 37, 63, 163).

Gower alludes politely to this controversy in her preface to *Milocca* (Chapman 1971:xv–xvi). Her research, she explains, documents the civic pride and

ties to their home community of the Milocchese and their neighbors, the socialist uprising of 1920, village religious processions, and "co-operative" inter-
class relations in what remained a largely feudal agricultural economy. "It is
likely that life is not much different from what it was when I was there, with
the same social stratification and local politics dominated by two rival factions." Recent literature, she observed,

> tends to stress the squalor and misery of Sicilian life . . . But I never got the im-
> pression that the Milocchese were unhappy with their lot. Nor did it occur to
> me that they should be unhappy. Nevertheless, behind the squalor and misery
> described by the modern writers, the Sicily I knew forty years ago is still recog-
> nizable: the importance of the family, the seclusion of unmarried women, the
> distrust of the government and its representatives, and strong pride. (Chapman
> 1971:xv–xvi)

Gower's 1928 Sicilian village study was three decades ahead of a burgeon-
ing interest by anthropologists and political scientists in southern Italian
peasant society, particularly in its class relations and land tenure patterns.
This scholarly focus likely resulted from the American invasion in World
War II and the anxieties of postwar American governments and powerful
funding agencies that Italy—particularly the impoverished south—might "go
Communist" (cf. Nader 1997; Wallerstein 1997). Others besides Banfield did
fieldwork in southern Italy and published influential works (Friedman 1953;
Lopreato 1965; Cronin 1970). Even Redfield joined the debate, proposing
that southern Italians were a special case: an exception to the peasant's characteristic "intense attachment to native soil; a reverent disposition toward
habitat and ancestral ways; a restraint on individual self seeking in favor of
family and community . . ." (1956:118, 140). Redfield cited Friedman's research, but not Gower's, still unpublished, though he had read it 20 years
earlier.

More generally, "peasant societies," and rural communities in the "circum-
Mediterranean," had grown to be significant locations for anthropological
research and theorizing in the postwar United States and Britain (Pitt-Rivers
1954; Boissevain 1965; Peristiany 1966; Potter et al. 1967). Charlotte Gower
missed the publishing wave of immigrant studies and background studies of
the 1920s by a few years, but Fred Eggan found the carbon copy of her manuscript just in time for her to catch the end of the next big wave of social scientific interest in Italians and their "problems."

Milocca, which was translated and published in Italy as well, met a respectful reception by Europeanists. Brian O'Neill has pointed out that Gower's
book was cited 15 times in John Davis's *People of the Mediterranean* (1977), a
volume which, as Joao Leal has remarked, "stands as one of the most influential books ever written on Mediterraneanist social anthropology." O'Neill describes *Milocca* to his students as " 'the first' modern-structured ethnographic

monograph of a European community, followed by Arensberg [1937] and others." And Leal notes that Gower, in addressing the issue of factionalism, "was the first anthropologist to notice its importance in Southern Europe, foreshadowing Boissevain's interest in the topic" in his classic monograph on Malta (1965). Gower's "observations on the contrast between female and male patterns of behaviour in Milocca," Leal continues, "anticipate the 'honor and shame' debate in Mediterraneanist social anthropology of the 1960s and 1970s."[6] The honor and shame debate later found its way into the new anthropology of gender and discussions of gender ideologies in cross-cultural perspective.

On Wisconsin

The conference room (also the library and archive) of the Department of Anthropology at the University of Wisconsin–Madison is decorated with a series of photographs of retired faculty dubbed the Rogues' Gallery by our emeritus colleague Aidan Southall. The line-up was all male until a few years ago when we finally persuaded Catharine McClellan and her husband, John Hitchcock, to contribute their portraits. To the right of the Bunn Coffee-Matic, the microwave, and the double sink, in pride of place near the door, is a large, indifferently executed, but still striking oil painting of unknown provenance. The portly, middle-aged sitter—in three-quarters view with a map of the world behind him, pipe in hand, and arresting dark eyes that catch the wandering gaze of present-day faculty members during long meetings— is Ralph Linton. A typed label, affixed after his death in 1953, gives a capsule biography.

Linton was the first anthropologist hired in a permanent position at the University of Wisconsin, in 1928. Although his Harvard Ph.D. was awarded only in 1925, for research on the prehistory of the Marquesas Islands of Polynesia, Linton had over a decade of prior ethnological, archeological, and museum experience. He was hired away from Chicago's Field Museum as an associate professor, at a salary of $4,250, and quickly promoted to full professor in 1930 with a raise to $5,000 (UWFEC 1928–30; Linton & Wagley [1971] give the promotion year as 1929).

Linton was joined at the University of Wisconsin in 1930 by Charlotte

6. I am grateful to George Stocking for eliciting and forwarding to me this information on *Milocca* and its reception from Joao Leal (e-mail JL/GS 3/25/99) and Brian Juan O'Neill (fax BO/GS 3/31/99). John Davis discusses *Milocca* and "Gower Chapman's" ethnographic accounts in his comparative overviews of Mediterranean societies and their sexual division of labor, occupational roles, factions, class systems, mechanisms of credit, political structures, states, fascism, kinship and residence patterns, godparenthood, fraternal rivalries, dowry, inheritance, and religion (1977:9, 44, 55–59, 78–79, 103–4, 141–42, 164, 178–79, 188–89, 228, 230–31).

Ralph Linton. (Courtesy of the University of Wisconsin–Madison Archives.)

Gower, recently returned from Sicily. Gower was hired as an assistant professor at a salary of $3,000 (UWB 1930–31). Her appointment was listed as
Assistant Professor of Physical Anthropology (UWAA 1929–30, 1930–31;
UWAC 1928–29, 1929–30; Wisconsin faculty shortly accepted a "waiver" of
14 percent of their salary as an alternative to the firing of 14 percent of the

faculty during the depression). Gower had learned physical anthropology, archeology, and associated laboratory skills as an undergraduate at Smith College, from Cole, and at the Field Museum in Chicago—where Linton had worked before Wisconsin and where he and Gower first met. But this is still a surprising job title for a scholar returning from a year and a half of pioneering ethnographic research. She and Cole stressed her four-fields training at Chicago: she was hired to complement Linton's course offerings, which were largely in ethnology, even though Linton had extensive archeological field experience. His title by 1930 was Professor of Social Anthropology.[7]

In 1928, Linton joined Wisconsin's Department of Economics and Sociology. The two departments split in 1929–30, and the latter became the Department of Sociology and Anthropology, remaining a joint department until 1958 (UWAA 1929–30, 1930–31; UWAC 1928–29, 1929–30; UWAP 1939; Sewell 1975).[8] During the 1930s, Wisconsin sociology and anthropology faculty continued to teach courses in what are nowadays separate departments or schools, such as rural sociology and social work, as well as in cognate fields to sociology such as social psychology and criminology. Senior faculty specializing in all of these areas passed judgment on the worthiness of their junior colleagues for contract renewal or promotion.

7. In 1928, while she was finishing her dissertation, Gower applied for a newly established assistant professor position at the University of Michigan. Even though he was one of her advisors, Edward Sapir wrote Leslie White, then in his first year of teaching at the University of Buffalo, "Carl Guthe, Univer. of Michigan, is trying to get a man to do some teaching and also museum work in anthropology at Univ. of Michigan. He tried to interest Linton, I hear, but Linton didn't go. Then Charlotte Gower suggested herself to him and I understand Guthe was struck by this as possible and is inclined to make her an offer. Because of her relation to me I am resisting my first impulse to take the initiative and write Guthe to get in touch with you. But I think it would be quite alright [sic] for you to drop Guthe a note asking for possibilities and refering [sic] to me as one prepared to back you up. He may be able to make you a better offer than he is prepared to make to Charlotte" (UMB: ES/LW 3/15/28). Boas' student Gladys Reichard also applied but failed to win the Michigan position. Julian Steward, Kroeber's student at California, was hired but left after one year. Leslie White took up the Michigan position in 1930 (William Peace, pers. comm. 1997; see also Deacon 1997:268; I thank William Peace for alerting me to this correspondence and providing me with copies of it). Sapir appears to be correct that Carl Guthe was "trying to get a man to do some teaching." Gower apparently never knew why her application to Michigan was unsuccessful.

8. The earliest anthropology courses were taught by Wisconsin's first lecturer in sociology, Jerome Dowd, in 1897, and by English archeologist Charles Henry Hawes in 1907. Chairman John L. Gillin explained, "In 1930, Gower was added to offer two courses in Physical Anthropology at request of Medical School and Department, the latter because of bearing of Physical Anthropology on race relations and on culture. The remainder of her time was devoted to Prehistory and to the growing enrollments in social anthropology" (UWAP 1939: Memorandum on Budget of Department of Sociology and Anthropology, 1939–41). Wisconsin's first woman anthropology Ph.D. (the only one through 1955) was Ruth Useem, in 1947, for her research on acculturation among Rosebud Sioux (Yearbook of Anthropology 1955:750).

The University of Wisconsin Bulletin, for the first year Charlotte Gower joined the faculty, lists her courses and Linton's separately, under the head-ing "Social Anthropology," which follows "Sociological Theory" in the bulle-tin.[9] Course titles and descriptions in the bulletin show that "Social Anthro-pology" at Wisconsin in the 1930s included what today would be considered biological anthropology as well as archeology. Miss Gower is listed as offering six new courses: Primitive Religion ("A study of selected primitive religions from the functional standpoint"), Theories of Culture, Human Pre-History, Introduction to Physical Anthropology, Advanced Physical Anthropology ("Training in laboratory methods with research on assigned problems"), and a graduate course on Problems of Culture ("Application of anthropological method to sociological research"). The University of Wisconsin teaching pro-gram title of Social Anthropology, and Gower's job title of Assistant Profes-sor of Physical Anthropology, were flexible: three of the four fields of anthro-pology were now represented in University of Wisconsin course offerings. Through Gower's teaching, so was functionalist theory—a recent and con-troversial British import in 1930—as well as Chicago School sociology, in close rapprochement with anthropological methods.

By 1931–32, Linton and Gower were co-teaching three courses to graduate students, the special-topics, generic Anthropological Problems plus two new courses. One, "The Individual in Cultural Change," has the intriguing cata-logue description, "The significance of the rebel in relation to the culture pat-tern." The other, "Fundamental Contrasts Between Oriental and Occidental Cultures," is undescribed, although Gower reports adding an emphasis on Japan to the course in the prewar year of 1937 (UWASIR). In 1937–38, social psychologist A. Kimball Young, plus Linton and Gower, offered "Language and Culture" to graduate students, and the Boasian four-fields mandate was fulfilled.

Adelin Linton, Ralph's widow, later recalled that 36 undergraduate stu-dents "began their anthropology with Linton," including John Gillin (whose criminologist father later became department chairman), Sol Tax, Lauris-ton Sharp, Clyde Kluckhohn, and E. Adamson Hoebel (Linton & Wagley 1971:36). These men, future U.S. Commissioner of Indian Affairs Philleo Nash, and others who later became well known in anthropology, studied as well with Gower, the only other anthropologist on staff. But she is nearly always omitted when her former students or their biographers and memo-rialists trace their intellectual descent and indebtedness. Since records left behind of Gower's teaching show she emphasized a creative synthesis of four-

9. The University of Wisconsin Bulletin has the confusing system of combining the General Announcement of Courses for the following year, here 1931–32, with the current year's cata-logue, here 1930–31:187–91).

CHARLOTTE GOWER   143

fields anthropology, empirical sociology (including the study of "personal documents"), and a focus on culture change; and since some of her former students became leading figures in major departments of anthropology by midcentury, this is a major omission that elides Gower's contribution to the formation and academic transmission of postwar American anthropology.[10]

Ralph Linton was by all reports a gifted and charismatic teacher, "a phenomenally successful lecturer to undergraduate classes" (Gillin 1954:278; cf. Linton & Wagley 1971:36–37; UWA: Tax 1989). W. W. Howells, who came to Madison in 1939, the year after Gower departed and two years after Linton left for Columbia, heard from students that Linton "was known for having a phenomenal memory and a sense of humor; he was a spellbinder who would lean back in his chair and lecture off the top of his head, to the deep satisfaction of his hearers. (I only knew him elsewhere, but I remember his style.)" Howells added, "Anthropology doubled in size in a few years with Charlotte Gower, also a lively person and a popular teacher" (UWA 1989).

In two memoirs, Sol Tax has recalled both Linton and Gower warmly, but focused far more attention on Linton, describing himself as Linton's first anthropology student (Tax 1988:1; UWA 1989).

> I should say a word also about Charlotte Gower, who taught not only courses in prehistory and archaeology . . . but also had an ongoing seminar, evenings at her apartment; the class I recall included, besides us, students in other departments, with whom we discussed problems beyond anthropology. I recall one of them whose consuming interest was landscape gardening, and more than once after class he took me aside to ask what its relation was to anthropology! Gower was of course writing her account of life in a Sicilian village, and we were impatient to see the results. I recall in one of my papers written for her in 1929 [sic] that I jokingly referred to her forthcoming book of '1949,' little dreaming that she would become a high ranking officer in the Women's Army Corps during World War II. (UWA: Tax 1989)

In a term paper, Tax teased his 28-year-old teacher not only about her uncompleted book but about being a "savior of the weak" by inaugurating the "Science of Background Studies." Now anthropologists would no longer have to risk "scalping and boiling" in order to do their fieldwork (UCRLT 1930). Tax's friendly, egalitarian, joking tone, and the evening seminars at Gower's apartment, suggest far less social distance than is customary even today between university faculty and their students. Since foregoing the privileges of

10. Tax, for example, became professor of anthropology at Chicago, Kluckhohn at Harvard, Hoebel at Minnesota, and Sharp at Cornell. Sharp was the undergraduate advisor of Ward Goodenough and David Schneider. Kluckhohn was Schneider's graduate advisor at Harvard (Marshall 1999). All these men played key roles in training the next generation of prominent American anthropologists.

conventional deference behavior and social distance from students can be dangerous to the careers of junior faculty, especially women, even at this end of the century, one wonders how Charlotte Gower's teaching style and relations with students were perceived by her senior male colleagues.

The close working relationship necessary for Gower and Linton, the only two faculty members in what Tax calls "the new anthropology emphasis," and who co-taught courses beginning in 1931, extended outside the confines of Sterling Hall. Gower is remembered by a daughter of Mrs. Antonina Paratore, the proprietor, as a drinking companion of Linton's in one of Madison's Sicilian-owned speakeasies (Herb Lewis, pers. comm. 1996), located a convenient four blocks from Gower's apartment. (Gower dedicated the published version of *Milocca* to Mrs. Paratore, "who brought the best of Sicily to her adopted country.")

The persistent story about Charlotte Gower, the one told over many years by friends and colleagues such as Fred Eggan and Sol Tax, is that she and Ralph Linton were lovers. Eggan and others told colleagues over the years that the relationship began not at Madison but during the time that Gower was a graduate student and Linton was based at Chicago's Field Museum (Ray Fogelson, pers. comm. 1996). If true, this would complicate the story of how Charlotte Gower came to be hired at the University of Wisconsin two years after Linton.

Linton's third wife, Adelin, in a biography written with Charles Wagley in 1971, says Linton's marriage to his second wife, Margaret, was "never a harmonious one, at least according to Linton, and it deteriorated further after the couple went to Wisconsin. They agreed to a trial separation in 1932." Margaret and their son moved to New York, and the couple divorced in 1934. Things moved rapidly on the marital front for Linton, though, who in 1935 married "Adelin Hohlfeld, a young widow who was at the time a columnist and book reviewer for the Madison Capital Times" (Linton & Wagley 1971:24). Mrs. Hohlfeld was the widow of the son of one of the most influential professors on the University of Wisconsin campus, Alexander Hohlfeld, chairman of the German Department (Cronon & Jenkins 1994:156, 162).

It is impossible not to wonder about Gower's relationship with Linton, her closest colleague, nine years her senior, a man in a disintegrating marriage, and a person many of his former (male) students recall as fascinating. It is also impossible not to wonder why the two never married, and what happened to their professional relationship after 1935, when Linton married someone else. And what effect did the new faculty wife and well-connected journalist—Adelin Hohlfeld was actually the society columnist—have on Gower's reputation and career? Adelin Linton's biography of her late husband mentions Gower only in passing, although it goes on at some length about Linton's

relations with other (male) faculty, and with both male and female students
(Linton & Wagley 1971:37).

John P. Gillin, his former student, alludes delicately to Linton's personal
entanglements in an obituary.

> As a man, Linton was a complicated personality. He had an extraordinary ca-
> pacity for friendship . . . He was a man who needed personal relationships, and
> many of his friends thought that he wasted himself in his constant wanderings
> about this country and abroad to contact them and to make new acquaintances
> . . . He exhibited a form of gallantry that made him attractive to women, many
> of whom lacked the faintest idea of what he was talking about. (Gillin 1954:278)

By 1937, Ralph Linton could be less than complimentary about Charlotte
Gower in private, at least as evidenced by a letter he wrote to Sol Tax. The
issue was which anthropologist should be hired at Wisconsin. Gower was
advocating for George Murdock. "Charlotte probably thinks she can lead
him around by the nose," Linton wrote, a remark that seems oddly subject
to Freudian interpretation. Or else, he continued, Gower wanted to bring in
(Raymond) "Firth, Malinowski's understudy. I have vetoed that and she has
threatened to resign if we bring in [Alexander] Lesser. I think it as well she
did. She is scared stiff without my help" (UCRLT: RL/ST 5/10/37). Gower
seems, from this passage, to have had a more shrewd and catholic perspective
on anthropology than Linton, since she was already championing two very
different young scholars who 20 years later would be counted among the most
influential figures in the discipline.[11]

Linton's letter shows he represented himself as the patron of a less-than-

---

11. Gower served as Malinowski's "more-or-less hostess" during an otherwise forgotten visit
he made to Wisconsin in 1935. McMillan (1986:217–18, 257, 261), who corresponded with
Gower in 1974 and 1976 regarding her experiences at Chicago, takes the view that Malinowski's lectures at Chicago, Northwestern, Yale, and Wisconsin from 1930 to 1940 had virtually no
intellectual impact on American anthropology, their content barely remembered by the former
students who heard them. "Gower . . . provides a typical account: 'He had a very childish tendency to try shock techniques on any new acquaintance or audience—mainly language of dubious acceptability. I recall his dismissing someone as a "tiresome bugger" for my benefit. Once I
explained that in my experience a "bugger" could be any small boy, I do not recall his having
worked that ploy again. For a new audience he usually began, "Anthropology is the Study of a
Man . . . embracing woman." He must have been a hypochondriac: When he was leaving Madison, I offered to help him pack. He accepted, but asked me to wait a few moments in the lobby.
When I eventually went up, there was little packing to do, except for a long array of medicine
bottles on the bureau. As he examined these before handing them to me, he usually finished off
the bottle, saying, "No use in carrying that bit." ' " It appears that Gower and Malinowski discussed functionalist theory and Firth's suitability for the Wisconsin faculty position. If Gower
had not been fired, perhaps Malinowski's intellectual influence, or at least memories of his visit,
would have survived at the University of Wisconsin.

fully-worthy Gower, and shows that he, Gower, and the administration knew he would be leaving the department. Linton departed from Wisconsin in the fall of 1937 for a visiting professorship at Columbia University. A few months later, he claimed the chairmanship of the Columbia Department of Anthropology, winning the position in place of Boas' choice, Ruth Benedict—who was vetoed on grounds of her sex by President Nicholas Murray Butler (Linton & Wagley 1971:47–49; Modell 1983).

Charlotte Gower lost her job at the University of Wisconsin about four months later, by January of 1938 (UCRLA: CG/FC 1/13/38). Linton may have publicly supported Gower both before and after his marriage, whatever their personal relationship, but have been unable, after his departure, to protect her from the new department chairman, John L. Gillin, who took office in the fall of 1937. Or Linton may have been privately critical of Gower to the new chairman, just as he had been to Sol Tax.

Linton's privately expressed hostility toward Gower by this point may have had a more personal origin. University of Chicago departmental legend has it that Gower had another lover, none other than A. R. Radcliffe-Brown (e.g. Robert Moore, pers. comm. 1995; Ray Fogelson, pers. comm. 1996; the story came from Fred Eggan). Radcliffe-Brown joined the Chicago faculty in 1931 and remained until his departure for Oxford in 1937 (Stocking 1979:21, 29, 1995:352–66). The story goes that Gower—clearly cast as anthropology's, or at least the University of Chicago's, femme fatale—was involved with the two men simultaneously. There are several variants of the same anecdote: one morning Ralph Linton knocked on the door of Charlotte Gower's Chicago apartment, only to find it opened by A. R. Radcliffe-Brown, wearing a silk monogrammed bathrobe. (In other versions, Linton finds the bathrobe hanging in her bathroom.)

Gower was a visiting faculty member at Chicago during the spring quarter of 1936, teaching physical anthropology, prehistory, and primitive religion "in exchange for Harry Hoijer, who went to Madison to teach Linguistics" (Chapman 1977b; UWASIR 1936). Her former student, Tax, was then an advanced graduate student at Chicago, and her former graduate school classmates, Redfield and Eggan, were on the Chicago faculty. Did Gower really have simultaneous, or serial, affairs with Linton and Radcliffe-Brown? Or was she pursued by both of these supremely self-confident older men and uninterested in one or both, either entirely or at a given point? Did she want to break off any involvement earlier than her suitor preferred? In any case, it could have been a professional disaster, the woman scorned being fully matched by the fury of the powerful man sexually rejected, or dumped before he can get around to it, by a junior female.

Gower's account to Stocking, decades later, revealed no hint of any personal connection with either Linton or Radcliffe-Brown.

A. R. Radcliffe-Brown, Sydney, Australia, ca. 1930. Photograph by Sarah Neill Chinnery. (Courtesy of Sheila M. Waters.)

Radcliffe-Brown was also [like Sapir] a "star" of sorts, someone whom Cole had acquired and exhibited with pride. I can imagine no other American head of a department of Anthropology who would have been happy with such a subordinate. I do not recall anything about his debate with Linton in 1933. My impression was that Linton regarded R. B. as a threat to orthodox American anthropology, with its stress on history (diffusion) and human nature as explanations of culture. Radcliffe-Brown appeared to discount explanations on terms of individual psychology (Fear first made the Gods) and search for explanations in terms of essential conditions for the survival of a society. Hence his emphasis on social structure, and his talk of social systems. He patently regarded psychological explanations as rather childish . . . When I returned to Chicago for a term (1936?) I believe that Radcliffe-Brown was in China. At least I did not have an opportunity to attend any of his classes. (Chapman 1978)

Nor does Gower indicate whether her own interest in China, about which she had lectured at Wisconsin, and where she later spent four years, relates in any way to that of Radcliffe-Brown, who had ambitions of launching a full-scale, comparative research program in China and Japan (McMillan 1986:156; Stocking 1995).

According to many people's reminiscences, Ralph Linton and A. R. Radcliffe-Brown loathed each other. Even Adelin Linton writes, "Linton disliked Radcliffe-Brown as a person, although he respected and assimilated many of his ideas" (Linton & Wagley 1971:39). If this is so, might the two professors have been rivals not only for the intellectual and personal loyalties of their respective students and the supremacy of their theoretical positions, but also for the attentions of Charlotte Gower?

Sol Tax (UWA 1989) has described "the famous rift between Ralph Linton and A. R. Radcliffe-Brown, another of my Chicago professors and one who 'picked a fight' with Boasian anthropologists including Linton." In 1933, Tax, as a Chicago graduate student, arranged what he accurately calls "a famous debate" on functionalism at Chicago between Linton and Radcliffe-Brown (Stocking 1995:354–55). Three years earlier, Gower was already discussing functionalism with her Wisconsin students, including Tax, who Linton worried by 1933 was becoming a convert to the functionalist views of Radcliffe-Brown. Tax had to go to a great deal of trouble getting each man to agree on the terms, conditions, and debate resolution. "Again, Linton worried . . . and five or six years later said quietly to me, 'Sol, remember the debate you arranged between me and Radcliffe-Brown? Well, tell me: who were you trying to get, me or him?'" (UWA: Tax 1989; UCRLT 1933).

Linton and Radcliffe-Brown also had a second intellectual duel, a "joint seminar session at the University of Wisconsin in 1936."

Radcliffe-Brown came to Wisconsin University accompanied by a collection of his devoted followers, and the session turned into a confrontation and was one of the most stimulating events that Wisconsin social sciences had produced. The two men provided quite a contrast on the rostrum: Radcliffe-Brown, tall and arrogant in beautifully tailored English clothes, a monocle, and a long cigarette holder; Linton, big and burly in rumpled unmatched tweeds and smoking a pipe. (Linton & Wagley 1971:39)

Gower probably helped to arrange this event in her home department, but no evidence survives concerning her reactions, intellectual or personal.

Publish or Perish

In the preface of what became his most widely read book, *The Study of Man* (1936:viii), Ralph Linton acknowledged "the constructive criticism" of departmental colleagues E. A. Ross, Charlotte Gower, and Kimball Young. It was logical that Linton should list Ross first: sociologist Edward Alsworth Ross was not only chairman of the department until his retirement in 1937, he was editor of the Century Social Science Series in which Linton's book appeared. But it seems likely that Gower, with whom he had been co-teaching classes, was the person who most closely discussed this work with Linton.

Their intellectual collaboration is substantiated in a letter Gower wrote to Cole: "I am sure it is no secret . . . that I am playing Waterman to Ralph's Kroeber in the preparation of a new source-book to accompany *The Study of Man*. It's freshening me up no end on my anthropological reading" (UCRLA: CG/FC 2/9/37). Linton, though, did not bother with citations in his book —which he dictated to the department secretary directly from his lectures in introductory anthropology—and there is only one footnote (see Linton & Wagley 1971). Presumably the "source-book" was intended to remedy these defects. And it seems clear that Gower saw herself as the junior partner in collaboration with a more famous scholar, as with T. T. Waterman's and Alfred Kroeber's work in California ethnology. Moreover, according to Eggan, Linton "tacked on" Charlotte Gower's anthropological bibliography, developed for her own teaching of introductory courses, to the back of *The Study of Man* (Ray Fogelson, pers. comm. 1996).

There is other evidence of Gower's influence on, or usefulness to, Linton. Her chapter in *Milocca* on "Sex and Age" discusses what since the 1980s anthropologists, and others, have called gender. "My sister has six children, two boys and four burdens," Gower begins by quoting, before launching an account of the life course of each sex, the sexual division of labor, husband-wife relations, "house-nuns" (unordained, chaste women), and priests (Chapman 1971 [1973]:30–49). Linton published two articles on "Age and Sex Categories," one entitled "A Neglected Aspect of Social Organization" (1940, 1942). His articles were recommended to me, during my graduate student years, by Elizabeth Colson, as work unduly neglected by anthropologists. Now, of course, I wonder how strongly Linton's discussions of sex and age were influenced by Gower's ideas, their collegial conversations, and even the second chapter of Gower's Sicilian village manuscript, completed five years earlier and still unpublished when Linton's articles appeared in the top two sociology journals in the country.

In 1935, Gower wrote Redfield, by then Dean of Social Sciences at Chicago, about her book manuscript on Sicily, which she finished by the end of the summer, asking him to comment on it and enlisting his help in getting it published by the University of Chicago Press (UCRLR: CG/RR 7/25/35). Early in 1937, she asked Cole to inquire about the fate of her manuscript: "It is nearly a year now that they have had the mss" (UCRLA: CG/FC 2/9/37). Cole contacted the editor, Donald Bean, but the University of Chicago Press finally rejected the manuscript in July of 1937.

Gower immediately submitted it to the University of Wisconsin Press, whose managing editor, Livia Appel, solicited and obtained letters of support for Gower's book from Cole and Redfield. Gower, who also wrote the two men to request letters, added that she planned to "make the same request of R-B. With recommendations from such outstanding people I feel the committee [on Publications at Wisconsin] should be duly impressed" (UCRLR: CG/RR 7/23/37). Any letter from Radcliffe-Brown seems to have vanished, but Cole wrote, "I consider it an important study—fully as important as *Middletown*. It is a scholarly contribution both in subject and method. Personally I believe the book would have a wide appeal to students of the Social Sciences and to others interest [sic] in immigrant and acculturation problems" (UCRLA: FC/LA 7/37).

Redfield too declared, "I have read the first six or seven chapters of this manuscript and take the liberty of expressing to you my opinion that they constitute a contribution to scholarship of unusual merit and that both the simplicity and quality of exposition and the subject matter make me feel that the book would have general appeal" (UCRLR: RR/LA 7/27/37). Six months later, he wrote Gower, "Someone told me recently that your book on Sicily was announced for publication by the University of Wisconsin. I hope that this is true. It certainly should appear" (UCRLR: RR/CG 1/3/38). But by December of 1937, the Wisconsin Committee on Publications had rejected Charlotte Gower's book as well.

That spring, Robert Redfield tried again to arrange for Gower's manuscript to be published by the University of Chicago Press, and this time Editor Donald Bean responded positively. "I think your idea of publishing Gower's *Milocca, A Sicilian Village* and the forthcoming Embree book on the Japanese village at one time is excellent, and if the Division [of Social Science] can finance the composition on all of them, we will undertake [it]" (UCRLR: DB/RR 4/27/38). There is a gap at this point in Redfield's surviving papers, but two other anthropological community studies, John Embree's *Suye Mura: A Japanese Village* and Horace Miner's *St. Denis: A French-Canadian Parish*, were published by the University of Chicago Press in 1939. Gower's manuscript remained unpublished. By 1940, Redfield had lost track of it. "Certain students here would like very much an opportunity to consult certain sections of Miss Gower's manuscript, in connection with their research. Do you know where the manuscript is, and where I might get permission to look at it? I understand that Miss Gower is in the Orient" (UCRLR: RR/LA 8/2/40).

Two people recall that Gower gave the original manuscript to Radcliffe-Brown, who left in 1937 for a professorship at Oxford, and who was supposed to help get it published at Oxford University Press (UWA: Tax 1989). Judge Eben B. Gower, who had been corresponding with Mrs. Ernestine Bingham, University of Chicago anthropology departmental secretary, about his daughter's lost manuscript, received a (last) letter from Charlotte in Hong Kong. "It seems that the first copy of her book on Sicily was left with Prof. Radcliffe-Brown in England, where it was being considered by the 'Clarendon Press'. She is writing to him about it" (UCRLA: EG/EB 12/17/40). This account, which seems to come directly from Charlotte Gower's letter to her father, also implies that she sailed from New York to England on the way to China in June of 1938, visited Radcliffe-Brown at Oxford, and gave him the manuscript herself. This of course implies that Gower and Radcliffe-Brown remained friends after he left Chicago.

The original manuscript has never surfaced again. Radcliffe-Brown is the last known person to have seen it. Buried among Robert Redfield's correspondence is one key answer to the puzzle. R-B did indeed, he reports, try to assist Charlotte Gower in getting her book published, but was stymied by the disruption of academic life in the early, disastrous years of World War II. His handwritten letter to Cole, written only a few weeks after the catastrophic bombing of London in the Blitz of December 1940, was passed on to Redfield by Ernestine Bingham.

I hear that you are enquiring about the M.S. of Charlotte Gower's book on Sicily. I have it here. In normal times the Oxford University Press would have published it. (They have read it.) But it is very doubtful when normal times will recur. I do hope you will be able to get it published at last. However, I will not send the M.S. till I hear from you. There is another copy somewhere but Charlotte does not seem to know where it is. I decided to make a small book of the ideas that I put before the seminar in Chicago and have been working on it at intervals. In present circumstances I cannot say when it will be printed. Oxford, so far, has not been bombed. But the work of the University is, of course, only carried on on a very reduced scale. (UCRLR: RB/FC 1/28/41)

Radcliffe-Brown's letter implies that he too had heard directly from Gower at some earlier point, in person or by letter, about the missing copy of her manuscript. We can only wonder if, with a book published by Oxford University Press, Charlotte Gower might have overcome the intensifying discrimination against women in academia after World War II and have returned to a faculty position in American anthropology.

Cole, Redfield, Kimball Young, Judge Gower, and Ernestine Bingham, exchanging letters in their continuing search for Gower's book manuscript, eventually recalled—correctly as it turned out—that the carbon copy was somewhere at the University of Chicago (UCRLA: 1939–41). It was this carbon copy that was found, in 1941, lost again, rediscovered in 1969, and finally published—in 1971.

Cole persisted in the effort to see Gower's work in print, asking Redfield if "we could include it in the publishing program of the department for next year? The series of peasant society books is going well and it seems to be desirable that it be not allowed to lapse. The manuscript is a good one" (UCRLR: FC/RR 4/1/41). Redfield responded by showing Gower's manuscript (the carbon copy) to William F. Whyte, W. Lloyd Warner, and A. M. Halpern. Whyte, though, compared it unfavorably to Edward Spicer's new book, the Yaqui village study (Spicer 1940). "Spicer addressed himself to a particular problem . . . Miss Gower tries to present a complete picture of village life, and her material becomes quite diffuse . . . Spicer was much more skillful than Miss Gower in his use of personal material." Whyte then went on to praise Horace Miner's statistical detail on family and social structure and criticize Gower's lack of such data. But then he made a concession.

> My very high opinion of Spicer's work may be influenced by some considerations apart from its scientific value. His thesis bears directly upon the problem of culture change in the district that I have studied . . . For all my criticisms of Miss Gower's work, I feel that the material which she does present on the social structure is important. Anthropologists ought to know about a society in which class lines are so definitely drawn that there is a different form of address for each class and yet in which it is possible for people to move up or down. Milocca fits into a category somewhere between societies like our own and the caste system. I don't know any other examples in this category among contemporary peasant or urban societies. (UCRLR: WW/RR 11/9/41)

"Your criticisms seem to me well taken," Redfield wrote (responding to an earlier, possibly verbal, critique by Whyte), "and make clearer to me the shortcomings of the manuscript. I suppose we must remember that the work was done a good many years ago, at a time when the questions asked in connection with community study were less penetrating than they are today" (UCRLR: RR/WW 10/29/41). A. M. Halpern's view of Gower's manuscript was also harsh. "As a general judgment, I find it a superficial piece of work . . . The approach appears closer to the old-line ethnographic approach than to any other. . . ." He criticized the lack of "a map and a census" but then concluded, "As to whether the department should recommend its publication, I should say that we should. Judged as an ethnography, it is up to standard in the reliability of the data reported and in inclusiveness. And it is potentially useful as background material for studies of either social change in Italy or Italian immigrants in the U.S." (UCRLR: AH/RR 12/5/41).

Ironically, back in 1928, Gower's Sicily research was funded precisely because it was part of the new "Science of Background Studies." But by 1941 that was far from a cutting-edge field in social anthropology. The intensity of criticism Gower's manuscript received shows she had missed her chance by many years to be applauded for her pioneering community study of a peasant society, or for her ethnographic approach. The fateful date of Halpern's letter, two days before the bombing of Pearl Harbor, suggests another reason why there is no more correspondence in the Chicago archives regarding the publication of Gower's book for nearly another 30 years. The university's publication program was cut back dramatically during wartime (*Yearbook of Anthropology* 1955:742).

Why was Charlotte Gower's book originally rejected by two university presses in 1936 and 1937? That was still the depths of the depression, but other scholars—mostly men, it is true—were managing to get their books published. Gower's book is beautifully written, documented innovative research, and could well have found a reasonably large audience for a scholarly book, as Cole believed, after the model of the Lynds' widely read community study of Middletown (1929; Wissler 1929; Holthoon 1995). Perhaps American concern with immigrants and their assimilation, and thus interest in their cultural roots in the Old Country, had abated since the 1920s, a delayed consequence of the passage of the immigration-restricting McCarran Act in 1924, and the ongoing economic crisis of the depression. Gower might have been better advised to publish with a trade press, as did Benedict, Mead, and Linton. But she might well have thought that since the University of Chicago Press had published the books of so many of her former graduate student classmates that, with Cole's and Redfield's support, the press would be interested in her work.

And how independent was the Committee on Publications at the University of Wisconsin Press from departmental and college politics, with their ongoing moves toward what is nowadays at the University of Wisconsin called "strategic planning," meaning cutting faculty positions? Gower's position in her department was already shaky by the fall of 1937, while her book manuscript was under review. In addition, she may well have been known to the third Mrs. Linton and her powerful former father-in-law, Professor Hohlfeld, as Linton's longtime mistress. Gower quite likely was a prime target for dismissal from the University of Wisconsin.[12]

By June of 1936 she was already considering her options. She applied for, but failed to win, a position at Hunter College in New York (UCRLA 1936: CG/FC 3/21/37). In her twice-yearly instructional report filed at the University of Wisconsin in March of 1937, in the space where faculty are supposed to list the subjects of their research, Gower described a new project, a community study of New Glarus, a Swiss American town about 20 miles from the university. She spent a month there in the summer of 1936, put in six weeks in Madison doing documentary research, and reported "some progress on analysis of newspaper material." (This research, with its classic Chicago School approaches to an immigrant community and their "personal documents," was never completed or published.) Gower also noted "preparation of material for source book in Anthropology—just begun." By contrast, Linton's instructional report lists, more forcefully, under Publications rather than Research, "Source book in Anthropology in Preparation" (UWASIR 1937). No such source book was ever published.

Linton collaborated in his "popular" book and article writing with his third wife, the former journalist. Adelin Linton and Charles Wagley (1971:24–25) have noted, "Sometimes such pieces were ghost written under Linton's name and sometimes both names appeared" and that Mrs. Linton posthumously completed one-third of Ralph Linton's monumental The Tree of Life (1955), based on her husband's lecture course. Adelin Linton says she "never participated" in "his serious scientific work." Did Gower collaborate with her friend and colleague on some of his articles, or even his 1936 book? And did she receive an acknowledgment in the book and no mention in the articles, rather than a co-authorship that might have improved her publication record and job security?

In her October 1936 report, Gower wrote, under Publications, "'A Sicilian Rural Community' in publishers [sic] hands, but date of publication as yet

12. To make matters worse, in 1937 conservative members of the Wisconsin state legislature, imitating the New York legislature's Rapp-Coudert Committee, launched an investigation of communism and immorality at the University of Wisconsin. The Red Scares of the late 1930s, especially targeting state schools, were direct precursors of postwar, McCarthy-era government investigations (Schrecker 1986). Worried about being investigated, what with his recent divorce and remarriage, Ralph Linton told Ward Goodenough in the early 1950s, he had paid one of his shady connections to entice one of the most aggressive upstate legislators into a downtown Madison hotel room with a young woman. A detective burst in on them, and that was the end of the investigation. It was the best $800 he ever spent, said Linton (Goodenough, pers. comm. 1997).

unknown." A year later she typed, "Research on New Glarus–no progress. (No assistance)... Sivilian [sic] Manuscript in hands of Univ. of Wis. Press" (UWASIR 1936–37).[13] With the departure of Linton and retirement of Ross, Gower seems to have had increasingly tense relations with the new depart-ment chairman, John L. Gillin, author of the ominously titled *Taming the Criminal* (1931). The university archives hold thick files of clippings of Gillin's newspaper interviews—he was a member of the State Board of Pardons—and his massive collection of "slides, photos, and movies" of prisons from Germany and the Philippines to Alcatraz. (For some reason his black eye-shade was filed with them.) Gillin's 1937 instructional reports (casually listing "[a] few commencement addresses last June") portended a gathering storm around the woman assistant professor who complained in her own report to the dean that same week of "No Assistance" for her research. Gillin summa-rized the hiring of Howard Becker on a three-year contract in sociology, and on the anthropology side, Alexander Goldenweiser (last of Reed College) for a one-year replacement for Linton, and Morris Swadesh to teach anthro-pology and linguistics for a year. He went on, "I am appointing a committee to give a thorough study to the courses offered in the department looking toward the closer coordination of the courses offered in sociology and an-thropology, eliminate any overlapping which may be found, to consider the possible elimination of certain courses and the introduction of new courses if, after a careful study, such changes are found to be desirable" (UWASIR 1936–37). My passes through multiple boxes of departmental files from the 1930s in the archives turned up no committee reports, meeting minutes, or correspondence spelling out just what happened next. But three months after Gillin formed his committee, Charlotte Gower was told her contract would not be renewed.

This was not a tenure review in the modern sense but an opportunity to renew a contract, promote, or fire a faculty member. The tenure system had been newly devised—at Harvard in the mid-1930s—as a supposedly im-personal, bureaucratic, and fair way to review faculty after seven years, and terminate the weakest in order to conserve institutional money during the depression. It became a standard system nationwide by 1941. A high propor-tion of its early victims were long-serving women faculty, often those teaching introductory or service courses (Rossiter 1982:194).

Gower wrote Cole,

13. Gower received no university research funding in 1937 (unlike her colleagues), and her summer funding for 1936 was markedly lower than that awarded to male faculty. "Each project presented is judged on its merits," John L. Gillin explained to Melville Herskovits, trying to lure him to Wisconsin. Gower in 1936 was awarded $368, (sociologist) McCormick $600, (social psychologist) Young $1,000, Gillin himself $2,000, and Linton $2,300 (UWAP: JG/MH 3/5/38).

I am very sorry to have to write you this letter, for it will probably distress you. To be brief, and only mildly euphemistic—I shall not be re-appointed here at Wisconsin when my present contract expires in June 1939. The department is, I gather, disappointed that I have not published more during the time I have been here. My research (unfortunately) has gone too exclusively into my courses. —There is also the possibility that they would like to have my courses attract more students. I am not sure that Prehistory and Physical Anthropology *should* be popular courses. However, this letter is not meant as a presentation of my defense. Their aims are not mine, apparently, and I shall need a new job. Is there any hope at all, under the circumstances? I am very discouraged at the moment. Women are hard to place. A person who has lost a position is hardly in an advantageous position to get another . . . I am dreadfully sorry to be such a problem to my friends . . . The case has received no publicity, at all. (UCRLA: CG/FC 1/13/38)

"Perhaps the situation is not as discouraging as it appears at first," Cole replied.

Even though your book is delayed, you must have considerable material which will lend itself to articles suitable for the [*American*] *Anthropologist* and similar journals. Why not make a business of preparing at least two papers which will indicate what you have done? You might also think in terms of making Prehistory more popular to the undergraduate. It can be done, and if that is what Wisconsin desires, why not attempt it? I heard fine reports of your work here [teaching at Chicago], but perhaps you had a more advanced group to deal with. (UCRLA: FC/CG 1/26/38)

He went on, after hoping that "they may change their minds," to suggest, "What about Vassar or Smith?" and offered to try to "pull some wires" with "the probable successor to Linton [at Columbia]," and "to be on the watch for another opening" (UCRLA: FC/CG 1/26/38).

The Wisconsin senior faculty obviously had no intention of changing their minds. But Gower had no intention of continuing to teach at Wisconsin either, where she faced dismissal rather than a hoped-for promotion. Unmarried and nearing 36, Gower had supported herself through academic employment since the age of 20, with a hiatus of five and a half years for graduate study and her postdoctoral research fellowship in Sicily. It is unlikely, on a yearly salary of $2,580, that she had much money in savings. The option of returning to Judge Gower's house in Kankakee must have been an unbearable one to her. With one more year to go on her final contract, she was already applying, by March of 1938, for a position at Lingnan University in Canton, on the south coast of China. This was for a teaching position in sociology, according to the dust jacket of *Milocca*. The only anthropology job in the United States was another vacancy at Hunter College, but it was just a one-year position. In order to avoid remaining on sufferance with the professional colleagues who had dismissed her, or retreating in humiliation to her childhood home, Charlotte Gower took a huge risk.

"The Chinese opening rather terrifies me," she wrote Cole. "They are entirely frank about bombs, the uncertainty of the situation, and so on. But after all, why not? . . . I am neither more nor less bomb-proof than anyone else. I suspect it would all be a very valuable experience. The one catch is the marked missionary character of the Institution. Having made affiliation, I am committed to the support of the Christian Church in China . . . Will you be taking girls into the field this summer? I have two students who are interested" (UCRLA: CG/FC 3/15/38). I suspect that fewer "girls" from the University of Wisconsin got field experience in archeology after Gower left.[14]

The Lingnan job had been listed at the University of Chicago Placement Bureau. Professor Ogburn of sociology suggested Charlotte Gower for the vacancy, even though she hesitated to ask him for a letter of recommendation because, as she confessed in a letter to Redfield, "I hardly know him . . . and can see no reason why he should know anything more about me than my name and difficulties . . ."

I should have written you long ago to confirm the unpleasant news I sent by Mr. [Harry] Harlow [University of Wisconsin psychologist]. Please excuse my negligence. Writing was depressing, given the subject matter, and provided too tempting opportunities for self-justification and self-pity. So I avoided it . . . I am very much interested in the Lingnan position, bombs and typhus notwithstanding. The consideration that I have had occasion to give to problems of acculturation has aroused my curiosity about detached communities living under foreign social environments — and the Lingnan community sounds like a convenient unit for observation. The uncertainty under which it now exists is abnormal, of course — but the effects of "terror" should in themselves be interesting. I should expect, off-hand, to find the group more closely knit than usual. In any case, I hope I get the position, whatever its disadvantages. And my interest in it is not entirely the result of my knowledge that openings for me will be few and far between. You know, perhaps, that Wendell Bennett is taking Ralph's position here. As yet, I have heard no discussion of who will replace me in 1939 if not this year. (UCRLR: CG/RR 4/6/38)

Her letter, besides demonstrating her courage, shows that one of Gower's responses to her personal crisis and limited professional options was a growing intellectual curiosity about what anthropologists 60 years later variously label the anthropology of warfare, disaster, and terror.

Robert Redfield wrote Gower the next day that he was sending a letter

14. Gower earlier asked both Redfield and Cole to help find financial support at Chicago for "my prize female student . . . If women students are worth bothering about, she probably is" (UCRLR: CG/RR 8/19/35). Gower's efforts were unsuccessful: the student never attended graduate school.

to Lingnan, commenting about Wendell Bennett, "I think they have a good man." Bennett was a Chicago Ph.D. as well, with a 1930 archeological dissertation on the Hawaiian *heiau* (temple). Gower is "intelligent, and a thoroughly experienced teacher of Anthropology," Redfield testified, "competent both in physical and cultural Anthropology. Her unpublished work on the Sicilian Peasant which I have read assures one as to her scholarship. It seems to me that Dr. Gower's interest in peasant peoples represented by this Sicilian research constitutes a special qualification for work in a Chinese community. Her colleagues at the University of Wisconsin report to me that she has been a successful and well-liked teacher" (UCRLR: RR/Trustees of Lingnan University 4/7/38).

The American director of Lingnan University, Olin Wannamaker, asked Cole for a letter as well. "Under normal circumstances, an American who teaches in China must be friendly, adaptable, patient as well as dynamic. Under the present abnormal circumstances all these qualities must be heightened. Our institution is entirely non-sectarian and extremely liberal, but we do value an earnest Christian attitude of mind. If you can comment on this aspect of Dr. Gower's qualifications, we shall appreciate this." Cole's letter of recommendation masterfully dodges the earnest Christian attitude of mind issue. "Miss Gower" is, he believed, Episcopalian. "She entered so fully into Sicilian life and customs that she was able to give us an excellent interpretation of religious beliefs" (UCRLA: FC/OW 4/12/38).[15]

This testimony to her participant observation skills and cultural relativism may not have been exactly what Wannamaker wanted to hear. But there were undoubtedly few applicants for a teaching position in a foreign country already invaded by the Japanese, who had conquered Manchuria in 1937 and were advancing south along the China coast. By the time the University of Wisconsin regents accepted Gower's letter of resignation in June of 1938, she was already sailing for China.[16]

---

15. Cole also called Gower "a superior student . . . one of the two most able women we have had in this department." Since there were so few women in the anthropology graduate program at Chicago in either the 1920s or 1930s, this seems a bit equivocal. Perhaps it reveals that even sympathetic senior male faculty like Cole perceived women as a separate and unequal category of anthropologist, not to be ranked alongside the men. On the other hand, he was writing to a Baptist missionary about Gower's suitability for life in China. Cole stresses her adaptability as exemplified by "her dealings with the Sicilians both here and abroad" and how, during Gower's two summers of archeological fieldwork, "under the somewhat trying conditions of field excavations, she was always cheerful and one on whom we could always depend" (UCRLA 1938).

16. Wisconsin initially hired three part-time, short-term lecturers to replace Gower (UWAS 1938). The department, reported John L. Gillin to George Sellery, dean of Letters and Science, suggested Melville Herskovits as a replacement for Linton. "Careful attention should be given to the man chosen in order to maintain at this time the prestige of the department which Linton has given it." Gillin's offer to Herskovits ("The department is looking for a man to take the place

One letter survives from this period. Living in Hong Kong, Gower asked for Redfield's help obtaining a fellowship for a Chinese senior colleague to study at Chicago.

There have been rumors here that R-B is coming out to China with some purpose of finding out what has been done with some books which England has been supplying to the refugee universities. . . . Possibly with the war on, the plan is changed. In any case I have heard nothing of or from him for well over a year. But I basked in his reflected glory a bit this summer when I went up to Yunnan and saw some of the Yenching people. I have been retired from pharmacy and returned to the teaching staff. Someone had to teach Social Psychology, so I have taken that over. And next semester I am to attempt to guide them through the mazes of Social Statistics . . . But I laugh a bit hollowly when I remember that when I came out I was rejoicing in the opportunity to really settle down and specialize in social anthropology. (UCRLR: CG/RR 11/10/39)

Backstage in a War

Sol Tax's memoir of anthropology at Wisconsin (UWA: Tax 1989) glossed over the upheavals and reversals in Gower's life and told a romantic tale. "She did indeed finish the manuscript, and sent it off to the Oxford University Press in England, and herself set off on a trip to China to do research. While on board ship, however, she and the ship's captain were married, and I do not

---

of Professor Ralph Linton in anthropology"; UWAP: JG/MH 3/5/38) was unsuccessful. The two finalists of the remaining "men on the list" of candidates (Gillin's words; the list itself is missing from the Wisconsin archives) were Eggan and Bennett. Eggan had "rather limited experience in fieldwork. I have one report on him," Gillin confides, "that he is rather sissified and dandified." (One begins to suspect how the flamboyant and female Charlotte Gower rated with a man of Gillin's sensibilities.) Sapir, Gillin says, approved Bennett as "the best man in sight at this time." Sociologist Louis Wirth agreed that "if we want an archaeologist he is the man," and Clark Wissler, his supervisor at the American Museum of Natural History, concurred. Bennett "has the finest personality of any of the men I met," Gillin concludes (UWAP: JG/GS 2/2/38). "We are looking for a man in anthropology who will ultimately take the place of Professor Ralph Linton," Gillin (UWAP: JG/WB 3/23/38) wrote Bennett in Peru, who accepted the "one year or two year" appointment as associate professor, which later became permanent. In the fall Gillin offered William W. Howells, then at Harvard's Peabody Museum, "the position left vacant by the resignation of Dr. Charlotte Gower . . . We want a man who is primarily an ethnologist but prepared to give this amount of physical anthropology [as background for archeology students]" (UWAP: JG/WH 10/7/38). Howells (a gifted physical anthropologist but obviously, like Gower, an adaptable younger scholar when presented with an employment opportunity) joined the Wisconsin faculty in 1939. Gillin's (and, reportedly, Wirth's and Wissler's) unselfconscious use of the formula, "looking for a man," like Sapir's identical usage in 1928, is characteristic of the period, and emblematic of the prejudices and expectations that Charlotte Gower and other women scholars have faced for most of this century as obstacles to winning and keeping academic positions.

know what, if anything, she did in China, which was soon to be torn by warfare." Howells' (UWA 1989) reminiscence noted Linton's departure in 1937, then added, "As for Charlotte, she went to Ling-Nan University in China, was captured by the Japanese in Hong Kong in 1941, was exchanged and came back to become one of the first officers in the women Marines and, I think, eventually married a sea captain and settled in Kankakee. A very American story."

Gower did meet Captain Savilion H. Chapman, and they married in 1947, but she did not settle in Kankakee. Her story, which was in fact "very American," took another startling turn in the postwar years. A small handful of yellowed newspaper clippings in her Wisconsin "faculty file" gives a remarkable account of Gower's experiences, some of it in her own words. The first carries the headline "Charlotte Gower 'Safe' in China." Gower, "former member of the University of Wisconsin anthropology staff," "was thought to be safe in Japanese occupied Hong Kong on the basis of information received today by Madison friends." The American sponsors of Lingnan "wrote that all Americans on the staff were reported to be safe and 'not subject to harsh treatment' on Jan. 30. The Chinese president of the college and some Chinese members of the staff escaped to Free China before the Japanese took over the British colony Dec. 25 [1941]" (*Wisconsin State Journal* 2/16/42).

Correspondence in the University of Chicago archives picks up the story next. Olin Wannamaker wrote to Clarence Dykstra, president of the University of Wisconsin, sending a carbon copy of his letter to Judge Gower in Kankakee, who forwarded it to Cole. "Dr. Gower has been among the Americans interned by the Japanese after the fall of Hong Kong. She is expected to arrive here [New York] on the S. S. Gripsholm about August 20. I write you for the reason that the head of your Department of Anthropology will be well acquainted with Dr. Gower and may be interested in securing her return to her former position." Judge Gower sent his own letter to Cole, asking for help in finding a job for his daughter. Cole responded, "I communicated with Dr. John A. Wilson, Chief of the Division of Special Information in Washington.... I hope that Charlotte will be getting home soon and if she is interested in a place in Washington, I think she had best write Mr. Fahs" (UCRLA: OW/CD 7/24/42, EG/FC 7/28/42, FC/EG 8/24/42).

This exchange implies that Charlotte Gower, who was returning from four years in what was now enemy-occupied territory and who spoke Cantonese, was, through Cole's Washington connections, recruited for wartime government intelligence work. Cole, an old Asia hand, was himself training Army and Navy officers in the Civil Affairs Training School for the Far East (Eggan 1963:643).

In January of 1943, Charlotte Gower returned to Madison to speak to "nearly 500 women at the monthly meeting of the Madison Civics club" on the topic of "Backstage in a War." Lingnan University, then in Canton, was "'shot from under' her almost as soon as she arrived, when the Japanese conquered the city," reporter Eva Jollos wrote. "For nearly a year she became a pharmacist in the refugee hospital which was set up on the campus, and was forced to observe the cruelties inflicted on the Chinese by their conquerors, she said." In 1939 Gower left for Hong Kong, where Lingnan University had regrouped, to resume teaching. "British women and children were ordered evacuated in 1940, but the American officials remained optimistic until Dec. 6, 1941, she said . . . 'We had bombs for breakfast the next morning, but there was no panic' " (*Capital Times* 1/10/43).

Gower described resuming her work as a pharmacist (her training in physical anthropology and her experience teaching all those advanced lab courses at Wisconsin no doubt coming in handy). She also organized a hospital on the Lingnan campus. " 'At that point the war still seemed faintly like cops and robbers or Gilbert and Sullivan,' " but Japanese bombing intensified, and "Miss Gower was forced to brave a hail of shrapnel to get from the consul's house where she had found shelter to the hospital where she worked." Gower, on evacuating this section of Hong Kong, then worked as a nurse in a different hospital. As reported in the *Capital Times*,

> Christmas eve the hospital staff had a party, and on Christmas day the island surrendered, Miss Gower continued. "Ours was a terribly hopeless situation when the news came," she said. "We sat all night waiting for the Japs to come, not knowing what to do, or what would happen" . . . on Jan. 5 all "enemy aliens" in Hongkong were rounded up, and after several weeks of crowding into various Chinese brothels, they were interned in the prison community on the other side of the island. "We had a fairly decent camp, but it was terriby crowded," she pointed out. "The crowding was next worst to the constant, gnawing hunger. From January to March we were almost always hungry. At first our diet was fixed at 1,000 calories per day, and if most of us had not brought extra supplies, we would have died." (*Capital Times* 1/10/43)

Gower tutored other prisoners in "Chinese" (Cantonese) until she was released in a prisoner exchange (*Milwaukee Journal* 3/19/43). " 'I was rather afraid when the Japanese inspected the luggage that they would discover the diary which I was smuggling out,' Miss Gower revealed. She had cunningly concealed the written sheets, and they were not discovered" (*Capital Times* 1/10/43).

The next dramatic development is an announcement by the Navy. "Captain Charlotte Day Gower, former dean of women at Lingnan university, Hongkong, China, had been named director of training for the women's reserve of the marine corps." Newspaper photographs of Captain Gower show her — 41 and less than six months out of a prison camp — as thin and pale, with short, dark hair combed carelessly back, rimless glasses, and a slight smile. She and three other woman officers had "begun a recruiting drive to enlist 18,000 women and 1,000 officers. Enlisted reservists will start training Mar. 6 at [ironically] Hunter College" (*Wisconsin State Journal* 2/18/43; *Milwaukee Journal* 3/19/43; *Milwaukee Sentinel* 3/19/43).

There are few anthropological sightings of Charlotte Gower until the publication of *Milocca* in 1971 found her "living in retirement with her husband in Washington, D.C." (Eggan 1971:xii). She wrote from Kankakee in 1947 to Cole and Redfield to arrange the sale of most of her anthropology books to the Chicago department, acknowledged congratulations on her recent marriage, and moved with her husband to Washington (UCRLR: CGC/FC 3/13/47, CGC/RR 3/27/47). Sol Tax, after writing of Gower's sailing to China, continued,

> The next thing I recall was a telephone call from a downtown hotel where she had arrived with her husband. This was at least ten years after the war, and I was heavily engaged in teaching and in innumerable projects, but of course I was happy to see her and to try to help her when she explained that her manuscript had been irrevocably lost years before in England. On investigation, it turned out that my colleague Fred Eggan had seen a carbon copy of it somewhere, and we were able to locate it and get it published, finally, in 1971. (UWA: Tax 1989)

Tax's last sentence somehow seems inadequate to describe the additional gap of 15 or so years before Gower's book, completed in 1935, was finally published.

Gower herself, in the 1977 Stocking questionnaire, filled in most of the holes in her story in a few tantalizing lines. Under Job History, for the years 1943–45, she wrote, "Training Officer for US Marine Corps, Women's Reserve. (I welcomed the opportunity for military service. During 1944–45, I was assigned to duty with OSS, working mainly with the Far East.)" Gower also reported returning as "Assoc Professor, Lingnan University Canton, China" in the summer of 1946. A discreet gap in her job history followed, before she typed, "1948–65 Analyst, CIA."

The woman anthropologist who was forced out of academic life by senior colleagues at Wisconsin, and by wartime occupation at Canton and Hong Kong, turned out to have skills and knowledge that were highly valued in another kind of anthropological career: military intelligence officer and Central Intelligence Agency analyst. Charlotte Gower had long-term field experience, contacts, analytical experience, and vernacular language capabilities in two countries, China and Italy, that were under imminent risk of "Communist takeover." It seems likely that during her 1946 return to China—a year after officially leaving the Office of Strategic Services, and only three years before Mao's entry into Beijing—Gower was acting not only as associate professor of sociology and dean of women, but as an American field intelligence operative. In joining the newly organized CIA, she anticipated the Cold War career choice of many another American anthropologist who was unable to secure a permanent faculty position, or who was in search of research funding opportunities in "the field" (Wolf & Jorgensen 1970; Nader 1997). Again, Charlotte Gower was "backstage in a war."

Charlotte Gower Chapman died of a heart attack in 1982 in Washington, D.C. Her obituary in the *Washington Post* states that she joined the CIA in 1947, when it was founded, and retired in 1964. Her husband, Savilion H. Chapman, survived her, dying in 1992 at the age of 88. His obituary in the *Post* reveals that he, too, was "a retired official of the Central Intelligence Agency," as well as "a former captain in the merchant marine" for the Isthmian Line. Born in Hartford, a graduate of the U.S. Merchant Marine Academy, he "served at sea through World War II. In 1946, he moved to Washington and joined a forerunner of the CIA, which came into existence in 1947. He was an operations officer in the field of maritime affairs. He retired in 1966." Savilion Chapman's obituary notes that his son, Robert R. Chapman, died in 1981, the year before his wife. S. H. Chapman was survived by two grandchildren and two great-grandchildren. I do not yet know whether Robert Chapman was Gower's son by birth or adoption or a stepson through her marriage at the age of 45.

Shadows of Our Forgotten Ancestors

Charlotte Gower's experiences—while she had some spectacularly bad luck —are examples of the obstacles that early-twentieth-century women faced as scholars and as women living unconventional personal lives. Her career as an academic woman gives a fresh slant on the early years of anthropology and the newly professionalized social sciences. It displays some of the inner workings of two great research universities, one public and one private, both famous in the development of the social sciences in the United States (Curti & Carstensen 1949; Faris 1967; Stocking 1979; Bulmer 1984; Cronon & Jenkins 1994). Gower's experiences illuminate the "statuses and roles" of these influential universities, their customs and their institutional workings, from an unusual perspective: that of the junior, the marginal, and the academically unsuccessful. This is a perspective not generally found in standard histories of higher education or histories of science.

Gower's "very American story" brings into focus the history of early- and mid-twentieth-century American anthropology. Her intellectual biography exemplifies the discipline's roots in four-field, Boasian approaches; anthropology's early institutionalization; and its rapprochements with other newly formed social science disciplines, particularly sociology. Her training, research, and teaching, and that of her colleagues at Chicago and Wisconsin, reveal the influence of Chicago School sociology on anthropology, and document rapidly shifting approaches to studies of social change, "acculturation," and community. Her failure to get her research published and to keep the faculty position she had won against the odds sheds light on the ways that anthropology and the social sciences were bureaucratizing in American universities during the pivotal years from 1935 to 1941, a period which largely dictated the shape of the rapid expansion of the social sciences, fueled by federal dollars, during the post-Sputnik, Cold War era.

Charlotte Gower was pushed out of academic anthropology, like most other women scholars of the 1930s, in a systematic and continuing sex discrimination which left the number of women faculty in anthropology and other disciplines lower in the 1960s than it had been in the 1920s (cf. Rossiter 1982, 1995). Gower responded by seeking employment in China in hopes of studying the "acculturation" of a community in terror and under threat of war, and herself became an early victim of World War II. Like Benedict and Mead, her more famous women colleagues, she volunteered her anthropological skills to the wartime American government. Gower too studied "Culture at a Distance," probably with the heavy reliance on personal documents, life histories of immigrants, and local newspapers advocated by Chicago School empirical sociology (see Benedict 1946).

But Gower apparently continued her studies, both at a distance and in the field, after the war, returning to China and then joining the newly formed Central Intelligence Agency. She had become one of the earliest field researchers on the anthropology of warfare and terror as forms of social change, as well as an early practitioner of what came to be called applied anthropology. She wrote her analyses not for her anthropological peers but for her OSS and CIA superiors. American global "security" interests during the Cold War afforded Gower a venue for her anthropological skills and a professional living—though one invisible to her former colleagues—and helped to generate a professional audience for her book on Sicilian villagers 35 years after it was written.

The near total erasure in the United States of Charlotte Gower's memory and work parallels the omission of many earlier women anthropologists from histories of the discipline, its subfields, and their intellectual debates. This erasure continues, in complicated ways, in late-twentieth-century anthropology, as documented by research on women's roles in the history of anthropology (Lurie 1966; Babcock & Parezo 1988; Gacs 1989; Lutz 1990; Parezo 1993; Behar & Gordon 1995). The more recent of these collections and essays have found a wide and appreciative readership among female anthropology faculty and students, but they have had little impact on mainstream anthropological teaching of the history of anthropology, or on assessments of the intellectual traditions of anthropological theory. As a result, we are currently creating a sexually stratified history of anthropology, particularly at the graduate level. The majority of male students learn a 1990s/millennial take on the anthropological canon that largely remains a narrative of patrilineal intellectual descent. Many women students, in the United States and elsewhere, but relatively few men, take anthropology of gender courses, or learn histories of anthropology that incorporate the lives and works of more than the handful of women who became professors at major universities. (Of course, another question much discussed in anthropology departments these days is how much present-day graduate students are actually learning—or are interested in learning—about the history of anthropology before the last decade.) But we need to integrate far more on the history of women in the discipline—their ideas and intellectual biographies—into standard and required courses, texts on anthropological theory or method, and books on the history of anthropology.

We also need to consider more carefully the experiences and intellectual legacies of other categories of less conventional—or less conventionally successful—kinds of anthropologists, female and male. These include contract ethnologists, early non-European American scholars and anthropological collaborators, museum anthropologists, government employees, and so on. Incorporating accounts of these scholars, their careers, and their ideas into our disciplinary histories would give a more complex picture, to ourselves and to our students, about what anthropology was, and what we are becoming.

Acknowledgments

Portions of an earlier draft of this chapter were presented at the session "Fashioning the Past: Feminist Predecessors, Genealogies and Generations," at the American Anthropological Association Annual Meetings, San Francisco, California, November 20–24, 1996. I thank Deborah Gordon, Barbara Babcock, and other session participants for their comments. My thanks also go to George Stocking and Richard Handler for their comments on drafts of this chapter, and to Richard Handler for his skilled editing. Many thanks to Ray Fogelson, George Stocking, and Robert Moore for telling me oral histories of Charlotte Gower at Chicago, and special thanks to George Stocking and Robert Moore for helping me track Gower in the University of Chicago Archives. James Richardson did a fine job of assisting me at Regenstein Library. I thank W. W. Howells for his memories of Charlotte Gower, which got me launched on this research, and Herb Lewis and John Hitchcock for information on Gower's life in Madison. T. Douglas Price in 1989 elicited invaluable written and oral testimony about the history of anthropology at Wisconsin. Ward Goodenough, visiting assistant professor at the University of Wisconsin in 1948–49, and Ruth Goodenough contributed accounts of Gower and Linton. William Peace offered comments on an earlier draft, archival information, and leads on Gower, Leslie White, and the intellectual milieu of the University of Chicago in the 1920s and 1930s. Mac Marshall helped me trace the academic lineages of some of Gower's former students. Robert Brightman suggested sources of information about Gower and commented on an earlier draft. J. Frank Cook, University of Wisconsin archivist, helped in locating documents. Alice Oleson has provided me tremendous help by collecting books, articles, and documents in the University of Wisconsin libraries, and by commenting on this essay. I thank her, and all the University of Wisconsin students in my Anthropology by Women classes from 1988 to 1998, for their enthusiasm, discussions, and moral support of this research. Kirin Narayan and Dale Bauer have long encouraged me in this research on our predecessor at the University of Wisconsin, and discussed my discoveries with me. Much of the archival and bibliographical research for this paper was carried out while I was a Vilas Associate Professor at the University of Wisconsin–Madison. I gratefully acknowledge the support of the William F. Vilas Trust.

References Cited

Arensberg, C. 1937. *The Irish countryman: An anthropological study.* New York.

Babcock, B., & N. Parezo. 1988. *Daughters of the desert: Women anthropologists and the Native American Southwest, 1880–1980.* Albuquerque, N. Mex.

Banfield, E. C. 1958. *The moral basis of a backward society.* Glencoe, Ill.

Behar, R., & D. Gordon, eds. 1995. *Women writing culture.* Berkeley, Calif.

Benedict, R. 1946. *The chrysanthemum and the sword.* New York.

Boissevain, J. 1965. *Saints and fireworks: Religion and politics in rural Malta.* London.

Bulmer, M. 1984. *The Chicago School of sociology: Institutionalization, diversity, and the rise of sociological research.* Chicago.

Buzaljko, G. 1993. Isabel Kelly: From museum anthropologist to archaeologist. *Museum Anthropology* 17(2):41–48.

Cattell, J. M., ed. 1933. *American men of science: A biographical dictionary,* 5th ed. New York.

Cattell, J. M., & J. Cattell, eds. 1938. *American men of science: A biographical dictionary,* 6th ed. New York.

Cavan, R. S. 1929. *Business girls: A study of their interests and problems.* Chicago.

Chapman, C. G. 1971. *Milocca: A Sicilian village.* New York. Reprinted in a hardcover edition in London (1973).

Chapman, C. G. 1977a. Completed questionnaire returned to George W. Stocking, Jr. Chicago.

Chapman, C. G. 1977b. Letter to George Stocking, 8 October 1977. Original in the possession of George W. Stocking, Jr. Chicago.

Chapman, C. G. 1978. Letter to George Stocking, 27 February 1978. Original in the possession of George W. Stocking, Jr. Chicago.

Cole, F-C., R. B. Dixon, & A. V. Kidder. 1929. Anthropological scholarships. *American Anthropologist* 31:571–72.

Cronin, C. 1970. *The sting of change: Sicilians in Sicily and Australia.* Chicago.

Cronon, E. D., & J. Jenkins. 1994. *The University of Wisconsin: A history. Vol. 3: Politics, depression, and war, 1925–1945.* Madison, Wis.

Curti, M., & V. Carstensen. 1949. *The University of Wisconsin: A history, 1848–1925.* 2 vols. Madison, Wis.

Darnell, R. 1990. *Edward Sapir: Linguist, anthropologist, humanist.* Berkeley, Calif.

Davis, J. 1977. *People of the Mediterranean: An essay in comparative social anthropology.* London.

Deacon, D. 1997. *Elsie Clews Parsons: Inventing modern life.* Chicago.

Eggan, F. 1963. Fay-Cooper Cole, 1881–1961. *American Anthropologist* 65(3):641–48.

Eggan, F. 1971. Foreword. In Chapman 1971, xi–xii. New York.

Embree, J. 1939. *Suye Mura: A Japanese village.* Chicago.

Faris, R. 1967. *Chicago sociology, 1920–1932.* San Francisco.

Fox, G. 1928. Central Section, American Anthropological Association. *American Anthropologist* 30:524–32.

Freire-Marreco, B., & J. Myres, eds. 1912. *Notes and queries on anthropology,* 4th ed. London.

Friedmann, F. G. 1953. The world of "la misèria." *Partisan Review* 20(2):218–31. Reprinted in Potter et al., 324–36. 1967.

Gacs, U., ed. 1989. *Women anthropologists: Selected biographies.* Urbana, Ill.

Gillin, J. L. 1931. *Taming the criminal: Adventures in penology.* New York.

Gillin, J. P. 1954. Ralph Linton: 1893–1953. *American Anthropologist* 56(2), Part 1:274–81.

Godoy, R. 1978. The background and context of Redfield's Tepotzlan. *Journal of the Steward Anthropological Society* 10(1):47–79.

Gower, C. D. 1923. A contribution to the morphology of the apertura pyriformis. *Journal of Physical Anthropology* 6(1):27–36.

Gower, C. D. 1927. The northern and southern affiliations of Antillean culture. *American Anthropological Association Memoirs,* No. 35.

Gower, C. D. 1928. The supernatural patron in Sicilian life. Doct. diss., Univ. of Chicago.

Holthoon, F. L. van. 1995. Robert Lynd's disenchantment: A study of Robert Lynd's cultural criticism. In *Small town America: A multidisciplinary revisit,* 30–59. Amsterdam.

Linton, A., & C. Wagley. 1971. *Ralph Linton.* New York.

Linton, R. 1936. *The study of man: An introduction.* New York.

Linton, R. 1940. A neglected aspect of social organization. *American Journal of Sociology* 45(6):870–86.

Linton, R. 1942. Age and sex categories. *American Sociological Review* 7(5):589–603.

Linton, R. 1955. *The tree of life.* New York.

Lopreato, J. 1965. How would you like to be a peasant? *Human Organization* 24(4):298–307. Reprinted in Potter et al., 419–37. 1967.

Lurie, N. 1966. Women in early American anthropology. *Pioneers of American an-*

thropology. American Ethnological Society Monograph Series 45:31–81, ed. June Helm. Seattle.

Lutz, C. 1990. The erasure of women's writing in sociocultural anthropology. *American Ethnologist* 17(4):611–27.

Lynd, R., & H. Lynd. 1929. *Middletown: A study in contemporary American culture.* New York.

Marshall, M. 1999. Ripples from a Micronesian sea. In *American anthropology in Micronesia: An assessment*, ed. R. C. Kiste & M. Marshall, 387–431. Honolulu.

McMillan, R. 1986. The study of anthropology, 1931 to 1937, at Columbia University and the University of Chicago. Doct. diss., York Univ.

Mead, M. 1972. *Blackberry winter: My earlier years.* New York.

Meyerowitz, J. 1988. *Women adrift: Independent wage earners in Chicago, 1880–1930.* Chicago.

Miner, H. 1939. *St. Denis: A French-Canadian parish.* Chicago.

Modell, J. 1983. *Ruth Benedict: Patterns of a life.* Philadelphia.

Murray, S. 1986. Edward Sapir and the Chicago School of sociology. In *New perspectives in language, culture, and personality*, ed. W. Cowan, M. K. Foster, & E. F. K. Koerner, 241–92. Amsterdam.

Nader, L. 1997. The phantom factor: Impact of the Cold War on anthropology. In *The Cold War and the university*, ed. N. Chomsky et al., 107–46. New York.

Parezo, N. 1993. *Hidden scholars: Women anthropologists and the Native American Southwest.* Albuquerque, N. Mex.

Peristiany, J. G., ed. 1966. *Honour and shame: The values of Mediterranean society.* London.

Pitt-Rivers, J. 1954. *The people of the Sierra.* London.

Potter, J., M. Diaz, & G. Foster, eds. 1967. *Peasant society: A reader.* Boston.

Powdermaker, H. 1966. *Stranger and friend: The way of an anthropologist.* New York.

Redfield, R. 1928. Among the Middle Americans: A Chicago family's adventures as adopted citizens of a Mexican village. *The University of Chicago Magazine* 20(5):243–47.

Redfield, R. 1930. *Tepoztlan, a Mexican village: A study of folk life.* Chicago.

Redfield, R. 1956. *Peasant society and culture: An anthropological approach to civilization.* Chicago.

Rossiter, M. 1982. *Women scientists in America: Struggles and strategies to 1940.* Baltimore, Md.

Rossiter, M. 1995. *Women scientists in America: From World War to Affirmative Action, 1941–1972.* Baltimore, Md.

Scheville, M. 1993. Lila M. O'Neale and the Yurok-Karok basket weavers of northwestern California. *Museum Anthropology* 17(2):67–71.

Schrecker, E. 1986. *No ivory tower: McCarthyism and the universities.* New York.

Sewell, W. 1975. Development of research in the social sciences, 1949–1974. In *The University of Wisconsin: One hundred and twenty-five years*, ed. A. Bogue & R. Taylor, 218–27. Madison, Wis.

Social Science Research Council. 1928. Social Science Research Council. *American Anthropologist* 30:553–54.

Spicer, E. 1940. *Pascua: A Yaqui village in Arizona.* Chicago.

169

Stocking, G. W., Jr. 1979. *Anthropology at Chicago: Tradition, discipline, department.* Chicago.

Stocking, G. W., Jr. 1982. Gatekeeper to the field: E. W. P. Chinnery and the ethnography of the New Guinea mandate. *History of Anthropology Newsletter* 9(2):3–12.

Stocking, G. W., Jr. 1995. *After Tylor: British social anthropology, 1888–1951.* Madison, Wis.

Tax, S. 1988. Pride and puzzlement: a retro-introspective record of 60 years in anthropology. *Annual Review of Anthropology* 17:1–21.

Thomas, W. I., & F. Znaniecki. 1918–1920. *The Polish peasant in Europe and America.* 5 vols. Chicago and Boston.

Wallerstein, I. 1997. The unintended consequences of Cold War area studies. In *The Cold War and the university*, ed. N. Chomsky et al., 195–232. New York.

Washington Post. 1982. Obituary. Charlotte Chapman. Saturday, 25 September, B4.

Washington Post. 1992. Obituary. Savilion H. Chapman, CIA official. Monday, 9 March, D6.

Wissler, C. 1929. Foreword. In Lynd & Lynd, v–vii. 1929.

Wolf, E., & J. Jorgensen. 1970. Anthropology on the warpath in Thailand. *New York Review of Books.* 19 November:25–35.

Yearbook of Anthropology. 1955. Dissertations in anthropology submitted to educational institutions of the world in partial fulfillment of requirements for the Ph.D. degree or equivalent, 701–52. New York.

Manuscript Sources

UCRLA   Department of Anthropology Papers Series I, the Department of Special Collections, University of Chicago Library.

UCRLE   Fred Eggan Papers, the Department of Special Collections, University of Chicago Library.

UCRLP   Presidents' Papers, the Department of Special Collections, University of Chicago Library.

UCRLR   Robert Redfield Papers, the Department of Special Collections, University of Chicago Library.

UCRLS   Department of Sociology Papers and Interviews, Fay-Cooper Cole Papers, the Department of Special Collections, University of Chicago Library.

UCRLT   Sol Tax Papers, the Department of Special Collections, University of Chicago Library.

UMB   Bentley Library, University of Michigan.

UWA   Department of Anthropology Archives, University of Wisconsin–Madison.

UWAA   University of Wisconsin Announcements, University of Wisconsin–Madison Archives, Memorial Library.

UWAB   University of Wisconsin Budgets, University of Wisconsin–Madison Archives, Memorial Library.

UWAC   University of Wisconsin Catalogues, University of Wisconsin–Madison
          Archives, Memorial Library.
UWAF   Faculty Files, University of Wisconsin–Madison Archives, Memorial
          Library.
UWAG   John L. Gillin Papers, University of Wisconsin–Madison Archives,
          Memorial Library.
UWAP   Presidents and Chancellors; Acting President George C. Sellery, Presi-
          dent Clarence A. Dykstra, University of Wisconsin–Madison Archives,
          Memorial Library.
UWAS   Department of Sociology and Anthropology General Files, University
          of Wisconsin–Madison Archives, Memorial Library.
UWASIR   Department of Sociology and Anthropology Instructional Reports,
          University of Wisconsin–Madison Archives, Memorial Library.
UWFEC   Faculty Employment cards, University of Wisconsin–Madison Ar-
          chives, Memorial Library.

"DO GOOD, YOUNG MAN"

Sol Tax and the World Mission
of Liberal Democratic Anthropology

GEORGE W. STOCKING, JR.

In the early spring of 1954, only weeks after President Eisenhower announced the explosion of the first United States hydrogen bomb and the prior announcement by John Foster Dulles of the policy of "massive retaliation" against the Soviet Union, Sol Tax sent a memo to his Chicago colleague Robert Redfield suggesting that the need might now be "sufficiently clear and urgent to all parties in the world struggle" to induce them to cooperate in providing "some insurance against complete loss of our cultural heritage, and possibly the species." Specifically, he proposed the establishment of a "world university" on a "distant island recognized as off-bounds to destruction," which could be "stocked with representatives of what might be lost with atomic devastation of the world (whether by war or accident)." While "selected plants and animals should be included," the emphasis would be on "fertile humans of all cultural, national, and racial heritages" chosen "from (and in some way by) all the peoples of the world," so that the islanders would "themselves be able to repopulate the earth." Although Tax did not specify the means of selection, he suggested criteria of education and age. Since the cultural purpose would be to create a repository "of human knowledge and cultural creations" that might be cared for and passed on, and since "under-

---

George W. Stocking, Jr., is Stein-Freiler Distinguished Service Professor Emeritus in the Department of Anthropology and the Committee on the Conceptual Foundations of Science at the University of Chicago. His works on the history of American anthropology include *Race, Culture, and Evolution: Essays in the History of Anthropology* (1968) and *The Ethnographer's Magic and Other Essays in the History of Anthropology* (1992). He was editor of *HOA* from the time of its founding in 1983 until 1996. In 1998, he received the Franz Boas Award for Exemplary Service to Anthropology from the American Anthropological Association.

standing and appreciation are necessary for a meaningful repository," those chosen "must in effect constitute a group of scholars" whose "age distribution would be like that of any university community"—though as in a university, the "particular individuals" might change "from year to year." The chances for implementing the plan would be improved if it were undertaken by the United Nations, to which it might best be presented by "delegations centering around India." This memo itself, along with "its author and all intermediaries," might better "be forgotten along the way" (56/5: 4/1/54; see below, 263 "Manuscript and Interview Sources").

Since the memo was dated April 1, we may assume it was a prank. But like any good prank, it was consistent with the character of the prankster—who from an early age had begun to invent himself as an activist in the solution of the world's problems, which he approached with a mix of liberal democratic enthusiasm, relativist humility, and universalist hubris. As manifest in the postwar decades, Tax's anthropological activism may be seen as both complementary and contrastive to dominant tendencies of American anthropology in the early Cold War period. Grounded in the Boasian anthropological tradition, Tax was responsive both to its shifting emphases and to its countertendencies. Although his own ethnographic work focused on Native Americans, in a period of expanding anthropological horizons he was in the vanguard of efforts to enlarge the still-enclosed world of American anthropology as both a discipline and a community. But in contrast to some other anthropologists (most of them also liberal democrats), Tax was not involved in research projects linked to the global expansion of United States economic, political, and military power. In contrast, his evolving vision of liberal democratic anthropology was directed to the creation of a multivocal world community, for which anthropology would provide both model and dynamic, and within which traditionally disempowered peoples might effectively sustain their cultural independence in a rapidly changing world. In examining his anthropological career, and the personal biographical dynamic that motivated it, we may thereby cast a reflective light on the anthropology of the Cold War period—a period perhaps richer and more complex than some present-day retrospects would suggest.[1]

---

1. This essay was conceived of as part of a larger project tentatively entitled "Anthropology Yesterday: Essays on American Anthropology in the Cold War Years, 1945–1973"—each essay biographically focused, and envisioned (in the metaphor of a colleague) as a series of overlays, cumulatively illuminating many aspects of anthropology in the Cold War period. As methodology, the overlay metaphor does not work so well in the isolated case of a single figure, in which necessary contexts must be immediately provided, and the biographical dynamic is more demanding. If each of the dozen or so anthropologists I had in mind were to be treated at this length, the book would be very long indeed, and not likely to be finished in my lifetime. In the shorter run, I hope to pair this essay, contrastively, with a similarly subtitled essay on Clyde Kluckhohn.

From Milwaukee to Guatemala:
Activism and Science in Tax's Earlier Years

Although he was born in 1907 to "mildly Zionist" Russian immigrant parents whose antecedents included "a line of rabbis," Tax later recalled having been "thoroughly secular-minded" from his "early high school days" (280/10: "Creation and Evolution"; cf. 5/1), more influenced, perhaps, by the political milieu of Milwaukee, where his socialist parents must have supported the candidate who in 1910 was elected as the first Socialist mayor in the United States. Small and shy as a child, Tax had "Walter Mitty dreams of greatness" associated "with somehow or other saving the troubled world" (1988:2); by one account, he and his younger brother Erwin used to "spend hours planning how they would bring reason to the world and institute reforms in the interest of peace and world brotherhood" (Blanchard 1979:420). By the time he was 12, however, Tax's more practical entrepreneurial, organizational, and reformist predilections were also manifest. "Cited" by a member of the "Newsboy's Republic" for selling newspapers without their permission, he became actively involved in the group, serving as editor of the Newsboy's World— which through the city's schools had a circulation of 5,000 (5/6; cf. Blanchard 1979:420; J. Bennett 1998:342).

Upon his graduation from high school in 1925, Tax went with his elder brother Archie to Florida, hoping to make money in the land boom to pay for college; after serving four months as assistant circulation manager of the Miami Daily News, he entered the University of Chicago in the spring of 1926 (5/6; 273/12). His "failure" that summer as house-to-house salesman left him unable to afford increased tuition fees, and he was forced to transfer to the University of Wisconsin (5/8). Having neglected his studies for extracurricular activity in the Hillel Foundation, he was asked in the spring of 1927 to withdraw until he had "gotten academic credit again elsewhere," and he spent the next year selling advertising for the Milwaukee Sentinel and taking courses at the Milwaukee State Normal School (5/1; 5/7). Reentering the University of Wisconsin in the fall of 1928, he continued active in Hillel and joined in the founding of the student Wisconsin Liberal Club. But in the summer be-

---

The more sharply outlined image of Cold War anthropology which my own is intended to nuance is a generalized one, drawn from a variety of readings and interactions with colleagues and students, constrained no doubt by my own experientially conditioned ideological predispositions (see below, 246), which I hope to discuss in an essay entitled "Glimpses into My Own Black Box." For entry into the small but growing body of specifically relevant literature, consult Nader 1997 and Price 1998, as well as Price's Web site (Price n.d.). A useful general historical source is Gaddis 1997. Just as the present essay leaves untouched or only briefly mentioned various aspects of Tax's career not clearly related to its major themes, so also there are many issues of Cold War anthropology untreated here that may surface more clearly in other essays I hope to write.

fore his return, he had chanced to read Robert Marett's *Anthropology* (1912), and when Ralph Linton offered the university's first anthropology course that autumn, the first two lectures made Tax forget "about other careers" (1975c:507; 18/2: ST/E. Banks 10/63). Anthropology, he later recalled, "critically coincided with philosophical values" he had adopted in high school, when he had spent an evening reviewing the "different conclusions of great thinkers" as to whether there were "knowable absolutes." Concluding that "the very diversity" of their views "settled the question in favor of relativism," he "never wavered" from that position (1988:3)—though this did not prevent him from activism consistent with a personal "absolute value" expressed in catch phrases of American democratic culture: "live and let live," "equality and justice" and "freedom and self-determination for all" (280/10: "Creation & Evolution").

The anthropology Tax embraced—and from which he also never wavered —was the "four field" anthropology that Linton shared with more ortho-dox Boasians, encompassing physical anthropology, archeology, linguistics, and what was then still called ethnology (cultural anthropology) (18/2: ST/E. Banks 10/63; cf. Stocking 1976, 1995b). By the time Tax began graduate work at the University of Chicago in the fall of 1931, he had already spent four months in Algeria on an archeological expedition sponsored by the Beloit College Logan Museum, followed by two months in France with the American School of Prehistoric Research and a summer at a Laboratory of Anthro-pology field school led by Ruth Benedict among the Mescalero Apache (cf. Stocking 1982). In giving himself to anthropology, Tax did not abandon his activist commitment, but merely put it off to the future. Distinguishing be-tween a "therapeutic" and a "pure science" interest in "the study of culture," he argued in his undergraduate thesis at Wisconsin that the former must be based on "the best knowledge of its subject," and that a "pure science anthro-pology must furnish that knowledge" (in Blanchard 1979:421). By the time Tax entered graduate school, anthropology had "pushed everything else into the background," and for 17 years he pursued study and research in "pure sci-ence"—sustained by the faith that it would "one day provide an answer for social problems" (18/2: ST/E. Banks 10/63).

Although Tax later suggested that if he were anyone's "disciple," it would be Linton's (Rubinstein 1991a:181), he came under two other major influences at Chicago. A. R. Radcliffe-Brown, soon to be known as "R-B," had just arrived from Australia to replace the leading American Boasian, Edward Sapir, who had left to accept an appointment at Yale. Strongly committed to the estab-lishment of a "scientific" social anthropology as an alternative to Boasian "his-torical" approaches, R-B wanted to extend to American Indian ethnography the comparative sociological study of kinship and social organization he had previously carried on in Australia and South Africa, in the hope of eventu-

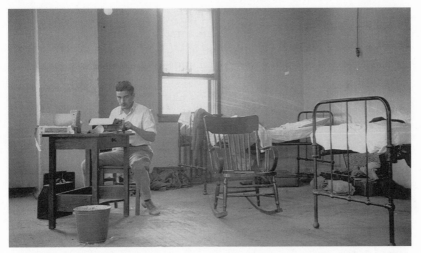

Sol Tax, during his participation in the Laboratory of Anthropology summer field school led by Ruth Benedict in 1931 among the Mescalero Apache. (Courtesy of the Department of Special Collections, University of Chicago Library.)

ally deriving "laws of human society" (Stocking 1995a:352–60). Recruited as R-B's research assistant, Tax was delegated to mine the existing literature of Native American ethnography for comparative material, orienting himself to the history and theory of kinship studies by reading Lewis Henry Morgan's *Systems of Consanguinity* (Morgan 1871). During the summers of 1932 and 1934, Tax also carried on his own fieldwork among the Fox (Mesquakie) Indians of Iowa and among related tribes extending northeastward to Ontario, in preparation for a thesis on "Primitive Social Organization with Some Description of the Social Organization of the Fox Indians"—portions of which were published in the festschrift presented to R-B upon his departure in 1937 to accept the chair at Oxford (Tax 1935, 1937a, 1937b).

In coming to Chicago, Tax did not sever his connections with Linton. On weekend visits with his future wife, Gertrude, back in Madison, Tax took along synopses of R-B's lectures, and in 1933 he arranged a debate between Linton and R-B "on the proposition that laws are possible in anthropology" (Stocking 1978). When Linton subsequently incorporated some of R-B's thinking into *The Study of Man* (1936)—the most influential anthropological textbook up until the publication of Melville Herskovits' *Man and His Works* in 1949—he read every chapter to Tax as he wrote it, and they "argued about it and discussed it" (Rubinstein 1991a:181).

The third influence on Tax, and in some respects the most important, was Robert Redfield, who by the later 1930s had become a dominant figure in Chicago anthropology, his role strengthened by his service as dean of the Social

Sciences Division between 1934 and 1946 (Stocking 1980). In 1934, Redfield invited Tax to participate in the Middle American ethnographic project he was carrying on under the sponsorship of the Carnegie Institution of Washington. Redfield had studied four communities in Yucatan which he placed at different points on a scale of modernization; he wanted Tax to do comparative work in Guatemala (Redfield 1941:358). During the next seven years Tax, assisted by his wife (and for a time in collaboration with Redfield), carried on intensive fieldwork in the highland communities of Chichicastenango and Panajachel, focusing on problems of world view and economy and on ethnic relations between Indians and Ladinos (Rubinstein 1991b). In 1940, Tax was made a research associate of the Chicago department, although he continued to be associated with the Carnegie Institution until 1947.

Between 1942 and 1944, Tax was professor at the Instituto Nacional de Antropología y Historía in Mexico City, where he was involved in training students in social anthropology and ethnographic fieldwork, an activity accepted as war service by his draft board (Blanchard 1979:425). In preparing the students for fieldwork in Chiapas, Tax tried to organize the daily life of the team along " 'democratic' lines." The effort, however, failed because the students (all of them "liberals," and two or three with "communist tendencies") had "no notion of group initiative and self-government" and "the idea of collective responsibility — in practice — was foreign to them" — a failure he later used to demonstrate the deep cultural roots of "the problem of democracy in Middle America" (Tax 1945b:197–98). In the same cultural tradition, however, the students later approached him to ask how, working with Indians who were "poor, diseased, and exploited," he could see "what they were seeing and not *do* anything about it?" Tax responded that nobody could "do anything about it" without being "very clear what 'it' really is" — which was the job of the scientist to determine. Recalling the incident in print, he drew on Mill's *System of Logic* to insist on the difference between "is" and "ought." In the spirit of Radcliffe-Brown, he suggested that "science as such is immoral," and that the anthropologist was interested in the specific community he studied only as a geneticist might be interested in "a bottle of fruitflies." The administrator and the "social philosopher" (or "planner") might be concerned with "social problems" or make recommendations about "social policy" on the basis of "goals and values that are set outside of science," but in principle these roles must be kept distinct, and their overlapping in practice was, to say the least, problematic (Tax 1945a).

Within a few years, however, Tax's own role as a serious theoretical scientist came effectively to an end. Reminiscing 40 years later, he felt that he had made important contributions in two areas: the study of kinship and the study of the kinds of society he and Redfield had investigated in Middle America (1988:18–19). In each case, however, the impact of Tax's work was limited by delays in publication. The "ego-less" kinship chart he developed in his doctoral research has been seen by others as anticipating the development of componential kinship analysis in the 1950s (Rubinstein 1991a:175), but the only portions of his dissertation actually published were those two essays in R-B's festschrift, augmented in the second edition by an account of the history of the study of social organization (Tax 1955). Similarly, Tax's Guatemalan fieldwork revealed "more impersonalism in social interaction than Redfield had found" among the Yucatec Maya—thereby "raising questions about the origins of impersonal, atomistic, and pragmatic social relations in urban, industrial society" (Hinshaw 1979c:762). But a decade-long delay in the publication of *Penny Capitalism* limited the impact of the theoretical implications suggested by its title, and it was never followed into print by the volumes on world view and social institutions mentioned in its preface (Tax 1953b).[2] Even before its appearance, Tax had turned from "pure science" to an action-oriented anthropology on two fronts: work with, and on behalf of, Native American communities, and organizational and editorial activities extending out from the Chicago department to the American anthropological profession and beyond to a world community of anthropologists.

2. A review of economic anthropology by one of Tax's students in 1965 cited *Penny Capitalism* as one of three foundational works in the establishment of the field, demonstrating by "comprehensive and detailed study of a peasant economy" the efficacy of "ordinary anthropological means and fieldwork methods" in the study of economic phenomena (Nash 1965:123); but a survey of a dozen likely sources suggests that Tax's work was little mentioned in the subsequent literature. Tax's Guatemalan fieldwork notes have been available on microfilm since the early 1950s, and notes and drafts of chapters for a book on world view are preserved in his papers (276-80). In commenting later on its failure to achieve publication, Tax emphasized the diversion of his energies to professional and action anthropological activities. Correspondence with Redfield, however, suggests that Redfield's sending another student to work on world view in Panajachel—with Tax's generous (though obviously reluctant) consent—had an inhibiting effect on Tax's completion of the work (RRP: ST/RR 7/14/52, RR/ST 7/18/52, ST/RR 7/25/52). Over the years Tax did continue to work on the world-view manuscript, which was considered for publication by the University of Chicago Press in 1964 (under the titles "The Other Side of the Coin" and "Practical Animism"), but was withdrawn by Tax when he got a grant for a follow-up study with his student Robert Hinshaw. Slightly revised, the manuscript was submitted in 1977 as "The World of Panajachel," but publication seems to have been forestalled by the editor's requests for substantial shortening (276/3). A note Tax later clipped to this correspondence (presumably intended for the research assistant helping to organize his papers) bears the illuminating comment "I think I indicated several months ago that I should indicate some of my failures and lost causes, and publication of The World View of Panajachel would be one of them." In the same spirit, I note here that Tax's early ethnographic work is one of several topics given cursory treatment in this essay.

Tax and Postwar Anthropology:
Acculturation in Evolutionary Perspective
and in the Modern World

Although he had previously been a part-time instructor in the college, Tax's permanent association with the Chicago faculty began early in 1945, when he was given a half-time two-year appointment, during which he was to have primary responsibility for the development of a new graduate anthropology curriculum, in anticipation of a postwar influx of returning veterans (RRP 35/2: F. Cole/R. Tyler 2/10/45; ST interview 5/29/76). Conceived by Tax on the model of the Chicago collegiate core curriculum, it became a three-year required sequence in which contemporary social anthropology was placed in an evolutionary world-historical perspective. The opening course, Human Origins, introduced in the fall of 1945, was planned by Tax, the physical anthropologist Wilton Krogman, and the archeologist Robert Braidwood (in occasional consultation with outside specialists, including the British evolutionary archeologist V. Gordon Childe). This was followed in 1946 by Fred Eggan's encyclopedic review of world ethnography, and in the fall of 1947 by a team-taught course covering a range of issues in social and cultural anthropology. For more than a decade, the 220-230-240 sequence provided the comprehensive training in general anthropology that was the hallmark of Chicago students (Stocking 1979b:33).

In the fall of 1945, Tax also assisted Redfield in planning a course on the transformation of "folk society" in the process of "civilization" (RRP 35/2: 11/45); and it was this transformation, articulated in the theoretical rhetoric of "acculturation," that in the later 1940s was the focus of his professional anthropological involvement outside the Chicago department. First schematized by Redfield, Linton, and Melville Herskovits in a memorandum for the Social Science Research Council in 1936, the acculturation paradigm was the outcome of a gradual shift in Boasian anthropology from historical to psychological problems, and from cultural elements to cultural patterns, under the changing circumstances of field research and Native American life (Stocking 1976). In tandem with the culture and personality approach, and with a residue of evolutionary assumption, it was to be a major tendency in American anthropology in the first decade after World War II. Given the historically rooted interethnic situation in Middle America, the acculturation paradigm seemed especially suited for that area, where Redfield had worked and where his "folk-urban continuum" provided both a conceptual framework and a focus of critical reevaluation (Stocking 1980). It was in this context that Tax entered the larger field of professional anthropological activity in the postwar period—a field that was becoming more complex in both its geographical range and its internal demography.

It was only during and after World War II that American anthropology moved decisively into the international arena—in a pattern largely coincident with United States strategic interests and programs of economic development, and marked organizationally by the efflorescence of "area studies" (W. Bennett 1947; Hall 1947; Lambert 1973; Wallerstein 1997). There had already, of course, been a long-standing interest in the archeology and ethnology of lands south of the border. By 1875, the International Congress of Americanists had held the first of its biennial meetings in France, although it was two decades before it actually met in the Western Hemisphere (Comas 1954:xiv). In 1910 Franz Boas joined with scholars from several nations in founding the International School of Archaeology and Ethnology in Mexico (Godoy 1977). While there was little if any direct involvement of the United States government in Latin American research, the long-standing American strategic interest in the area had precipitated a professional crisis in anthropology as early as 1919, when Boas accused some Latin Americanist anthropologists of having spied for the United States during World War I (Stocking 1968). During the interwar period, however, work in the region continued to be carried on under nongovernmental auspices—most notably, by the Carnegie Institution, which sponsored archeological work in Yucatan in the 1920s and after 1930 extended this to include Redfield's comparative ethnographic enterprise (Sullivan 1989).

With the onset of war in Europe, there were signs of a more general anthropological interest in Latin America. In 1940, the National Research Council Division of Anthropology and Psychology began a review of research, and in March 1941 there was a preliminary meeting of a Committee on Latin American Anthropology. It was early in 1946 that Tax was invited to join, as alternate to Redfield (49/4: C. Guthe/ST 3/18/41; 282/4: "1984"), and at the meeting that November he initiated a plan to collect relevant manuscript materials on microfilm. The main concern of the committee, however, was the "critical" situation of anthropology in South America, where a number of local anthropologists had been "displaced because of new political regimes"—notably, that of Perón in Argentina. On this issue, however, the committee felt that "any protest should better come from the AAA," to which a communication was to be addressed. Of more immediate concern was the generally sad state of anthropological research in the region, including Mexico, where "pure anthropology" seemed to have "very little future." To address this situation, a new subcommittee on Academic Relations was instructed to "explore conditions," to advertise "the qualifications of our colleagues there," to pursue "all possibilities of interchange," and to seek foundation support. There was also informal discussion of the "desirability of assessing past, present, and possible future trends in Latin America, particularly in regard to areal studies in general" (49/5: C. Wagley, CLAA minutes, 11/30/46).

Six weeks later, Chairman John Gillin reported that he had been "reli-ably informed" that the recently established "Bureau [i.e., Office] of Naval Research" was interested in investigations of "the basic patterns of modern Latin American culture," but would "prefer that such a project be actually sponsored and administered" by the Research Council Committee on Latin American Anthropology (49/4: JG/CLAA 2/13/47). Before the creation of the National Science Foundation in 1950, the Office of Naval Research was the "principal federal agency supporting academic science," and in its early years adopted a very flexible and permissive policy in the encourage-ment of "basic" rather than "applied" research (Sapolsky 1990:37). Among the anthropological programs it supported were George Peter Murdock's Coordinated Investigation of Micronesian Anthropology (Bashkow 1991) and the Columbia University Research in Contemporary Cultures project of Ruth Benedict and Margaret Mead (Mead & Metraux 1953). The Latin American proposal, however, seems to have run aground. Tax himself was concerned about the Office's apparent reluctance to sponsor the research di-rectly, which he felt might become the subject of congressional concern (as in-deed it later did). Instead, he offered suggestions for a project along the lines of the recent study of "the race problem in the United States" by Gunnar Myrdal (1944). Although it would use Latin American researchers where possible, in the end it "should be frankly a North American anthropological interpre-tation"; enclosing a topical outline, Tax suggested that research should be pursued "empirically," without even assuming that "there is a Latin American culture" (49/4: ST/JG 2/25/47). Although a later budget proposal circulated by Gillin acknowledged the existence of considerable cultural variation, it nevertheless assumed "that a new type of western civilization"—which Gillin called "Creole culture"—was developing from three historical sources: the culture of Spain and Portugal at the time of the Conquest, the indigenous cultures of Latin America, and "the cultures of modern western Europe and North America" (49/4: JG/CLAA 9/20/47). The project as such apparently foundered because the National Research Council committee was "not au-thorized to originate or promote research and to try to sell it to other depart-ments of the government" (49/4: JG/CLAA 9/20/47). However, the idea of a study of creole (or "criollo") culture continued to be discussed in the com-mittee (27/7: JG/ST 2/24/48; Gillin et al. 1949), and, along related lines, an acculturation project was pursued by Tax himself.

Among the members of the Latin American committee was Paul Fejos, a Hungarian-born Renaissance man whose scarcely credible career included stints as fighter pilot, medical doctor, biological researcher, and innovative film director, both in Hollywood and in ethnographic film projects in South-east Asia and the Amazon (Dodds 1973; STP 282/4: "1984"). In 1937, during a tiger hunt in Southeast Asia, Fejos had saved the life of the Swedish industrialist (and putative Nazi sympathizer) Axel Wenner-Gren, whose American business ventures subsequently entangled him with the Internal Revenue Service. When Wenner-Gren established the Viking Fund in 1941—apparently in the false hope that he might thereby shelter funds the IRS was suing him for—he made Fejos its research director (Dodds 1973:78–79). Shortly after the war, Wenner-Gren's name was removed from the State Department's "proclaimed list" of those barred entry to the United States, and in 1950 the Viking Fund was renamed after its founding benefactor. The Wenner-Gren Foundation for Anthropological Research was to be a major source of funding for the discipline in the postwar period, and through Tax (and his colleague Sherwood Washburn) maintained a close relationship to the Chicago department (Silverman et al. 1991). As fellow members of the Research Council's Latin American committee at the end of the war, Tax and Fejos were both aware of the need for external funding to underwrite a synthesis and evaluation of current anthropological knowledge of the area, and by April 1949 they had joined in planning a seminar on Middle American ethnology to be held at the Viking Fund offices immediately preceding the meetings of the International Congress of Americanists in New York that September (212/1: ST/PF 4/18/49, PF/ST 4/21/49).

Early in the planning, Tax articulated a conception of the mechanics of conferences that, with slight variations, was to be implemented in a series of symposia and conferences he organized and stage-managed over the next four decades. In the paradigm case, major topics of discussion were defined in advance, including cultural and subcultural areas, race relations, social change and acculturation, social organization, economy and technology, the Spanish or Indian provenience of cultural traits or elements, the life cycle, the calendar, shamanism and sorcery, politico-religious organization, and personality and culture. Each was assigned to one anthropologist charged with drafting a short paper characterizing the region as a whole and suggesting smaller regional differences. The papers were circulated to all participants beforehand for comment, so that the seminar itself could be devoted entirely to the discussion of major issues and of differences of opinion, with papers then revised to function as a "guide to further research" (212/1: ST/J. Fuente 3/8/49; cf. ST/PF 4/18/49, ST/R. Beals 8/1/49). The "whole thing," as Tax suggested to George Foster, was to be "a highly cooperative enterprise" (212/1: ST/GF 5/13/49).

In the event, the seminar drew together 32 scholars, 10 of them from institutions south of the border, with a half day devoted to discussion of each of seven papers on specific topics, ranging from economy to ethos. After this, there was general discussion of acculturation and social change, which were to be the defining themes of *Heritage of Conquest*, the semipopular volume Tax subsequently edited. Rather than treating "the ancient glories" of Middle

America, it dealt with "the people today, mostly the uneducated rural people" (Tax 1952a:7) and incorporated a considerable portion of the verbatim transcript of the seminar. The first of two generalizing sessions focused on the problems of classifying existing cultures and the periodization of historical changes; the second was devoted to the report of a committee, chaired by Tax, offering a mapping of 20 different communities by "degrees of acculturation," according to an "index of acculturation" based on the "retention" of four major "trait" categories from "pre-Columbian times": monolingualism, technology, social organization, and religion (262–63). This was followed by discussion of the report to be presented to the Americanist congress, focusing on the degree of acculturation in different areas and among different groups and the possibility—suggested by Oscar Lewis's ongoing restudy of Redfield's Tepoztlán (Lewis 1951)—of "before and after" studies of the same people. Worth noting in all this, by contrast to the perspective of Tax's soon reemergent activism, in his implicitly evolutionary suggestion that "the places which have retained Indian culture are those where there wasn't much to start with"—that is, those which were "marginal to the great societies of the old days" (Tax 1952a:269)—as well as his functionalist conception of the advisory role of the anthropologist: "people who are interested in planning ought to have some notion from us as to what parts of the culture they can change without changing other things that they don't want to change" (276).

The International Congress of Americanists, to which the Viking Fund seminar summary was offered, was much more constrained by the retrospective traditions of nineteenth-century European scholarship. But even here, the discussion of acculturation became the telos of the three congress volumes that Tax edited, with resonances of the tripartite evolutionary structure of the new core curriculum at Chicago. The implicit starting point (logically, though not by publication date) was *The Indian Tribes of Aboriginal America* (1952b), which were marginal to the "highest cultural development" of *The Civilizations of Ancient America* (1951b:1), culminating in *Acculturation in the Americas*—offered by Tax as evidence that "anthropologists have moved fully into the problems of the world in which we live" (1951a:v). It was to these present human problems that Tax was to devote the major portion of his energies in the years that followed.

Appraising Anthropology Today and Celebrating Darwin: Tax and Mainstream Professional Anthropology in the 1950s

Before tracing the path along which Tax's activism led him to reject the acculturationist paradigm and to distance himself from some of the major tendencies in American anthropology during the postwar period, it would be well to consider also the ways in which his activist impulse continued to be channeled into the organizational life of the discipline, along lines that in fact forwarded some of those tendencies. Once reactivated, his organizational urge was irrepressible, and although it found various outlets, they were all expressions of his desire to sustain and increase the visibility, power, and efficacy of a broadly embracive, integrated, and organizationally unified discipline of anthropology.

When the American Anthropological Association met in Chicago in 1946, after a period of internal discussion about how to organize effectively to meet the challenges of the postwar period, Tax chaired the local arrangements committee. In the reintegrative spirit of the constitutional provisions that were to be passed at the meeting, he took the initiative in getting the professional societies of the linguists, the physical anthropologists, the folklorists, and the applied anthropologists to meet concurrently—to the end of countering the centrifugal tendencies of the interwar years, during which the "four fields" had tended to develop distinct professional identities (Stocking 1976:173). A similarly ecumenical spirit is manifest in his intra-university activity in this period. Upon his appointment as full professor in 1948, he began a stint as associate dean of the Division of Social Sciences, serving also as chair of its curriculum committee—in which role he was a leader in establishing a general social science course on the model of Anthropology 240. After interacting "intensely" for five years with "150 colleagues of every social science discipline" (Tax 1988:2), he went on to serve as director of a self-study of the university's behavioral sciences programs, one of five such programs commissioned by the Ford Foundation at major university centers (Tax et al. 1954). Before that, however, Tax's involvement in professional activities outside Chicago had also entered a new phase.

When Tax took on the editing of the Latin American volumes in 1949, he had already had some publishing experience, first in Mexico, where he helped to bring about translations of Linton's *Study of Man* (1936) and Redfield's *Folk Culture of Yucatan* (1941), and then in Chicago, where he got the fledgling Free Press to publish out-of-print books used in the new graduate anthropology curriculum (Tax 1988:6). In 1952, when the Wenner-Gren Foundation sponsored an International Symposium on Anthropology, the papers prepared in advance were collected separately as *Anthropology Today: An Encyclopedic Inventory*, under the general editorship of Alfred Kroeber (1953). But when plans for a second synthesis volume seemed not to be working out, Kroeber coopted Tax to serve as chief editor of a radical condensation of the 1,900 pages of typed transcriptions of the discussions. Rejecting the title "Anthropology Tomorrow"—because he felt there was not enough innovation in the book to warrant it (77/1: ST/ALK 8/8/52)—Tax eventually settled on the more simply descriptive *An Appraisal of Anthropology Today* (Tax et al. 1953).

Later that year, when Melville Herskovits resigned as editor of the *Ameri-*

can Anthropologist and the editorial board had to choose a successor, the selection was apparently influenced by Tax's Chicago colleague Sherwood Washburn, who, like Tax, was discouraged by the "conservatism" of the Wenner-Gren symposium (77/1: SW/ST 8/8/52) and who felt that the discipline's journal had long been moribund (CKP: SW/CK 1/29/53). Having served as associate editor since 1951, Tax was an obvious choice for the revitalization project, and he took it on with characteristic entrepreneurial enthusiasm. In the first number under his editorship, he announced plans to "vastly improve scholarly communication" by increasing the journal's frequency to six issues a year, and its size "by at least 50%," along with four separate monographs a year, addressed to four concentric circles of readership, inside and outside anthropology. All of this was to be funded by various economies of printing and format, including a greater press run for an expanded association membership, as well as the exploration of external funding—in the event, primarily from the Wenner-Gren Foundation (Tax 1953a). In a democratically delegational spirit, Tax encouraged symposia evaluating the status of research in particular areas, with the papers distributed over several numbers, or as theme numbers under a special editor. Over the next several years, there were numbers on museums, on the Southwest, and on Latin America—culminating in one proposed and edited by Margaret Lantis as a contribution to the American Studies movement: "The U.S.A. as Anthropologists See It" (77/1; 37/4: ST/ML 5/18/53). When Tax retired as editor at the end of 1955, after he became chair of the Chicago department, his successor noted that the "ambitious hopes and policies" of his "four year program for enlarging the size and scope" of the *Anthropologist* had in fact been accomplished in only three years (Goldschmidt 1956).

In chairing the Chicago department, Tax worked closely with Washburn, who had preceded him as chair and who also had close ties to the Wenner-Gren Foundation, which from its inception had had a strong interest in biological anthropology and human evolution (Silverman et al. 1991:6–30). When Washburn arrived in the department, during the second year of the new postwar program, he came as the leading representative of the "new physical anthropology" then emerging in response to the neo-Darwinian "evolutionary synthesis" of the 1930s (Smocovitis 1996). But he was also a staunch proponent of the Boasian critique of racism, which in 1950 and 1951 was embodied in two Statements on Race promulgated by scientists meeting in Paris under the auspices of the United Nations Educational Scientific and Cultural Organization. Taken together, these two tendencies (the modern evolutionary synthesis and the critique of race) helped to constitute what has been called the "UNESCO vision of man"—an anthropological world view Tax shared with Washburn (Haraway 1988). Upon his arrival in Chicago, Washburn had taken over the Human Origins course in the sequence

Tax had organized, and quickly became, along with Redfield, one of the two intellectual leaders in the Chicago department. Working closely with Tax, he envisioned its becoming a counterforce to the "conservatism" he felt had been manifest at the Anthropology Today symposium (cf. CKP: SW/CK 1/29/53, 2/12/54; STP 77/1: SW/ST 11/15/56, 1/9/57).

Tax was troubled by what he called the "split personality" of anthropology as it had developed in the aftermath of Franz Boas' critique of nineteenth-century racial and cultural evolutionary assumptions (cf. Stocking 1976:118–27). Although he was Boasian in a general sense, and wholeheartedly anti-racist, cultural and biological evolutionism were persistent and recurring countertendencies in Tax's own version of "four-field" anthropology. On the one hand, he argued that the "complete separation" (mediated by Boas) "of man as an organism from man as a member of society and bearer of culture" had "resolved the common confusion between race and culture" that had culminated in "Hitler's disastrous mythology." But on the other, he was concerned that as a consequence of the belief that culture was " 'superorganic' and quite independent of 'blood' or 'race,' " a "generation of students had grown up convinced that biological and cultural anthropology needed each other mainly to demonstrate the limitations of the biological in man"—with the result that the two "specializing" branches of anthropology "have tended to draw apart from each other" (1960:271–72). In 1955, while Tax was still editor of the *American Anthropologist*, he conceived a project that he hoped might bring them back together.

While attending a "supper conference" at the Wenner-Gren Foundation on issues in physical anthropology, Tax was provoked by the mention of Charles Darwin to think about the impact of the *Origin of Species*, the centennial of which was only four years off. Why not celebrate it at the University of Chicago, with anthropology at "center stage"? Anticipating competing celebrations in England, he managed to keep the world spotlight focused on Chicago by inviting Julian Huxley, grandson of Thomas Henry and one of the major articulators of the "modern evolutionary synthesis," along with the mathematician grandson and namesake of Darwin himself. Washburn worried that "an elderly group of famous and very able Englishmen" would direct the gaze of the symposium back to the past, rather than stressing "the younger and future" in order to generate "new thinking and a new synthesis" (77/1: SW/ST 9/5/56). But Tax, who was as much impresario as entrepreneur, was thinking more expansively of the impact and logistics of an evolutionary extravaganza—which, in the event, was a very large event indeed (see, in general, Smocovitis 1997).

Held over a five-day period around Thanksgiving 1959, beginning on the very date the *Origin* had been published a hundred years before, the celebration attracted over 2,500 registrants, including two-time Democratic presi-

Sol Tax, Ilse Veith, A. L. Kroeber, and Julian Huxley discussing evolutionary issues for the radio program "All Things Considered" during the Darwin centennial celebration, November 1959. (Courtesy of the Department of Special Collections, University of Chicago Library.)

dential candidate Adlai Stevenson. Of these, 350 were delegates from 14 countries and 184 institutions, including, after negotiations with the State Department, a number from behind the Iron Curtain. The preparatory "media blitz" was so effective that Tax, fearing the university's facilities would be "over-taxed" (sic: 1960:276), arranged for the proceedings to be broadcast to two venues other than Mandel Hall, where the five panels were actually held: one on the origin of life, one on the evolution of life, one on man as an organism, one on the evolution of the mind, and one on social and cultural evolution. Following the pattern established in previous symposia in which Tax participated, the papers were not read, but were circulated ahead of time and then discussed by the panelists; audience members were oriented to the discussions by a 64-page booklet of summaries included in each registration packet. Also in the packet was a complicated ticket, punched to indicate which panels and sideshows the registrant would be admitted to:

among them a lecture by the paleontologist Louis Leakey, an institute for high school teachers of biology, an institute on science and theology, centennial and Thanksgiving dinners, and a film called *The Ladder of Life*. There was even a musical production performed on three of the conference evenings. Frustrated in his hope to stage the Scopes-trial play, *Inherit the Wind*, with Melvyn Douglas as Clarence Darrow, Tax had sketched his own plans for a musical modeled on the Broadway hit *Oklahoma!*, which would have celebrated futuristic themes of progress and maintained (in apparent tension with the evolutionary theme of the conference) that "human nature does not change; whatever it is, it is irrelevant" (Smocovitis 1997). In the event, however, the play actually performed was a musical reenactment of Darwin's life story entitled *Time Will Tell*, composed and sung by local faculty talent (and available on a long-playing recording for $8.00). Julian Huxley, who at one point apparently thought he would play a leading role in the musical, later had the stage all to himself at the final convocation in Rockefeller Chapel, where he offered a vigorously secular sermon entitled "The Evolutionary Vision," which, as the focus of newspaper coverage, precipitated a flood of letters from outraged midwestern religious traditionalists (see, in general, Smocovitis 1997).

Despite a deficit of some $7,000 (in a budget of $57,000 raised from the National Science Foundation, the Wenner-Gren Foundation, and the National Institutes of Health), the conference was generally felt to have been a great success. But as Washburn had feared, and a recent commentary has agreed, it did not bring "new insights into the evolutionary picture," and the "discussions and contributed papers were surprisingly flat" (Smocovitis 1997). The anthropologists included several leading figures in the "new American evolutionism" that had emerged in the postwar period at several institutional loci besides Chicago (cf. Wolf 1964). A. I. Hallowell, a broad-ranging psychological anthropologist from the University of Pennsylvania, joined the biologists and psychologists on panel 4 to discuss "The Evolution of Mind." Panel 5, "Social and Cultural Evolution," included Leslie White and Julian Steward, the leading figures of postwar cultural neo-evolutionism, as well as two civilizational archeologists (Robert McCormick Adams and Gordon Willey), and several biologists. The panel was chaired, however, by Clyde Kluckhohn and Alfred Kroeber, who in 1952 had produced an ambitious and extensive "critical review of concepts and definitions" of the culture idea, and who were by no means neo-evolutionists. Indeed, what is striking about the final panel is the degree to which it still emphasized discontinuities between biological and cultural evolution, both in the preamble statement and the discussion itself.

Most of the issues, however, were defined in terms sufficiently general so that all the panelists could agree. White, who for 30 years had been wielding cudgels against anti-evolutionary Boasians, was pleased to discover that "most of my fellow anthropologists" now professed to have been evolutionists "all along" (Tax & Callender 1960:234). Kroeber, surviving doyen of Boasian anthropology, was reciprocally surprised to discover that he and White had been "sleeping in the same bed for thirty years without knowing it" (235)—only to have White insist that there were in fact "two beds" (236). Even so, a rather blandly good-spirited discussion continued until the very end, when the geneticist Herman Muller—supported by Huxley—pursued the problem of "negative feedback" between culture and biology, raising the charged and divisive issue of eugenic improvement. By then, however, the time allotted for the session was almost up, "just at the point when all of us have something to say and would like to say it"—and it was "a good thing, too," commented Kluckhohn in closing the panel. Foregoing the summary he had been assigned, he simply quoted George Gaylord Simpson on the process of evolution in general: "There is both order and disorder in it" (Tax & Callender 1960:242–43).

In the meantime, the "new evolutionism," propelled by Washburn and supported by Tax, seemed on the verge of becoming the defining feature of the Chicago department. With the encouragement of Bernard Berelson of the Ford Foundation, whom he met at the Center for Advanced Study in the Behavioral Sciences early in 1957, Washburn drafted a grant proposal on behalf of the department. Drawing heavily on the experience of his own field studies of wild baboons and on his functionalist approach to anatomy, he hoped to synthesize anatomy, anthropology, comparative psychology, and zoology in a study called "The Evolution of Human Behavior." By combining observational, anatomical, and experimental approaches, the project would investigate "the origin of walking, talking, and thinking," with the goal of assisting the "social scientist" in understanding human behavior in the present. Chicago was the place to do this, because it was already "more ecologically, genetically, and behaviorally oriented" than comparable institutions. Berelson was enthusiastic, and within weeks, the Ford Foundation had committed itself to a $75,000 grant over a three-year period (77/1: SW/ST 2/4/57, 3/27/57).

Although Washburn took the lead in articulating the Chicago variant of the "new evolutionism," Tax was encouraging from the outset, and there were other initiatives during his chairmanship that were cast in similar or related terms—notably, the multidisciplinary Chicago Chiapas project, which was formulated in the first year of Tax's chairmanship, and funded by the National Science Foundation under the title "Man in Nature" (103/11: press release 8/7/59; cf. 87/13).[3] Early in January 1957, Washburn congratulated Tax for

3. Originally cast in ecological terms, as a study of "the variation through space and time of small indigenous populations in a variety of natural and human environments," the Chiapas project rapidly evolved into a linguistic anthropological study of dialect variation ("both geographically and socially") among Tzeltal and Tzotzil populations with varying degrees of acculturative contact, both with each other and with European populations (87/13). The tension

leading the department into "a new phase of its existence" (77/1: SW/ST 1/9/57), and two years later he thanked Tax, then president of the American Anthropological Association, for having encouraged research that was opening up "a new era in primate studies" (77/2: 9/24/59).

In the event, however, the evolutionary turn fostered by Washburn and Tax in the Chicago department was soon to lose momentum, as it did in anthropology generally. As late as 1964, in a volume prepared for the Princeton Studies of Humanistic Scholarship in America, Eric Wolf could still speak of "the new American evolutionism" as evidence of anthropology's growing "scientific maturity" (1964:31). By that time, however, shifts had taken place in the Chicago department which suggest that the general postwar resurgence of evolutionism in American anthropology may better be regarded as a momentary phase of rapprochement in the ambivalent interaction of biological and cultural anthropology. Within months after receiving the Evolution of Human Behavior grant, Washburn left Chicago for Berkeley, and though his interests were carried on by his student Clark Howell, the subdisciplinary center of gravity in the Chicago department shifted dramatically when a "counter-raid" on Berkeley brought to Chicago three promising young sociocultural anthropologists: Lloyd Fallers, Clifford Geertz, and David Schneider (63/7: M. Singer/ST 3/10/58; 23/8: F. Eggan/ST 12/20/57, 2/6/58). During the first half of the 1960s, the department's rapidly enlarging sociocultural wing carried Chicago away from the embracively integrative evolutionist orientation encouraged by Washburn and Tax (Stocking 1979b:41–45). For those committed to a theoretically oriented sociocultural anthropology, "four field" anthropology seemed a survival from the anthropological past, and as the years went by, Tax became something of an exiled elder in his own departmental homeland. Already by 1960, however, he himself had for more than a decade been pursuing an activist and internationalist agenda that took him beyond the Chicago department.

Action Anthropology and the End of Acculturation: Toward the American Indian Chicago Conference

In 1968 Tax wrote a piece he called "Last on the Warpath," one of a number of retrospective essays or fragments, published or in manuscript, in which

---

between grant application rhetoric and actual research agenda raises, by implication, a more general issue: the extent to which the evolutionary, ecological, and other "scientistic" tendencies of anthropology in the 1950s articulated with the research priorities of funding agencies, and especially those of the National Science Foundation, where the role of the "social sciences" remained problematic throughout that decade (Lyons 1969:269–77), and where anthropology may have had an early competitive advantage by virtue of the natural scientific orientation of several of its component fields.

he traced the development of his interest in "action anthropology" (64/8; cf. 282/2). In this one, he recalled a description of the Fox (or Mesquakie) Indians in his master's thesis as "on the whole, a happy lot, with something of interest to do every hour of the day, something to call them forth at the dawn of the next." In the rhetoric of a latter-day rural primitivism, he had spoken of the Indians as rising "for an early hunting expedition," working "in the farm or garden," gossiping with "their white friends," dressing in their "finery" for a ceremonial, playing baseball, enjoying "social dances in the evening over at the Pow-Wow grounds"—following a "round of life" marked by "births and loves and deaths." Looking back, he noted that "there was almost no suggestion that these people had either personal or community problems" (64/8). This, despite the fact that in 1934 he had written a letter to John Collier, Commissioner of Indian Affairs, warning him that "the Indians were in a furor," and planned to "blockade their roads so that the school bus could not even enter their lands" to take their children to a school off the reservation, rather than "to their own community schools" (123/2: 9/4/34).

The "last on the warpath" of Tax's 1968 retrospect were not the Indians, however, but the anthropologists, and the account was that of his own consciousness-raising. Although there had been a movement within American anthropology toward "applied anthropology" during the New Deal and World War II years (Stocking 1976: 159–68), it was not encouraged in the Chicago department. In 1943, when Rachel Reese (Sady) proposed a dissertation on "the application of anthropological knowledge and methodology to the administration of public services in native areas"—specifically, on the basis of eight months' work on the Menominee reservation in Wisconsin—Tax, as her dissertation advisor, warned her that "it is almost sure to be turned down" because "it contains no anthropological problem" (59/2: Reese/ST 5/28/43, ST/Reese 7/2/43). Although Reese refused to accept the proposition that "administration can be separated from culture as a thing apart," she tried to follow Tax's advice "and think up a nice orthodox thesis topic," and did eventually receive her doctorate for a study of "the function of rumor" in a Japanese relocation center in Arkansas, where she worked in 1944 (59/2: Reese/ST 7/6/43). But as late as September 1945, Tax reported to her that the department was still discussing how "to get your 'applied' anthropology into the picture." Personally, he would "never approve of the conception, which seems to be held in Washington, that there is a 'field' of 'Applied Anthropology' somehow coordinate" with the other four fields. Granting that "anthropological findings are presumably useful to society," the person who interprets them, or who helps to solve practical problems, ought simply to be called an "anthropologist" (59/2: ST/Sady 9/25/45). Tax never changed his opinion of applied anthropology, but he was soon to define an alternative form of anthropological activism.

During the winter of 1947–48, when the first cohort of postwar students was fairly far along in its training, the Chicago department asked Tax to investigate the possibility of leading a field party to the Fox reservation, near the town of Tama, Iowa, within a day's drive from Chicago. Unlike many other Native American groups, the Fox had resisted allotment, and although they were now farmers, still held land in common. When last there 12 years before, Tax had been impressed that their culture was "live enough" to enforce traditional modes of behavior, although he feared its breakdown as the younger generation tried to "move forward according to white standards" (in Gearing et al. 1960:6). When he broached the field party scheme to John Provinse, a prewar Ph.D. of the department by then Assistant Commissioner of Indian Affairs, Provinse was in fact concerned about a recent "breakdown" of law and order, in the form of factional disputes occasioned by the federal government's plan to transfer jurisdiction over law enforcement to the state of Iowa. When Tax went to the reservation early in May, however, he found it "remarkably little changed": the ex-servicemen had formed an American Legion post, but during the two days of his visit there had been "both a peyote ceremony and a Bear Clan festival." Nevertheless, he assured Provinse that among the major problems his students would study would be those "of interest to you in establishing policy for the Reservation": specifically, "relations to neighboring whites," "acculturation," "mechanisms of social control and their effectiveness," and "factions"—which Tax thought had existed among the Fox for at least a hundred years (in Gearing et al. 1960:26–28).

When Tax's six students arrived in Tama, they were more impressed than he with the current problems of the Fox. Writing to Provinse, Redfield's daughter Lisa Peattie attributed pressure for the change in law enforcement to "the local DAR and the county attorney"; she was concerned that the enforcement of laws against the sale of liquor to Indians was stirring up resentment among ex-servicemen and that any attempt to enforce the letter of Iowa law "in the matter of marriage" would create "great havoc" (in Gearing et al. 1960:29). By midsummer, the students had begun to question their "pure science" orientation: "what this community needs is a group of anthropologists staying here all the time, organizing group activities and building Gemeinschaft" (33). Although Tax first rejected the idea of systematic student interference when Peattie pursued it by phone, within several days he wrote back reversing his decision (Blanchard 1979:429). His ideas about "the relations of research and social action" had been "a little up in the air in the last couple of years," but they were "coming down to earth gradually"—in response, as he later recalled, to "Hitler, the War, and the Bomb" (1988:8; cf. 1958b). And "whether they're right or wrong, at least I now have some conclusions": namely, "I don't believe that you can do 'pure research' among the Fox except if you also do what has sometimes been called 'action research.'"

From this point of view, the "'participant observer' method might very well be taken to mean 'interferer observer' method," since any observation would be a form of interference, and one might as well take "full advantage of it": "Let us simply recognize that we want to do something about our society and get ourselves into positions of relative power . . . and start doing it, observing what happens as we do it, and thus learning about the society in a way that is comparable to a controlled experiment" (in Gearing et al. 1960:32–33).

It took a while, however, to consider the implications of the "interferer observer" method, and to conceptualize it as "action anthropology." Initially, what came to be called "the Fox Project" was discussed in terms reflecting the pervading acculturationist assumptions of postwar American anthropology. It was taken for granted by Peattie (one of the more activist participants) that it was useless to try to "preserve the old culture" and that the Fox faced a "typical acculturation situation" (in Gearing et al. 1960:36, 50). Similarly, Lloyd Fallers (one of the more theoretically inclined) believed that what was at issue was rather "the rapidity and the mode of assimilation" (37). After the first summer's work Robert Reitz, who later served as field director of the project, posed the issue in "social engineering" terms, as a problem of "social disorganization" with seven "types" of "individual adjustment" (110, 98, 99). In the early phases, the project was conceived of in means-ends terms: the Fox had "economic wants," which could be treated as the "ends of project activities"; from this point of view, their "interpersonal relations" were simply "means"—or obstructions, in the case of "factionalism"—to the accomplishment of the project's "ends" (85–86, 98–99, 120).

From the beginning, however, the question of "alternative values" and "socially relevant value judgments" (Gearing et al. 1960:35, 37)—including those of anthropologists and of "science" itself—was a central concern, whether pragmatically (in the case of the activists) or theoretically (in the case of the Weberian Fallers). In seeking foundation support for the project in 1949 (after the department had bought a 58-acre farm as a continuing base of operations), Tax emphasized the impossibility of separating science from values, the "basic value position" of not treating people "simply as things," and the assumption that "the values pursued in a given community should be derived, as completely as possible," from "the needs and desires of the community members themselves," without at this point saying how this was to be accomplished, given the diversity of opinion among the Fox and the "definite" value notions of anthropologists who had abandoned the illusion of value "neutrality" (92–93).

By the third year, in the context of "a variety of experiences" of the effects of "coercive" administrative power over "cultural enclaves," the emphasis of the Fox Project was shifting in ways that reflected a rethinking of the means-ends approach to the value problem. Instead of seeing the Fox as "passively having things done to them by white contact," they were increasingly seen as "active agents" in their own adaptation, and project activity shifted away from economic programs to "the education of Indians and whites about each other" (Gearing et al. 1960:120; cf. 182). By this time, the project had produced an offshoot on the Fort Berthold Indian Reservation in North Dakota in an area that was to be flooded with the construction of the Garrison Dam. By arrangement with the Bureau of Indian Affairs, Robert Reitz worked for several years to assist the three tribal groups involved and the BIA personnel in developing a plan for resettlement and in negotiating problems that might arise in the process (Blanchard 1979:431–32).

At the meeting of the American Anthropological Association in 1951, Tax drew on the accumulating experience at Tama and Fort Berthold to articulate a conception of Action Anthropology, which he explicitly saw as a reversal of the position he had taken in 1945 on "pure science" and "applied anthropology." Insofar as applied anthropology "presupposed a body of scientific knowledge" available for application at the request of managers or administrators, action anthropology differed radically. The action anthropologist could "have no master," and was less interested in applying "general knowledge" than the "clarification of goals and the compromising of conflicting ends or values." For action anthropologists, community research was "justifiable" only insofar as the results were "imminently useful to the community and easily outweigh[ed] the disturbance to it." Because they were interested in "the dynamics of acculturation," in which the body of existing theoretical knowledge always fell "far short of the needs of effective action," action anthropologists must have a dynamic, pragmatic approach to theory. Working in complex situations that characteristically included "a dependent people" split into "factions," a powerful bureaucracy, and surrounding communities of "a different culture," the action anthropologist's goal was to educate them all "to their own and each other's goals, to mediate them, clarify them, and eventually make them effective." They must therefore "constantly guess and improvise," developing theory in relation to practice, accepting the risk that colleagues would accuse them of giving up "building an edifice of theory" and engaging instead in "social work." Although it was unlikely that "thousands" could be trained to "work with Point 4 teams, the Indian Service, [and] the Trust Territories," Tax nevertheless hoped that a few academically trained and dedicated action anthropologists, working in key areas, would influence others, "since education has a way of spreading." And because this could happen only in a democratic society, it was probably impossible "in some colonial situations." Accepting "that limitation as long as it exists," Tax hoped that elsewhere in the world action anthropology would become "a force to be reckoned with" (Gearing et al. 1960:167–71).

A year later, Tax took the further step of explicitly rejecting the anthropo-

logical and administrative paradigm of "acculturation." He had in the meantime traveled in the Southwest, where he visited the Hopi, who were generally
thought to be among the least acculturated Indians, but who seemed to him
"no more permanently Indian than the Mesquakies" (1988:9). In the spring of
1952, at a meeting of the Central States Anthropological Society, he made the
"very bold statement" that "acculturation does *not* occur" among the "small
enclaves" of North American Indians, and that the Navaho, the Fox, and
the Iroquois would be "with us for a thousand years." As first formulated, his
hypothesis depended on distinguishing between changing "outer forms" and
resistant "inner meanings," and between "assimilating individuals" and "un-
acculturated Indian communities." Rejecting the sociological "theory of the
melting pot," Tax argued in pan-Indian terms (and with romantic primitivist and implicitly evolutionary resonances) that there were fundamental differences between "Western European culture" and that of the North American Indians. Recasting the biblical story of the expulsion from paradise as
Childe's "Neolithic Revolution" (the transition from "the food-gathering
stage of human culture" to a "full agricultural economy"), Tax suggested that
North American Indians (as opposed to those of Middle America and much
of South America) were "among the few people on earth who never became
in any sense peasants." Connected to Europeans only "by the most remote
fork in the historic tree of culture," they had escaped the "slavery to property
and to time" which over "thousands of years" had habituated Europeans to
the ethic of "work-and-save." Still retaining the "habits of thought" of "the
hunt," they had been "rightly perceived" (rather than stereotyped) by Europeans as "noble red men" who were "free in some sense they were not" (in
Gearing et al. 1960:173–76).

A month or two later, Tax presented his ideas at a conference on assimilation organized by the Association on American Indian Affairs. The meeting
was intended to "persuade Congress and the B.I.A. that they should slow
down the increasingly destructive withdrawal of reservations" being carried
on under the termination policy, which—reversing the priorities of the "New
Deal for Indians"—encouraged a relocation of Indians from reservations to
urban centers (Tax 1988:10–11; cf. Prucha 1985:67–71). Tax later recalled
that the Indian leaders present had at first made the by then standard argument that assimilation was inevitable, but that in the meantime they needed
help. But when Tax insisted that there was "no scientific evidence" for the
inevitability of assimilation, and that such an assumption in fact supported
"the damaging value judgment" that some Indians were "progressive" and
others "backward," each of the Indian leaders arose to "vehemently" recant—
leaving Tax to conclude that he had been "the boy who said that the Emperor
wore no clothes" (1988:10; cf. 131/6: "1952").

Tax made explicit a further implication of the developing action anthropology agenda in a commencement address he gave in 1954 at the high school graduation of his elder daughter (12/6: "The Freedom to Make Mistakes"). After discussing parent/child relationships, he turned to "dependent communities," which were not children, which had more "collective adult wisdom" than administrators, and which did not share the same cultural assumptions. The attempt to impose the values of the "dominant culture" on such communities was fundamentally misguided. Furthermore, it had ramifying consequences in the sphere of colonial policy, since "we are now in an era when, in many parts of the world, colonies which are not given the freedom to make their own decisions, will take that freedom"—a prediction Tax left unelaborated, but which suggests an awareness of impending colonial transformation not generally characteristic of early 1950s anthropology (in Gearing et al. 1960:249–50).

After having previously been turned down by both the Ford Foundation and the Wenner-Gren Foundation, the Fox Project received funding from the reform-oriented Schwartzhaupt Foundation in 1954. Although Tax continued to act as advisor, on-site activities were left in the hands of the various summer student groups and the several early participants who maintained a continuing relation to the project—notably Robert Reitz, who became field director in 1955. Throughout this period the participants carried on extended discussions of general policy issues (the means-ends problem, the problem of competing values, and the freedom to choose) as well as of more conventionally theoretical aspects of their work, including its implications for a "looser" actor-choice concept of culture—anticipating, in a general way, theoretical tendencies of the 1990s (Gearing et al. 1960:167, et passim). Given the predominant impulse to activism, however, and the orientation of the Schwartzhaupt Foundation, such theoretical concerns were subordinated to a series of activities that to the external observer might well have seemed like conventional race relations and social welfare work. These included seminars and media programs intended to raise the consciousness of the local white community, a scholarship program to encourage Fox young people to go to college, and a native craft industry called Tamacraft, all of which, in one way or another, ran up against the ideology of assimilationism either in the white community or among the "traditionalist" and "progressivist" factions among the Fox. Furthermore, despite the emergent emphasis on Fox agency, projects were characteristically initiatives of the anthropologists. They were not insensitive to Fox response: when Tax arrived unannounced with a film crew to make a documentary of a peyote ceremony, in order to demonstrate that it was a legitimate church, and the Fox debated among themselves whether this larger goal was worth "defiling" a single ritual, Tax quickly withdrew—realizing suddenly that his plan was "akin to asking a man to deliver his wife to a lecherous creditor to save the family from ruin" (Gearing et al. 1960:305–

6). Major projects, however, depended heavily on the participation of the anthropologists. When Reitz, the organizer and manager of the Tamacraft program, moved to Chicago in 1958, to serve as director of the American Indian Center, the program fell apart, and could not be resurrected when local white businessmen sought to reestablish it as an assembly line enterprise (Foley 1999).

By that time, the Fox Project itself had come to an end, without producing a synthetic volume or a final evaluation.[4] The second edition of the *Documentary History* compiled by several key project members ended in ambivalently self-critical indeterminacy, and a sharply critical evaluation volunteered by a University of Iowa economist was never published (Gearing et al. 1960:422–26; Spence 1973; cf. Foley 1999). More generally, the missionary optimism of some of Tax's earlier presentations of action anthropology at professional meetings contrasts sharply with the "Reflections on Action Anthropology" he drafted 20 years later: "we have generally found ourselves faced with intractable human situations, for which reason we could be useful not in solving community problems but in learning and understanding, with the people, that they were indeed intractable"—with the consolation that "a community of people in trouble likes it when somebody understands that it isn't their fault" (282/2; cf. Tax 1958b:18). In 1986, a sympathetic evaluation of the action anthropology movement offered several reasons for its failure to enter the mainstream of anthropology. In an era given to theory building and "social science as social physics," it was seen as neither theoretically fruitful nor rigorously scientific. Because Tax's leadership was permissive, action anthropology was unable to constitute a "core of coherent tradition"; because his students either chose to work outside of or had difficulty finding jobs in academic departments, they remained outside "the reward structure" of anthropology. In this context, action anthropology was unable to establish itself in the important centers of graduate anthropological training—including, most strikingly, the University of Chicago (Rubenstein 1986:270, 273).

From the point of view of disciplinary ideology, action anthropology was caught in the contradictions of cultural relativism and universalism in a period of neo-evolutionary resurgence. Critics at the time, notably Tax's mentor Redfield, were troubled by the possibility of "people self-determining themselves to be cannibals," or the Fox asking for "political self-determination and admission to the United Nations" (Redfield 1958:22; Tax 1958b:19). Tax's students, on the other hand, saw themselves as defenders of the "rich-

---

4. In this respect, it was not atypical of long-term projects of the 1950s, including notably Kluckhohn's comparative study of values in five southwestern cultures, and Redfield's comparative study of civilizations. From this and other points of view, it would be interesting to compare the various collaborative and comparative projects initiated in the postwar period, a number of which are discussed individually in Foster et al. 1979.

ness of cultural variability" at a time when the "pendulum seems to have swung to a theoretical position antithetical to cultural pluralism" (65/5: C. Sutton/ST 5/21/56; cf. 132/3: N. Lurie/ST 1/31/64). However, the tension between cultural relativism and cultural evolution was manifest also in Tax's own thinking. He objected on several occasions to the use of the modifier "primitive" to describe any presently existing group (e.g. 26/3: ST/F. Gearing 10/29/59) and insisted on the cultural specificity of each. But in his pan-Indian moments, he tended to characterize American Indians as a whole in terms of value contrasts resonant of the polar oppositions of nineteenth-century evolutionism—notably, communitarianism as opposed to individualism—and to gloss this contrast in what might well be called "soft primitivist" terms: not only was "Indian culture" better for Indians, it would be "better for many of us," ameliorating "some of the evils of our own culture" (64/8: "Last on the Warpath"; cf. Lovejoy & Boas 1935).

Well before the end of the Fox Project as such, the focus of Tax's anthropological activism on Native American issues had shifted from the local community of the Fox to the national community of an emergent pan-Indianism. In 1954, as editor of the *American Anthropologist*, he helped organize a Wenner-Gren Supper Conference bringing together John Provinse of the Bureau of Indian Affairs and a group of anthropologists, to "examine objectively" the "basic assumptions of our national approach to the Indian problem" (Tax 1954:387). The conferees were in "complete agreement" that the prediction of total assimilation was "unwarranted" and that the government role was to "develop" rather than to "manage" reservation resources, with an added acknowledgment that greater attention should be paid to "the assumptions held by the Indians themselves" (Provinse et al. 1954:388, 393; cf. STP 215/7). As Indian voices grew louder and more radical in the years after 1960, Tax continued to speak out on matters of Indian policy in various contexts. During the Johnson administration he served on a presidential task force on Indian policy (112/4: ST/Ablon 11/4/66; 152/7); in 1968 he organized a session of the Anthropological Association on hunting and fishing rights (135/6: ST/ W. Chino); in the early 1970s he was active in support of the Indian occupation of Alcatraz and on the issues of Indian land claims (155/6: ST/M. Wax 5/21/71, 7/8/71). But his most significant activist contribution was his role in initiating the American Indian Chicago Conference in 1961—an action anthropological extravaganza on the scale of the Darwin Centennial, but oriented toward the future rather than the past, and in the long run a more fruitful realization of the principles of action anthropology than the Fox Project.

The Chicago conference was conceived in the spring of 1960, when the Schwartzhaupt Foundation indicated that it had money available for a conference and Tax thought that the time might be ripe for a general reconsideration of Indian policy.[5] After mulling the matter over during the summer, and after several meetings with Carl Tjerandsen of the foundation in the early fall, Tax forwarded a proposal on November 10. With a new and more receptive administration in Washington, the time seemed ripe to produce a general policy document, analogous to the Meriam report, which in 1928 had laid the basis for the "New Deal for Indians" (Prucha 1985:62). Such a document would draw on the experiences resulting from that earlier policy and on the subsequent development of the social sciences, in a world situation which required "that we resolve our domestic 'colonial' problems" (in Lurie 1961:482). When Tax arrived at the Denver convention of the National Congress of American Indians on November 14, he received word that the foundation had agreed to provide $10,000, and later that night "got [the] idea for the first time that Indians might write [the] first draft [of such a] report" (217/3: "Diary"; cf. Tjerandsen 1980:64). Presented in these terms, the conference proposal won the unanimous approval of the Indians present, and at the conclusion of the Denver convention Tax discussed further plans with Helen Peterson, director of the National Congress, and D'Arcy McNickle, who as chair of an all-Indian steering committee was to play the leading role in drafting the conference program document (217/3: "Diary"; Tax 1968; Parker 1992:192–93).

From this point on Tax conceived of his own role as that of coordinator of a pan-Indian event. He played it, however, in a characteristically activist manner, with the help of a small staff of current and recent students associated with action anthropology, including Reitz as associate and Nancy Lurie as assistant coordinator. Within several days of the Denver convention Tax and McNickle had arranged for the annual Summer Workshop in Indian Affairs — a program for Indian college students Tax had helped to organize in 1956 to develop a pan-Indian leadership cadre — to meet in Chicago at the time of the conference (217/3: "Diary"; cf. Wax 1961; Parker 1992:187). By a week later, Tax had gained the cooperation of a number of anthropologists at the American Anthropological Association meetings, and broached with the National Broadcasting Company the possibility of television coverage for what was originally called the American Indian Charter Convention but was soon retitled when the last two words seemed likely to discourage participation by some Indians (Lurie 1961:482–83). Over the next six months he and his staff served as a money-raising, publicity, and local arrangements committee, developing a mailing list of more than 5,000 (4,000 of whom were Indians), and preparing a series of information packets with materials on his-

5. In reconciling minor discrepancies among several accounts of the conference (Ablon 1979; Blanchard 1979; Lurie 1961; Tjerandsen 1980), I have relied on Tax's "Diary" of the genesis and early organization of the conference (217/3: a copy of a document included in conference materials he deposited in the Smithsonian's National Anthropological Archives in 1969).

torical, legal, and economic issues, including a map showing the present distribution of Indian population that two of Tax's graduate students, Sam Stanley
and Bob Thomas, had prepared in 1956 to document the persistence of tribal
groups. By the time of the conference in June, these materials, along with
drafts of other documents, had helped to focus discussion at nine regional
and more than two hundred local community, tribal, or intertribal meetings.
These discussions were summarized in six "progress reports," edited by Lurie,
and Tax as coordinator sent out several letters which, by articulating what
"everybody seems to want," sought to smooth over "factional" differences between "traditionalists" and those who favored "working with Congress and
the Administration" on economic, educational and health programs (216/11;
cf. Lurie 1961:483, 488–91; Ablon 1979:447–49).

In the end, "everybody" came, including 467 Indians from 90 tribes or
bands, swelled by several hundred relocated Chicago Indians who joined in
feasting and dancing at Pow Wow events on the Midway long into the night.
There were also about 150 white observers—anthropologists, lawyers, and
representatives of religious and Indian rights groups, including members of
a Department of the Interior Task Force on Indian Affairs—all of whom sat
quietly in the plenary sessions, and after some debate on the floor, were also
allowed, on the same basis, to attend small group meetings. Discussions were
open-ended and upon occasion heated, and decisions were in principle almost
overly rule-governed, with tribal delegates guaranteed 60 percent of the total
vote and the remainder given to those (including non-reservation Indians)
who came without formal delegate status. But in practice issues were decided
quite informally, by voice vote or a simple show of hands, after something
approximating consensus had been achieved by talking.

As finally approved, the Declaration of Indian Purpose called for the end
of termination and for the adoption, as "official policy," of "the principle of a
broad educational process" intended to remove "the disabilities which have
presented Indians from making full use of their resources"—both advanced
in terms of "a positive national obligation to modify or remove the conditions
which produce the poverty and lack of social adjustment" which were "the
outstanding attributes of Indian life today" (AICC 1961:5). Specific proposals relating to economic development, health, welfare, housing, and education anticipated the programs of the subsequent "war on poverty"—with a
strong emphasis on the active participation of Indians in the planning process, conceived as a "total program" (7, 19). Quoting Chief Justice John Marshall on treaties as compacts "between two nations or communities having
the right of self-government," the document affirmed the "universal desire
of all Indians that their treaties and trust protected lands remain intact and
beyond the reach of predatory men" (16, 15). To this end, it called for the
"return in trust" of those parts of the public domain deemed "excess" or "non-

Clyde Warrior and Ben Bearskin, Sr., leading Sol Tax to the stage of Mandel Hall at the American Indian Chicago Conference, 1961. (Photo by F. Peter Weil. Courtesy of the Newberry Library.)

essential" to the purpose for which they had been "originally taken," or which had been "consumed by termination policy." To counter recent federal and state attempts to tax Indian property, it proposed legislation clearly exempting any "income received by an enrolled member of an Indian tribe, which is derived from tribal, allotted and restricted Indian lands" (15). One of the major potential lines of division—between reservation and relocated urban Indians—was smoothed over by recommendations that the needs of "off-reservation Indians," while not specified, must be "taken into account" (17–18). Another division, between assimilationists and defenders of traditional identity, was bridged in three opening statements: a Creed, a brief Statement of Purpose, and an American Indian Pledge," the latter a victory for the "patriotic American Indians," but adopted, as Tax later recalled, by "voice vote without noticeable dissent" (Tax 1968a).

Taken together, these preliminary passages may be read as an attempt to find an energizing rhetoric to unite the otherwise divisive forces of factionalism. Affirming the "inherent right of all people" to "spiritual and cultural" autonomy, they insisted on the need to "defend our Indian culture" from "being absorbed by American society." To this end, however, they appealed to the principles of American democracy ("life, liberty and the pursuit of happiness" in a "free society")—prefaced by a pledge, at "this critical hour of human history," to offer "our lives, our property and our sacred honor" in its defense, and to resist "the promoters of any alien form of government" in their effort to "plant upon our shores or within any of our institutions" a contrary "ideology or way of life" (AICC 1961: inside cover, 4–5). Whatever the specific authorship or motivation of these exhortations, they represented a rhetorical compromise consistent with the facilitative style of the conference coordinator, who at the final Pow Wow was presented with an enormous peace pipe, and at the close of the conference the next day, with a feathered headdress (Lurie 1961:498). Although President Kennedy had not accepted an invitation to send a personal representative to receive the final document, the incoming Secretary of the Interior, Morris Udall, arranged for Indian leaders to present it to him at the White House, an event that Tax attended with some reluctance, having initially felt that it should be "an all-Indian ceremony" (216/10: ST/W. Wall 8/6/62).

Neither all Indians nor their action anthropology facilitators agreed about the Chicago conference's accomplishments. In contrast to Tax's recollections of relatively easy accord, Lurie's contemporary "official" account indicated that there had been changes in the three drafts of the declaration, in which an original call for the abolition of the Bureau of Indian Affairs was gradually softened until the version passed at the conference offered only the "urgent" recommendation that its "present organization" be "reviewed" (1961:484–45). To Lurie, traditionalists who at one point spoke out against American

citizenship and sought a restoration of sovereign tribal status and treaty agree-
ments represented a "factionalism based on absolutely irreconcilable basic assumptions," in sharp contrast to the position of "politically shrewd" assimilationists, who regarded such demands as "seditious." She predicted that those
who hoped the conference would establish "a new nation or series of nations"
would "naturally consider the AICC a total failure" (495). On the other hand,
the leading assimilationists later viewed their achievement of the "pledge" as
having "frustrated an un-American conspiracy"—and were in turn regarded
by more radical action anthropologists as having "disrupted" the conference
(119/6: ST/L. Morrisett 1/14/66; 156/6: ST/M. Wax 1/21/72). Indeed, the
Carnegie Cross-Cultural Education Project carried on by several Tax-trained
action anthropologists in eastern Oklahoma between 1962 and 1968 was almost run aground by charges from the Cherokee establishment (headed by
an executive of the Phillips oil company) that the project was an attempt at
retaliation by Tax (a "Zionist Communist" from the "'pink' University of
Chicago") for their role at the Chicago conference (A. Wahrhaftig in Pavlik
1998:96–97; cf. Wax 1971:279–362).

A radically different view of the Chicago conference was taken by a newly
emergent group of young pan-Indian activists, some of them members of the
Summer Workshops in Indian Affairs who at Tax's initiative had been invited to Chicago. According to their later recollection, they at first regarded
the conference as a gathering of "Uncle Tomahawks" who offered "the old
song and dance to a slightly new anthropological tune" (Clyde Warrior in
Steiner 1968:36). Meeting among themselves as a "youth caucus," however,
they were "soon chairing many of the conference committees," and they led
in forestalling an attempt to table the statement of purpose—which as passed,
"had mostly what we wrote" (Mel Thom in Steiner 1968:37). Whatever the
factional specifics of its authorship, the statement ended with a ringing affir-
mation of Indian intention to hold on to "the few poor parcels they still retain"
of the American continent "as earnestly as any small nation or ethnic group
was ever determined to hold to identity and survival" (AICC 1961:19). And
within weeks of the Chicago conference 10 of the young radicals had recon-
vened in Gallup, New Mexico, to found the National Indian Youth Council,
which played an important leadership role in the activist struggles of the 1960s
and 1970s (Steiner 1968:303–5; cf. Ablon 1979; Cornell 1988; Pavlik 1998).

Having previously offered action anthropology as a response to colonial
liberation movements, Tax was by no means unsympathetic to the new pan-
Indian radicals, who saw their movement as part of a country-wide youth rebellion "in an era of resurgent nationalism among dark-skinned people the
world over" (Vine Deloria in Steiner 1968:44). But his most important contribution to the pan-Indian political activism that was "kicked off" by the
conference and rose to a peak over the next 15 years had surely been his role

in organizing the Chicago conference itself (Cornell 1988:188–89). The various facilitating processes he led in developing—the progress reports (with their summaries of tribal and intertribal pre-conferences), the packets of information (with their material on economic and legal issues and their historical accounts of land seizures and treaty negotiations), the mailing lists themselves (which were later used to build the circulation of a national newspaper, *Indian Voices*), along with the "mingling and mixing" and the political debate of the conference itself—taken together, helped to constitute a supratribal communication network which was a vehicle for the emergence of a new pan-Indian self-consciousness (Ablon 1979; cf. Steiner 1968:37; Cornell 1988; Lurie 1999).[6]

From *Current Anthropology* to Tamu Tamu: Tax as Grassroots Impresario of a Multivocal World Anthropology

During the same decade when Tax was developing the method of "action anthropology," he was also enlarging the stage upon which it was to be enacted, until by the time of the American Indian Chicago Conference, that stage encompassed all the world. In general, the internationalization of American anthropology in this period was closely tied to American overseas interests, and in a broadly contextual way this could perhaps be argued as well for Tax. But unlike many other anthropologists in this period, he was not involved in governmental anthropology during World War II or in the various "development" or defense-related governmental enterprises of the post war and Cold War period (see below, p. 253). In contrast, Tax's international involvement grew much more directly out of his professional and action anthropology commitments.

As early as the 1940s, Tax's Latin Americanist activities had a distinctly international flavor, both in the encouragement of anthropological work by Mexican students and in the multinational participation in the 1949 Americanist Congress. In retrospect, however, he dated the beginning of his involvement in "world anthropology" to the 1952 Wenner-Gren symposium. Tax had not been involved in the planning for this "World Survey of the Status of Anthropology." It was originally conceived by Paul Fejos, the foundation's director of research, and developed by A. L. Kroeber and a com-

---

6. As is the case with some other spheres of Tax's activity, many aspects of his involvement in Native American affairs go unmentioned here, including his role in the Chicago American Indian Center (STP 113, 114; Tax 1988:20) and the Native American Educational Service (STP 137–42).

mittee including anthropologists of the various subdisciplines and major academic centers—on which the Chicago representative was Washburn. Nor did
Tax contribute one of the "inventory papers." But his presence as a participant and his leading role in editing the appraisal volume greatly enlarged the
international sphere of his activities: of 81 participants in the symposium,
27 were from countries outside the United States, ranging beyond Europe
and Latin America to include India, Thailand, Indonesia, and Japan (Tax
et al. 1953:377–79; Fejos 1953). Retrospectively, he saw the conference as "a
launching pad for a new career" (282/1: "Do Good, Young Man").

As a follow-up to the symposium, the Wenner-Gren Foundation experimented with a *Yearbook of Anthropology*, one volume of which was produced
in 1955, and reprinted in part as *Current Anthropology* the following year
(Thomas 1955, 1956). Feeling that this had been too great a drain on the foundation's resources, Fejos asked Tax (who had recently completed his term as
editor of the *American Anthropologist*) to develop an alternative plan to "continually keep scholars abreast of new knowledge" (Tax 1965:243). Tax's own
contribution to the *Yearbook* had been a historical and programmatic defense
of the "integration of anthropology," both as a disciplinary tradition and as
an international "group of intercommunicative scholars" (1956a:315, 321).
Having recently presented to the Philadelphia meetings of the International
Congress of Anthropological and Ethnological Sciences a plan for a world
journal to be called *Humana*, Tax saw Fejos' proposal as an opportunity "to
develop new patterns of worldwide intercommunication in the profession"
(78/5: ST/G. Willey 5/6/58). At first he thought in terms of biennial review
volumes leading in a decade to a follow-up volume to *Anthropology Today*,
a concept later realized as the *Biennial* and *Annual Review[s] of Anthropology*
(Siegel 1959–65). Reluctant, however, to implement this plan without discovering what "the scholars of the world" thought "most useful," Tax embarked on what was to become a transglobal series of regional conferences.
After preliminary meetings in the United States, he crossed the Atlantic in
July and August of 1958 to meet with anthropologists in six western European
countries, culminating in a gathering of 14 at Burg Wartenstein, the Austrian
castle recently renovated to serve as a Wenner-Gren conference center. What
emerged from the discussion was the journal *Current Anthropology*, which Tax
edited for the first 15 years of its existence.[7]

7. Unless otherwise specified, the present account is based on "The History and Philosophy
of *Current Anthropology*" (Tax 1965), which incorporated material from the "pre-issue" of the
journal (Tax 1959a), along with the text of a long paper Tax presented to the 1964 Moscow Congress of Anthropological and Ethnological Sciences. An illuminating perspective is provided
also in a later course lecture in which Tax reflected more systematically (and retrospectively) on
CA as an application of the principles of action anthropology, in the context of his early editorial activities, as well as his emerging thought on "non-hierarchical" principles of "community
development" (Tax 1975b).

Although there was to be much subsequent discussion, and a series of evolutionary modifications, the fundamental character of *Current Anthropology* was established at the Burg Wartenstein meeting. Representing the "changing sciences of man," the new journal would facilitate "intercommunication among students of man wherever in the world they are working." It was to be "unitary," treating "a single set of cross-cutting materials" available to all students of the sciences of man, "speaking to one another on the same pages in the same language." And it should be "fast and convenient," so that scholars (or "scientists") could easily and quickly "share knowledge of their current activities." To encourage prompter and more flexible communication, *Current Anthropology* would be a journal rather than a yearbook, published in English, because that was "the language currently read by more scholars than any other." Rather than trying to resolve the variation of terminological and disciplinary definition in different national traditions, it would include among the "anthropological sciences" not only physical anthropology, ethnology, prehistory, folklore, linguistics, and social anthropology, but "all of their subsidiary and related sciences by whatever names." It would feature two types of material: "major reviews of subjects of considerable scope" (with an emphasis on "the growing points of anthropology and new evaluations rather than syntheses of what has become well known") and a variety of "current news and reference materials," including news of "research activities and discoveries," surveys of "guides to materials," and requests for information (Tax 1965: passim).

With the basic orientation defined, Tax put the principle of intercommunication into peripatetic practice, emplaning on a series of four trips that during the next year carried him (still by propeller-driven craft) through "all of Europe, Asia, Central and South America, and Africa." Although every two or three days brought "a new country, new language, new time, new money, new people," the format was more or less standard: advance planning through some colleague or personal friend, a meeting around a long table in some local institution, an hour-long presentation by Tax, four hours of questions and discussion, a luncheon or dinner, with more discussion, followed often by a party. Careful notes were taken at each stop, so that new developments could be incorporated into the next presentation of the plan — although once beyond the western European orbit, "very few changes were suggested." By Tax's account, the response was always enthusiastic: overcoming "cultural and national and political barriers and economic inequalities," the conferees saw themselves as "architects of a new structure": evidence that "the world over" anthropologists shared "the same values" (Tax 1965).

Returning "still breathless" from his "fourth long journey" as the Johnny Appleseed of World Anthropology, in September 1959 Tax sent out to some 3,000 anthropologists a 16-page "pre-issue" of *Current Anthropology: A World Journal of the Sciences of Man*, in which he included a list of the 650 people he had met with, the dates and places of 44 meetings, a world map of his stops, and pictures of the gatherings, along with a brief history of the project, and most important, a Letter to Associates. For though *Current Anthropology* invited nonassociates to subscribe, it was intended as a "social experiment": the establishment of a "community" of "professional anthropologists" (all of whom were to be listed in the first number). The associates would receive the journal for 20 percent of its published subscription rate, in acknowledgment of their responsibilities as members of the community: to enlarge it by nominating "eligible persons" (including students at a special rate); to pay their associates' fees without reminder or bill; to read the journal "as soon as it was delivered" six times a year; to use the enclosed Associate Reply Letters to respond to questions the editor raised; to offer suggestions for future articles ("or other material"), including those they might provide; and to "respond promptly" to the editor's requests, including those for "comments on articles" (Tax 1959a).

What evolved as the "CA* Treatment"—the comments published with particular articles—was perhaps the most distinctive feature of *Current Anthropology*, and one of many topics of continuing discussion in the Letter to Associates enclosed in every number, in which Tax summarized the Associate Reply Letters and addressed the issues raised in them. Originally, Tax had thought of review articles as symposia "without having to travel," a means of "pooling capabilities" in areas "increasingly difficult for one person to cover single-handed," and of "drawing in people at the borderlines of our science." Once "provisionally accepted," review articles would be duplicated and sent to readers, including names suggested by the author and by other experts in the particular field or at its margins. After reading the comments, the author would advise Tax whether they were best incorporated into the argument with acknowledgment or included with rejoinder, so that each review article would include a core statement, supplementary information, and rebuttal. Over the first several years, however, this scheme was modified, in part because of the expense involved, and in part because of complexities of authorship—including the responses of readers incorporated into the revised version. In the end, what emerged, after considerable discussion in the pages of the journal, was a simplified pattern of article, responses, and rebuttal—preserving community interchange, but not at the expense of individual authorship (Tax 1965).

The problem of CA* Treatment was only one of a number of issues considered in the continuing exchange of letters between Tax and the associates: they discussed whether to print book reviews, whether to reprint articles from other journals, whether to print translations, the length of articles (generally, much longer than in the normal journal), whether purely local events should be included in a calendar, what kinds of institutions should be included in a directory of anthropological institutions, whether to include a section on the travel plans of associates (so that they could contact other associates along the way). There were also, however, more systematic preoccupations, including notably the criteria of group membership: the definition of an "amateur" or a "student" (which, given different educational trajectories, varied from country to country); whether an associate who failed to participate should continue as such, or pay the higher rate of a nonassociate "reader"—with Tax, true to character, favoring a permissively inclusive policy. And there was a continuing discussion of language: whether abstracts should be printed in several languages, and if so which ones; whether (given that the publication language was English) British or American spellings should be standard; how to avoid localisms in the use of English; whether the word "primitive" should be used; how to find "non-partisan" and "objective" ways to refer to matters with a political charge (this, in relation to a discussion of research among a group in South Vietnam); whether ad hominem arguments should be allowed (having concluded that his editorial admonition of one Polish scholar for inappropriate language was perhaps his own ethnocentric response to differing national standards of scholarly discourse, Tax was then warned by another Pole that the offender's ad hominem language was not in fact "characteristic" of Polish scholarly discourse). Finally, there was the matter of the predominant role played in the journal by American anthropologists, which Tax met by an appeal to universalist nationality-blindness and editorial optimism. Insofar as the CA community was a "group of individual scholars associated together without respect to national lines," then the "nationality of authors should not concern us." Because it originated in the United States, where geography, language, and culture made "communication easier," it was natural that in the beginning, associates from that country should dominate; fortunately, however, their proportion was less than 40 percent, and in the "latest issue" (in October 1961) "not a single U.S.A. Associate" was listed among the authors (Tax 1965).

All of these questions had in one way or another to do with the nature of the community that was being created, how within it to relate the local and the global, and how to balance the pragmatic demands of publication, the ideal of democratic process, and the goal of scientific truth. Tax spoke of CA as a "new species of scholarly institution"—not a "formal institution" but one "permitted to evolve after the fashion of a 'natural institution,' like the family or a hunting party, with which anthropologists are so familiar." Although he rejected the accusation that CA was "my journal," and resisted playing the role of "umpire," the production of a journal within constraints of time and budget required that he play a more active role than that of coordinator, as he had characterized his contribution to the American Indian Chicago Conference. He rejected manuscripts, he proposed experiments, he resolved discussions of policy, sometimes siding with the minority opposing some change, on the grounds that they were a substantial group and had made arguments that had to be taken seriously. Some associates complained that he was too "democratic" when he believed he was simply being "empirical" — trying always to achieve a "workable compromise between 'democracy' and 'practice,'" trying to "learn what our needs are and to satisfy them, while continuing to ask whether I have correctly interpreted and effectively acted upon the data" (Tax 1965).

Reviewing CA's first five years, Tax clearly felt that democratic empiricism was working well: "if it is true that science thrives to the degree that exchange of knowledge is free, CA does something for the sciences of man." Indeed, he was so pleased with its success that he proposed a kind of pyramid scheme: if each associate would seek out 20 nonanthropologist specialists in surrounding fields, the network of communications might be extended to 60,000; discounting duplications, one could still imagine "10,000 or more biologists, geologists, social scientists, philologists, artists, musicians, historians, philosophers, etc., etc.," who would be interested in the journal (Tax 1965:250). That vision was never to be realized, and although his hopes for CA remained high at the time of his resignation as editor in 1974 (Tax 1975b:1), it seems likely that over time Tax himself might have felt that CA had lost some of its reformist dynamism. But he surely appreciated the rising proportion of its subscribers who by the early 1980s came from outside the United States (Stocking, personal correspondence with the University of Chicago Press 4/20/81), and, from a later perspective, the way in which his venture may be seen to anticipate some of the possibilities of scholarly interchange in the age of fax, e-mail, and the World-Wide Web (Tax 1988:20; cf. Harnad 1997:1048). And in the 1960s and early 1970s, it was an important forum in the discussion of issues raised by the radical critique of postwar anthropology: notably, the problems of relativity, relevance, reflexivity, and ethics in ethnography (e.g. CA 9:391–436: "Social Responsibilities Symposium").

During the same period, Tax was busily engaged in pursuing his vision of a "world anthropology" in other venues of international scholarly organization: specifically, the International Congress of Anthropological and Ethnological Sciences. Founded in 1934, the congress met twice before World War II, first in London and four years later in Copenhagen. After a 10-year lapse, it met again in Brussels in 1948, where an organizing committee was established to create an international scientific union of the sort UNESCO was then encouraging. Although the committee had not completed its work by the time of the 1952 Vienna meeting of the congress, the International Union of Anthropological and Ethnological Sciences was formally established at the Philadelphia meeting in 1956, and in 1968 the union and the congress were officially integrated. In the later retrospective outline of his career,

Tax included under the heading "warp threads" brief phrases about each of the congresses he attended: "The Philadelphia Congress, 1956—thoughts of the whole world"; "The Paris Congress, 1960—Czech rebellion"; "The Moscow Congress, 1964—worth it?"; "The Tokyo Congress, 1968—opportunity for a TEST" (282/1: "Do Good, Young Man"). To be tested was whether the congress, which even in Tokyo was "international" only with respect to Europe and the United States, could actually become globally international. Funded largely by Japanese industry, the Tokyo meeting was "beautifully hosted" but "small," and it seemed "genuinely problematic" whether countries like India, Nigeria, or Brazil "could ever host a full-scale Congress." Indeed, "the concept of International Congresses itself seemed endangered." At the Moscow meeting in 1964, Italy and West Germany had competed for the right to be host in 1973, but in 1966 both withdrew for "lack of local financial support," and the United States delegation stepped into the breach. Elected president of the International Union at the Tokyo meeting, Tax took on the responsibility for planning the 1973 meeting in Chicago (282/1: "Do Good, Young Man").

Given his previous experience and his expansive personality, it followed almost inevitably that Tax would conceive of the Chicago congress as not only "truly international," but also as "the most ambitious ever"—even, as he described it later in a newspaper interview, "mammoth" (Hafferkamp 1973:2).[8] The first and critical hurdle was to find funding, a challenge complicated by the fact that, because this was the second International Union meeting in the United States, the "usual sources" were likely to provide only token support. Tax's solution was to reconceptualize the congress, so that its three major components were seen not as money-spending, but as money-raising, activities. Rather than being the outcome of the congress, the production of books would be its generative telos; Tax accomplished this transformation by convincing the Dutch publisher Mouton to provide $200,000 for "general expenses" as an advance on the royalties of the series of books that the congress would produce. Taking advantage of the fact that "in this generation" the topically focused scientific conference with precirculated papers had become "a major means of scientific development," Tax enlarged the scope of the congress to include a series of "pre-Congress conferences" that might command funding from particular sources, thereby defraying the travel expenses of con-

8. One possible way of interpreting Tax's career is as a series of explosions in the arenas of his activist impulse, a reiterative pattern, each instance of which foreshadowed some aspect of the succeeding manifestation, all of them culminating in the 1973 Chicago meetings of the ICAES—from this point of view clearly the climactic event of his career. The present account is derived largely from my own file of ICAES documents, augmented at points by Tax's account in STP 76/2, and informed also by materials in the 23 boxes of congress records (see Manuscript and Interview Sources, ICAES).

gress delegates and producing books whose royalties could go to general congress purposes; modified as a way to support particular topical sessions, this approach provided over $200,000 more. A third innovation, the financial impact of which was less easily measured, was to have postcongress "cooperative programs" involving individual scholars and educational and research institutions in the Midwest, as a further means of supporting their travel expenses (GS/ICAES; STP 76/2; cf. ICAES Box 14).

Nominally integrated around the theme "One Species, Many Cultures," the content of the congress was generated from below, in a grassroots style that Tax himself spoke of as "coordinated anarchy" (Hafferkamp 1973:2). By January 7, 1972, the early announcements of the congress had elicited almost 100 proposals for conferences, and over 800 individually volunteered papers, which Tax and his staff sorted into 19 major groups, ranging from "history, theory and research methods" through topical concerns in sociocultural anthropology, to major subdisciplinary areas, and then to nine categories devoted to major geographic areas—with 149 papers left over as "undecided or unclassified." Recruiting session organizers and volume editors (usually the same person performing both functions), Tax encouraged each of them to "creatively imagine his good book," to "fill in gaps" by soliciting papers, and "with our help to influence the direction in which the papers are written." Since the precirculation of the papers would in effect constitute a form of publication, it should be possible for the editor "without too much damage to eliminate a few of what he thinks are very bad papers from the published volume": instead of "officially rejecting papers," they "could simply be returned to authors for revision" (GS/ICAES; ICAES Boxes 9 & 17).

Within this framework, congress activities developed in hypertrophic manner. There were 3,000 (later, "close to 4,000") participants from a hundred foreign countries, all of them kept track of by a "computerized registration system." Those without adequate funding had been assisted by "extra fancy invitations which look[ed] so impressive that a poor but enterprising anthropologist could use it to finagle money from his own government or university" (Hafferkamp 1973:3); upon arrival in Chicago they were greeted with a $300 subsidy to cover local expenses. To accommodate the delegates, the congress preempted Chicago's largest hotel, with overflow at the nearby YMCA. The inaugural plenary session was held in Louis Sullivan's gilded architectural-landmark Auditorium Theatre. All told, there were 2,200 papers, precirculated to session participants, so that the sessions themselves could be devoted entirely to discussion, with provisions for tape recording. There were also 40 translators in four rooms offering simultaneous translations of some sessions into English, French, German, Russian, and Spanish, as well as translators for other languages, who "could enter the system through intermediary translation." Aside from the academic sessions, there were concerts by Pete Seeger's

American Folk Concert Singers and the Chicago Children's Choir, as well as ethnographic films and a feature-length video about Chicago's ethnic groups, with visits to Chicago's ethnic communities. Harking back to the American Indian Chicago Conference, there was a Native American Pow Wow and a Youth for Mankind conference, with high school representatives from 17 countries. And for evening entertainment, there was an opera, specially commissioned for the occasion (76/2; ICAES Boxes 5 & 11).

The idea had come to Tax early in the planning, as a way to kill two birds with one stone: on the one hand, to memorialize the occasion by the creation a cultural pluralist artwork "on the order of Leonard Bernstein's 'Mass,' which had been commissioned by the Kennedy family"; on the other, to raise money from its performances, and from educational TV, and perhaps even from commercial networks. So he wrote to Gian Carlo Menotti, who first thought it a joke, but then signed on for $25,000. In the spirit of *Amahl and the Night Visitors*, the plot involved a family of Indonesian war victims "somehow magically transported" to the apartment of a Chicago family, and the ensuing problems of cultural communication as the two families "bickered with one another in English and Indonesian" (Hafferkamp 1973:2–3). Unfortunately, the libretto and music for *Tamu, Tamu* (roughly, in Indonesian, "The Arrivals," or "Guests") arrived in Chicago only shortly before the congress opened, and the production suffered as a result. Unfavorably reviewed by critics—who apparently misheard Indonesia as Indochina—*Tamu, Tamu* sold less than a third of the seats during 16 performances at the Studebaker Theater over the 10 days of the congress. Far from raising money, it was responsible for a hefty $130,000 loss to the congress's budget deficit. Nor was that the end of the congress's financial difficulties. The indeterminate number of books that were to have been money-raisers mushroomed to nearly a hundred, which took some years to produce, and 15 years later had still not sold well enough to realize the advance on royalties provided by Mouton (ICAES, Boxes 5 & 12).

Given the pragmatic optimism that filled and overflowed the spaces of his personality, it was unthinkable that Tax should have regarded the congress as other than successful. Reminiscing in 1988, the "only disappointment" he acknowledged was that the volume of congress proceedings which was to have been sent free to all members "was denied publication by the Berlin firm" that in the meantime had purchased a bankrupted Mouton (Tax 1988:8). Among the 92 titles that were actually published, it is worth noting that, although the congress papers had been originally categorized in rather conventional terms, a number of them did in fact reflect the late 1960s radical critical cry for a more "relevant" anthropology. And as Tax himself argued, the congress did substantially advance the globalization of the discipline: although roughly 82 percent of the papers were by "scholars identified with the industrialized

Sol Tax, Margaret Mead, and Gian Carlo Menotti, seated in the lounge of the Studebaker Theater at the opening performance of *Tamu, Tamu,* August 1973, in front of two unidentified anthropological opera lovers. (Courtesy of the Department of Special Collections, University of Chicago Library.)

world," there were substantial numbers from the rest of the globe, including about 9 percent from Asia-Oceania, 5 percent from Africa (excluding South Africa), and 5 percent from Latin America. At the opening session, Tax had been able to announce that the 1978 congress would be held in India; and it was not until 1998 that the congress again met in Western Europe or the United States. Insofar as world anthropology exists today as an organized entity, it can safely be said that Sol Tax did more than any other individual to bring it into being.[9]

Saving Hyde Park: A Revelatory Local Moment in the Global Trajectory of Action Anthropology

It is tempting to look at Tax's career as series of local community involvements, shifting in site, growing in extent, until they encompassed the world. These included, among others, the Newsboy's Republic in Milwaukee; the local departmental community of Chicago anthropology in the 1930s, reconstructed in the postwar period and transformed after 1960; the larger academic community of Hutchins' University of Chicago, reaching outward over the radio "roundtable" and in the pages of the *Bulletin of Atomic Scientists*; the Native American community of the Mesquakie in the 1930s and the Fox Project in the 1950s, moving beyond to a pan-Indian community at the Chicago conference; the community of Latin Americanist anthropologists, expanding to that of professional anthropologists in the United States, and then stretching beyond to the world community of professional anthropologists through *Current Anthropology* and the International Union of Anthropological and Ethnological Sciences—an expanding life historical sequence of relations between the "local" and the "global."

To further illuminate the geographical and political trajectory of Tax's action anthropology, however, it may help to consider a particular place and moment in this sequence that stands out because of its personal immediacy: the 1950s struggle to "save" Hyde Park, the local community of the University of Chicago. It was a period when the future of the local community itself seemed at risk, and in contrast to his role in the Fox Project, Tax was in-

9. After meetings in Delhi (1978), Quebec and Vancouver (1983), Zagreb (1988), and Mexico City (1993) the congress met in Williamsburg, Virginia, in 1998. Tax would surely have been disappointed that the Williamsburg meeting was minimally funded and poorly attended, with only 800 anthropologists of the predicted 3,000 showing up for its 304 sessions, and with a high percentage of "no show" speakers from the host country—leading one British observer to suggest that "the failure of a significant number of anthropologists and of institutions to support the ICAES would seem to indicate that it simply doesn't count, as it is for the most part a congress of anthropologists from the 'less developed' countries" (Bowman 1998).

volved not only as an anthropologist, but as a resident and citizen whose children went to the neighborhood school and who himself could walk from his home on Woodlawn Avenue to his job at the university. Recounting the episode in 1958, in rhetoric still redolent of the sense of "panic" and "doom" that pervaded Hyde Park in the early 1950s, Tax recalled the "tidal wave of population from the segregated, long-contained black belt" that threatened to "engulf" the community from the northwest in the aftermath of the 1948 Supreme Court decision outlawing restrictive covenants, the means the university and other property owners had previously used to "keep Negroes out." Large apartments were being broken up into small ones, "turning middle-class buildings into rows of tenements along streets rapidly becoming slums." Faced with a "rash of new crimes," people "could not safely walk the streets in the evening except in groups." Increasing numbers of middle-class whites were moving out, and rumor had it that even the university itself had "secretly decided to abandon the neighborhood." Conscious of "the 'changes' that were occurring at the north end of our neighborhood," the "community council" made up of representatives from a variety of local organizations appointed a committee, but "nothing was done." Elsewhere in Chicago, the response had been "rioting, violence, and bombs to keep the Negroes from moving into a white area"—but in "our liberal community, that was unthinkable," and "never even whispered." Instead, in 1949 another community group was formed, "specifically to develop an interracial community of high standards": the Hyde Park–Kenwood Community Conference. In contrast to the community council, it had a more grassroots character, including "middle-class Negroes, as well as whites," and Tax was active in it from the beginning (Tax 1959b:22–23; cf. Hirsch 1983:171).

For several years, the Community Conference organized "block groups," carried out "community surveys," and "developed techniques to control illegal uses of property." But despite "all the work and good will," whites were still leaving, and "the overcrowded black ghetto continued to spill over." The "great breakthrough" came in the spring of 1952, when "planning was still a bad word" and "'race' was still embarrassing," but "everybody was against crime." The conference set up an "emergency committee" (on which Tax played a leading role) to organize a mass meeting. Mobilized by leaflets ("Are You Next? Are You Afraid? Only You Can Smash Crime!") and traumatized by the attempted rape of a university employee's wife, some 2,500 Hyde Parkers came to Mandel Hall on May 19. Immediately before the meeting, the university, which had previously had its head "still in the sand," joined in the planning, and at the meeting itself a resolution was passed forming a new organization, the South East Chicago Commission, which was to be chaired by the chancellor of the university. Although it came to be referred to by some as the Crime Commission, Tax, who drafted the founding resolution, recalled specifically rejecting that negatively charged "bogey word," because the goal was to deal instead with "the causes of crime" ("neighborhood deterioration, etc.") by systematic planning—although that charged word, too, had been avoided (Tax 1956b). Under the aggressive leadership of Julian Levi as executive director, the commission became effectively an arm of the university, using both legislation and "rough, though legal, means to keep out crime and unethical real estate operations." Although the Community Conference "preferred education, grass roots understanding, block organization, good public relations, often pulling the Commission's chestnuts out of the fire," the two groups nevertheless managed to work together—"not always too peacefully—for the same ends." Even so, the neighborhood "continued to change at a dizzying pace": between 1950 and 1956, 20,000 "presumably middle-class people, mainly whites," left Hyde Park, "replaced by 23,000 people, almost all of them presumably poor Negroes." Despite all efforts, "we were really losing our war" (Tax 1959b:25; STP 4/11; cf. Rossi & Dentler 1961:102–55; Abrahamson 1959).

By Tax's account, the turning point came in 1956, three years after he had withdrawn somewhat from community activism upon taking on the editorship of the *American Anthropologist*. That fall he "happened to sit in" on a meeting of the Community Conference committee "charged with maintaining an interracial neighborhood," at which discussion focused on a "new Tenant Referral Service" created to place "white families in dwellings where they were needed to stem the tide." Having learned from experience that "mixed buildings did not work," because of white fears that they inevitably "turn," the committee concluded that the "next line of defense, if we were to have integration," was to have "mixed blocks," in which some buildings would be Negro, and others white, with departing whites replaced by "another white family." While the Referral Service would also attempt to place "middle-class Negro families in blocks which were exclusively white," the committee (which was "interracial") was aware that the new system would inevitably "discriminate in favor of whites." But however "painful" the decision, these "dedicated liberal people" realized that in order to establish "a good mixed neighborhood," they must agree to "a program of racial discrimination which, for any success, implied some sort of quota system." The same moral issue arose in relation to the planning for extensive urban renewal that was being developed at this time. "Any plan to save our neighborhood physically would require reducing the density of population," and since "the most deteriorated parts" would be razed, the people forced out would be "the poor newcomers, the slum dwellers, almost all of whom were Negroes" (Tax 1959b:25–26; cf. Abrahamson 1959:300–304).

Faced with this "moral crisis," Tax had feared that the "great urban renewal program" might fail because "our moral position before the world would become clouded," jeopardizing federal and city approval of the redevelopment plan. To prevent this, it was necessary that "we make clear in our own minds, and for all to see, that we wanted, and would have, a mixed neighborhood in which people of both races, and even poor people of both races, would live and work together"—and this would require "community discussion of the frankest kind on the most delicate issues, out of which would come basic agreement that the kind of community for which we were working was indeed this ideal." Fortunately, however, "exactly this" had occurred "in the past twelve months," and as a result "we cemented our compact with the future." On November 7, 1958, the Chicago City Council approved the redevelopment proposal, and "our plans for an interracial community, which appeared impossible in 1948, a fighting chance in 1952, a nip and tuck possibility in 1956" now seemed "to be well on the way" (Tax 1959b:26).

Although Tax had offered his account as "the whole story" of this struggle, there was one notable and revealing elision: the resistance to redevelopment mounted by the South West Hyde Park Neighborhood Association—a resistance all the more striking in that it was led by St. Clair Drake, one of the several African Americans who had gained a Ph.D. from the Chicago Department of Anthropology, and whose classic work Black Metropolis (co-authored with Horace Cayton) in fact provided the demographic and cartographic base point for Tax's account. Returning in 1955 from a two-year stint of teaching in Ghana, Drake had tried unsuccessfully to buy or rent in the all-white area east of the university, and had instead bought a house in the area that was to be redeveloped. In the summer of 1956, he was elected president of the Neighborhood Association, and in ensuing months led the group's opposition to the university's "heavy-handed" procedures in implementing the redevelopment plans. Drake was apprehensive that the underlying purpose of the whole venture was not community integration, but the restoration of the area "to its former all-white character"—as evidenced by the failure of the South East Chicago Commission to take "a clear stand for 'open occupancy'" in still existing all-white areas (Drake in Rossi & Dentler 1961:167, 184; cf. Drake 1978:98). Troubled by some of the same issues ("do we represent only the well-educated, somewhat liberal, mostly white, middle class and upper middle class?"), leaders of the Community Conference became concerned that the redevelopment plan had "engendered tremendous bitterness and opposition in our community" (Rossi & Dentler 1961:174). However, they continued to support the renewal proposal, which the city's Neighborhood Redevelopment Commission approved in November 1956 by a vote of 2 to 1 (the lone Negro member). Although Drake's Neighborhood Association launched a court fight, it was defeated in October 1958, when the U.S. Supreme Court, by refusing to accept jurisdiction, in effect upheld the legality of the procedures—shortly before the city council vote that

Graduates of the Department of Anthropology of the University of Chicago, at the Twenty-Fifth Anniversary Reunion, 1955, including Robert Armstrong (far left), St. Clair Drake (second from left), Sol Tax (fourth from left), Fay-Cooper Cole (seventh from left) and Fred Eggan (ninth from left). (Courtesy of the Department of Special Collections, University of Chicago Library.)

was the culminating moment in Tax's account (Rossi & Dentler 1961:180; Tax 1959b:26).

Drake was not insensitive to the difficult moral choices faced by participants in the redevelopment struggle, but he saw them in different terms, with a very different existential weighting: it was "unfortunate" that "fate" had put Community Conference leaders (both "white and colored") in a position "where they have to defend their racial liberalism while trying to build an interracial community"; by contrast, however, "every Hyde Park Negro leader is almost driven schizophrenic trying to decide whether to act as a 'Race Man' or in terms of his social class position." Preferring to "fight the germs of malaria" than "the germs of prejudice," Drake left Hyde Park for West Africa, where for several years he headed the sociology department of the University of Ghana (in Rossi & Dentler 1961:180–81).

Tax felt that his own experience in the redevelopment struggle had perhaps been "as much the source of the method and theory of our so-called 'action anthropology' as the work that my students and I have done with American Indians" (1959b:23). But there were significant differences between the situation in Hyde Park, where he participated as "both citizen and anthropologist" in the community in which he lived, and that on the Fox reservation, which he and his students approached from the outside, and to which, however empathic, they remained always outsiders. Obscured by Tax's elision of Drake's Neighborhood Association, these differences have to do with the nature of what Tax referred to as "our" community, the problem of competing values, and the issue of empowerment. Although Tax at several points included "middle-class Negroes" among those in "our" community, his rhetoric suggests that the possessive pronoun did not include the incoming "tidal wave" of ghetto blacks whose "race" and "class" were one (1959b:22–23). Similarly, his references to "overcrowding" do not reflect a relativist awareness of what a contemporary sociological study described as "the conflict of housing values" between those of upwardly mobile in-migrants from the ghetto—for whom overcrowding in a converted Hyde Park apartment might seem, relatively, "luxurious"—and those of the "upper-middle-class whites" whose housing standards were being used to justify condemnation proceedings (Rossi & Dentler 1961:175–76).

There is evidence that Tax (with whom Drake corresponded in regard to the court review [23/4: SCD/ST 9/28/57, ST/SCD 10/2/57]) was not insensitive to some of the issues Drake had raised. In February 1957, speaking to the local council of churches and synagogues on "Color, Class, Culture, and the Conscience of Our Community," Tax suggested that "we liberal intellectuals" faced "a moral crisis" insofar as the Tenant Referral Service would involve "acting for the good end of non-segregation by employing the evil means of racial discrimination." Fortunately, however, it was possible to sidestep the moral compromise implied by the Referral Service, "provided that an absolutely bad criterion like color is assiduously avoided, and provided we remain respectful of legitimate cultural difference" (hanging laundry in the front yard, as opposed to honking to rouse a friend at 5 A.M.—which was in any case illegal), and relied instead on class differences, with the hope that "we" might also find "a means to subsidize poor people we want for neighbors," just as universities provided scholarships for otherwise qualified low-income students (265/7: "Color, Class, Culture, and the Conscience of Our Community," 6–8; cf. 4/1).

Looking to the future in the concluding passage of his later published account, Tax counseled the need for continuing "moral unity," which would be "possible only if for the purpose of racial integration," and which in "the next phase" would "have to face the issues of class differences as well," and eventually, even the "issue of cultural differences," by deciding that "in our particular community, not even middle-class definitions of social behavior are the only ones which we can tolerate." On this basis, "the whole result will be the culmination of a process which proves that a community of people can write its own destiny" (Tax 1959b:27). That they had the power to do so depended, however, on the achievement of moral unity rather than adoption of the tactics of confrontation.

The contrast between confrontation and moral unity achieved through discussion is evident in Tax's reminiscent account of his relation to the Wood-lawn community immediately south of Hyde Park, where Saul Alinsky, the radical community activist of the 1930s "Back of the Yards" struggle, began organizing about 1960 (Brazier 1969:24-30). Although Alinsky was a friend of Tax's, and had been a speaker at the 1952 mass meeting on crime, his approach to community work differed radically. In sharp contrast to the "search for consensus" that had been seen as characteristic of the Hyde Park–Kenwood Community Conference, Alinsky worked by "establishing an enemy—a method related of course to Union labor strategy" (5/4: 5/14/88). Sometime after the Woodlawn campaign began, the University of Chicago Student Government organized a debate between Tax and Nicholas Von Hoffman, who had taken over the management of the Alinsky project, and, according to Tax, "was blaming the university for all the problems of Wood-lawn." When the two were invited by the sponsors to lunch together before-hand, Tax thought that a "friendly discussion in advance would improve the debate," only to discover that Von Hoffman "refused any conversation—playing to the hilt the enemy theme." Tax, however, refused to be cast in the role of "the enemy"—and at the debate itself was supported by his friend Alinsky. But his "conscience nevertheless hurt" when the subsequent success of Alinsky's activity showed that "our local failure to 'do something' about Woodlawn" during the Hyde Park renewal campaign "was not—as I have previously thought—because there was no community organization there through which to work." It was only after his appointment as dean of the Extension School in 1963 that Tax was able to "assuage that guilt" by estab-lishing weekly meetings with the Woodlawn Organization, and offering "the help of a friendly University" in seeking government grants (5/4: 5/14/88).

By 1968, however, Tax's understanding of the relations of blacks and whites in the local community and the nation at large had undergone significant fur-ther development, now explicitly informed by experience in Native Ameri-can action anthropology. Taking advantage of a provision of the Higher Edu-cation Act of 1965 providing funds "to strengthen community service pro-grams of colleges and universities," and drawing on "the experience of the American Indian Center in Chicago as a major example in analyzing for others the problems, limitations, and potentialities of developing indigenous participation," he organized an eight-month-long Community Service Work-shop in which 80 community activists and welfare workers met periodically with "guest discussants" drawn from an equal number of relevant profes-sionals, including local politicians, police officials, welfare and educational administrators, and members of the university faculty (none of them, how-ever, anthropologists). In the style of other Tax conferences, there were plenary sessions, lectures, panel presentations, large and small group dis-cussion sessions, feedback sessions, work sessions—all ultimately brought together in a single volume, including texts of lectures and abstracts from the tapes of the discussions. Although the workshop was designed to bring together "Negroes, Appalachians, American Indians and many others," it "soon became evident that the Negroes were a special group of the disestablished." Their views "dominated the discussions," which took place at "a critical time" in their "independence movement"—as manifest in a shift "from the term 'Negro' to 'Black'" during the course of the workshop. Reflecting on the event in the preface to the published volume (*The People Against the System: A Dialogue in Urban Conflict*), Tax described it as a "happening" in which "establishment" participants (himself included) "learned in part by shock." After "ten years of waning hope," two successive summers of rioting in urban ghetto communities had revealed "the basic nature" of the race relations problem: "these were not race riots in the sense that a white man need feel unsafe in the streets," but "a state of warfare, albeit unorganized, with an implicit demand for complete independence from the colonialist establishment," which Negroes now saw as "forcibly" maintaining "an economy, a 'system,' which does not benefit them" (Tax 1968b:i–iv). Though Tax thought of himself as having been "all my life a great liberal and a nonracist," the concept of "institutional racism"—the "idea that people of goodwill could be part of institutions that made equality impossible"—had "never occurred" to him, but could only be learned "from blacks (then Negroes) from their point of view" (in Rubinstein 1991a:180; cf. STP 274/4:10–14).

Humble Hubris: Politics, Identity, and Personality in the Creation of Community

Some might read Tax's role in the "saving of Hyde Park" simply as a narrative of white middle-class liberal reformism, with a movement from anxious self-interest to paternalistic moralistic activism to gnawing guilt to belated consciousness-raising and compensatory rhetorical involvement. But while this reading might satisfy certain ideological tastes, more omnivorous historiographic appetites may find its image of Tax stunted and anemic, and look for interpretation in more rounded and chromatic terms. Tax was a middle-class liberal academic, but there was radical tendency in his make-up and early experience, which came again to the fore after 1950, and then even more obviously in the later 1960s. And while it was was ultimately and frankly utopian, to be realized in discourse rather than confrontation, it motivated a significant departure from the mainstream of cultural anthropology in the Cold War period. To understand that turning, it may be helpful to look behind the episodes of Tax's professional life to certain underlying aspects of his anthropological persona: his political sympathies, his ethnic identity, and his unique personality. Taken together, these may contribute to an understanding of the potent mix of relativist humility and universalist hubris that impelled his action anthropology through ever larger circles of community.

The earliest surviving statement of Tax's political orientation is an essay written during the spring of 1926 for an English course he took during his quarter at the University of Chicago, entitled "A Proposal for a Union of Humanity: Its Possibility, Probability, and Inevitability" (7/1; cf. 273/12). In the preface, Tax suggested that "the only way to insure lasting peace, and the only means of securing the greatest economic and social benefits from our civilization is to set up a permanent *union* of all people, a union as strong as that which binds the United States of America." What is especially noteworthy about the ensuing argument is its social evolutionary structure: the "striking resemblance between existing savages and man at one stage of evolution" was evidence both for the probability that, "if they survive, they will achieve our stage of civilization," and for the fundamental uniformity of "human nature," which made it "inevitable" that "the race should have done definite things at certain times and under certain circumstances." On this basis, Tax traced a "transition from savage to civil society," and thence by "definite stages" to "unions of societies" and ultimately to "internationalism"—of which the United States was "the world's greatest example": "a union of forty-eight nations, a conglomeration of all races, peoples, nations and religions," within whose borders were "forgotten most provincial prejudices." Just as the Articles of Confederation laid the basis for the United States Constitution, so the League of Nations (lacking an executive branch) would be succeeded by a stronger world union. And while this, too, might be only temporary, over time such imperfect experiences of interdependence would bind nations closer together, until a permanent union would inevitably be established, from which nations would be unable to withdraw or go to war, because they would "no longer be self-sufficing." It was not, however, only economic interdependence that knit together union. Just as the world was already a unit economically, so also was it in morals, "with the same code in force": "all nations are becoming melting pots of races, language, and religion." Paralleling this unity of morals was a developing unity of tolerance and understanding: just as personal dislike was a product of ignorance, so racial hatreds and national prejudices arose "simply because we do not know or understand the people in question." And just as in daily human experience "the longer and the better you know" individuals you dislike, "the more you like them," so also "with nations and races." Indeed, the mere passage of time, enhanced by the "the advent of the printing press and the rapid means of communication and transportation," would itself gradually impel nations to "learn to know, understand, respect, and love every other people on earth." War—"the chief enemy of international understanding and 'good will toward men'"—might for a while recur, but with the growth of understanding the vicious circle of prejudice and war would be replaced by the counter circle from "union to peace to lack of hatred to good fellowship [back] to union," leading inevitably to "the desired results: better conditions of social well-being" (7/1; 273/2).

Viewed from the retrospective standpoint of his life career, Tax's modest "Proposal" can be seen as an intellectual/ideological matrix in which are embedded many of the distinguishing features of his later anthropological activism: the ideal of world fellowship as the inevitable outcome of a universal historical process, foreshadowed by the emergence of civilization out of savagery and the experience of American democracy, impelled by the growth of tolerance and understanding, mediated by advances in communication, within an ever enlarging community of the anthropologically enlightened. Over time, however, this matrix was to be modified in certain crucial respects, which can better be understood in the context of Tax's political and social experience during his years at the University of Wisconsin.

The "better conditions of social well-being" that were the "desired results" of Tax's peace plan reflected his socialist upbringing, which predisposed him to participation in the radical liberal subculture—"communists, atheists, and what not" (6/10)—that he encountered at the University of Wisconsin (Cronon & Jenkins 1994). In the spring of 1928, during his year of enforced leave, Tax had spoken out at a "mass meeting" on behalf of David Gordon, a member of the first class of Alexander Meiklejohn's Experimental College. Gordon had been imprisoned in New York when a judge declared "obscene" an anticapitalist poem he published in the Communist Party's Daily Worker, but after a month had been freed on probation to return to the university (New York Times 5/11/28; cf. Cronon & Jenkins 1994:179–80). In the aftermath of the mass meeting, Tax and two radical friends he had met at the Milwaukee normal school (and who much later "went into the Stalinist underground") founded the Wisconsin Liberal Club (6/8: 1/71). That fall, the three of them, joined by Tax's brother Erwin, who had just entered the Experimental College, began to publish the Wisconsin Student Independent as an organ of radical liberal critique. Tax's own pet political project—an outgrowth of his earlier pacifist "Proposal"—was the "Percentage Peace Plan," a rather complex system whereby individually signed pledges not to participate in war between two nations were to take effect only when a "proportional computation" indicated an equivalent commitment among the population of each nation. The plan, however, was resisted by the "small handful" of communists in the Liberal Club, on the grounds that "a world revolution is necessary before peace can be attained." Although Tax's plan was adopted as Liberal Club policy, after being twice rejected, this provoked a communist takeover at the next annual election of officers, in a successful effort to "kill the Club" (6/9: WSI 1928–29; 6/8: 1/71). Before that happened, however, the issue had been

posed in the *Student Independent* as one of ends and means: in 1917, the bolshe-
viks had "killed the Russian Czar"; in 1929, the British socialists had "kissed
the English King's hand"—an accommodation that noncommunists within
the Liberal Club justified in the hope that "out of free discussion" the "benefits of socialism" might be realized "throughout the civilized world," without
resort to the "alternative" of "armed revolution" (6/9: *WSI* 6/3/29, p. 4).

Tax later recalled the communist takeover as a "lesson in tactics" (Blanchard 1979:421) which by one account convinced him that "revolutionary
ideology was inappropriate for reformist advocacy in American Society"
(J. Bennett 1998:342). But at the time he clearly retained a certain sympathy
for communism as an ideal, practicable in certain groups under certain historical circumstances. In the spring of 1930, while with the Beloit archeological expedition to Algeria, he wrote a short paper arguing that the daily camp
arrangements were "an unconscious experiment in communism," which "in
a week" had changed "our whole culture-pattern" from "the capitalistic to the
communistic" (10/8). And there is evidence to suggest that Tax thought this
new culture-pattern, with its implicit slogan of "from each according to his
abilities, to each according to his needs," was once a general world historical phase like that of "primitive communism." Reviewing a Hollywood film
called *White Shadows in the South Seas*—a story of "primitive happiness" finally
"wrecked" by the "white shadow" of civilizing uplift—he described it as an
answer to "our Imperialists," a "demonstration of why a certain kind of communism could work," and as evidence of "the folly of sacrificing the end of
progress for the supposed means" (6/9: 11/14/28).

However, the same Algerian experience that Tax glossed in terms of a universalist communist ideal also led him to appreciate the relative value of specific ethnic identities. In 1985, Tax recalled that he had "always identified
as Jewish," and had all his life "at least nominally kept Jewish dietary habits
and restrictions and the major holidays." But he had "never been a religious
believer," and cautioned lest "an account like this give an exaggerated impression of my Jewishness, which I never thought of as important in my life"
(5/1: "Jewish-ness File"). Yet on one occasion, he himself suggested a link between his Jewish experience and his anthropological orientation (1981:309),
and unpublished materials from his early manhood suggest that his Jewish-
ness was a more significant factor in the formation of his intellectual identity
than later published autobiographical reflections suggest (e.g. Tax 1988).

His Orthodox parents—who spoke Yiddish "when we four children were
not supposed to understand something"—sent him to Chaider (Hebrew
school), and in 1929 he recalled having learned "enough to become bar mitz-
vahed—and just laugh at the whole thing": "I think I was born an atheist . . .
there never was any conflict" (6/10: "Trad. Sermon"). Apparently autobiographical literary fragments from the same period suggest, however, that he

Sol Tax, as photographed for the invitations to the celebration of his Bar Mitzvah on October 31, 1920. (Courtesy of the Department of Special Collections, University of Chicago Library.)

attended Chaider for five years, that the rabbi punished him physically when he "faltered" in the Hebrew lesson or "dared to question the things that were told *as fact*," and that his father "refused to recognize that any doubt in the matter could exist," so that he was left by himself "to evolve a philosophy that suited his conceptions of the true and the false" (6/11). He knew he "was a Jew," and was "embarrassed" and "a bit scared when passing thru a Polish district" and someone shouted "Dirty Jew." But in high school it was with gentiles that he "argued and played and talked" and had his "puppy love affairs." In short, he led "a typical American life in most respects": he was "a Jew, and a Socialist and a Pacifist, too" but the socialism and pacifism "were more important in my life than the Judaism" (6/10: "Trad. Sermon").

When he was at the University of Wisconsin, however, Tax's Jewish identity took on a greater personal significance. For the first time, most of his friends were "the first American born generation" children of Jewish immigrants. In Hillel, these were "mainly Midwesterners, with scant Jewish education" who had joined largely for social reasons, and, in his own case, also "to release a lot of excess energy which I have always had." But in addition, there were also political friends of the "Greenwich Village intelligentsia" (Easterners attracted to Wisconsin by the university's progressive reputation), most of them "communists, atheists, and what not" who "happened to be Jews" because "most University intelligentsia *is* Jewish," but who laughed at the "Jewish Babbitry" of his Hillel associates (6/10: "Trad. Sermon"; Tax 1981:301–2). In the fall of 1928, there was an outbreak of what Tax later called "gentlemanly anti-Semitism" at the university (1981:300; cf. Cronon & Jenkins 1994:119), to which he responded in an editorial for the *Hillel Review*. Arguing that this prejudice was "so deep in the social fabric" there was "little hope" of soon ending it, he suggested that the task of Jews was to "adjust" and "adapt" to "conditions as they exist." Adaptation did not mean losing "our individualities" or squelching "the thinkers and individualists among us"; neither did it imply adopting an assertive "We're Jews and we're proud of it" stance. Between "these extremes," Tax sought "a place for ourselves where we have *the maximum amount of freedom and expression and still cause a minimum of friction.*" If, to avoid friction, "Jews should not attend public dances in such numbers that the Gentiles have to leave," Tax nevertheless insisted that "we should begin to fight, if we must, for things which are necessary and worthwhile," including "scholarship, and research, and leadership in social movements and in the Arts and Letters" (6/10: 12/14/29).

The critical moment in the history of Tax's "Jewish-ness" came in 1930, while he was in Algeria. It was his first trip outside the United States, and his shipboard diary opens with comments on the cultural contrasts he had expected to find between the "generally more civilized Europeans" and the "cocksure" carriers of the "American spirit," with its "democracy and its laws and its inveterate 'necessity.' " Tax, however, was clearly one of the latter: he could not understand why an attractive Jewish woman he met on the boat and later accompanied (somewhat reluctantly) to the Folies-Bergère ("third rate vaudeville") could have chosen to leave California to return to Poland. But at the expedition camp in Algeria, where he prided himself on being the best cook, he surprised Alonzo Pond, the expedition leader, by serving him a "good old-fashioned Jewish style dinner" (10/3). At his request, Pond told a Jewish merchant in the nearby town that one of his crew was Jewish, and Tax was invited to join the merchant's family for the first and last days of Passover (Tax 1981:308). It seems to have been an epiphanal experience of identity, more richly recorded in a typescript composed at the time than in his later published account (10/7: "The Jewish Community of Ain Beida" 5/5/30; cf. Tax 1931).

Having lived for almost two months with "a group of real Americans, Nordics or what have you," Tax was struck by the "great, great similarity of the mental makeup of the Jews here with those at home." Although his hosts conversed with him in French, Tax felt that he "might just as well have been back at the Hillel Foundation bull-sessions," or "in the very Jewish Liberal Club": there was "the same quickness," the "same eagerness," and "above all, there were the same premises—premises which all but the two exceptional members of our expedition [the anthropologists-to-be John Gillin and Lauriston Sharp] utterly lacked—that my Jewish friends at home have, the fundamental belief in Social Justice as the necessary goal, and the ultimate perfection of mankind as the desired end." It was in this context that Tax rejected his earlier "first impression" of the assimilative changes that "a few hundred years make in the Jew—how completely he conforms to the culture of his neighbors." Instead, he now emphasized "the feeling of the universality of the Jew": how alike the Algerian Jews were in speech, action, and appearance to "the Jews at home," how "unlike any other people I had ever seen," how "exactly the same, essentially, had remained the traditions and observances of the Jewish faith and the Jewish life through the centuries." (10/7: "The Jewish Community of Ain Beida" 5/5/30; see also 262/5; Tax 1931, 1981)

Tax did not, however, regard Jewish identity as primarily religious. As religion, Judaism was simply another "mythology," providing "answers to our unanswerable curiosity" and an "outlet" for a fundamental "emotional drive," analogous to those of hunger and sex—just as atheism did for communists in Soviet Russia, and as "the Myths of Science" did for him personally. Nor did Tax consider Jewishness based on biology, though he had once been inclined to see that as the explanation of the Jews' disproportionate share of "the geniuses of the world." Rather, Jewish identity was "tribal" in an ethnic or cultural sense, and "the retention wherever we are of that tribal pattern" over the centuries was both cause and consequence of "the social prejudice against us." And it was a good thing, too, to keep "our culture intact," because of its "peculiar fixations" on the pursuit of knowledge and its "messianic complex": its belief in the possibility of "a heaven on earth." If there were "so many Socialists, Communists, etc. and social reformers" among Jews, it was because "we are all Prophets." Thus for "the sake of humanity" in general, it was important to "keep our unity as an ethnic group," and "not mix culturally or biologically"—"that is why I am a segregationist" (6/10: "Trad. Sermon").

By the time Tax returned to the United States, however, this newly awakened sense of universal Jewish identity had been shaken by a "feeling of dread." He later recalled having witnessed "brownshirts marching in the streets" of Munich (1981:300), and in a long fragment written upon his return he avowed a "complete pessimism" jarringly at odds with the optimism fundamental to his personality. During his absence, America had been wracked by "unemployment, wars on communists, [and] crop failures," and "as far as the Jews were concerned, I became even more pessimistic." Whereas the campus response to the "bit of anti-Semitism" of the preceding year sustained an "optimism" that "we might yet adjust ourselves and be happy," Tax now predicted that "the next thirty years" would see "a complete breakdown" in "our adjustment to our gentile environment," just as was occurring "in some European countries today." Before the Great War, "we had visions of a cultural melting pot" to which Jews would "contribute our share," and "the result would be America." But since then "the idea of America" had changed; the passage of immigration restriction laws and the rise of "100% American doctrines" made clear that henceforth "America was to be Anglo-Saxon," and other elements "already here were to become Anglo-Saxonized." Tax feared a time when American Jews would be subjected to the same treatment as Jews in Poland and Romania, "without hope of adjustment in their Gentile environment," and praying only "for the time when they will be in their own land, in *Eretz Israel*" (6/10: "What lies before us?").

Apparently intended as a talk at Hillel, the document broke off suddenly after the observation that the same fate "is crashing down upon us in America." Another fragment, however, focused specifically on Zionist issues (6/10: untitled). Before his trip abroad Tax had addressed these as a member of the Avuka debating team (along with Max Wax, Moe Max, and Maurie Zox), which, against a visiting team from Oxford University, had argued "the negative side of the proposition that the establishment of a Jewish homeland in Palestine would end anti-semitism in the world" (5/1: 4/12/85). But when the British Labour government "and Sidney Webb, Lord Passfield, the great Socialist leader," suggested in October 1930 that Jewish immigration to Palestine be halted and Jews forbidden to acquire more land as long as Arabs remained landless and unemployed, Tax's political commitments and his recently intensified Jewish identity were brought into sharp conflict. On the one hand, he defended "British Socialist motives" as "quite in sympathy with International Justice" and the plight of landless Arabs, who "must be taken care of as the Jewish settlement continues or there cannot be more Jewish settlement"; while Jews might have "a legal *right* under the mandate to push the Arabs out, they haven't the *moral* right." But there was also "another side of the story": a part of Palestine once belonged to Jews, and after centuries of hardship, indignity, and even massacre, "Zionism was the only hope, the only saviour," especially for "millions of Jews in Poland and Romania"—and now that hope was to be "rudely shattered." And yet, "Jew that I am," Tax was willing that the Jewish case be considered "on an equal basis" with that of the Arabs: both "the British Socialists and the Jews alike must strive" for "the greatest justice." But after toying with the solution of encouraging migration of "displaced Arab families" to Transjordania, Arabia, and "perhaps even North Africa," Tax avowed that it was "quite inconceivable" and "a bit unfair" that they be "taken bodily to [an]other land": "People can't be moved as if they were cattle—!" And there, the second fragment, like the first, was broken off—Tax's Jewish identity having run up against the radical liberal politics that it itself had engendered (6/10: untitled).

It was in the following autumn that Tax began graduate work at the University of Chicago, and by his own account, his "Jewish-ness"—like his political activism—seems to have been put on hold while he devoted himself wholeheartedly to the "science" of anthropology. In his correspondence with Redfield in the 1930s Tax referred in passing to the "present German-Jewish situation," and later to the events of Kristallnacht in November 1938 as "a real Pogrom in Germany," but with little apparent sense of strong personal identification (Rubinstein 1991b:108, 244). He later recalled that during his protracted fieldwork in Guatemala, "the 'Jews' were mythical beings connected with the creation, and Indian people never associated us with the *Judeos*, and we never had occasion to proclaim our 'identity' other than as North Americans." And in working among North American Indians, "there was no occasion that I remember when the question arose," nor did he recall ever having "talked about it" with non-Indians with whom he worked—all of whom "were 'liberal' and respected all religions" (5/1: "Jewish-ness File").

Although Tax did not achieve tenure at the University of Chicago until a decade after receiving his doctorate, his career was by then a step ahead of the cohort of the American Jewish intellectuals who were able to establish themselves academically only in the 1950s (Hollinger 1996). Mentored by Redfield, who was personally close to President Robert Hutchins and who served for 12 years as dean of the Social Science Division, Tax had become associate dean under Redfield's successor in 1948. Aside from his frequent participation in the Hillel Foundation's whimsical Latke-Hamentasch debates, his Jewishness (as his own accounts suggest) was largely a familial matter (4/4:

Sol Tax, at the 1961 Hillel Foundation debate, to which he brought "all the makings of potato *latkes* and [having begun them, in this background photo] finished the 'frying' as a demonstration to make the point of their simplicity as compared with the complex hamentosh" (STP 4/4). Smiling on Tax's right is Professor Harry Kalven, of the Law School, while Professor of Political Science Herman Finer makes his case at the podium. (Courtesy of the Department of Special Collections, University of Chicago Library.)

"Vitae 1980"; 5/1; Tax 1981); insofar as it was publicly manifest, it was along liberal assimilationist lines. Late in 1945, he participated in a panel on Planning for Jewish Cultural Adjustment at a conference sponsored by the American Jewish Committee (211/5). Early in 1946 he wrote to Ashley Montagu on behalf of his brother Erwin's proposal for a statute making "race defamation" or "group libel" illegal (47/9: 1/8/46; ETP 1/2: AM/ST 1/31/46). In 1956, he served on the national advisory board of ICHUD, an organization devoted to the "tragic problem of Arab refugees" and the encouragement of Arab-Israeli friendship. In 1964, it was with some reluctance that he agreed to identify Jews on a list of fellows of the American Anthropological Association for an article David Bidney was writing on Jews in anthropology, and in the same year he was "conscientiously unable" to support a "Board of Jewish Education"—since he had "not yet become reconciled to parochial schools" (5/1).

As that "yet" may suggest, Tax did later in life come to feel that his "basic point of view in anthropology" might have been "influenced by my Jewish background" (1981:308), and there is confirming evidence in his thinking about primitiveness, cultural continuity, and cultural relativism. After attending a lecture on Menstrual Pollution in Judaism and Christianity early in 1986, Tax recalled his reaction three decades previously to Redfield's *Primitive World and Its Transformations* (1953). Explicitly embracing "a double standard of ethical judgement" as "part of my version of cultural relativity," Redfield had argued (following Alfred Kroeber) that an "infantile obsession" with "blood and death and decay" was a marker of primitiveness, which over "thousands of years" had been transcended in the process of civilization. In the margin of his own copy, Tax had commented: "[he is] wallowing in valuation: is this [to be] the alternative to strict cultural relativism?" Later recalling another reaction he had not noted in the margin at the time, Tax suggested that his own Orthodox grandmother "had doubtless used the MIKVA," and that this was evidence that in his own family, civilization must have taken place, not over thousands of years, but in a single generation (282/4: 1/18/86; 23/3: ST/S. Diamond 5/23/62; cf. Redfield 1953:159–65). And for a colloquium on Jewish Life in the United States in 1979, Tax used his own life experience as "a naïve participant" to offer "Perspectives from Anthropology." Drawing an analogy between the "miracle of Jewish survival" and that of North American Indian societies "surviving against impossible odds with their basic religion and world view intact," he quoted his early paper, "An Algerian Passover," as foreshadowing his tendency "in my subsequent professional theories" to see "cultural continuities as stronger than fluctuations from environmental changes." Building upon this original experiential template, he came to realize, both among "Maya Indian villagers" and among "bands and nations of North American Indians," that "a unique world view maintains its integrity precisely because it is resilient and permissive of a large variety of particular beliefs and practices which can change in response to external changes or be passed from one [culture] to another or [received] from a wholly different culture" (1981:307, 309–10).

The relativism of Tax's later thinking about particular "world views" existed, however, in a certain tension with his persisting predisposition to envision the world in universal evolutionary singularity, whether construed in scientific or political terms. In a fragment on "relativism" written in 1949, before the Fox Project was well underway, Tax took a "middle ground": since the "absolute value" of the freedom of a cultural group to choose its values assumed a knowledge of "the full consequences" and the "full context of their choice," social scientists had both "the right and obligation" to "make and spread knowledge" about the consequences of choosing one set of values "rather than another" (264/3). During the next few years, however, the experience of the Fox Project convinced Tax that cultural groups should have "the freedom to make mistakes," and by 1970 he went even further, defending the necessity of biting one's tongue when Native American activists unfairly lumped sympathetic anthropologists with those opposing self-determination (155/6: ST/M. Wax 5/21/70). Nevertheless, Tax continued to think of world views in terms that would have been recognizable to traditional evolutionists. Although early opposed to the use of the term "primitive" to describe contemporary groups, he did not abandon a more positive "primitivism" when it came to comparing their values with "ours." Contrasting the people of "the bow"("so-called" tribal hunters) and the people of "the hoe"("so-called" peasant villagers) with "the people of the urban industrial world," he defended their rejection of the values of work ("our materialism and our achievement motivation") in favor of the "virtues of sacrifice, generosity, and cooperation" that "subjugate our egos to a larger whole"—and which were "expressed and rewarded in different ways in every culture." It was only in "recent years" that "some members of the species" had begun to understand "the larger whole" to which "our moral responsibility is supposed to extend," and crucial among these were anthropologists: "just as our general ethic accepts the sacredness of the person, the special lesson of anthropology is that it is necessary to the person to treat as equally sacred the continued existence of the group— and its culture. . . ." The solution of "general social problems in the whole world" therefore depended on simultaneously defending "cultural heterogeneity" and developing "a global ethic" (Tax 1975c:507–8).

Aside from his activism on behalf of Native American self-determination, Tax's political commitments during the decade of the 1950s were limited in scope, and by no means radical. The public presence of Adlai Stevenson at the Darwin Centennial may perhaps be taken as marker of Tax's own liberal democratic political sympathies, the limits of which were manifest on the touchstone political issues of domestic anticommunism and American overseas involvement. As the later response of Cherokee tribal leaders to the Carnegie Cross-Cultural Education Program suggests, Tax was not immune to charges of communist sympathy. His youthful radicalism, however, was far enough in the past so that he felt comfortable assuring his contact at the Carnegie Corporation that his "personal record" was "fortunately pure" (119/8: ST/Morrisett 1/14/66). Furthermore, the "lesson in tactics" that he recalled learning in the Wisconsin Liberal Club may have sustained a caution regarding institutional association with communists in the height of the McCarthy period. In the fall of 1953, Tax was himself involved in evaluating the political "purity" of a Chicago graduate, Robert Armstrong, to whom Redfield had promised a fill-in appointment during his own year's leave of absence, but whose appointment was forestalled at the last minute on the basis of information given to the university by the Federal Bureau of Investigation. At Tax's suggestion, Armstrong prepared a political autobiography detailing his membership in and break from the Communist Party, and then "talked the whole matter through" in a painful interview with Tax, Eggan, and Dean

Ralph Tyler. Tax and Eggan decided to continue with the appointment, but first to submit it to the Board of Trustees because of its "controversial" nature. Before that could happen, however, the appointment was withdrawn when it was vigorously opposed by Washburn upon his return from summer research to resume the department chair (RRP: RA/RR 10/5/53).

Overseas, the revelatory case was Guatemala, where Tax's attitude was a mixture of indigenist empathy and anthropological opportunism. Years later, he recalled his excitement at the "overthrow" of the dictator Jorge Ubico in 1944 and the "new very liberal constitution," soon followed by the founding of the Instituto Indigenista Nacional. The head of the new institute was Antonio Goubaud, who had been a primary ethnographic informant of Tax's during the later 1930s, and who (after receiving an M.A. from Chicago in 1943) had gone on to become Guatemala's ambassador to the United States and representative to the United Nations (276/6; Rubinstein 1991b:47). In 1951, however, Tax was "shocked" by an ambassadorial speech that attacked the United Fruit Company, but contained no mention of the Instituto Indigenista or of United States assistance in social welfare programs (RRP 56/5: ST/RR 4/16/51). Later that year, however, when Goubaud returned to Guatemala for the inauguration of Jacobo Arbenz, he found himself in "political difficulty" as the new government took "a sharp turn away from domination by the U.S.A.," and committed suicide by slashing his wrists. After the Arbenz government was itself overthrown in 1954, in one of the more "successful" of the Central Intelligence Agency's anticommunist interventions (Prados 1986:98–107), Tax recalled being impressed by the fact that the new government of Castillo Armas "recognized anthropology as none had ever done before," sponsoring the Seminar on National Integration that led to Tax's own return for the first time since 1944 (276/6). Judging from the case of Guatemala, it would seem that Tax's fear of nuclear war in 1954 did not imply a systematic critical posture toward American overseas involvement.

Until late in the 1960s, Tax tended to exempt the United States from even moderately radical critique. In a short fragment called "The Colonial Situation" written in the spring of 1960, he suggested that there was "nothing theoretically impossible about a large class-less society," and that "in fact we [in the United States] tend to have it, with considerable mobility" (266/5). Over the next few years, however, Tax moved beyond his interest in Native American self-determination to respond to issues of broader global political concern. In the early stages of the Cuban missile crisis, he took the initiative in organizing a series of regional conferences of anthropologists to see whether there might emerge a consensus on issues of war and peace that could be regarded as a "clear 'anthropological' position [such] as we tend to have on race, colonialism, and American Indians" (218/5: ST/P. Fejos 11/23/62); ultimately, however, they focused on the narrower problem of nuclear "Deterrence Strategy"

(218/5: 2/4/63). As an activist dean of Continuing Education (253/13: ST/G. Beadle 5/6/63), in 1966 he organized major conferences on contemporary communist China (320/4) and on the draft—the latter, in response to a student sit-in opposing "the use of course grades" to determine induction priorities for service in Vietnam (321/3; Tax 1967:vii). A year later, when several of the more radical Columbia University anthropologists responded to the "crisis of conscience" brought on by "our Vietnam involvement" by organizing a symposium on war and peace at the meetings of the American Anthropological Association—only in the event to wonder whether they had inadvertently created "a fink-out" rather than a "teach-in"—Tax contributed a historical analysis of the conditions under which Americans might seriously consider alternatives to the draft, which he described as "a policy that violates our sacred values of both freedom and equality" (Fried et al. 1968:ix; Tax 1967:207; STP 223/1, 2).

Tax's growing awareness of the war in Vietnam is recounted in one of a number of reflective fragments he composed during the year he spent at the Palo Alto Center for Advanced Study in the Behavioral Sciences in 1969–70. In the earlier 1960s, he had worried that Southeast Asia might "become a trap for us," and "sometime later" had signed a petition against "our use of napalm in South Viet Nam." The decision to send in ground combat forces "seemed to me insane," he wrote; the Tonkin resolution and the bombing of the north left him "much concerned," and after reading Robert Scheer's radical critique of United States involvement he began to "speak out loudly of Vietnam as a tragic mistake" (cf. Scheer 1965). But only in 1969, after the "stories about the Mai Lai massacre broke," did he realize that such incidents were not "aberrations" but "commonplace and even at some levels in the military [were in fact] 'policy' "; and "the most horrible truth of all now emerged—that a large segment of the American population and many of our national leaders would support the war knowing all this." It was "clearly not enough to be against the war, to dissociate oneself from those who supported it, and await the opportunity to express opposition at the polls." And there, the holograph manuscript broke off—at the point when liberal discourse and democratic process seemed no longer to be enough (273/9: 7/24/70).

But for Tax, these were sine qua nons of his political and anthropological activism, which was in turn an extension of his personality. During the same year at the Center, he composed a fragment, cast partly in the form of a dialogue (implicitly between himself and his alter) on the problem of "how does one develop a new or better institution needed by people?" Queried by alter, Tax quickly rephrased the question as "how does it happen?" and substituted for the individual agency of "one" (himself?) a presumed "natural process," specifying its operation within a "society with equalitarian democratic ideals" like "many tribal societies" and "our own in 1776." The problem was to discover "the environment in which, and the process by which, the people themselves" create new institutions. Acknowledging alter's charge that "even that smacks of megalomania," Tax argued that present global necessity was "so urgent, the mother of invention may need a Caesarian!" and went on to offer the model of *Current Anthropology* in a series of processual tropes. CA was "an intellectual free market" ("editor only writes the figures on the board"); a "town hall meeting by mail" ("editor is neutral chairman"); "a sort of Darwinian process of natural selection" ("editor welcomes/seeks variations to offer"); "an orderly anarchy" ("editor working hard to have no power"); with the result that CA was "what associates wish to tell one another" ("editor provides opportunities [never pressure] for more to 'speak' "). Granting that it was not "a democracy" in the vote-counting sense, Tax suggested that it was rather a matter of taking "interests into account," describing "data to all," drawing "a conclusion," and getting it "ratified or changed"—and by these means, presumably, performing the Caesarian (273/9; cf. 274/5: "History of *Current Anthropology*").

Tax was aware of the expansive tendencies of his own personality: his congenital optimism, his need to be constantly active, his pleasure in "the excitement of experiment," even, perhaps, a tendency to megalomania (273/9). During the two decades of his anthropological apprenticeship, these were counterbalanced by a certain self-doubt. In the privacy of notes he later wrote on "the question of high standards," Tax averred that he had "never felt confident, and eventually have had to use reason to convince myself that I am not a fraud." Nor was he reassured by Redfield's respect, which might simply have been "because I was useful to him." In the late 1940s, however, "something happened," and he realized that his tenured membership on the faculty of "a great University" was "not a mistake, a dream from which I would awake" (281/1: 11/25/76)—rather, perhaps, a position from which the world-reforming dreams he had shared with his brother Erwin might begin to be realized in action.[10]

But as his comments on the editor's role suggest, they were to be realized in

10. Erwin Tax, at the time owner of the Decker Press in Prairie City, Illinois, was shot to death on May 10, 1950, by the daughter of the previous owner, who then committed suicide (*Chicago Tribune* 5/11/50). Erwin's surviving papers contain a number of documents suggesting that his world-reforming impulses continued strong during and after his short career as a graduate student in sociology at the University of Chicago (e.g., "A Liberal Manifesto" and "Ten Errors of Marxism"—which he described to Dwight McDonald as a "prescription for the ills of the leftist world" [ETP 1/2: ET/DM 10/7/46]). Sol Tax intervened on his brother's behalf on a number of occasions, notably in seeking a publisher for an Arthurian/Celtic epic poem Erwin composed while serving overseas in World War II (it was published in 1948 by the Decker Press as *The Wraith of Gawain*). Whether Erwin's death, coming in the early phase of Sol Tax's turn from scientific to action anthropology, may have been an added motive for that redirection remains a matter for speculation.

a manner that was in principle self-effacingly antihubristic, and might even be characterized as humble. When Tax late in life offered "explanations" for his activism, it was in terms of two deeply engrained "personal characteristics." The first was "an almost lifelong reluctance to do only one thing at a time"—which he felt was related to "a willingness to let things happen or grow"—and less obviously, to "a desire to improve institutions." The second was a "deliberate indecisiveness," which he associated with his "generally relativistic philosophy" and his "immersion in action anthropology," and which manifested itself in a "trial and error" style, so that "it became my peculiar virtue to be able to accept and quickly internalize and recombine the ideas of others." Ideas, he felt, came to him in "profusion," and he expressed them "quickly and enthusiastically," so that he might "even appear to be promoting them," when in fact he had a corresponding "quick willingness to accept their rejection happily." Granting that he was a problem solver, he insisted that he was not "a 'planner,' in the sense of one who sets goals and then determines means to achieve them" (1988:16–17).

Not all who knew him would have agreed with Tax's self-effacing representation of his activist personality. There were some who found him indirectly quite directive, among them one who felt that it was Tax's own unstated prior goals that usually emerged from apparently open-ended democratic discussion; another who characterized him as "the Holy Ghost looking for a Virgin Mary." In solving problems, he seems to have learned something of the tactics of Chicago ward politics: his mentor once congratulated him on "stacking" a committee "with Redfields" (56/4: RR/ST 8/25/53). And there were times when individuals chafed, or even felt exploited, when limited resources were rationed in the cause of a common good: one associate of the 1950s recalls Tax as "an artist at getting people to work for little or nothing" (M. Wax, pers. comm.). In a satirical document a more defensive and humorless ego might well have suppressed, but which Tax chose to preserve for posterity, he was presented as a huckstering entrepreneur: "Honest Sol, Chicago Southside Wheeler-Dealer," parlaying "front-wheel drive & shiftless new ideas" and "late model abstractions" through a worldwide organizational network, graphically represented in an organizational chart of lines and boxes descending on one side to "all publishing companies," the Federal Reserve System, the New York Stock Exchange, the World Bank, the Vatican, and B'nai Brith, and on the other side down through UNESCO and the "Prime Ministers of All Countries Everywhere"—with branches to the NSF and the CIA: "Today, the Cooperative, Tomorrow, the World, Next week, the Universe" (270/5: L. Moss[?]). In a general way, however, Tax's own more modest self-portrait is not inconsistent with the person I first met in 1963.

I am reminded, though, of a comment he made at a planning session for the 1973 congress, which I recall as "if you cast bread upon the waters, you've got

to expect some of it may come back soggy." Among its resonances are a tolerance for softer thinking, buttressed by a confidence that out of a generative
profusion of ideas, some will turn out to be productive. Tax (who sometimes
fell back on biological analogy in speaking of process) was a tender-minded
intellectual Darwinist, eclectic and pragmatic, who saw intelligence inher-
ing in the group, but allowed himself (if he did not claim) a privileged role
as agent in its articulation, even as he abjured "the power to decide history"
(273/9). And despite his denial that he selected goals, there were nevertheless goals implicit in what he himself called the "method" of *Current Anthropology*. Characteristically, they were goals that were realized in the process of
pursuing them: goals of facilitating, extending and maximizing participation,
intercommunication, understanding, mutual respect, and of course knowledge, in both a scientific and a practical interactional sense—all of which, in
Tax's view, would lead to empowerment. They were perhaps better regarded
as "values" than as goals, insofar as they governed both ends and means, and
were widely held in the culture of which Tax was a part, loosely cohering in
what may be regarded as a version of American Liberal Democratic Ideology: the equal right of every person to participate and every voice to be heard
in the town meeting, of every point of view to be evaluated in the free market place of ideas—out of which would come "somehow," "as if by magic," an
adaptive consensus.

It was not, however, a democracy of majority vote, but a democracy of egalitarian like-mindedness based on the tolerance and discursive mediation of
difference—a modern recuperation of the like-mindedness of the undifferen-
tiated antihierarchical societies of the paleolithic. Undermined by socioeco-
nomic and technological developments since the neolithic revolution, this
original human social state was still discernable in the United States of the
founding fathers, and exemplified in the present among surviving "peoples of
the bow." Although Tax came to eschew the word "primitive," he remained
all his life an evolutionist in the spirit of V. Gordon Childe, and a primitivist
in the positive Rousseauistic sense. Despite the socially corrupting impact of
the agricultural revolution, the emergence of urban class societies, and the
rise of industrial capitalism, despite the increasing gap between social understanding and technological knowledge—all culminating in the multifaceted
planetary crisis of the postatomic world—it was still possible that a kind of
globally pluralistic equivalent of primitive like-mindedness might be recover-
able by the creation of "autonomous local communities" within a worldwide
information system.

Organizing Good Guys:
The Tasks of World Anthropology
and the Future World Order

It took some time, however, for that possibility to reassert itself as the focus of Tax's anthropology in the aftermath of Hiroshima—one of several moments in his life when his congenital optimism deserted him.[11] Ruminating on the implications of this "immense leap in the preposterous acceleration of man's technology," Redfield recounted to his daughter Lisa how Tax, in preparing the department's new core course, had been constructing a chart of technological development from "the flint handaxe to—whatever was the latest up to the atom bomb." The rate of recent acceleration was "so enormous" that it would take "a strip of paper sixty-eight feet long" to get it all on one chart, at the end of which the ascent was almost vertical—and then the bomb was dropped. Tax's interpretation, according to Redfield, was "this is where we get off. Another nova, another sun—the first made by man—and the cycle begins again somewhere" (in Stocking 1979b:30; cf. Boyer 1985).

Although Tax's post-hydrogen-bomb fantasy of a Pacific Island ark anticipates in certain key respects his later dreams of a new world order, it was not until the following decade that he began systematically to envision the tasks of anthropology in global terms. By the later 1960s, he had concluded that "the coming new trend in anthropology will be work on such species wide problems as war, colonialism, destructive nationalism; gross inequalities, racism, poverty; technological and urban overdevelopment, and irreversible environmental destruction; overpopulation; alienation, anomie, and discontinuity of generations; and so on." Within this larger frame—but in a way consistent with his own evolving anthropological orientation—he specified "three tasks of world anthropology [that were] equally urgent": the "mitigation of the human problems of forced acculturation and the physical destruction of peoples who seem to be in the way of stronger peoples"; "analysis of the scientific problems of the rapidity of change of traditional forms"; and the "speedy education of people of all nations, including statesmen, scientists, planners, and engineers in the anthropological points of view which are needed both to make more effective programs of modernization and to ameliorate their negative human consequences" (25/4: ST/M. Freedman 8/31/70).

---

11. In addition to the "complete pessimism" he had felt upon his return from Europe in 1930, and the evident pessimism of the postwar period, there was also a period in the early 1980s, after a heart attack and stroke, when Tax questioned as "vanity of vanities" the "optimistic outlook" he had held "since childhood" that "man's immortality is in the legacy he or she leaves behind": "how vain is *how much* of human accomplishment?" (282/5: "Immortality").

From 1965 on, Tax was involved in a series of ventures that sought to bring together anthropologists and the anthropologically-minded (the "good guys" of the world) in the pursuit of these tasks, and especially in the propagation of "anthropological points of view" on a global basis.[12] At the Anthropological Association meeting in the fall of 1965, he showed some colleagues a plan to "apply the ideas developed in *Current Anthropology*" to teaching anthropology in colleges and universities, by developing a two-part journal (one for students, one for teachers) that would "keep up with new knowledge" on a "less professional level." Teachers who needed further help answering questions could submit them by airmail or telephone to a "cooperative of the world's anthropologists from all research frontiers," who on the basis of "classroom feedback" would "continually produce material to fill the lacunae"—materials that would doubtless interest some commercial textbook publisher. Anticipating sales of $120,000 a year, Tax expected that the plan might be self-supporting, and even enable those anthropologists who earned money by writing to "earn at least as much" while avoiding "the pitfalls of the raw competitive world" (270/2: ST/Dear colleague 6/2/66). The response, however, was at best mixed, and over the next several years the journal idea was transformed into a project for a textbook, to be called *Creative Anthropology*. But in the end, that, too, received mixed prepublication reviews, and Tax returned to each member of the cooperative his or her original investment, except for those who had contributed only a dollar, which would not have covered bank and postage costs (270/5: ST/Karen, n.d.)

In the same year that he initiated the anthropological cooperative, Tax took the lead in organizing a conference for the Council for the Study of Mankind, a group of liberal academics from American universities, a number of them from the University of Chicago, which had been formed 20 years before in the "family of man" spirit of the early UNESCO years. Tax, who had recently become involved as a member of the council's executive committee, saw the conference as the means of making a "general breakthrough to the American intellectual system." Adopting the format he had used for other conferences at the Center for Continuing Education, he hoped to develop it "as a major means of education on a national scale." There would be a core group of "major figures from all over the world who have been concerned with Mankind" who would face one another before a "strategically invited audience," with an emphasis on participation by "the younger generation"

12. I owe the "good guys" reference to Carol Bowman Stocking, who was present sometime in 1966 or 1967 when Tax came to the National Opinion Research Center with the idea of creating a worldwide directory of organizations that might be sympathetic to one of his projects, and who recalls that a colleague also present spoke of this as a "good guy list." Although not from Tax's mouth, the phrase well exemplifies his various attempts to mobilize the "anthropologically minded"—who were, clearly, the "good guys of the world."

(223/6: ST/ G. Hirschfeld 5/16/66). Although there was division within the council as to whether the conference should "develop into an action organization," Tax felt that "since my view of 'action' involves mostly education in various forms, perhaps the differences are not great" (223/6: ST/J. Seeley 11/14/66, ST/G. Hirschfeld 11/28/66). In the event, the conference was co-sponsored by the Center for Advanced Intercultural Studies, a similar group on whose board Tax also served, and was entitled "Education for Mankind: A World Conference on the Understanding of Different Cultures and Forming Human Community" (223/7: Minutes 10/20/67). Echoing his student "Proposal for a Union of Humanity" of 1926, Tax saw the meeting as an opportunity to consider the "cohesive forces" which have impelled the "idea of mankind" and the "divisive forces" which have inhibited it from "serving as a general criterion for the conduct of men and of nations," the forms of its manifestation in different cultures and disciplines, and "the ways it can be applied without reducing diversity to uniformity, or transforming pluralism into divisiveness and antagonism" (224/1: ST/S. O. Adebo 2/20/68). Although the six-day conference in April of 1968 drew together 30 overseas guests, most of them from outside the major Euro-American powers, and several times that many American educationalists, it was longer on rhetoric than results, and failed to realize what one participant called "Sol Tax's brilliant idea of an international community of scholars and intellectuals concerned with education for mankind, who would be bound together by a magazine rather than a formal organization" (224/4: F. Young/R. Moore 5/2/68, W. Stanford/R. Moore 6/13/68).

By the time of the Education for Mankind conference, Tax was involved in planning yet another program for the global development and propagation of anthropology: the Center for the Study of Man. Its roots went back to 1965, when the two long-standing anthropology units of the Smithsonian Institution, the Bureau of American Ethnology and the United States National Museum Department of Anthropology, were merged in a new Office of Anthropology. Tax was invited by the secretary of the Smithsonian to head the new unit, but agreed only to help develop programs while retaining his position at Chicago (200/7: [1971]).[13] After several years experiencing "the extreme factionalism" built into the new Office (W. Sturtevant, pers. comm.), Tax recommended the reconstitution of a Department of Anthropology and the establishment of a new Center for the Study of Man, in which a number of Smithsonian anthropologists continued to participate. Before the Center's first full-scale meeting in early May of 1969, Tax offered as a basis for

13. In writing about the Center for the Study of Man, of which I was for several years a member, I have relied primarily on materials in my own files, as well as on William Sturtevant's helpful responses to several queries, and on several documents from the seven boxes of materials in the Tax papers (200–207).

discussion "A Modest Proposal" embodying his vision of the three "equally urgent" tasks of world anthropology (cf. above, 237), enlarged to encompass three "urgent problems" threatening the "survival of the [human] species": "War in a Nuclear age—The Population spiral—The growing pollution of our planet." As a precondition for addressing these problems, Tax suggested that it was necessary to "organize world anthropology" on a new basis, using the newest computer technology to create quickly accessible global directories of anthropologists and anthropological institutions, and a comprehensive, "up-to-date inventory" of anthropology literature. In this context, the tasks of the new Center would be to coordinate research, to encourage cooperation and dialogue, and to educate: "we cannot manipulate nor engineer, we can only educate" (200/6, 7; 273/5).

Although many of the anthropologists participating in the first full meeting added their bit to the rhetoric of good liberal global intentions, in practice the Center for the Study of Man became the legatee of a hodgepodge of programs already underway or in the proposal stage—as well as the hostage of bureaucratic and factional tensions within Smithsonian anthropology and of the politics of congressional funding. There was a program in Urgent Anthropology, a plan for a multivolume *Handbook of North American Indians*, an American Indian program, a Current Anthropological Bibliography program, a plan for an Anthropological Film Archives, an Archives and History of Anthropology program, a Computerization program, a National Folklife Study program, and, most ambitiously, a plan for a Museum of Man (200/7, 8). While some of these (urgent anthropology, anthropological bibliography, and computerization) clearly reflected the global interests of Tax, others reflected traditional Smithsonian Americanist concerns, and there were recurrent turf-tensions over institutional arrangements and resources—exacerbated, perhaps, because Tax continued to function as an occasionally commuting acting director and most of the members of the Center were non-resident anthropologists (seven of them international) who participated by mail and at an annual meeting.

By the time of the 1970 meeting, Tax had reenvisioned the Center as a Center for Advanced Studies with interdisciplinary senior fellows and graduate-student junior fellows; it would organize a series of conferences on particular social problems, to be pursued by "limited-time task forces" whose members would become fellows during periods when they were in Washington (200/6: ST/Colleagues 4/3/70). Although a task force on population was established before the 1970 meeting, the continuing tension between the expansive impulse of Tax's global vision and the institutional inertia sustaining local perspectives was not then resolved. Soon thereafter, there was a separation of functions, with the educational ventures (the traditional Smithsonian museum-oriented programs) remaining in Washington, and Tax becoming resident director of a research branch in Chicago, where he supervised a bib-liographic program of data coordination and planned a series of additional task forces. In addition to one on population and a second on the environment, Tax looked forward to others on such then highly "relevant" problems as "War; Racism; Colonialism; Poverty; [and] Generational discontinuities under conditions of rapid social change." To facilitate the work of task forces he proposed a three-part Center research agenda to develop "necessary new information on 100 societies and/or part societies": new field studies (at an average cost of $15,000), "re-cycling" studies of existing ethnographic material ($10,000) and "piggy-back" studies on already on-going studies ($5,000) —which, at an average of $10,000, plus money for administrative expenses, would require grant funding of $1,300,000 (200/6: 4/2/71, 4/27/71).

The 1971 conference at Chicago, however, brought to the surface various methodological issues facing the task forces: the utility of data abstracted from existing ethnographies versus the initiation of new problem-oriented fieldwork; the value of anthropological holism versus specialist expertise (or as one overseas anthropologist unkindly put it, the "articulation of anthropological enthusiasm with what other people are doing"); the absence of human biologists among task force personnel; the possibility of general application of the "effective strategies" developed by tribal and peasant people; and the inadequacy of existing theoretical approaches. In characteristically activist fashion, Tax suggested that the need for a new "systems analysis paradigm" be delegated to an afternoon workshop: "my ideal is to get out a mailing next week" (Stocking notes 5/15/70). Although Tax felt that the conference had been a "splendid" success, and the published report represented it in optimistic terms, the continued resistance of professional specialists and the failure of foundation funding forced Tax again to rethink the Center's mission (202/2: ST/Colleagues 5/24/71, Kunstadter/Hackenburg 6/3/71; cf. Shea & Emmons 1972).

Ever resilient and resourceful in pursuing his global vision, Tax responded by turning from center to periphery. Taking advantage of foreign currency funding available through the Smithsonian for overseas conferences, he invited 50 anthropologists, the great majority from Third World countries, to go to Cairo, Egypt, the following May for a Conference on Anthropology, Cross-Cultural Data Retrieval and Pressing Social Problems—specifically, education in the modernizing world, social integration in new nations, social dislocation caused by urbanization, industrialization, and population growth, and physical and mental health and social well-being in different cultures (202/7: 5/17/72 press release). Because scholars from industrialized countries —however much they might sympathize with the "have nots"—had always dominated international conferences in the past, Tax proposed to start from the other end, giving the developing nations a "predominant presence." This, to counter the "colonialist notion that anthropologists in a single world tradition 'study' other peoples" by the view "that they learn from one another." Toward these ends, he proposed a "pilot project" of a hundred descriptive monographs (toward an eventual 1,200) which would be addressed in a series of comparative cross-cultural books. These were to be developed in conjunction with the forthcoming Ninth Congress of the International Union of Anthropological and Ethnological Sciences, according to a detailed schedule that anticipated the publication of five books and 100 monographs in 1974, an equal number in 1975, and a "second generation" in time for the Tenth Congress in 1978 (202/7: "Reflections," "Draft"; 202/10: "Remarks").

Tax's project was partly realized at the omnium gatherum of world anthropology in Chicago, where a number of preconferences, as well as some of the published congress volumes, were in fact devoted to "social problem" issues that had been posed in Cairo. And in 1974 the Center for the Study of Man sponsored a small Seminar on the Cultural Consequences of Population Change in Bucharest, Romania (203/1–4). But late that year, authors who had completed the proposed descriptive monographs were being told that the program "had not been active since the summer of 1973," and that because contacts with publishers had been unsuccessful, the "project was reluctantly being held in abeyance for the foreseable future" (203/7: Douglas/ST 3/3/75). By 1976, the "withering away" of the Center for the Study of Man, anticipated early on by Smithsonian traditionalists, was marked by the announcement that its activities had "evolved" to the point where they could be "integrated" with those of the National Museum of Natural History and the still unrealized Museum of Man, with the director of those two institutions serving henceforth also as director of the Center (200/6: S. Stanley/ST 11/2/76).[14]

During the same period in which Tax pursued his plans for a world anthropology through the Center for the Study of Man, he also became involved in a venture expanding the range of his anthropological vision even further, both in time and space—beyond the immediate future of pressing global social problems into the not-too-distant future of "extraterrestrial anthropology." In August 1966, Magoroh Maruyama, a polymathic cybernetic philosopher attached to the sociology department of a California state college, sent to Tax and several others (including Margaret Mead) a manuscript on "nonhierarchical organizations" (modern analogues of tribal societies, mediated by computers). Resonant in some respects of Tax's editorial method in Current Anthropology, it was a vision that he found congenial, and over the next

14. A number of the projects gathered together within the Center, including the Handbook of North American Indians, the American Indian program, the Anthropology Film Archives and the Folklife program are still active in one form or another (William Sturtevant, pers. comm.).

decade he became involved in several of Maruyama's "futuristic" (or "futurological") activities, and in efforts on behalf of his nomadic academic career (which at one point involved seven different appointments in as many years). After serving as nonhierarchical chair of a session run in Quaker meeting fashion at the 1970 spring meetings of the Society for Applied Anthropology, Tax intervened on Maruyama's behalf to get symposia on Cultural Futurology on the program of American Anthropological Association meetings for several years in the early 1970s. In a preface to a book Maruyama co-edited in 1971 on *Human Futuristics*, Tax recalled comments he had made at the 1956 Wenner-Gren symposium on Man's Role in Changing the Face of the Earth, where he had spoken of the "second great crisis in human history," in which man faced not simply "his individual mortality," but also that of the species and the planet (Tax 1971:vii–viii; cf. STP 265/5). In 1973, he asked Maruyama to organize a symposium on The Future of the Human Species as Seen by the Entire Species at the ICAES Chicago congress, and later he contributed a brief Afterword to the published papers of the 1974 Anthropological Association futurology symposium, suggesting the significance of "the inception of extraterrestrial anthropology" for a "full understanding of the possibilities and limitations of human cultures" (Tax 1975a:203). That same year, Maruyama wrote for Tax's festschrift an essay on "non-hierarchical epistemology," which Tax described as "splendid" (43/1: ST/R. Hinshaw 11/5/75; Maruyama 1979).

Tax's own contribution to futurology came in 1978 at a conference Maruyama had organized on "extraterrestrial community design." Assuming that the year 2000 was the target date for moving 10,000 people into the first settlement in outer space, Tax suggested that there was no time to lose in preparing a pool of 100,000 "heterogenistic, mutualistic, and symbiotic people" from which the actual colonists might be chosen. Representing a wide range of "classes/cultures/nations," they would be "grouped in a variety of ways in geographically isolated earthly colonies enjoying a network of Radio-TV-Computer communication." There would also be "a center for the whole"—"so like a University that we might as well call it that"—where the "best and/or representative" among the 100,000 would "discuss, research, and disseminate" to the rest "information, ideas, and proposals." The "immediate task" was "to develop the University" as an "autonomous, international, or even world-wide non-governmental institution," which, though it might "delocalize itself both electronically and psychologically," would be at least "partly sited" geographically. Here then was the furthest reach of a lifetime of creating community, realized or imagined, local, global, and now extraterrestrial (43/3: ST/MM 1/4/78; cf. above, 235: "Next week, the Universe").

At the energizing center of Tax's community-creating efforts was the community of anthropology itself, which, ever since he first encountered it at the University of Wisconsin, had been the community most important to his own identity. To Tax, it was a distinctive and in the broadest sense integrated community, insofar as professionals in the four fields, related disciplines, and "*any other specialists* find meaning enough in the whole study of man to maintain their intercommunication" (1956a:316) It was an inherently expansive community, "bounded only by the limits of what anthropologists do and use" (319)—a looseness that dismayed fellow anthropologists who preferred to see their discipline in more structured and less immediately functional terms. But it was held together because its members shared "a particular set of intellectual preferences and habits" (which Tax spoke of also as "values"), as well as "a 'liberal' view of other peoples and cultures which puts them on the side of the 'underdog' generally and of native peoples particularly" (320–21).

In April 1977, upon receiving the Malinowski Award of the Society of Applied Anthropology, Tax embodied this notion of the anthropological community in a rambling and reminiscent "grand review of the views I have developed over a lifetime"—an apologia for the anthropological faith he had embraced 50 years previously. Entitled "Anthropology and the World of the Future: Thirteen Professions and Three Proposals," it explicitly recalled the "Eighteen Professions" in which A. L. Kroeber in 1915 had insisted on a paradigmatic separation "of biology and psychology on one side from history and culture on the other." Tax, however, was less interested in defining professional boundaries than in moving his profession to action. His "professions" were keyed to specific "proposals," each related to a long-standing interest and expressed in an "action" initiative. To systematize anthropological knowledge, he proposed a "transformation into modern terms of the 1953 *Anthropology Today* [as an] international review of our sciences," to be accomplished in the 18 months before the 1978 Delhi meeting of the International Congress. To enlarge the "communication network" of anthropologists, he proposed the establishment of "new journal, perhaps called *Practicing Anthropology*," to be produced at the University of South Florida, as a means of intercommunication among nonacademic or "potential" anthropologists, and of "bringing anthropology into the everyday social and occupational structure." Finally, in the defense of North American Indian rights, he urged the "special obligation of American anthropologists," in cooperation with the International Union Commission on Ethnocide and Genocide, to assist North American Indians, "if invited," in entering into negotiations with "local governments and interests to improve Indian resources and opportunities" (274/10; Tax 1977).

It was in relation to the second (or "intercommunicative") proposal, however, that Tax offered suggestions about a utopian form of community that might overcome the "contradiction between a rapidly approaching single, interdependent world economy" and the continued existence of "competing nation states with lethal power." In paragraphs he quoted verbatim on several later occasions, he described a new world order that would exist on two levels, on the ground and in what today might be called cyberspace. At the former level, the geographical space of the world would be redivided into about 10,000 relatively self-sufficient "localities" (subsequently renamed "autonomous local communities") averaging 500,000 people, with "full local control," which might develop different "kinds of cultures." The second level would consist of "a system of public electronic communication which keeps track of all that happens in the interrelations of the localities." The "System"—here, in the original text, capitalized—would be set up in such a way that "every person or family or institution can initiate input," but would be programmed to represent "every changing interest" in an "egalitarian and libertarian manner" that would "limit the growth of power of individual localities" or alliances. As was often the case in his more visionary moments, Tax was vague about how we might get to the world of the future from the world of today: "multinational corporations" might have the power to "veto war" and encourage "a fast evolution"; technology, though it seemed to have led to a "dead end," would be the means to carry us beyond; and finally, there was "anthropology, in which I also believe" (Profession #13), and which if pursued along the lines of his professions and proposals, would play the essential educational role (274/10; 307/4; cf. Tax 1977). Here, then, a half century further on, was Tax's early universalistic and evolutionary "Proposal for a Union of Humanity," informed by the pluralism and relativism of his subsequent anthropological experience, with the local and the global now mediated, paradoxically, by the exponential technological progress that in 1945 had made him think we "must get off" and "begin again somewhere."

Six months before offering his anthropological apologia, Tax had become emeritus professor at Chicago. In January 1979 he suffered a mild heart attack, followed by a stroke that affected his peripheral vision and caused alexia. During the following decade he continued to attend department meetings and dissertation proposal hearings on Native American topics (at which his queries usually focused on the nitty-gritty details of ethnography). He also consulted on the publication of his ethnographic correspondence with Robert Redfield (Rubinstein 1991b), and worked on the organization of his own papers. His last publication, in 1988, was "Pride and Puzzlement," a "retro-introspective" essay review of his own career. On three occasions in the early 1990s, he came for an evening to my seminar as an elder oral informant on postwar anthropology, always cautioning, however, that we should corroborate and supplement his still quite serviceable memory by consulting the archives. What was perhaps his last participation in formal department activities was at a dissertation defense seven months before his death of a heart attack early in January 1995. Appropriately, the topic was the role of traditional Chippewa values in their conflict with whites in the 1980s over the right to spearfish in waters adjacent to their reservation in northern Wisconsin (Nesper 1994).

Cold War Counterpoint, Millennial Resonance: Sol Tax in Transhistorical Context

Every human life can be given many meanings, by different actors and interpreters, at different moments and from different points of view—the possibilities permuted or constrained by the selection and narrative juxtaposition of different "facts" or "events," by their contextual or metanarrative framing, and by the very choice of words used to represent them (including, even, such stylistic preferences as alliteration). The multiplicity of meanings is perhaps even larger for a life so locally rich and globally various, and so well documented, as that of Sol Tax—the more so since many moments here unmarked, or themes touched upon in cursory fashion, might elicit further meanings. Among these meanings are readings of Tax's life and work that might be generated from less empathic or more critical points of view. To the cynically inclined, his Wenner-Gren–supported world anthropological venture may seem (in the recent words of a colleague) tainted by "Nazi blood money," and the very idea of "world redemption through anthropology" itself "a form of imperialist arrogance." Others, rejecting the implication of knavery, might think of Tax as rendered naïve by history: in the words of another colleague, he was "a classic embodiment of the aspirations, limitations, and contradictions of anthropology's great age of world consciousness and growth," but by the end of his life had become a tragic anachronism in a world in which "anthropology is no longer a community and perhaps not even a recognizable discipline, all borders and structures are in contention, [and] there no longer exists a suitable platform (in the Archimedean sense) from which to move the world with an anthropological lever." My own existential trajectory—from communist activism through disillusionment to academic liberalism and disciplinary marginality—predisposes me to a less assured interpretive posture: aware of my own metanarrative predispositions, but suspicious of metanarrative simplification, attentive to a range of contexts, but seeking historical ground always in textual material, empathetically recuperative, but with a touch of irony and skepticism. This, with the hope that those who knew Tax (and he himself, were he still alive) might recognize his voice and experience— but with an ear open also for unappreciated or unexpected resonances of meaning, and the expectation that other readers seeking other meanings will find in my narrative material with which to construe or sustain them.

In contemplating the larger meanings that Tax's life may elicit or confirm, it may be helpful to have in mind several broader contextual frames. To begin with, we may reconsider Tax's relationship—both complementary and contrastive—to other anthropological tendencies in the Cold War period. Having resituated him in the anthropology of his day, it may then be useful briefly to consider ways in which his unique counterpoint to other Cold War themes may resonate with recurrent motifs in the history of American anthropology, over its *longue durée* and down to the present millennial juncture.

Trained in the Boasian Americanist tradition in the decade of its opening to a wider range of conceptual and methodological influences, Tax came of professional age at the beginning of its expansive postwar moment, when, in the aftermath and face of holocaust, and the sharpening division of the world into antagonistic ideological camps, there was nevertheless a strong sense of disciplinary optimism. Sustained by new funding possibilities, the prospect of institutional expansion, the renewal of interdisciplinary initiatives, and the opening of overseas ethnographic fields—and surfing on the wave of American global power—American anthropology entered a larger world, carrying with it the glowing hope that a unified and universalistic "science of anthropology," in the spirit of UNESCO, might assist in the reduction of world tensions and the unification of "the family of man." Along with such figures as Margaret Mead, Tax exemplified this optimistically expansive anthropological spirit.

By the 1950s, the notion of a unitary science of anthropology embracing the cultural, physical, linguistic, and archeological variety of humankind was sustained in the American tradition more by disciplinary ideology and institutional inertia than by day-to-day anthropological practice. But if Tax himself did no work in three of the four fields, he was and remained an ardent proponent of the "integration of anthropology." Characteristically, if not uniquely, American, this integrative tradition stands in sharp contrast to the traditional continental European separation of "anthropology" (as physical anthropology) and "ethnology," and of "social anthropology" from the rest of anthropology within the twentieth-century British tradition (cf. Stocking 1995a, 1995b). When Tax embarked upon his global travels in the propagation of "world anthropology," he carried with him the baggage of this embracive and expansive American disciplinary ideology, and insofar as "world anthropology" exists today as an institutionalized entity, it still bears the birth markings of that ideology.

Within the cultural anthropological field already in the 1950s and still today dominant in American anthropology, Tax was not at the time highly regarded as an anthropological theorist, and it would be difficult today to recuperate him. While some (including Tax himself) might point to his early "ego-less" kin chart, or to the "actor/choice" view of culture that can be seen as emergent in the Fox project, or to other tendencies within action anthropology as potentially fruitful conceptually, these are hardly enough to counter the view of his contemporaries (at points in effect acknowledged by Tax) that he had abandoned theory for action in the organization and propagation of anthropology and in support of cultural self-determination among native peoples. Similarly, his contribution to ethnography—the focus of his energies for the first decade of his anthropological career—was to a considerable extent forestalled by delays in publication and by his turn to activism (cf. above, 176 and note 2). Nevertheless, to illuminate both his own career and that of postwar anthropology, it may be helpful to consider briefly Tax's relation to major postwar tendencies in American cultural anthropology: acculturation and culture change, neo-evolutionism, culture and personality, and the study of world view and values, and, more generally, the universalistic scientism of the period.

Acculturation was systematically articulated in the 1930s as an outgrowth of the dominant Boasian diffusionist tradition (Stocking 1976:142–44), and by the 1950s it represented a pattern of cultural theory which seems in retrospect already to have been near exhaustion (to await reincarnation in diasporic and transnational interests of the 1990s [e.g. Apter 1991]). But if a change in conceptual terminology from "acculturation" and "culture contact" (among the structural-functionally inclined) to the more dynamic and inclusive "cultural change" had already begun by the time of the Wenner-Gren symposium of 1952, "acculturation" was still prominent among the conclave's major processual categories (Beals 1953). And when Robert Redfield, in the discussion that followed, found some merit in Tax's "perfectly outrageous hypothesis that acculturation never occurs," it was only with the caution that he could not be speaking of acculturation in "the ordinary sense" (Tax et al. 1953:128). Although acculturation was variously problematized in the symposium review, and increasingly weighted toward psychological processes, acculturation studies nevertheless continued to be carried on throughout the decade. Indeed, it was not until the middle 1960s that the supercession of "acculturation" by "cultural change" was decisively manifest in the conceptual categories of the *Biennial Review of Anthropology*. And in that process, there was no mention of Tax's "outrageous hypothesis," which had been put forward in the realm of action and applied rather than theoretical anthropology.[15]

15. Tax's work on the Fox Project is given brief mention in Spindler & Spindler 1959:52, but without reference to his rejection of acculturation. There is evidence, however, to suggest that at the time, Tax's volte face was favorably received by some anthropologists (131/6: "1952")— and that others were independently critical of the concept. While Tax himself did not pursue the issue theoretically, at least one student of his who did not go into action anthropology was involved in ethnographic research that demonstrated resistance to acculturation, and went beyond Tax to argue the complexity of the processes involved (Edward Bruner, pers. comm.). In contrast, it is worth noting that Redfield's work was a major reference point in general anthropo-

In contrast to acculturation, the neo-evolutionism that flourished for a decade or so after 1950 represented a substantial departure from Boasian anthropology, which had defined itself in the critique of Lewis Henry Morgan and nineteenth-century evolutionism (Stocking 1976:124, 135; Wolf 1964). Tax's relation to the reemergence of evolutionism from the prewar margins of professional anthropology was somewhat ambiguous. On the one hand, his role in curriculum revision and the Darwin Centennial, as well as his support of Washburn's evolutionary interests in primate studies, reinforced an evolutionary view of the emergence of human culture. On the other hand, his rejection of acculturation was itself anti-evolutionary, insofar as such studies had an implicit evolutionary tendency, with relative acculturation interpreted in terms of psychological characteristics differentiating the more traditional or "native-oriented" individuals or groups from those adapted to urban or "White man culture"—differences sometimes laid out in geographical sequence along a line of increasing distance from some outpost of Western civilization (Spindler & Spindler 1971; Hallowell 1955:307–58). Writing to Stanley Diamond in 1962, Tax recalled that he had "for a time worked within the Folk-Urban framework," but during the Fox Project "lost interest" in "hypothesized stages of any kind—even as ideal types." Indeed, his subsequent world travels had convinced him that "anthropology had gone wrong by associating itself with the study of 'primitives'"—a word that inevitably had "pejorative" connotations (23/3: 5/23/62). Even so, there was, from 1926 on, a continuing evolutionary undercurrent in Tax's own thinking, which articulated with the cultural polarities favored by Redfield, insofar as Tax (like many anthropologists before and since) continued to see tribal peoples in "soft primitivist" terms as polar oppositional other-worldly alternatives to Western urban industrial civilization. But if Tax did not systematically anticipate the longer-term reaction against evolutionism that began in the middle 1960s, it is important to note that his action anthropology commitment to cultural preservation and self-determination involved a distancing from the evolutionism inherent in "modernization" and "development" anthropology (Tax 1963).

Neither Redfield nor Tax was closely associated with the culture and personality movement—another extension of the Boasian tradition that as a paradigm, came upon hard times in the 1950s (Stocking 1986:9). But in trying to give meaning to Tax's "outrageous hypothesis" at the Wenner-Gren symposium, Redfield pointed to the work of A. I. Hallowell "and others" as demonstrating the "peculiar stability" of "personality type" through historical time

---

logical discussion during the 1950s, especially in relation to peasant societies (Geertz 1961:23). Paradoxically, in view of Redfield's reservations about the enterprise, he was also an important theoretical influence on action anthropology (Pavlik 1998:57, 107, 128–31, 136, 229).

(in Tax et al. 1953:128). In Hallowell's ethnographic work on the Berens River Ojibwa, the study of personality type was closely associated not only with acculturation, but also with the study of "world view" (1955:112–82), which (in an evolutionary framework) was also a central concept in Redfield's later anthropology. A further link in this chain of conceptual affinities is suggested by Redfield's reference, after quoting Clyde Kluckhohn's definition of "value" at the Wenner-Gren symposium, to the idea that "all sectors of Pueblo life are bound together by a consistent, harmonious set of values which pervade [the] categories of [their] world view . . ." (Tax et al. 1953:322–24). At that point, we are close to the definition of culture offered a year previously by Kroeber and Kluckhohn in their "critical review of concepts and definitions," in which "values" were "the essential core of culture" (1952:181). And at this point, we are close as well to the essential core of Tax's anthropology and of American anthropology generally in the early Cold War period.

Approaching that core, it is important to keep in mind that each of the anthropological tendencies considered here may be interpreted in terms of its presumed function in support of American national or imperial interests in the Cold War era: acculturation and evolutionism insofar as they imply a universal teleological developmental process in which American economic, political and, cultural forms were the highest manifestation; culture and personality — in the form of national character studies — in more directly instrumental terms (Mead & Metraux 1953). In each case, Tax's relationship was qualified: for acculturation, by his critical turn; for evolution, by his residual soft primitivism; for culture and personality, by his noninvolvement. And despite his early experience with structural-functionalism in the Radcliffe-Brownian mode and his late futuristic references to "the system," Tax seems also to have had little interest or involvement in systems theory, in either its Parsonian or its more generalized mode—which, although not treated here, was perhaps the most important of the more "scientistic" tendencies in American social science during the early Cold War period.

But it is in relation to the problem of "values"—a widespread concern in post–World War II American social science, and especially in anthropology (Edel 1988)—that Tax's particular position in Cold War anthropology comes most sharply into focus, especially, perhaps, when considered in relation to that of Clyde Kluckhohn. Despite significant differences, Tax and Kluckhohn shared enough in life experience and anthropological orientation to make a comparison historically suggestive, given the central role of value in the thinking of both men.

Born in the same year in adjacent midwestern states, near-contemporaries at the University of Wisconsin, they were both anthropologically eclectic within the Boasian tradition. Each was involved in a postwar long-term team-research project (cf. Foster et al. 1979)—and each with mixed results, in terms of his ultimate objectives. Both were cultural relativists convinced of the relevance of anthropology to the problems of modern life. And, most important, both were liberal democrats with a sense of the world historical significance, in a particular world historical moment, of certain fundamental American cultural values (cf. Taylor et al. 1973).

Tax might well have accepted Kluckhohn's suggestion that "the crisis of our age is a crisis of value," and would surely have agreed that "the world must be kept safe for differences," and that the "democratic solution is that of orchestrated heterogeneity" (Kluckhohn 1949:270). But there are significant contrasts in their thinking about values, in terms of motive, method, and meaning. Both men responded to the mind-wrenching ethical and eschatological issues raised by Nazism and the atom bomb, which gave a poignant urgency to the recurrent intellectual problem of rationalizing cultural relativism with panhuman standards of morality, civilization, and scientific knowledge. But the weighting and the trajectory of their concerns were quite different. Kluckhohn worried about the limits of relativism and the possibility of panhuman moral standards: for him, toleration of "other ways of life" was demanded only "so long as they do not threaten the hope for world order" (1949: 268). The "key question [was] that of universal human values," and Kluckhohn felt that "in principle, a scientific basis for values [was] discoverable" (285–86). It was with this goal in mind that he designed and directed the Harvard Comparative Study of Values in Five Cultures, an ambitious empirical study of the cultural variability of values in an environmentally homogeneous area of northwestern New Mexico, a project whose methodology clearly reflected the positivist scientism of the 1950s (Powers 1997).

In contrast, Tax seems to have experienced little or no contradiction between his growing cultural relativism and the panhuman value assumptions that were implicit in the method of action anthropology and sustained by his underlying evolutionary optimism. For Tax, who in the early 1950s repudiated "pure science," differing cultural values were more likely to be revealed in interaction with the ethnographic subject rather than derived in the analysis of data by a disinterested scientific observer—whose values as scientist were also very much at issue. But perhaps the most meaningful comparison between Kluckhohn and Tax is the difference in the oppositions that framed their value thinking. For Tax, it was the contrast between the values of tribal societies and those of Western culture; for Kluckhohn, it was that between American democratic and Nazi or Soviet totalitarian values.

That contrast is foreshadowed in their wartime and early postwar careers. Tax's institutional connections and professional activities in this period did not involve close relations with the United States government, and his developing activism on behalf of native American self-determination tended in fact to place him in an oppositional role. Kluckhohn, on the other hand,

Clyde Kluckhohn, pondering an issue raised by his tabular characterization of value-emphases in five southwestern cultures (cf. Kluckhohn 1956:127), at a roundtable discussion chaired by Sol Tax on the occasion of the twenty-fifth anniversary of the dedication of the Social Science Building at the University of Chicago, November 11, 1955. (Courtesy of the Department of Special Collections, University of Chicago Library.)

had been one of the many anthropologists actively involved in the war effort, serving as co-chief of the Foreign Morale Analysis Division of the Office of War Information (Taylor et al. 1973). His wartime intelligence work segued easily into an advisory role to the defense establishment in the early Cold War period—the more easily in view of the close linkages that already existed between northeastern academic institutions and the government. By early 1951, Kluckhohn was refusing anthropological commitments because of his heavy involvement in defense-related government work, for which he had "top secret" clearance, and which included advising the Air Force not only on the selection, training, and evaluation of personnel, but also on the morale factors in the choice of potential bombing sites in the Soviet Union (CKP: Box 4490.5). As the founding director of the Harvard University Russian Research Center, he sometimes encouraged students in projects of specific interest to the Central Intelligence Agency and other governmental agencies without informing them of this fact (Diamond 1992:59, 109).

The point, however, is not to stereotype Kluckhohn as an ardent "cold warrior" or a "true believer" in the ways and means of the national security state (cf. Price 1998). Both he and the issues he faced were too complex (both at the time and in historical retrospect) for such simplified ideological characterization. It is rather to suggest how, in the postwar and Cold War period, two anthropologists who shared a serious commitment to the values of a liberal democratic anthropology might be led along very different paths of action in the world. More generally, one might argue that future historical interpretations of American anthropology in the Cold War period should take into account not only the divergent experiences of Tax and Kluckhohn, but also those of others whose intellectual, ethical, ideological, and activist commitments and trajectories may differ significantly.

Thinking about such dissimilar experiences requires also sensitivity to historical transitions or phases and to the way in which these affected historical actors at the time. For Kluckhohn and many other anthropologists, the transition from the struggle against totalitarianism in World War II through the brief "new world order" optimism of the early United Nations moment to a renewed antitotalitarian commitment in a repolarizing world—whether or not viewed as "service to the national security state"—reflected, in its conscious ideological aspect, not simply anticommunism, but a consistent belief in the values of American liberal democracy. The sense of a radical dissociation between those values and United States international policy came at different times for different actors, but was not widely evident in the anthropological community until the later 1960s.

From the anti-Vietnam War perspective of that later moment (which is the implicit interpretive standpoint of much subsequent radical critique), some might regard the participation of anthropologists in Voice of America broadcasts as politically problematic if not morally questionable (cf. Nelson 1997). But the matter did not present itself in these terms in 1961 when the United States Information Agency, in an effort to respond to recent criticism of VOA (and worried lest it be seen as a waste of time and money better spent "on this business of who is ahead in the space race") asked Sol Tax to organize a series on anthropology as "an example of how we in the United States look at the world" (267/2: W. Nichols/ST 9/15/61). Tax took it as an opportunity for the discipline's "younger, most creative men" to present its "new frontiers" (still strikingly neo-evolutionary) to listeners whom he imagined as a "general audience at the University of Moscow" (Tax 1964:6). While clearance was apparently a problem in the case of one "questionable nominee," those invited—two of whom were in fact women—do not seem to have been reluctant to participate (267, 268).[16] This, even though a number of them were later

16. Expressed here rhetorically ("creative men") and qualified in the event, the exclusion of women is one of several exclusionary processes that would require exploration in a more gen-

among the more vigorous critics of American overseas involvement in Latin America and Southeast Asia and among the advocates of a "reinvented" anthropology that would study "dominated cultures" and "cultures of power" (Hymes 1972; Horowitz 1967; Wakin 1992). The point, of course, is that while there were intimations of a radical critical consciousness even in the 1950s (e.g., Manners 1956), it was not until the mid-1960s that radical critique became a significant force in American anthropology—and that many issues often now perceived in that context did not present themselves in the same terms to most actors before 1964.

To advocate an empathic sensitivity to the experiential perspective of historical actors (analogous to that of an ethnographer for the beliefs and behavior of ethnographic subjects in the present) is not to deny the historiographical legitimacy and fruitfulness, for certain purposes, of present perspectives—even, in a limiting methodological and epistemological sense, their inevitability. There are, and should be, metanarrative frameworks that may facilitate a more generalized transhistorical understanding, beyond the vision of most historical actors. For a disillusioned Marxist turned pessimistic academic liberal like myself, the most salient of these metanarratives are in fact the radical critical ("the rise of the national security state" and the global interests of "American imperialism"). That salience is constrained, however, by methodological and ethical anxiety lest simplification obscure the perspective and the experience of the historical actor. If there is understanding to be gained by viewing Tax as an actor, witting or unwitting, in the imperial theater of the "American Century," it seems "experience nearer" (in a historical as well as an anthropological sense) to think of him as very much in the "American Grain" (cf. Geertz 1974:58). This, not in the tradition of "manifest destiny," but rather that of the "city on a hill" and town meeting democracy—manifest even in the way Tax's vision of the world community of anthropologists resonates to the "participatory democracy" of 1960s student radicalism (cf. Gitlin 1993).

In placing the life and work of an individual in a broader interpretive framework, there is something to be said for an idea of "resonance"—especially for

eral treatment of anthropology in the Cold War period. One measure of its power might be to compare degree lists of the 1950s with faculty lists of the 1970s; a similar comparative yardstick might be the lists of participants in the various team projects. The exclusionary impact of anti-Communism is also worthy of more systematic study (cf. Schrecker 1986; Price 1998)—with reference as well to the underground role of Marxism in certain theoretical tendencies, research projects, and institutional loci (most notably, perhaps, Columbia). The exclusionary impact of race is evident in the biographical essays collected in Harrison & Harrison 1999. As for the impact of homophobia, it is worth noting the suggestion that Kluckhohn's relation to the defense establishment may have been enforced by knowledge the FBI had of his homosexuality (Diamond 1992:296–97) one who prefers the suggestive in-(*or* over-)determinacy of "context" to the assertive determinism of "cause." As opposed to the idea of "impact" (implying compellingly demonstrable effect) or "influence" (implying convincingly discernable connection), an idea of "resonance"—whatever its general historiographic utility—seems especially appropriate in the case of Tax, given his marginalization from mainstream anthropology during the last three decades of his life.[17] This is not to imply that his work was without impact during the period of his greatest activity: at the very least, it can be said that his contribution to the modern American Indian movement, if underappreciated, is undeniable; so also, his role as organizer and propagator of world anthropology. But in turning to action anthropology, in a period when the discipline was busily seeking scientific legitimation, Tax effectively forestalled any contribution he might have made to anthropological theory or method. And in a period when even the more scientifically legitimate idea of applied anthropology had distinctly secondary status within the discipline, Tax's more radical program of action anthropology was kept at the margins—and was still there when the radical resurgence began in the later 1960s.

Although Tax's essay, "The Integration of Anthropology," is cited several times in the introduction to *Reinventing Anthropology* and also on the issue of "relevance" in one of the chapters, his name goes unmentioned in the rest of the volume—even in the chapter on cultural change and resistance among Native Americans, where it might have been most relevant (Hymes 1972). Two and a half decades further on, David Maybury-Lewis, the founder of *Cultural Survival* (a venture quite consistent with Tax's preservationist orientation) did not remember Tax as an influence (pers. comm.), though in 1971 he had in fact consulted him as "the doyen of activists in anthropology" (46/6: DM-L/ST 10/27/71). Similarly, it was only upon hearing the eulogies at Tax's memorial celebration that Terry Turner, for 25 years a colleague in the same department and an activist in the 1990s movement for the empowerment of indigenous peoples, appreciated the fact that they had both been involved in the same enterprise (pers. comm.). At this point, we are more in the realm of resonance than of influence or of impact.

Lingering for a moment longer in that methodologically problematic

17. In using the word "resonance," what I intend it to convey is a sense of resemblance-in-recurrence across historical time, when a specific medium of transmission is not easily or at all determinable—a resemblance-in-recurrence of ideas that may differ in original content and context, but which sound (or re-sound as) familiar, and are susceptible of amplification (and distortion) in later contexts, to purposes that seem to the hearer in significant respects the same as those of the original speaker. Resonance may refer to the voice of a particular past individual speaker, or the echoes of a particular era; resonance may also be transhistorical in a broader sense, insofar as it refers to leitmotifs of human thought, re-sounding in the zeitgeists of different eras. Both senses are germane to the present interpretation of Tax.

realm, one may briefly call attention to themes in Tax's career as action anthropologist that are still resonant today and may resonate on into the new millennium. Over the shorter historical span of the last half century, echoes may be still be heard, and may perhaps be amplified, in present conceptual and methodological notions of agency, empowerment, globalization, ethnicity, identity, multiculturalism, reflexivity, relevance, voice—as well as other topics reflected in the tables of contents of the *American Anthropologist*. Such resonances reverberate more loudly as one moves into the recently refurbished arena of action, where "what is relevant in anthropology" has been the theme of the *Anthropology Newsletter* for 1998–99, and "public interest anthropology" is the latest incarnation of the activist impulse (Sanday 1999). Younger anthropologists who lament the "virtual absence of an anthropological voice in US public debate" and the "skepticism" with which "the likes of Margaret Mead have been historically met" within the discipline, now find themselves "seeking the modern Margaret Mead" (*AN* 39 [7]:1). In that context, it is quite possible that Tax may be recovered as a resonant kindred spirit.

Over a wider and longer transhistorical span, Tax's activist anthropology resonates with Franz Boas' "anthropology as *Kulturkampf*" (Stocking 1992) and, more distantly, with E. B. Tylor's "reformer's science" of ethnology (Stocking 1995a:xiv, 370). In somewhat different ways, both these founding figures may be heard as sounding a number of enduring and familiar contrapuntal themes that resonate throughout the further reaches of the Euro-American anthropological tradition: progressivism and romanticism, universalism and relativism, pragmatism and utopianism, vindication and critique, identity and alterity. How long into the next millennium they will be sounded in association with the name and career of Sol Tax remains to be heard.

Acknowledgments

A draft of the first half of this essay was written and presented orally during my term as Fellow of the Dibner Institute for the History of Science and Technology at the Massachusetts Institute of Technology (January–March 1998); it also benefited from discussion at a meeting of the Morris Fishbein Center Workshop in the History of the Human Sciences, University of Chicago, May 19, 1998. The larger research project of which the essay is a part is supported by a grant from the Wenner-Gren Foundation for Anthropological Research. I would like also to thank the staffs of the research archives mentioned below (and especially of the Regenstein Library Department of Special Collections), without whose assistance I would not have been able to prepare this essay. Others who were helpful in various ways include my research assistants, Stephen Rosecan and Kevin Caffrey, the staff of the Department of Anthropology, and a number of colleagues and friends, including Robert McC. Adams, Grant Arndt, Edward Bruner, Matti Bunzl, Harvey Choldin, Noah Efron, Raymond Fogelson, Richard Handler, Dell Hymes, John Kelly, David Maybury-Lewis, Norman McQuown, Rob Moore, Murray Murphey, Manning Nash, Lisa Peattie, Barbara Rosenkrantz, Sam Schweber, Carol Bowman Stocking, Terry Straus, William Sturtevant, Terry Turner, and Murray Wax—as well as Raymond Smith, who managed to rescue several pages of painfully produced text that had vanished, unsaved, into the bowels of my computer. Susan Tax Freeman and Marianna Tax Choldin graciously encouraged and assisted my interest in their father without inhibiting it in the slightest respect.

References Cited

Ablon, J. 1979. The American Indian Chicago Conference. In Hinshaw 1979a:445–56.

Abrahamson, J. 1959. *A neighborhood finds itself.* New York.

AICC. 1961. Declaration of Indian purpose. American Indian Chicago Conference, University of Chicago.

Apter, A. 1991. Herskovits's heritage: Rethinking syncretism in the African diaspora. *Diaspora* 1 (3): 235–60.

Barbachano, F. C. 1979. The influence of Sol Tax on Mexican social anthropology. In Hinshaw 1979a:103–9.

Bashkow, I. 1991. The dynamics of rapport in a colonial situation: David Schneider's fieldwork on the islands of Yap. In *Colonial situations: Essays on the contextualization of ethnographic knowledge,* ed. G. W. Stocking, Jr., HOA 7:170–242.

Beals, R. 1953. Acculturation. In Kroeber et al. 1953:621–41.

Bennett, J. 1998. Applied and action anthropology: Problems of ideology and intervention. In Bennett, *Classic anthropology: Critical essays, 1944–1956,* 315–58. New Brunswick, N.J.

Bennett, W. 1947. *The ethnogeographic board.* Washington, D.C.

Blanchard, D. 1979. Beyond empathy: The emergence of an action anthropology in the life and career of Sol Tax. In Hinshaw 1979a:419–43.

Bowman, G. 1998. ICAES, Williamsburg. *Anthropology Today* 14 (6): 22.

Boyer, P. 1985. *By the bomb's early light: American thought and culture at the dawn of the atomic age.* New York.

Brazier, A. 1969. *Black self-determination: The story of the Woodlawn Organization.* Grand Rapids, Mich.

Comas, J. 1954. *Los congresos internacionales de Americanistas.* México, D.F.: Instituto Indigenista Interamericano.

Cornell, S. 1988. *The return of the native: American Indian political resurgence.* New York.

Cronon, E., & J. Jenkins. 1994. *The University of Wisconsin: A history. Vol. 3: Politics, depression, and war, 1925–1945.* Madison, Wis.

Diamond, S. 1992. *Compromised campus: The collaboration of universities with the intelligence community, 1945–1955.* New York.

Dodds, J. W. 1973. *The several lives of Paul Fejos: A Hungarian-American odyssey.* New York: Wenner-Gren Foundation.

Drake, St. C. 1978. Reflections on anthropology and the black experience. *Anthropology and Education Quarterly* 9:85–109.

Drake, St. C., & H. Cayton. 1945. *Black metropolis: A Study of Negro life in a northern city.* 2 vols. New York.

Edel, A. 1988. The concept of value and its travels in twentieth-century America. In M. Murphey & I. Berg, eds., *Values and value theory in twentieth-century America,* 12–36. Philadelphia.

Fejos, P. 1953. Report of the Director of Research. In *Report on Foundation activities for the year ended January 31, 1953.* New York: Wenner-Gren Foundation.

Foley, D. 1999. The Fox project: A reappraisal. *Current Anthropology* 40:193–210.

Foster, G., et al., eds. 1979. *Long-term field research in social anthropology.* New York.

Fried, M., M. Harris & R. Murphy, eds. 1968. *War: The anthropology of armed conflict and aggression.* Garden City, N.Y.

Gaddis, J. 1997. *We now know: Rethinking Cold War history.* Oxford.

Gearing, F. 1970. *The face of the Fox.* Chicago.

Gearing, F., R. McC. Netting & L. R. Peattie. 1960. *Documentary history of the Fox project: A program in action anthropology.* Chicago.

Geertz, C. 1961. Studies in peasant life: Community and society. In Siegel 1961:1–41.

Geertz, C. 1974. "From the native's point of view": On the nature of anthropological understanding. In *Local knowledge: Further essays in interpretive anthropology,* 55–70. New York.

Gillin, J., et al. 1949. Research needs in the field of modern Latin American culture. *American Anthropologist* 51:149–54.

Gitlin, T. 1993. *The sixties: Years of hope, days of rage.* Rev. ed. New York.

Godoy, R. 1977. Franz Boas and his plans for the International School of American Archaeology and Ethnology in Mexico. *Journal of the History of the Behavioral Sciences* 13:228–42.

Goldschmidt, W. 1956. From the editor's desk. *American Anthropologist* 58:1–3.

GS/ICAES. George W. Stocking, Jr., personal collection of pre-Congress notices.

Hafferkamp, J. 1973. Man, oh mankind, what a happening. *Chicago Daily News,* Panorama, 11–12 Aug., pp. 2–3.

Hall, R. 1947. *Area studies: With special reference to their implications for research in the social sciences.* SSRC Pamphlet 3. New York.

Hallowell, A. 1955. *Culture and experience.* Philadelphia.

Handler, R. 1990. Boasian anthropology and the critique of American culture. *American Quarterly* 42:252–72.

Haraway, D. 1988. Remodeling the human way of life: Sherwood Washburn and the new physical anthropology, 1950–1980. In *Bones, bodies, behavior: Essays on biological anthropology,* ed. G. W. Stocking, Jr., HOA 5:206–60.

Harnad, S. 1997. Learned inquiry and the Net: The role of peer review, peer commentary and copyright. *Antiquity* 71:1042–48.

Harrison, I., & F. Harrison, eds. 1999. *African-American pioneers in anthropology.* Urbana, Ill.

Herskovits, M. 1949. *Man and his works.* New York.

Hinshaw, R., ed. 1979a. *Currents in anthropology: Essays in honor of Sol Tax.* The Hague.

Hinshaw, R. 1979b. Preface. In Hinshaw 1979a: ix–xvii.

Hinshaw, R. 1979c. Sol Tax. *International encyclopedia of the social sciences* 18:760–63.

Hirsch, A. 1983. *Making the second ghetto: Race and housing in Chicago, 1940–1960.* Cambridge.

Hollinger, D. 1996. *Science, Jews, and secular culture: Studies in mid-twentieth-century American intellectual history.* Princeton, N.J.

Honigmann, J. 1959. Psychocultural studies. In Siegel 1959:67–106.

Horowitz, I., ed. 1967. *The rise and fall of Project Camelot.* Cambridge, Mass.

Hymes, D., ed. 1972. *Reinventing anthropology.* New York.

Kluckhohn, C. 1949. *Mirror for man: The relation of anthropology to modern life.* New York.

Kluckhohn, C. 1956. Toward a comparison of value-emphases in different cultures. In L. White, ed., *The state of the social sciences,* 116–32. Chicago.

Kroeber, A., & C. Kluckhohn. 1952. *Culture: A critical review of concepts and definitions.* Cambridge, Mass.

Kroeber, A., et al. 1953. *Anthropology today: An encyclopedic inventory.* Chicago.

Lambert, R. 1973. *Language and area studies review.* Monograph 17 of the American Academy of Political and Social Science. Philadelphia.

Lewis, O. 1951. *Life in a Mexican village: Tepoztlán restudied.* Urbana, Ill.

Linton, R. 1936. *The study of man: An introduction.* New York.

Lovejoy, A. & G. Boas. 1935. *Primitivism and related ideas in antiquity.* Baltimore, Md.

Lurie, N. 1961. The voice of the American Indian: Report on the American Indian Chicago Conference. *Current Anthropology* 2:478–500.

Lurie, N. 1999. Sol Tax and tribal sovereignty. *Human Organization* 58:108–17.

Lyons, G. 1969. *The uneasy partnership: Social science and the federal government in the twentieth century.* New York.

Manners, R. 1956. Functionalism, realpolitik, and anthropology in underdeveloped areas. *America Indigena* 16:7–33.

Marett, R. 1912. *Anthropology.* London.

Maruyama, M. 1978. Toward human futuristics. In Maruyama & A. Harkins, eds., *Cultures of the future,* 33–59. The Hague.

Maruyama, M. 1979. Transepistemological understanding: Wisdom beyond theories. In Hinshaw 1979a:371–90.

Mead, M. 1959. *An anthropologist at work: Writings of Ruth Benedict.* Boston.

Mead, M., & R. Metraux, eds. 1953. *The study of culture at a distance.* Chicago.

Morgan, L. 1871. *Systems of consanguinity and affinity of the human family.* Osterhout, N.B., Netherlands (1970).

Myrdal, G. 1944. *An American dilemma: The Negro problem and modern democracy.* New York.

Nader, L. 1997. The phantom factor: Impact of the Cold War on anthropology. In N. Chomsky et al., *The Cold War and the university: Toward an intellectual history of the postwar years,* 107–46. New York.

Nash, M. 1965. Economic anthropology. In Siegel 1965:121–38.

Nelson, M. 1997. *War of the black heavens: The battles of western broadcasting in the Cold War.* Syracuse, N.Y.

Nesper, L. 1994. Waswagonniniwug: Conflict, tradition and identity in the Lac du Flambeau band of Lake Superior Chippewa Indians spearfishing the ceded territory of Wisconsin. Doct. diss., Univ. of Chicago.

Parker, D. 1992. *Singing an Indian song: A biography of D'Arcy McNickle.* Lincoln, Neb.

Patterson, J. 1996. *Grand expectations: The United States, 1945–1974.* New York.

Pavlik, S., ed. 1998. *A good Cherokee, a good anthropologist: Papers in honor of Robert K. Thomas.* American Indian Studies Center. Los Angeles.

Powers, W. 1997. The Harvard five cultures values study and post war anthropology. Doct. diss., Univ. of New Mexico.

Prados, J. 1986. *Presidents' secret wars: CIA and Pentagon covert operations since World War II.* New York.

Price, D. 1998. Cold War anthropology: Collaborators and victims of the national security state. *Identities* 4(3–4):389–430.

Price, D. n.d. http://www.stmartin.edu/homepages/fac_staff/dprice/

Provinse, J., et al. 1954. The American Indian in transition. *American Anthropologist* 56:388–93.

Prucha, F. 1985. *The Indians in American society: From the Revolutionary War to the present.* Berkeley, Calif.

Redfield, R. 1941. *The folk culture of Yucatan.* Chicago.

Redfield, R. 1953. *The primitive world and its transformations.* Ithaca, N.Y.

Redfield, R. 1958. Values in action: A comment. *Human Organization* 17:20–22.

Redfield, R., R. Linton & M. Herskovits. 1936. Memorandum for the study of acculturation. *American Anthropologist* 38:149–52.

Rossi, P., & R. Dentler. 1961. *The politics of urban renewal: The Chicago findings.* Glencoe, Ill.

Rubinstein, R. 1986. Reflections on action anthropology: Some developmental dynamics of an anthropological tradition. *Human Organization* 43:270–79.

Rubinstein, R. 1991a. Conversation with Sol Tax. *Current Anthropology* 32:175–83.

Rubinstein, R., ed. 1991b. *Fieldwork: The correspondence of Robert Redfield and Sol Tax.* Boulder, Colo.

Sanday, P. 1999. Public interest anthropology. *Anthropology Newsletter* 40 (3):32.

Sapolsky, H. 1990. *Science and the navy: The history of the Office of Naval Research.* Princeton, N.J.

Scheer, R. 1965. *How the United States got involved in Vietnam: A report to the Center for the Study of Democratic Institutions.* Santa Barbara, Calif.

Schrecker, E. 1986. *No ivory tower: McCarthyism and the universities.* New York and Oxford.

Shea, M., & M. Emmons. 1972. Anthropology and social problems: Population; environment; education. *Current Anthropology* 13:279–83.

Siegel, B., ed. 1959–65. *Biennial review[s] of anthropology.* Stanford, Calif.

Silverman, S., et al. 1991. Reflections on fifty years of anthropology and the role of the Wenner-Gren Foundation. In *Report for 1990 and 1991. Fiftieth anniversary issue,* 5–70. New York: Wenner-Gren Foundation.

Smocovitis, V. 1996. *Unifying biology: The evolutionary synthesis.* Princeton, N.J.

Smocovitis, V. 1997. Celebrating Darwin: The 1959 Darwin Centennial Celebration at the University of Chicago. MS prepared for a volume of *Osiris.*

Spence, A. 1973. The Fox project. MS in STP 26/4.

Spindler, G., & L. Spindler. 1959. Culture change. In Siegel 1959:37–66.

Spindler, G., & L. Spindler. 1971. *Dreamers without power.* New York.

Steiner, S. 1968. *The new Indians.* New York.

Stocking, G. W., Jr. 1968. The scientific reaction against cultural anthropology, 1917–1920. In *Race, culture and evolution: Essays in the history of anthropology,* 270–307. New York.

Stocking, G. W., Jr. 1976. Ideas and institutions in American anthropology: Thoughts toward a history of the interwar years. In Stocking 1992:114–77.

Stocking, G. W., Jr. 1978. The problems of translating between paradigms: The 1933 debate between Ralph Linton and Radcliffe-Brown. *History of Anthropology Newsletter* 5 (1): 7–9.

Stocking, G. W., Jr. 1979a. Anthropology as *Kulturkampf:* Science and politics in the career of Franz Boas. In Stocking 1992:92–113.

Stocking, G. W., Jr. 1979b. *Anthropology at Chicago: Tradition, discipline, department.* Chicago: Regenstein Library.

Stocking, G. W., Jr. 1980. Redfield, Robert. *Dictionary of American biography,* Supplement 6, 1956–1960:532–34. New York.

Stocking, G. W., Jr. 1982. The Santa Fe style in American anthropology: Regional interest, academic initiative, and philanthropic policy in the first two decades of the Laboratory of Anthropology, Inc. *Journal of the History of the Behavioral Sciences* 18:3–19.

Stocking, G. W., Jr. 1986. Essays on culture and personality. In *Malinowski, Rivers, Benedict and others: Essays on culture and personality,* ed. G. W. Stocking, Jr. HOA 4:3–12.

Stocking, G. W., Jr. 1987. *Victorian anthropology.* New York.

Stocking, G. W., Jr. 1992. *The ethnographer's magic and other essays in the history of anthropology.* Madison, Wis.

Stocking, G. W., Jr. 1995a. *After Tylor: British social anthropology, 1888–1951.* Madison, Wis.

Stocking, G. W., Jr. 1995b. Delimiting anthropology: Historical reflections on the boundaries of a boundless discipline. *Social Research* 62:933–66.

Sullivan, P. 1989. *Unfinished conversations: Mayas and foreigners between two wars.* Berkeley, Calif.

Tax, S. 1931. An Algerian Passover. *The American Hebrew,* 3 April, p. 548.

Tax, S. 1935. Primitive social organization with some description of the social organization of the Fox Indians. Doct. diss., Univ. of Chicago.

Tax, S. 1937a. Some problems of social organization. In F. Eggan, ed., *Social anthropology of North American tribes,* 3–32. Chicago.

Tax, S. 1937b. The social organization of the Fox Indians. In F. Eggan, ed., *Social anthropology of North American tribes,* 243–85. Chicago.

Tax, S. 1945a. Anthropology and administration. *America Indigena* 5:21–33.

Tax, S. 1945b. The problem of democracy in middle America. *American Sociological Review* 10:192–99.

Tax, S., ed. 1951a. *Acculturation in the Americas: Proceedings and selected papers of the XXIXth International Congress of Americanists.* Vol. 3. Chicago.

Tax, S., ed. 1951b. *The civilizations of ancient America: Selected papers of the XXIXth International Congress of Americanists.* Vol. 1. Chicago.

Tax, S., ed. 1952a. *Heritage of conquest: The ethnology of Middle America.* New York (1973).

Tax, S., ed. 1952b. *Indian tribes of aboriginal America: Selected papers of the XXIXth International Congress of Americanists.* Vol. 2. Chicago.

Tax, S. 1953a. Editorial. *American Anthropologist* 55:1–3.

Tax, S. 1953b. *Penny capitalism: Guatemalan Indian economy.* Smithsonian Institution Institute of Social Anthropology Pub. 16. Washington, D.C.

Tax, S. 1954. Wenner-Gren Foundation supper conference. *American Anthropologist* 56:387–88.

Tax, S. 1955. From Lafitau to Radcliffe-Brown: A short history of the study of social organization. In F. Eggan, ed., *Social anthropology of North American tribes,* 2d ed., 445–84. Chicago.

Tax, S. 1956a. The integration of anthropology. In Thomas 1956:313–28.

Tax, S. 1956b. No 'crime' in SECC. *Chicago Maroon,* 30 March, p. 4.

Tax, S. 1958a. Action anthropology. Reprinted in *Current Anthropology* 16:514–17.

Tax, S. 1958b. The Fox project. *Human Organization* 17:17–19.

Tax, S., ed. 1959a. *Current Anthropology: A World Journal of the Sciences of Man.* Pre-issue.

Tax, S. 1959b. Residential integration: The case of Hyde Park in Chicago. *Human Organization* 18:22–27.

Tax, S. 1960. The celebration: A personal view. In Tax & Callender 1960:271–78.

Tax, S. 1963. The importance of preserving Indian culture. STP 267/1.

Tax, S., ed. 1964. *Horizons of anthropology.* Chicago.

Tax, S. 1965. The history and philosophy of *Current Anthropology. Current Anthropology* 6:242–69.

Tax, S., ed. 1967. *The draft: A handbook of facts and alternatives.* Chicago.

Tax, S. 1968a. Last on the war path: A personalized account of how an anthropologist learned from the American Indians. STP 64/8.

Tax, S., ed. 1968b. *The people vs. the system: A dialogue in urban conflict.* Chicago.

Tax, S. 1968c. War and the draft. In Fried, Harris & Murphy 1968:195–207.

Tax, S. 1971. Preface to M. Maruyama & J. Dator, eds., *Human futuristics,* vii–ix. Honolulu.

Tax, S. 1975a. Afterword: The inception of extraterrestrial anthropology. In M. Maruyama & A. Harkins, eds., *Cultures beyond earth,* 200–203. New York.

Tax, S. 1975b. History of *Current Anthropology.* Course lecture by Sol Tax transcribed by Gay Neuberger. STP 247/5.

Tax, S. 1975c. The bow and the hoe: reflections on hunters, villagers, and anthropologists. *Current Anthropology* 16:507–13.

Tax, S. 1977. Anthropology for the world of the future: Thirteen professions and three proposals. *Human Organization* 36:325–34.

Tax, S. 1981. Jewish life in the United States: Perspectives from anthropology. In J. B. Gittler, ed., *Jewish life in the United States: Perspectives from the social sciences*, 297–312. New York.

Tax, S. 1982a. Creation and evolution. Paper prepared for conference on "Science, the Bible and Darwin," SUNY Buffalo, 16–17 April. In STP 280/10.

Tax, S. 1982b. Planning Utopias. *Cultural Futures Research* 7 (1).

Tax, S. 1988. Pride and puzzlement: A retro-introspective record of 60 years in anthropology. *Annual Review of Anthropology* 17:1–21.

Tax, S., & C. Callender, eds. 1960. *Issues in evolution* (Vol. 3 of *Evolution after Darwin*). Chicago.

Tax, S., et al., eds. 1953. *An appraisal of anthropology today*. Chicago.

Tax, S., et al., eds. 1954. *A report on the behavioral sciences at the University of Chicago*. Chicago.

Taylor, W., et al., eds. 1973. *Culture and life: Essays in memory of Clyde Kluckhohn*. Carbondale, Ill.

Thomas, W., ed. 1955. *Yearbook of anthropology*. New York: Wenner-Gren Foundation.

Thomas, W., ed. 1956. *Current Anthropology: A supplement to "Anthropology Today."* New York: Wenner-Gren Foundation.

Tjerandsen, C. 1980. *Education for citizenship: A foundation's experience*. Santa Cruz, Calif.: Emil Schwarzhaupt Foundation.

Wakin, E. 1992. *Anthropology goes to war: Professional ethics and counterinsurgency in Thailand*. Madison: University of Wisconsin Center for Southeast Asian Studies.

Wallace, A., & R. Fogelson. 1961. Culture and personality. In Siegel 1961:42–78.

Wallerstein, E. 1997. The unintended consequences of Cold War area studies. In N. Chomsky et al., *The Cold War and the university: Toward an intellectual history of the postwar years*, 195–233. New York.

Wax, R. 1961. A brief history and analysis of the Workshops on American Indian Affairs conducted for American Indian college students, 1956–60. In STP 157/8.

Wax, R. 1971. *Doing fieldwork: Warnings and advice*. Chicago.

Wolf, E. 1964. *Anthropology*. New York.

Manuscript and Interview Sources

This essay is based primarily on research in about half of the 307 boxes of manuscript materials in the Sol Tax Papers in the Department of Special Collections the Regenstein Library at the University of Chicago, which are systematically catalogued, and in some folders include retrospective comments by Tax himself. These materials are here referred to by box and folder number (without the archival acronym given to other manuscript sources, except where its omission would leave the reader in doubt), with names of correspondents abbreviated where appropriate, and with modifications for documents other than dated letters. More generally, I have drawn on a variety of historical materials collected over the three decades of my membership in the Chicago department. These include interviews with Tax in seminars devoted to the history of anthropology at Chicago, materials collected in the late 1970s for an unrealized history of the department (including questionnaires, texts, and tapes from former students), the reminiscences of colleagues, and my own interaction with Tax over a quarter of a century, both personally and in writing. I have also taken occasional advantage of prior or current research in related materials in the Department of Special Collections: the papers of the University of Chicago Department of Anthropology (cited here as UCDA; cf. Stocking 1979b); the Robert Redfield Papers (RRP; cf. Stocking 1980); the Current Anthropology Papers (CAP); the Darwin Centennial Papers (DCP; cf. Smocovitis 1997); the International Congress of Anthropological and Ethnological Science Papers (ICAES); and the Erwin Tax papers (ETP); as well as ongoing research in the papers of Clyde Kluckhohn (CKP) in the Harvard University Archives.

"IN THE IMMEDIATE VICINITY A WORLD HAS COME TO AN END"

Lucie Varga as an Ethnographer of National Socialism—
A Retrospective Review Essay

RONALD STADE

Introduction

Lucie Varga died at the age of 36. She left a few traces in the sands of time: a daughter, personal memories and testimonies, a short list of publications. What she did *not* leave was a scholarly legacy. And what she did *not* receive during her lifetime and after her death was academic recognition. Almost half a century passed before someone discovered her writings. In 1991, historian Peter Schöttler published *Zeitenwende: Mentalitätshistorische Studien, 1936–1939* ("Tides Turning: Studies in the History of Mentality, 1936–1939"), a volume devoted entirely to Lucie Varga's life and work. Schöttler had come across Varga's name during his research on the relationship between the early Annales School and German historiography, and realized that she represented a personal link between the two. Apart from "discovering" Varga's writings, Schöttler translated several of them into German and provided an extensive introduction to them in *Zeitenwende*. By doing so, he wanted to

Ronald Stade is Associate Professor at the School of International Migration and Ethnic Relations, Malmö University, Sweden. His work focuses on political anthropology, and in particular on the connection between international institutions and cultural trends and local politics. His publications include *Pacific Passages: World Culture and Local Politics in Guam*, "The Production of Sovereignty: Cultural Readings of an Ambiguous Concept," and "Designs of Identity: The Politics of Aesthetics in the GDR."

document the biography and historiographic contribution of a member of the Annales group. My ambition in this essay is more limited. Here I focus on Lucie Varga's ethnographic investigation of the emergence of the National Socialist movement in Germany. Given the fact that Varga's life was structured by the historical processes that led to the Nazi succession to power, the intertwining of her life and work becomes obvious.

A European Biography

Lucie Varga was born as Rosa Stern on June 21, 1904, not far from Vienna.[1] Her Jewish family had roots in Hungary but had assimilated to the German culture of the Habsburg Empire, and her mother tongue was thus German. Rosa, it seems, according to marital records in Vienna, belonged to the Protestant faith.[2] Whether this means that the entire family had converted to Christianity or only Rosa (maybe in later years) is unclear. The conversion of the whole family, however, would not be inconsistent with the assimilationist habitus the Stern family seems to have displayed in other matters.

Malvine Tafler-Stern, Rosa's mother, divorced her husband Gyula (Julius) Stern, who lived in Budapest, and she, Rosa, and Rosa's two elder siblings lived outside Vienna. The family enjoyed an upper-class life style, with servants and a British tutor who taught the children both French and English. Rosa attended a liberal private school in Vienna where the unconventional ideas of the youth movement of the time were allowed to flourish. On a whim, Rosa changed her name to Lucie, despite the mocking remark by one of her teachers that Lucie Stern must be considered a tautology. Soon after graduating from school, Lucie married a physician, Josef Varga, a man 12 years her senior. He too came from a Jewish-Hungarian family, albeit one with considerably fewer assets.

Lucie had suffered from diabetes since her last year in school, and the illness interrupted her university studies, as did the birth of her only child, Berta. Eventually, though, she majored in history and art history and took courses in philosophy and psychology. Her doctoral thesis was a critique of the stereotype of the "Dark Age." In this investigation, she also attacked the simple inversion of medieval prejudices by the Enlightenment: the medieval polemic against heretics, who were described as people who spread false dog-

---

1. Lucie Varga's biography has been synthesized from the following secondary sources: Jay 1973; Lange-Enzmann 1996; Löwenthal 1957; and Schöttler 1991.

2. Lange-Enzmann (1996:56), quoting John Tashjean, who for his unpublished 1962 doctoral thesis interviewed a Hanns Jäger-Sunstenau, whose mother had been a close friend of Lucie's second husband's family. A source is given: Heiratsregister, Evangelisches Pfarramt Helvetischen Bekenntnisses, Wien I (Trauungen 1933/34), Blatt 31, Reihenzahl 57.

mas for the sake of worldly fame, she argued, was inverted by the Enlightenment denunciation of popes, priests, and clerics as power-hungry and fraudulent. Already at this stage one can detect a structural bias in her writing, a
refusal to grant excessive agency to individuals in social analysis.

Franz Borkenau and Paris

In 1932, the Vargas separated. Berta and Lucie moved in with her mother
in Vienna. The following year, Lucie met a fellow historian, Franz Borkenau, who, with a scholarship from the Frankfurt Institute for Social Research,
was conducting research on "The transition from the feudal to the bourgeois
world view" (as the book resulting from this research is entitled, cf. Borkenau 1934). Borkenau's family background was similar to Varga's. His parents
belonged to the Habsburg monarchy's stratum of enlightened civil servants
and judges. Franz's father, Rudolf Pollack, was of Jewish descent but had been
baptized Roman Catholic (many Austrians considered conversion to Christianity a necessary first step toward appointment to higher office). Franz was
adopted by a great-aunt to rid him of the Jewish name Pollack; thus he became
Franz Borkenau. He attended a strict Catholic school, joined a rebellious
youth movement, and eventually received a doctoral degree in philosophy
from Leipzig University. He also joined the German Communist Party and
began working for the Comintern, and under an alias, he became the leader
of the German Communist Student Organization. In connection with his
Comintern tasks, he traveled to England, Belgium, and Spain, establishing
contacts that would prove valuable.

Through Borkenau, Varga was introduced to the Marxian debate on the
dominating question of those years: Why and how could fascism have become
so successful in Europe? Borkenau published an article on the "Sociology
of Fascism" in 1933, arguing that fascism was one stage in an ongoing class
struggle. A key factor in that struggle was societal structure, and, more precisely, the relationship between political and economic developments (what
today might be termed the relationship between state and market), but Borkenau's analysis was not strictly Marxian. Rather, it took into account the kind
of structural contradictions and dynamics analyzed by scholars like Simmel
and Weber. Completely missing from Borkenau's article was detailed ethnographic and historical material. Without pursuing his argument, though, one
can keep his style of analysis in mind when we turn to Lucie Varga's ethnographic study of National Socialism. The differences between Borkenau's and
Varga's approaches will be striking.

Aware of the imminent danger that the rise of Hitlerism posed, Borkenau and Varga decided to emigrate to Paris, where Varga wanted to pursue

her research on the French branch of catharism, a religious movement she had encountered during her doctoral research. With the financial help of Varga's mother, Lucie, Franz, and Berta were able to take all their belongings from Vienna to Paris—"It was almost like a normal change of address," writes Schöttler. Before leaving Vienna, Borkenau converted to Protestantism, and he and Varga were married.

In Paris, Varga began working as Lucien Febvre's assistant. Borkenau was given the opportunity to publish in the *Annales d'histoire économique et sociale*, edited by Febvre and Marc Bloch. Nevertheless, Borkenau realized that his chances of obtaining an academic position in Paris were limited, and in fact, the acceptance Varga had found in Paris was highly unusual. Generally speaking, the French did not welcome the appointment of German scholars in their midst, and it took courage to work openly on behalf of German refugees.

Nevertheless, some people—among them, Maurice Halbwachs and Célestin Bouglé—possessed such courage. They were, however, a minority. Even when emigrés were welcomed and invited to contribute to ongoing research —as Febvre had encouraged Borkenau—profound misunderstandings between established French and German scholars occurred. For instance, Borkenau, while in exile, was part of the resistance group Neu Beginnen ("Beginning Anew"), named after a brochure published by Walter Löwenheim under the pseudonym "Miles." The group consisted of former communists, socialists, and social democrats who split off from the underground resistance movement ORG (Leninist Organization Group). But the Marxist debates among the various emigrés and resistance factions appeared marginal to Febvre. When Borkenau submitted a reply to Henryk Grossmann, who had reviewed Borkenau's "The Transition from the Feudal to the Bourgeois World View" (1934) in a highly critical and orthodox-Marxist fashion, Febvre opposed its publication. Instead of understanding the debate in the context of the developments in Europe, and of how German Jewish intellectuals positioned themselves toward those developments, Febvre saw it as purely theoretical quibbling.

Just a few years later, Marc Bloch would himself write about the "revolutionary transformation of French society" and take part in the struggle against fascism. In 1944, after close to a year in the Resistance, Bloch (whose *nom de guerre* was "Narbonne") would be arrested, tortured, held captive for three months, and finally executed by the Gestapo and its French accomplices (whereas Febvre survived the war and lived to see his protégé and friend, Fernand Braudel, assume the head of the Annales and of the Sixth Section of the Ecole Pratique des Hautes Etudes).

The Annales Connection

After a few weeks in Paris, Borkenau went to London, where he had had contacts since his Comintern years, and obtained a position teaching international politics in the adult education section of the University of London. It must have been under these circumstances that he met Bronislaw Malinowski, and indeed, it is known that Borkenau hoped to receive a position in South Africa, and that he therefore attended Malinowski's seminars. Varga visited Borkenau in London on several occasions, and thus she, too, may have come into contact with Malinowski, since in the first footnote of her ethnographic study about social and cultural change in an Austrian valley, she thanks him for his "helpful suggestions" (1936b:1). Furthermore, she begins the article about the Austrian valley by referring to ethnological methods: not taking anything for granted, not forcing analytical concepts on the ethnographic material. Nothing, she states, should escape scrutiny: "Every detail must be noted and recorded: family structure as well as forms of child rearing, patterns of thought as well as forms of religious belief, ideas about luxury and work as well as the rhythm of labor and leisure" (ibid.). Etic concepts, she continued, should not be substituted for emic ones, a precautionary measure which, if employed by historians, could save them from terrible anachronisms. Recognizing Malinowski's methodological teachings in Varga's statements requires no great leap. Interestingly enough, though, one can also recognize Lucien Febvre's distaste for the use of transhistorical concepts. Thus Varga's work offers one instance in which different varieties of a search for empirical and analytical authenticity came together, and the family resemblance between the early Annales and the Malinowskian programs becomes apparent.

Eventually, Borkenau accepted a position in the Sociology Department at the University of Panama. The position did not pay well enough for the entire family to resettle, so Borkenau left Europe by himself, only to return six months later. An English newspaper gave him the job of covering the Spanish Civil War, but by this time, his long separation from Lucie and Berta had resulted in a definite split. In the meantime, Lucie Varga had established rapport not only with Lucien Febvre but with his wife and children. Both Lucie and her daughter became close friends with the Febvre family and were included in many of its activities, and at one point, Lucie took 13-year-old Henri Febvre with her daughter on vacation in the Montafon Valley in Vorarlberg. The trip resulted in Varga's 1936 ethnographic study, "A Valley in Vorarlberg—Between Past and Present," to which I shall turn shortly.[3]

Professionally, Varga performed the work expected of an assistant in those days: preparing excerpts and summaries from books, translating from Ger-

3. See the section entitled "The City Enters the Village: 'In a Vorarlberg Valley.'"

man into French, locating references. Eventually, though, she was entrusted
with authoring reviews and articles for the *Annales* and the *Revue de Synthèse*.
Varga and Febvre even planned to write a book together (in the *L'Évolution
de l'humanité* series edited by Henri Berr). In his correspondence with Bloch
about this project, Febvre nevertheless gives a not entirely flattering description of Lucie Varga:

> She heads directly for the 'Great Ideas' that are simple and leap to the eye; well,
> she is *undisciplined*, a trait which we only value when we all too often have to
> regret its absence abroad. But apart from this, she is alert; she is extremely well
> read (if not in a systematic manner); she has a sense of the Text and of texts;
> this last point is very noticeable. I notice it when she works for me. She has
> the tendency (an excellent tendency indeed) to put aside the comments in the
> specialist literature and to engage directly with the text. For her it is one and
> the same; at the moment she devours the complete writings of Saint Bernard.
> (quoted in Schöttler 1991: 28)

Like Borkenau, Varga led the restless life of an emigré. She traveled frequently: to London to see Borkenau, to Toulouse for her catharism research,
to Vienna to visit her mother, and to Germany "to inform herself about the
mental state of the natives," as Febvre put it in a letter to Bloch.[4] In Germany,
she conducted what must be termed ethnographic fieldwork: "she talked and
listened to the natives, and recorded things that probably only a woman could
observe, pick up, and provoke; a woman who speaks German with a con-
spicuous Austrian accent, and who is accompanied by a little ten year old
girl."[5]

This fieldwork resulted in an article and a number of reviews, which were
published—together with contributions from Henri Mougin, Marc Bloch,
Charles-Edmond Perrin, Henri Brunschwig, Lucien Febvre, Maurice Halbwachs, Paul Leuillot, and Albert Demangeon—in the November 1937 issue
of the *Annales* that internally was referred to as the "Germany issue." Because
Febvre and Bloch had refused to satisfy the demand by Armand Colin, the
conservative publisher of the *Annales*, to include a pro-Nazi article in the issue
for the sake of "objectivity," the *Annales* was published autonomously beginning in January 1939. Since Varga's contribution was the opening article of
the issue, and since this article was presented as an interpretation of National
Socialism from an Annales perspective, the 1937 "Germany issue" marked
Varga's full recognition by, and inclusion into, the Annales circle.

4. Correspondence Febvre-Bloch, pp. 502–4; quoted in Schöttler 1991:28. The correspondence between Febvre and Bloch from the period 1928–1943 can be found in Bloch's estate documents in the *Archives Nationales* in Paris, available on three microfilm reels (signature: 318 Mi
1–3); Febvre's letters to Bloch, paginated continuously, are on the second and third reels.
5. Correspondence Febvre-Bloch, p. 369; quoted in Schöttler 1991:35.

Love and Science

If this article was the apex of Varga's academic career, it also turned out to be its finale. By the time the *Annales* issue came out, the cooperation between Febvre and Varga had come to an abrupt halt. Through their close collaboration, Febvre and Varga had fallen in love, and in the spring of 1937, Suzanne Febvre, Lucien's wife, had demanded that he choose between herself and Varga. Always cautious, always concerned with avoiding "unnecessary" risks (as Marc Bloch would later learn, when Febvre convinced him, the "incriminating" Jew, to resign as editor of the *Annales*), Febvre chose the security and predictability of his bourgeois family life.

Soon afterward, Febvre went alone to South America. This maneuver not only disturbed the relationship between Bloch and Febvre for the remaining years of their collaboration, it marked the termination of the contact with Varga, though as fate would have it, Febvre, on the return trip to France, met Fernand Braudel, who became his close friend and successor. For Varga, the sudden break was catastrophic. She had to start over again without social and economic capital (after the *Anschluss* of Austria, the flow of money from her mother in Vienna dried up). While Febvre consoled himself with an excursion to the New World, Varga had to earn a living as a saleswoman for kitchen appliances and as a factory worker. In order to circumvent the increasingly restrictive regulations for emigrés, Varga arranged a sham marriage, whereby she gained French citizenship and yet another new name: Rose Morin.

All the while, Varga never stopped researching and writing, which resulted in two articles about the cathars in the *Revue de l'histoire des religions* (1938a, 1939b). In addition, she wrote about catharism for an issue of the *Encyclopédie Française* that never came out. She also wrote a novel for serial publication in *L'Œuvre* (1938b). The protagonists were Hermann Gierlich, a Hitler youth, and Hermine, the girl with whom he fell in love at the Nuremberg party congress. Since Hermine was easily conquered, and since she was not a virgin, Hermann eventually jilts her and marries another. Hermine is the abandoned mistress: was that supposed to make Lucien Febvre a Hermann Gierlich?

The Last Year

In 1939, Varga managed to be employed by the official news agency (Agence Havas) where she translated and summarized German news. The following year, the French government left Paris and moved to Bourdeaux, dissolving the Agence Havas, and giving all employees three months' pay as a final gesture. Lucie and Berta Varga went to Lourdes, where Lucie accepted a job teaching the children of a wealthy farmer and doing agricultural chores. Later that year, Lucie and Berta moved to the village of Pibrac, outside Toulouse. Lucie tried canning spinach and selling it and keeping chickens. She also had a student in Toulouse to whom she taught some German—although even raising the fare for the streetcar between Toulouse and Pibrac was difficult.

After the Vargas had settled in Pribac, an old acquaintance, Albert Mentzel, together with his wife and three children, moved in with them. A Communist Party member, a student at the Bauhaus academy in Dessau, and a Jew, Mentzel had fled Germany after Hitler came to power. In Pibrac he earned a living carving wooden frames. After the war, he made a name for himself—under the pseudonym "Albert Flocon"—as illustrator, engraver, and author, and in the mid-1960s, he became professor at the Ecole Nationale des Beaux-Arts in Paris.

Toward the end of 1940, Lucie Varga's health deteriorated. Not only was the supply of insulin irregular, Varga also developed insulin resistance.[6] The village physician failed to recognize the diabetic pre-coma, instead suspecting an illegal abortion. When Lucie Varga finally was taken to the clinic in Toulouse, she was beyond help. Thirty-six years old, she died on April 26, 1941.

Mutual friends of Lucien Febvre and Varga offered to take in the 15-year-old Berta. Another friend wanted to make arrangements for Berta to follow her to the United States. Berta's father and her grandmother, however, were the first to arrange a ticket and travel documents for Lucie's child, and she wound up in Budapest with them, eventually establishing herself as a neurologist.

Necropolis

Lucie Varga did not survive the Nazi regime she had described. Neither did her mother, Malvine Tafler-Stern. In late 1944, she was drowned in the Danube River by members of the Hungarian Nyilaskeresztes (Arrowcross) Party, who had zealously helped the Germans to "solve" the Hungarian "Jewish question."[7] Lucie Varga's ex-husband, Berta's father, Josef Varga, was shot by German soldiers in the fall of 1944, together with 300 other Jewish forced laborers. Although Albert Mentzel survived the war, his wife Lotte Mentzel and their eldest daughter were deported from Pibrac to Auschwitz, where they were murdered. Marc Bloch was tortured and executed. The Nazis and fascists in Europe and beyond created a vast necropolis, the extent of which is only matched by the abyss that this rupture in history has produced.

6. Schöttler (1991:49) believes the insulin resistance might have been related to tension, exhaustion, and irregular, low-quality meals.
7. Hungary had provided the last asylum for East European Jews up to April 1944.

Lucie Varga and the Analysis of National Socialism: The Rationalization of Fanaticism

A few years before the occult-industrialized mass murder of the European Jews was set in motion, its early development in Germany might have looked threatening without necessarily pointing in a single direction. As Varga wrote in the opening lines of her article "The Birth of National Socialism: Social-analytical Notes": "In the immediate vicinity a world has come to an end. A new world emerges with yet unknown contours" (1937b:529). Varga saw this uncertain historical situation as an opportunity: the historian could work as an ethnographer, directly observing what went on in Germany, instead of having to rely on incomplete source material. The historian "can live in the country he researches to understand it in the context of its traditions of thought and patterns of behavior" (ibid.).

In her article, Varga listed the common explanations given in the 1930s for the rise of National Socialism. Marxian approaches saw Nazism as a surface phenomenon beneath which actual class antagonisms were at work, or as a movement of the "déclassés from all classes" (1937b:529). As we shall see, Varga subscribed to this explanation, but refused to accept the idea that these déclassés actually constituted a new class of some sort. Another explanatory model viewed National Socialism as a mass psychosis—something Varga rejected out of hand. Varga also mentioned Toynbee's notion of Nazism as a modern religion of the state. Again, this is an idea that she incorporated into her own thesis, despite her complaint that Toynbee never answered the questions of *how* this modern religion had emerged. Finally, Varga mentioned a history-of-ideas explanation: National Socialism as a syncretic form was produced out of old ideas (in particular, those of Nietzsche, Pareto, and even Chamberlain). But, Varga asked, what if neither class nor ideas have enough explanatory value? Schöttler believes that Varga, instead of offering an explanation of her own, moved to even more highly empirical terrain. Yet, as will become clear, Varga did indeed offer a model of her own—one that took into account communities of memory, social honor, structural history, and social organization.

Varga continued: "let us turn to the facts ... Before us lies a pile of files about the first followers of National Socialism in the years from 1922 to 1932. Let us open the files" (1937b:530). And then, using the technique of fictive speech, she summarized individual narratives about conversions to Nazism. There is the engineer from a small town, coming from a *deutschnationale* family, who lost his job during the depression and was converted to National Socialism when he accidentally walked into a meeting. There is the *déclassé* baron, now a traveling salesman, who heard the Nazis using the same core symbolic words about duty and discipline his father had always stressed. Finally, Varga tells the story of the soldier who felt alienated by the transvaluation he found upon his return to the Weimar Republic. Not only had the Great War been lost, it was now declared to have been a bad idea in the first place. In Germany, such soldiers organized into volunteer corps, and when these corps were disbanded in 1923, the soldiers continued to organize in militaristic, antisocialist, anti-bourgeois associations—and, in important ways, continued the war experience and the will to act. Since the associations lacked political programs, the organizing principle was one of personal followership, something that eventually would facilitate the men's loyalty to Hitler. "Playing soldier turned into reality," Varga wrote (1937b:532).

These stories feature *déclassé* individuals, but Varga also showed that even civil servants with the privilege of a permanent position joined the Nazi party. She argued that hyperinflation and economic depression had changed the future expectations even of this sort of person: "A diffuse danger threatened him. Who would protect his children? Should he throw them into an un-known world that was determined from the outside, and in which he had no ability to intervene?" (1937b:533). In this context Varga introduced the anthropological concept of social honor. Referring to the potlatch, she asked rhetorically: "But does not such a sense of social honor exist in our societies as well?" And then, moving in a social psychological direction, à la George Herbert Mead, she continued: "The fear of losing one's standing . . . the frustration and anger resulting from a feeling of being superfluous, of being increasingly pushed aside and becoming an outcast: all this stirs up hate and resentment" (ibid.). Implicitly translating her argument into Hegelian and Meadian terms, Varga argued that it was the fact and sense of social misrecognition and marginalization that prepared the ground for conversions to Nazism. Yet her analysis did not stop here.

In every revolution, Varga wrote, the extremists do not belong to the socially rising, but to the declining classes. Yet she did not conceptualize this social category as a class in itself, with consciousness of itself as a class: "Only we [the researchers] can say that by comparing the biographies of the first Nazis one detects their common denominator: The sense of losing one's footing" (1937b:534). In the French original Varga used the German term *Erlebnis-gruppen*, experiential groups, for these people.[8] A term that better conveys what Varga seems to have meant to say, and that makes a fully appropriate connection to anthropological theorizing, would be *communities of memory* (as deployed by Barbara Myerhoff and Liisa Malkki). What held these communities together, once they had gone through a Nazi conversion, was the

---

8. As is often pointed out, there are two words in the German language for the English concept of experience. One, *Erlebnis*, distinctly connotes something one has lived through. The other, *Erfahrung*, is more general and comes closer to the word "experience" in English.

experience of desperation. Varga thus went on to describe the revolutionary dynamic that made the conversion to National Socialism a successful strategy of organizing a society in crisis. "Every revolution is contraction, retreat, reduction," she wrote. "Revolution: that means to simplify everything and to impose dualisms on everything: friend or foe, comrade in arms or antagonist, strength or weakness, You or I, hunter or hunted" (1937b:535). The more effective the Nazis became in their revolutionary strategy of reduction, the more the number of converts increased.

In the second part of her essay, Varga moved from a social psychological to a social structural analysis. She linked the Nazi revolution to the weak position of the German bourgeoisie, the fast pace of industrialization, and the continuity of anti-Semitic organizations in Germany since the nineteenth century. More important, she connected the romantic resistance against Napoleon and his rationalist legacy with the historical "immaturity" of the German bourgeoisie. The national-romantic figures and movements provided the German bourgeoisie, paradoxical as it may seem, with anti-bourgeois, conservative, and nostalgic ideals. In this context, Varga pointed to the influence of Julius Langbehn—a long-forgotten ancestor of Nazism who, in his book *Rembrandt als Erzieher* (1890), concocted a mix of racial mysticism, anthropometrics, ideas about the national essence of Germans, and worship of nobility—and of Friedrich Nietzsche, who functioned as an apostle for the national-romantic and rebellious youth movements of the time, such as the *Wandervögel*. With a reference to one of Borkenau's publications[9], she demonstrated the quantitative presence of these youth movements already on the eve of World War I.

If her essay so far has been an investigation of how and why many Germans could become National Socialists, Varga's final section presented her most original point: the Nazi state can be defined in terms of "the rationalization of fanaticism." Varga accomplished this by differentiating three social groupings within the Nazi state system. First, there were the veterans of National Socialism—most of them survivors of Hitler's June 1934 purging of Röhm and other SA-leaders—who refused to adhere to Hitler's proclamation of the end of the revolution. Instead, they continued their revolutionary activism in the positions of judges, editors, professors, and civil servants to which they had been appointed. Thus, they functioned as a fanatic element in the state apparatus. Second, there were the "technicians" of Nazism, mostly social climbers who filled the ranks of upper and middle management in the state, and who worked with all the enthusiasm and slyness of the dilettante (as Varga put it). These experts had the ethos of engineers rather than fanatics. "Under every tyranny, 'loyal servants' can make a career irrespective of birth and social tra-

9. Varga referred to a 1937 article published by F. Jungmann, one of Borkenau's pseudonyms.

dition" (1937b:543). Finally, there were the passive Nazis who in almost any life situation could take advantage of the comprehensive Nazi state welfare system. They acted as "free riders" of the system.

But what about those who, however passively, resisted the system? To resist the Nazis meant renouncing state benefits: no financial credit from the state upon marriage, no child allowance, no subsidized bus and train tickets, no subsidized vacations, no admittance to sport and cultural events, and so on. "To make the sacrifice of doing without all these essential benefits (because those who resist do, of course, not get any of them) takes a true hero" (1937b: 543). In the category of such heroes Varga placed, first and foremost, those Roman Catholics who put their commitment to the church before anything else. Second were those Protestants who wanted no part of the official church of German Christians, and instead organized themselves in the *Bekennende Kirche* (Confessing Church). Third were the democrats who went into "inner exile," as it would be termed much later, that is, those people who withdrew from societal life and who felt like *Tote auf Abruf,* "ready to be called for death" (1937b:544). After that, Varga listed a number of other social groups in Germany whose members may have had reasons for discontent with the regime: various industrialists, farmers, and workers, for example, all suffering from strict government taxation and regulations. Frustrated as these people may have been, Varga did not count them among the heroes who distanced themselves from National Socialism in public. The only ones who had done so, and who had suffered the consequences, were individual communists, wrote Varga, almost in passing.

In the conclusion to her essay, Varga again described "the rationalization of fanaticism." After 1933, antibourgeois sentiments and precapitalist nostalgia had to be done away with, and Germany had to compete in the international marketplace—which required stimulating enormous growth in industrial production through a strictly regulated economy and through rationalization and centralization. On the rhetorical level, however, the antidemocratic and fanatic version of Nazism could still be employed in the service of the state, in order to solve the economic and administrative contradictions that every modern state is faced with, Varga concluded.

The fact that Varga placed the concept of social honor at the center of her analysis of the genesis of National Socialism has both empirical and theoretical reasons. The empirical background is the explicit use of the concept by the Nazis themselves—the 1936 party convention in Nuremberg was called, *Parteitag der Ehre* ("The Party Convention of Honor"); Robert Ley, head of the German Labor Front, published his speeches under the title, "The Revelation of Social Honor"; and so forth. Varga took this empirically central concept and translated it into terms that resonated with early anthropological theories about honor,[10] as well as with Hegelian and Meadian versions of social recognition theory.

Without explicitly referring to recognition theory, Varga nevertheless accomplished the task of identifying an ontological dynamic at the heart of National Socialism's ascent. Choosing the dynamic of social honor or recognition in this context has the advantage of interpreting the problem in genuinely social terms, that is, in terms of intersubjectivity and structure rather than individual autonomy and agency. Consequently, Varga did not fall for simplistic ideas about Hitler's charisma as an explanation for the success of the Nazi movement. Neither did she fall back on national character. Instead, she presented a complex picture of the historical situation in Germany: World War I created the preconditions for National Socialism; *déclassés* from all classes felt alienated in the New Germany of the Weimar Republic; not only the United States and neighboring European countries but the Weimar Republic itself was regarded in some quarters as an agent of social misrecognition; communities of memory organized themselves paramilitarily; key symbols and values, and a revolutionary reduction of complexity into dichotomies, resonated with certain aspects of private and public culture in Germany; the transformation of the Nazi movement into a state opened up new opportunities for those inside the system and shut out those who distanced themselves; the transformation from movement to state also made necessary the rationalization of fanaticism. Considering that this article was written in 1936, as things were evolving, and without the privilege of hindsight, the level of sophistication in Varga's analysis is striking.

The City Enters the Village: "In a Vorarlberg Valley"

In late September 1935, Febvre received in the mail an exercise book that contained an ethnographic study Lucie Varga had conducted while vacationing with her daughter and Febvre's son, Henri, in the Austrian Montafon Valley. In a letter to Bloch, Febvre suggested that the manuscript be edited for the *Annales*, and a few months later, it opened the January issue (Schöttler 1991:42). Since Varga, in the first footnote to the article, thanked Malinowski for his help in preparing the study (rather than the text), one may conclude that the ethnographic project had been planned for some time. Indeed, the vacation may well have been an excuse for conducting ethnographic fieldwork.

Malinowski's role in the project, and in particular his ethnographic com-

10. See, for example, Peristiany and Pitt-Rivers (1992).

petence, may have been associated with his own travels to the Alps: as Raymond Firth has told us, Malinowski had a villa in Oberbozen (in the Tyrol) where he spent most of the summer: "he usually worked on the balcony, often nude in the sun, with a green eyeshade, scrubbing himself with a solution of iodized salt in the intervals of discussion about Trobriand myth or family life" (1981:106). Whether Varga ever encountered Malinowski in this state we do not know. It seems apparent, though, that she had traveled in the Alpine region before she went to Vorarlberg.

Throughout her article on the Montafon Valley between past and present, Varga employed what Payne once called the "syntax of agency," and what otherwise is known as the ethnographic present. After opening remarks about anthropological methods and the geographical setting, Varga noted that the connection between the valley and the rest of the world is determined by economic and ideological changes emanating from such urban centers as Vienna and Zürich. Moreover, the cultural changes that had occurred in the valley had produced an acute sense of history in the local population, Varga wrote (1936b:3). Their narratives were structured in terms of a comparative dichotomy of "before" and "now." The concept of "before" connoted three periods: first, an "absolute past," encompassing the generation of the grandparents and all previous generations; second, the time before World War I, associated with the parents' generation and with a rural subsistence economy, which made it a "time of normality"; third, the recent 15 years (1920–35) when tourism, urbanization, and other trends created a "time of change."

Varga pointed out that even during the time of normality, the prewar years, the valley had not been isolated from the surrounding world. During summers, the men engaged in seasonal labor migration, returning home with experiences of countries without mountains, with other foods, other wines, and other women. During the months of male absence, something like a "summerly matriarchy" existed, Varga wrote. The labor migration might have led to changes in the valley, but nothing changed—"Absolutely nothing!"—and life went on as before (1936b:4). Not a single man brought with him a bride from the outside, and only two married in France and remained there.

The time of change began a few years after the war. The embroidery industry that had established itself in Vorarlberg faltered. Rumor had it that some men from the valley had sold the "secret" of the embroidery machines to America (there never was a "secret" to sell in the first place because these were ordinary machines). "It goes without saying that what was evoked here was not the real but a mythical America, one that was identified with 'business deals,' big industry, and brutal, irresponsible capitalist forces," Varga clarified in a most anthropological manner (1936b:6). Then came the German tourists, who volunteered suggestions to improve the organization and infrastructure of the valley villages. They climbed mountains and went skiing—something the village youth soon took to as well. Hotels were built and the number of inns increased. Their owners made social careers outside the agricultural social structure. The new village elite is made up of *nouveau riche* entrepreneurs.

This time of change brought new and intensive social conflicts. Men who could afford it began leading a double life in which the mistress in the nearest town consumed most of the new wealth. Villagers became litigious, as the land, water, and thoroughfare rights of the old class of rich farmers were challenged by their entrepreneurial successors. The priest, once considered "of the village," was ascribed a liminal position in the new urbanized village. A new semireligious concept, "progress," replaced much of the old faith. Progress stood for tourism, city ways, and Europe, that is, Germany and Switzerland. Austria, with its "red capital," Vienna, was rejected by the villagers, whose political affiliation always had been with the Christian-Social Party.[11]

Another visible change was in material culture, in particular in clothing. Varga observed odd constellations of German tourists wearing traditional *Trachten* ("costumes") and villagers walking around in city clothes. At ceremonial occasions, villagers might still put on the old apparel, but Varga overheard a young man, who was reprimanded for not having dressed in *Trachten* at his engagement party, reply: "Do you think I'm here to play the fool for you?" Varga pointed to a transformation of romantic and erotic ideals as one reason for the change in clothing practice: young men no longer desired peasant women; they wanted city women, or, at least, local women who had attained an air of urban sophistication.

While Varga thus enumerated some of the profound changes the valley had gone through, she nevertheless maintains that something like a *Nachbarschaftsmoral* ("neighborhood ethos") continued to organize social life in the village.[12] She does this by providing the example of Swiss agricultural entrepreneurs who had settled in the valley after World War I. Many of them seem to have come as tourists and then decided to purchase land and start up agricultural production. Even after 20 years, Varga wrote, these Swiss valley inhabitants had not become part of the valley neighborhood ethos, which, to a great extent, consisted of a sense and practice of reciprocity. What Varga refers to as "village amalgamation" thus had its limits. At the time she conducted fieldwork, the urbanization of the Montafon Valley had not yet severed the ties of neighborly giving and receiving.

11. To this day, the Alpine regions of Europe vote conservative. Since the end of World War II, for example, Bavaria has been ruled by the Christian-Social Party, which has enjoyed an absolute majority in every election.

12. One can relate Varga's concept to Arjun Appadurai's analytical metaphor of "neighborhood" (1996:178–99): particular neighborhoods are, in Appadurai's sense, the actual outcomes of modes of producing locality, of socializing space and time.

A turning of the tide occurred when the modernization of the valley was interrupted by the tremors of the global economic crisis. The prices for farm products dropped; opportunities for wage labor decreased; and, most important, the number of German tourists went down, until it finally reached zero after Germany closed its borders. What were the cultural consequences of this crisis, asked Varga. In some Alpine valleys the reaction to the crisis led to a form of millenarian return to "old values": old religion, old traditions, old authorities were to bring back the good days. In valleys like Vorarlberg, the *déclassés* embraced National Socialism as a way "forward" out of the crisis. Varga provided a biographical sketch of the first Montafon native who converted to Nazism (which in Vorarlberg first and foremost implied a conversion away from Roman Catholicism); the sketch of this individual's life complements the conversion stories Varga told in her article about the emergence of Nazism in Germany.

Varga's two ethnographic articles essentially tell the same story: National Socialism met with little resistance; to become a Nazi was more than anything a conversion of sorts; what was at stake in private and political life was the lack of social recognition ("social honor"); this facilitated a swift and general conversion process; the double nature of Nazism as movement and government opened up new opportunities for those on the inside. While Varga thus observes the general historical structure behind the rise of Nazism, she is also ethnographically sensitive to the particularities of this process. For instance, in Vorarlberg, the villagers, in the absence of a Jewish population, made Catholic clerics their major enemy, and, more important, "National Socialism in the village [was] a stage in the urbanization of the countryside" (1936b:16). Varga concluded from all this that one should take seriously the Nazi rhetoric about 1933 as the year of the "German revolution." A world had come to an end and what was ahead was uncertain: "The villagers' belief in progress, their political chiliasm, their courage born of despair—all that can change any time and turn into weary-of-life apathy and pessimist fatalism. Where will it lead? All we can do is observe. We are not prophets. In five, ten or twenty years we will know more" (20).

Names and Faiths

Lucie Varga was a trained historian. Her closest collaboration was with another historian, Lucien Febvre. Nevertheless, she conducted ethnographic fieldwork and wrote brief ethnographic accounts of the changes that occurred right before her eyes. Apparently, she felt compelled to do so because "in the immediate vicinity a world had come to an end." A new world was taking shape, but who knew what this shape would be? The old world had been one of empires rather than nation-states, subjects rather than citizens, hierarchical integration rather than democratic pluralism. In the end, the new world that was Nazism became little more than a mélange of an old imperial order and the new nationalist ideology. What this political and cultural bricolage made impossible was the old strategy of hierarchical integration through assimilation. Religious conversion was no longer a means of assimilation. Gone was the method of changing one's name in order to gain social acceptance. Any conversion to German blood had been ruled out. The gates were closed.

Then again, though, the closing of the gates had been a gradual process. The coming-to-an-end of a world that was nearby in time and space, the dissolution of the imperial world order, had taken place over a number of years. The rise of nationalist and racist ideologies had occurred over decades. The alienation all this caused is well known. Obviously it played an important part in the lives and work of Jewish intellectuals in Germany and Austria. How else can we explain the frequent name changes and uses of pseudonyms among them? Rosa Stern, Lucie Stern, Lucie Varga, Lucie Varga-Borkenau, Rose Morin: five names in a short life of 36 years. Franz Borkenau, born Franz Pollack, wrote under such pseudonyms as Wegner, Neurath, Georg Haschek, and Fritz Jungmann. Varga's friend Albert Mentzel became Albert Flocon; Max Horkheimer used the pseudonym Heinrich Regius; Theodor Wiesengrund became Adorno, and wrote under the pseudonym Hektor Rottweiler; Walter Benjamin wrote under the names Detlef Holz and C. Conrad—the list is long. One of the historians of the Frankfurt School, Martin Jay (1973:290), takes these naming practices to be symbolic of the status of Jewish intellectuals. Their ambiguous social identities and sense of alienation were manifested in a rather loose attachment to personal names.

Considering Varga's work also raises the historical legacy of assimilation. Converting one's name and religious affiliation had been common practice in the Hohenzollern and Habsburg empires, and it was even something of a tradition in assimilating Jewish circles. Is it a pure coincidence that Varga's main research interest was a persecuted, alienated religious group, the cathars, and that she placed Roman Catholics and Protestant members of the *Bekennende Kirche* before anyone else in her classification of German heroes who resisted the Nazi system? And what about her own and Borkenau's Christian background?

Whatever one makes of this connection between personal identity and scholarly writing, for Varga and many of her colleagues Hitlerism, persecution, genocide, exile, and intellectual reflection made unavoidable an interaction between life and work. In Lucie Varga's case it may have been this direct interconnectedness, rather than Malinowskian ideas about fieldwork, which urged her to travel to Germany and go directly to the people, asking them why and how they had become Nazis. The information she gathered, and the analysis she provided, should convince us to recognize Lucie Varga as one of anthropology's excluded ancestors. By so doing, anthropology might be injected with some of the nervous energy that shifting names and faiths can provide.

References Cited

Appadurai, A. 1996. *Modernity at large: Cultural dimensions of globalization.* Minneapolis, Minn.

Borkenau, F. 1933. Zur soziologie des Faschismus. *Archiv für Sozialwissenschaft und Sozialpolitik* 68:513–47.

Borkenau, F. 1934. Der Übergang vom feudalen zum bürgerlichen Weltbild. *Studien zur Geschichte der Philosophie in der Manufaktur-periode.* Paris.

Firth, R. 1981. Bronislaw Malinowski. In Sydel Silverman, ed., *Totems and teachers: Perspectives on the history of anthropology,* 101–39. New York.

Jay, M. 1973. *The dialectical imagination: A history of the Frankfurt School and the Institute of Social Research, 1923–1950.* London.

Jungmann, F. [F. Borkenau]. 1937. Autorität und Sexualmoral in der freibürgerlichen Jugendbewegung. In *Autorität und Familie. Studien aus dem Institut für Sozial forschung.* Paris.

Langbehn, J. 1890. *Rembrandt als Erzieher. Von einem Deutschen.* Leipzig.

Lange-Enzmann, B. 1996. *Franz Borkenau als politischer Denker.* Berlin.

Löwenthal, R. 1957. In memoriam Franz Borkenau. *Der Monat* 106:9 (July), 57–60.

Peristiany, J. G., & J. Pitt-Rivers, eds. 1992. *Honor and grace in anthropology.* Cambridge.

Schöttler, P. 1991. Lucie Varga — eine österreichische Historikerin im Umkreis der "Annales" (1904–1941). In *Zeitenwende: Mentalitätshistorische Studien, 1936–1939,* Lucie Varga. Frankfurt am Main.

A Complete Bibliography of Lucie Varga's Publications

1932   *Das Schlagwort vom "finsteren Mittelalter."* Baden bei Wien.

1933   Moyen Age et Renaissance. Review in *Revue de synthèse* 7:129–32.

1935a   Matèrialisme, idèalisme ou rèalisme historique? Review in *Revue de synthèse* 7:154–55.

1935b   Un testament politique. Review in *Annales d'histoire économique et sociale* 7:427.

1935c   Aristocratie et industrie en Angleterre. Review in *Annales d'histoire économique et sociale* 7:521.

1936a   La littérature viennoise. *Encyclopédie Française* 7:17/48/8–17/50/1.

1936b   Dans une vallée du Vorarlberg: d'avant-hier à aujourd'hui. *Annales d'histoire économique et sociale* 8:1–20.

1936c   Un problème de méthode en histoire religieuse: le catharisme. Review in *Revue de synthèse* 11:133–43.

1936d   En Amérique espagnole: métaux précieux, prix et travail forcé. Review in *Annales d'histoire économique et sociale* 8:570–74.

1936e   La recherche historique et l'opposition catholique en Allemagne 1936. *Revue de synthèse* 13:49–56.

1937a   Les luttes sociales en Allemagne et la génèse de la Réforme. *Science: L'encyclopédie annuelle* 14:5–6/57a–57d.

1937b   La génèse du national-socialisme. Notes d'analyse sociale. *Annales d'histoire économique et sociale* 9:529–46.

1937c   Pour connaître la France — ou l'Allemagne? Review in *Annales d'histoire économique et sociale* 9:602–4.

1937d   Luther, la jeunesse et le nazisme. Review in *Annales d'histoire économique et sociale* 9:604–6.

1937e   Sur la jeunesse du Troisième Reich. Review in *Annales d'histoire économique et sociale* 9:612–14.

1938a   Peire Cardinal était-il hérétique? *Revue de l'histoire des religions* 118:205–31.

1938b   Comment se fabrique l'hitlérien 100%. Scènes de la vie allemande. Histoire du jeune Hermann Gierlich, "enfant d'Hitler," élevé dans le mépris du cerveau, le culte du biceps, des parades et des chansons guérrières. Serial novel in *L'Œuvre* 16–30.

1939a   Sorcellerie d'hier. Enquête dans une vallé ladine. *Annales d'histoire sociale* 1:121–32.

1939b   Les cathares sont-ils des néomanichéens ou des néognostiques? *Revue de l'histoire des religions* 120:175–93.

MELANESIAN CAN(N)ONS

Paradoxes and Prospects
in Melanesian Ethnography

DOUG DALTON

Introduction

Melanesia has long been a privileged site for ethnographic inquiry, and as such, figures highly in the anthropological canon. Malinowski, Mead, and Bateson are just a few of the early prominent figures who did significant research in the region, and helped produce the extraordinarily abstract body of critical theory regarding exchange, gender, and the person for which the area is known today. Yet the history of theorizing in Melanesia is also known for its challenges to established anthropological canons.

In this essay, I will argue that Melanesia's privileged status is due in no small part to the apparent "acanonical" nature of Melanesian societies and to the way these societies exacerbate the inherent paradoxes of canon formation. By "acanonical" I refer to the fact that Melanesian cultures have been characterized by dynamic improvisation, flexibility, and fluidity—qualities which seem contrary to the ideas underlying the canon (Wagner 1981)—since the canon aims to fix great ideas and truths in the history of human thought, truths commonly assumed to be found almost exclusively in the prose of dead white European men. These writings functioned as oft-cited touchstones in the cumulative history of rational thought and civilization. Today, however, this notion of the Western canon is being challenged by those fighting so-called "culture wars" for "multiculturalism" in favor of including the cultural views and experiences of women, minorities, colonial subjects, and dispos-

Doug Dalton is Associate Professor of Anthropology at Longwood College. His current research concerns local-global dynamics among Rawa-speaking people in contemporary Papua New Guinea.

sessed peoples in the Western "canon." Multiculturalism so goes against the notion of a set progression of great inventions and discoveries headed by European patriarchs that Henry Louis Gates, Jr., finds it necessary to unhinge the idea of canonical fixity with the concept of "loose canons," applying an adjective once used to qualify the "structure" of Papua New Guinea societies (Gates 1992; DuToit 1962; Watson 1964, 1970).[1] Yet as Gates points out, those who, like himself, endeavor to establish an African American canon are criticized for wanting to establish any canon at all.

The problem of canon formation can be seen as one of attempting to fix and establish, retrospectively as well as prospectively, a particular language or theory against the movement of history.[2] The canon institutes time as a linear sequence and establishes a set of interrelated conundrums. Canonical texts must thus be thought of, paradoxically, as both the origin and end goal of humanity.[3] Because the canon is simultaneously prospective and retrospective, like Tylor's idea of "culture or civilization," it is supposed to be all-encompassing and universally valid, if not ultimately transcendental (Stocking 1968a, 1968b, 1968c; Tylor 1871). Yet clearly not everyone shares these supposedly universal truths or values the Western canon in the same way. Therefore, maintaining the timeline created by the canon requires parsing out of history people who don't share that canon, including most Melanesians (Fabian 1983). Historically, then, maintaining the Western canon at all in the face of such diversity, if not adversity, has required a political will to exercise force and violence.[4]

Melanesians, on the other hand, do not have these conundrums relating to the attempt to determine a progressive linear sequence. Instead they memorialize death and expenditure and approach time as an innovative sequence of events (Wagner 1981; Evans-Pritchard 1940). When anthropologists attempt to understand and construe Melanesian social and cultural "institutions" in Western linear rational terms, they therefore have to employ highly abstract

1. According to Gates, "Once we understand how they arose, we no longer see literary canons as *objects trouvés* washed up on the beach of history. And we can begin to appreciate their ever-changing configuration in relation to a distinctive institutional history" (1992:34). He instead offers this idea of the canon: "I suppose the literary canon is, in no very grand sense, the commonplace book of our shared culture, in which we have written down the texts and titles that we want to remember, that had some special meaning for us" (20).

2. By "canon" here I mean the Western written tradition of canonical texts. I suggest below that other cultures such as those of Melanesia have alternate ways of memorializing narratives and events in their cultures, each with its own set problems.

3. This paradox is explored by Derrida (1992a).

4. The claim I am making here is that canon formation and political colonial state building are linked processes, which I substantiate further below. Therefore, the formation and maintenance of the canon are predicated upon the political violence of the colonial state. For examples of colonial violence in areas of Melanesia, see Firth 1972, Kaplan 1995, and Keesing 1992.

theoretical notions to describe the creative symbolic, emotional processes that comprise them. This effort produces a curiously paradoxical canon that standardizes ideas of non-progressive process and motion rather than fixed progression, simultaneously encompassing non-Western cultural ideas into a Western epistemic frame yet allowing that frame to be relativized and destabilized by them. This intriguing effect however, does not account for the extraordinarily central place Melanesia has assumed in the anthropological canon, for other non-Western cultures also manage time as non-progressive movement. Melanesia's anthropological prominence must be viewed instead as the result both of its particular geographic and temporal location in the Western imagination and its colonial project, and of the way in which Melanesia articulated historically the inherent paradoxes of canon formation. In the following section I outline the development of Melanesia as a central part of the anthropological canon, paying special attention to the paradoxes that inform its history, and then discuss the political and literary problems faced by the canon in Melanesia.

The Canon and Melanesian History

In the early years of the nineteenth century when the concept of "race" and universal evolutionary laws were being used, even as they were being formed, as justifications for that century's European colonialism, "Papuans" were considered to be one of the least among the "lower races."[5] By 1855, though, while assuming the psychic unity of man, Herbert Spencer could write that Europeans must have "from ten to thirty cubic inches more brain that the Papuan" (Spencer 1855, quoted in Stocking 1987:141). So significant was this idea that 80 years later as important a European intellectual as the inventor of phenomenology Edmund Husserl, who was indirectly influenced by Leenhardt through his conversations with Lévi-Bruhl, could claim in a 1935 Vienna lecture that "according to the old familiar definition, man is the rational animal, and in this broad sense even the Papuan is a man and not a beast. . . . But just as man and even the Papuan represent a new stage of animal nature, i.e., as opposed to the beast, so philosophical reason represents a new stage of human nature and its reason" (Husserl 1970:290; Lévy-Bruhl 1975; Leenhardt 1979; Clifford 1982).[6] Traveling the Western Pacific about the same time as Spencer

5. The racial term "Papuan" is derived from the Malay "pua pua," meaning "fuzzy haired." The more modern term "Melanesian," meaning "black islands," continues the racism of this term (cf. Thomas 1989). I nevertheless use Melanesian because no other vocabulary is available.
6. While Derrida finds the racism of the Vienna lecture to be implicit in Husserl's *Origin of Geometry* and a reason for its critical rejection, Husserl's views would nevertheless become the basis for Mimica's recent study of a Papua New Guinea counting system (Derrida 1978:146 fn. 176; Mimica 1988).

was writing, the scientific explorer Alfred Russel Wallace concluded in 1869 that Papuans represented an earlier racial stage than the Malaysians because of "the loud, rapid, eager tones, *the incessant motion, the intense vital activity* manifested in speech and action" that made Papuans "the very antipodes of the quiet, unimpulsive, unanimated Malay"(Wallace 1869[1962]:318, quoted in Stocking 1987:101; emphasis added).

Wallace's assumption that Papuans "were remnants of the aboriginal population of a subsided continent, which the British geologist Phillip Sclater had called Lemuria, and which Haeckel suggested was 'the probable cradle of the human race'" led the early Russian explorer Maclay to settle in 1871 on the north coast of New Guinea with the hope of finding Lemurians still inhabiting the interior (Haeckel 1876:I, 361, quoted in Stocking 1991:14; see Webster 1984:28–30). Although Maclay was ultimately frustrated in his attempted forays into the interior, he became even more frustrated by encroaching European colonial empires, and he eventually failed in his attempt to have the region of New Guinea where he had settled set aside as a preserve, with himself as its foreign minister and advisor (Mikloucho-Maclay 1975; Stocking 1991). The ethnographic knowledge he had gathered was used instead to further the interests of the German Neu Guinea Compagnie in settling the north coast, which became a German possession in 1884, the same year that southern New Guinea was established as an English protectorate. Though Maclay's idealism at first led him to pursue evolutionary science through the physical measurements and specimens he collected—the science that would underwrite the ascendancy of the Western canon—he ended up disappointed, discovering instead another kind of "truth" about the power in history that is the canon's *raison d'être*: that abstract scientific truth serves European structures of power and colonial state-building interests.

When Maclay arrived on New Guinea's north coast, R. H. Codrington (of the strikingly egalitarian Melanesian Mission) was working in the island groups to the east. His studies of Melanesian religious concepts soon provided both Max Müller (in 1878) and Robert Marett (in 1900) data with which to attack Tylorian evolutionary assumptions: both men thought that Codrington had found in Melanesian *mana* an essentially human religious capacity that was in no way involved with Tylor's supposed religious origins of human rationality, Müller stressing its intangible and ubiquitous quality, as did Codrington, and Marett finding in it evidence of that "specific emotion whereby man is able to feel the supernatural precisely *at the point at which his thought breaks down*"(Marett 1909:28, quoted in Stocking 1987:319; Stocking 1995:167; Codrington 1891:118–19 fn. 1).

By the time that Codrington's information was being taken up in Marett's lectures, Alfred C. Haddon and William H. R. Rivers had returned from the year-long Torres Straits Expedition and were busy establishing the Cambridge School while challenging evolutionary anthropology on similar grounds through studies employing their own Melanesian data. Although Haddon was happy to have discovered in the Torres Straits what he thought was a geographical and architectural intermediary between the Australian lean-to and the Papuan pile houses, he also advocated the ethnographic study of limited areas where cultural comparisons could yield probable genetic connections, unlike evolutionary comparisons done across vast regions (Stocking 1987:105–7). Rivers, however, discovered that his kinship material could be explained only by assuming a historical mixing of cultures; indeed, he found Melanesian cultures to be "not homogenous," leading him to study patterns of diffusion and eventually to announce his conversion from evolutionism to diffusionism and ethnology (Rivers 1914:II, 209, quoted in Stocking 1995:207).

Papuans never played the central role that Australian Aborigine totemism and "hoards" did in the debates and models of Victorian evolutionary anthropology, and similarly the ethnographic results of the Torres Straits expedition never had anything like the impact of *The Native Tribes of Central Australia* that Spencer and Gillen had published the year of the expedition's return (1899). Unlike Aborigines, the Melanesians' "incessant motion" and heterogeneity were apparently better suited to challenge evolutionary laws than to support them. Therefore, despite its status as one of the most "primitive" places on the planet, Melanesia did not come to preeminence in the anthropological canon until Malinowski's self-fashioned humanist "revolution in the school of anthropology" came along with its model for intensive fieldwork. Despite having written a colonial situation out of his ethnography even more than Maclay had, Malinowski found himself dependent upon it and was forced to operate, in his words, "within the limits of truth and *realpolitik*" that defines the Western canon (Malinowski 1931:999, quoted in Stocking 1991:64). Identifying himself with a romanticized ideal of Maclay's first contact situation—the sympathetic ethnographer living alone among the natives—Malinowski nonetheless was forced to maintain the image of the "ethnographer's magic" through literary guile.

Malinowski's mature theoretical formulations were long in coming and his biologically and psychologically based functionalism was rooted ultimately in a profound understanding of how culture orchestrates passion and desire. Stocking points out that the 1920s saw a period following World War I when Victorian culture was subject to a wide-ranging antimodernist reassessment in which anthropologists could view tribal societies as viable romanticized alternatives to the problems of modern industrial society (Stocking 1989). A number of prominent scholars' works appear among the anthropological treatments considering so-called "primitive" societies as idealized alternatives to modernity: Malinowski's humanism, Leenhardt's characterization of Melanesian participatory "plentitude," the comparative work of Mauss at

least partly inspired by these two ethnographers, and the results of Mead's
early South Seas sojourn (Mauss 1967; Leenhardt 1979; Stocking 1991, 1995).
Although Malinowski saw himself as embarking upon the science of culture,
his distrust of bloodless "kinship algebra" and the Durkheimian submergence
of biological individuals in a collective "metaphysical entity" left his contemporary, Radcliffe-Brown, to formulate nomothetic functional social laws and
usher in British social anthropology's classical period, which combined Malinowskian field methods with what Malinowski considered to be Radcliffe-
Brown's theoretical "puritanism of prim precision" (Stocking 1995:364).

But Radcliffe-Brown's theoretical inventions did not fare well in Melanesia. If Melanesia was better suited to challenge (rather than to provide evidence for) evolutionary laws, the same can be said of its relationship to functional social structural laws. Bateson's ethnographic study of dynamic albeit
equilibrating processes of sustained differentiation was too theoretically explicit in ways that differed too much from Radcliffe-Brown's functionalist
ideas to be understood or have much influence at the time. For later Melanesian studies, however, his ideas seemed to represent the theoretical "golden
fleece" for which Melanesianists were searching (Bateson 1958; Forge 1972;
Wagner 1977; Lipset 1980). The discovery of a million "stone-age" people
living in the interior of New Guinea in the 1930s, their ensuing colonial pacifi-
cation, and the opening of the highlands to ethnographers after World War II
found Melanesian ethnography entering its classical era and J. A. Barnes
questioning the utility of Radcliffe-Brown's African models in Papua New
Guinea highlands societies (Barnes 1962). Entering into field situations as apparently pristine as Maclay's, and yet still as dependent upon their colonial
context as was Malinowski, ethnographers of Melanesia proceeded to produce texts that were to become canonical because of their contact fieldwork
situations and because of the theoretical innovations they found it necessary
to make.

The primordial field settings of the region seemed like perfect places to
explore the fundamentals of "exchange" when that concept became the guiding notion of Lévi-Strauss's structuralist social analysis. Yet as ethnographers
plumbed the principles of local cultures, they found Melanesia to be a place of
"loosely structured" social groups, transitory "big-men" or "great men," and
relatively incoherent spirit entities and religious beliefs, all of which are difficult to demarcate, much less account for, in Western rationalist terms or
through social scientific, functionalist laws.

Highland Papua New Guinea social groups have been dubbed "loosely
structured," "flexible," "plastic," and "open," and New Guinea marriages have
been characterized in terms of "complex," "asymmetrical," "dispersed" systems which are "basically 'open' " (Meggitt 1969:11). Social groups have been
found either not really to exist, except insofar as they are behaviorally elicited

and precipitated through named social distinctions, or to appear only fleet-
ingly, ephemerally, and often oppositionally in relations with other groups
that crystallize around particular exchange activities and ritual events and
then dissipate and disappear.

Melanesian leadership is also notoriously transitory as the fortunes of classic Melanesian big-men wax and wane in competitions with other big-men
who struggle to control the timing and thus capacities of other big-men to
produce food and wealth for ritual and ceremonial events (Strathern 1971).
Melanesian big-men are as dependent upon their followers as their followers
are on them for leadership and must successfully enact the roles of leaders
to provide for their followers, whose precarious prosperity is the big-man's
responsibility and may be his undoing (Clastres 1989). Classic Melanesian
big-men, moreover, "are a particular variety of great men" or leaders who gain
their power not so much from their proto-entrepreneurial manipulation of
regional wealth-exchange arrangements as from the relations they forge with
mystical powers and unseen entities in the course of becoming ritual experts
in men's religious cults (Godelier 1982; Godelier & Strathern 1991). Yet not
only are the powers capricious and uncertain upon which both big-men or
great men ultimately depend, the status of local leaders is entirely contingent
on their ability to elicit and produce effects and manifest community growth
and prosperity. The religious supernatural belief systems of Melanesia were
described by early observers as "idiosyncratic," randomly "irregular," "vari-
able," and relatively "incoherent" (Lawrence & Meggitt 1965). Indeed, they
are apparently best described not as beliefs at all but as a set of mystical techniques to gain knowledge of an unseen, intangible world of creative and trans-
formative imageries which can produce an imaginative symbolic language
for experiencing and expressing otherwise unarticulable, subliminal, creative
perceptions (Herdt & Stephen 1989).

Melanesians have thus been found to be creative, dynamic, episodic, improvisatory people who enact and manage "flow"; people who construct,
counterpoise, and interpret what is secret and hidden as opposed to what is
revealed and manifest, thereby obviating their own conventional constructions, and thus constituting essentially open, self-transforming, processual
societies (Wagner 1986; Strathern 1988). Anthropologists of Melanesia therefore found themselves adding to the anthropological canon by analyzing the
highly abstract aesthetic and symbolic processes regarding exchange, gender, and person for which the region is known today. These processes, however, concern such things as "meaninglessness," "entropy," "present absence,"
"the empty place," "contingency," the curse of mortality, "sorrow," and "lone-
liness" (Battaglia 1990; Errington & Gewertz 1987; Jorgensen 1980, 1985;
Schieffelin 1976; Strathern & Stewart 1999; Wagner 1967; Weiner 1991).

Such local Melanesian concepts are quite contrary to the notion of the canon: they emphasize existential contingency and mortality instead of a fixed progression of revealed abstract truths. Insofar as ethnographers take the Melanesian concepts seriously as valid alternative views and modes of being, they engage in a paradox of fixing within this supposed progression the truth of existential contingency and recognizing the impossibility of such progression or fixity. Indeed Melanesian anthropology has always apparently been at odds with itself: Melanesia's place in the Western imagination has long been to fill the "savage slot," a place thought to harbor people as ancient as the Australians and one discovered to be inhabited by "Stone Age" peoples, yet Melanesian ethnology's prominent role in anthropological theory has been largely to challenge evolutionary, functional, and structural scientific laws whereby the Western scientific canon would supposedly be advanced.

Flexible intellects will have no trouble supposing that the discovery of Melanesian heterogeneity and incessant movement may merely add to the progressive unfolding of truth in the Western canon, despite the fact that Melanesian cultures undermine its very idea. Yet it is still possible not to take Melanesian cultures very seriously, as implied by their place in the Western imagination; still possible to humanistically relativize the Western canon by including Melanesian cultures within its multicultural splendor; even more, still entirely possible to suppose that Melanesians help advance the truthful multicultural defamiliarizing of Western culture. Yet these latter alternatives suggest that Melanesian studies has arrived at the kind of paradox associated with the modern era that Kundera calls "terminal" (Kundera 1986). In his thinking, modern Western societies have entered an epoch in which their great legitimizing beliefs have disappeared: Western culture thus seems adrift in a godless universe as the triumph of rational science has instead produced pure irrational, unmotivated force willing only itself. Similarly, caught between Melanesian defamiliarization and Western epistemological assimilation (or between variability, transitory movement, and differentiation, on one pole and, on the other, social scientific laws) and between "truth and real-politik," the Melanesian canon seems to have reached an impasse. This canon *malgré lui* has therefore perhaps arrived at a kind of theoretical terminus in which it has come full force against the paradoxes of canon formation.

Why Melanesia has assumed such a prominent place in the anthropological canon is equally paradoxical. On the one hand, not once but twice—in the days when Papuans were thought to be remnants of the original rudest races and when a million Papuan language speakers were "discovered" in the inland regions of Australian New Guinea—Melanesia was thought to be the perfect place to study survivals of the earliest stages of mankind or foraging and tribal peoples unfettered by Western civilization. Yet on the other hand, Melanesian anthropology's role generally has been to contest evolutionary and functional social laws and to emphasize instead the messiness and imponderabilia of fieldwork, to offer feminist and other relativizing challenges, and the like. Melanesian cultures are ephemeral and contingent and therefore inherently challenge the great scientific laws that underpin the ideas of the Western canon. Yet they are assigned a fixed and permanent place in the historical archive, if not canon, in the unfolding of Western history (which, it must be noted, is Melanesian history as well). Because Western history is inextricably bound to the project of assimilating its Others to its political economic and literary epistemological structures, to account for the Melanesian canon requires an inquiry into the claims and suppositions by which the Western textual canon acquires and establishes its permanence and authority.

Forgotten Cannons

As soon as the question of the canon is posed, the most fundamental questions and problems of anthropology, cultural representation, and anthropological writing arise. These questions are rooted in the very idea and genealogy of "canon." The modern Western notion of the "canon" derives from the Greek root *kanna*, indicating a "reed," which derives from the Semitic Babylonian Assyrian *qanu* or "pipe." Although etymologists are hesitant to trace or recognize it, the Oxford English and American Heritage dictionaries suggest that *kanna* has two channels or patterns of derivation into the English language (via Latin and French): from the Greek word *kanon*, "rod" or "rule," comes the English word "canon," with one "n," of the literary or written sort; from the Greek word *kanna*, "reed" or "cane," comes the English word "cannon," with two "n's," of the military hardware sort. Because most etymological dictionaries fail to make the latter connection, it must be assumed that this second derivation is obscure or perhaps dubious.[7] However, the reason this genealogy is generally forgotten can be traced to the divergence between two

7. John Ayto, in his *Dictionary of Word Origins*, writes that "English has two different words cannon, neither of which can for certain be connected with canon" (New York, 1993:94). Most etymological sources agree that these two words are separate; among them are *The Oxford Dictionary of English Etymology* (Oxford, 1966), *A Comprehensive Etymological Dictionary of the English Language* by Dr. Ernest Klein (New York, 1966), *The Barnhart Dictionary of Etymology* by Robert K. Barnhart (New York, 1988), *An Etymological Dictionary of the English Language* by the Reverend Walter W. Skeat (Oxford, 1935), and *An Etymological Dictionary of Modern English* by Ernest Weekley (London, 1921). Unlike the previous works, however, Eric Partridge's *Origins: A Short Etymological Dictionary of Modern English* (New York, 1966) and Joseph T. Shipley's *Dictionary of Word Origins* (New York, 1945) list "canon" and "cannon" together and trace their origins back to a single source, as I do here. The etymological confusion which thus reigns is due to the ideological masking of the role of force and violence in the creation and administration of states. This masking protects the purity of state ideals and identifies states with justice rather than violence.

elements of Western culture that took place in the technological formation of modern Europe and the conceptual conundrums that accompany European state formation.

Between the years 1450 and 1520, two inventions were completed that set the course of early modern Europe. One, the printing press, was borrowed from China and perfected in several places in quick succession. The archive and canon soon followed. And the most notable publication of the period was, of course, the famed Gutenberg Bible. Simultaneously, the other invention, which Europeans adapted from the Chinese, using technology previously employed to forge church bells, is the military cannon. The first use of the written canon antedates the printing press and refers to any ecclesiastical rule, law, or decree of the church which underpinned the authority of the political rulers who developed the modern secular state. The earliest written canon was therefore the legal canon which codified and established the law of the state. Within 70 years of the perfection of the printing press, "canon" took on its more general definition of any rule, principle, or axiom governing a field of scientific or humanistic inquiry. The cannon followed a different etymological course than canon but nevertheless served the same purpose by serving the power of the state. Cannons and canon were thereby ideologically separated and the force underpinning the canon was masked.

The law of the state, of course, as the English idiom phrases it so well, must be "enforced" and, indeed, the emergence of the modern European sovereign territorial state coincided with the spread of both the printed word and explosive revolution in warfare technology. There is no such thing as law without the possibility and necessity of its enforcement, whether or not it is actually enforced. Canon and cannon proceed apace. As Derrida points out,

> law is always an authorized force, a force that justifies itself or is justified in applying itself, even if this justification may be judged from elsewhere to be unjust or unjustifiable. Applicability, "enforceability," is not an exterior or secondary possibility that may or may not be added as a supplement to law. It is the force essentially implied in the very concept of justice as law (droit). . . . there is no such thing as law (droit) that doesn't imply in itself, a priori, in the analytic structure of its concept, the possibility of being "enforced," applied by force. (Derrida 1992b:5–6)

But even though law and force are inseparable, law cannot be reduced to force, or to force willing itself. Otherwise, law is indistinguishable from force and violence that is arbitrary and unjustified. Laws, canons, and cannons require a foundation or basis in something other than and outside of this necessary relation between law and force. They require what Pascal, following Montaigne, referred to as the "mystical foundation of authority," i.e., "justice" (Derrida 1992b:11).

In Derrida's analysis, the concept of justice involves a paradox or aporia: there can be no appeal to "justice" without assuming or claiming an authority that is arbitrary and willed: "one cannot speak directly about justice, thematize or objectivize justice, say 'this is just' and even less 'I am just,' without immediately betraying justice, if not law (droit)" (1992b:10). Justice must be beyond law and beyond legal calculation in order to act as the basis of authority and law. "Justice" therefore cannot be named, specified, or traced to its origin without fixing and making it into a kind of "law," linking it with the possibility or necessity of arbitrary enforcement, and thus forsaking it: justice must instead be an impossible, unfounded, undeconstructable, incalculable, "mystical" force.

As Pascal wrote about justice, "Whoever traces it to its source annihilates it" (quoted in Derrida 1992b:12). Justice is an ideal that only appears as such in the negative violent reaction against arbitrary force willing itself or injustice—when the law becomes force willing itself, and so no longer just. Justice moreover shows itself only at the moment of pure performative, spontaneous, liberating, anti-authoritarian, revolutionary violence which Turner associated with the liminal or "redressive" phase of ritual social drama that founds a new order and a new law (Turner 1974, 1982). Derrida describes how justice and force coincide in these moments:

> What the state fears (the state being law in its greatest force) is not so much crime or brigandage, even on the grand scale of the Mafia or heavy drug traffic, as long as they transgress the law with an eye toward particular benefits, however important they may be. The state is afraid of fundamental, founding violence, that is, violence able to justify, to legitimate . . . or to transform the relations of law . . . and so to present itself as having a right to law. . . . These moments, supposing we can isolate them, are terrifying moments. Because of the sufferings, the crimes, the tortures that rarely fail to accompany them, no doubt, but just as much because they are in themselves, in their very violence, uninterpretable or indecipherable. This is what I am calling "mystique." (Derrida 1992b:34–35)

As soon as a new law and order are founded, however, the original founding performative violence for justice, or against injustice, is displaced by the law and its enforcement. Force and violence are then legitimized as maintaining a just law. The fact that the law is predicated on force rather than the justification for enforcement is thus forgotten and relegated to obscurity, despite the fact that enforcing the law itself creates the law. As the law is enforced it is applied to new contexts and interpreted, and new precedents are set. The canon is continually reinterpreted as new precedents and models are created, always in the name of existing "law" and "justice" but nevertheless founding and instituting it. Law thus quickly becomes force willing itself although force is yet rationalized as supporting a just law.

Justice and law are thus opposed and yet inseparable, and the possibility of justice must work within the understanding of this aporetic impossibility. If Derrida's view could be put in a series of propositions, the first would be that truth and justice are realities that cannot be expressed directly through language, law, or canons (or defended easily with cannons) without compromising and betraying them. This is because language and law fix things in such a way that they require force and violence for their maintenance. Yet it is also absolutely necessary to codify and express them, and one cannot do or suppose otherwise. Truth and justice therefore require their expression and codification with the understanding and cognizance that expression itself betrays them—that it irreducibly entails force and violence. This understanding therefore necessitates a view that the canon is inherently flawed, that at best it can only allude obliquely to truth and justice, and that its expression of truth, like the linguistic sign or cultural symbol, is arbitrary and therefore historically contingent and transitory.

Writing and Canon Fever

The Melanesian canon comes very close to this formulation. I have argued that it appears as the canonization of the acanonical—the discovery, formulation, and canonization of the creativity of Melanesian cultures and Melanesians' symbolic elicitation of this creativity, that is, of corporeally embodied cosmological capacities. Malinowski, Bateson, Mead, Wagner, Marilyn Strathern, and no doubt others thus assume prominent roles in the anthropological canon, and we could add Rappaport in the field of ecology and Weiner's feminist rethinking of Malinowski's corpus to this list as well (Rappaport 1968; Weiner 1976). Determining which "classics" from within a regional specialty are read more widely in the discipline always proves difficult. But the Melanesian canon has without question provided anthropology with a profound understanding of cultural relativity, the workings of symbolic forms, and cultural invention with regard to a variety of critical anthropological matters such as gender and the gift.

Given that Melanesian studies has in recent years come to a powerful and important understanding of Melanesian cultures, it is difficult to discern why particular works should be canonized or should return and continue to inhabit the present discourse. The answer may lie in Dumont's "writing matters" and what Malinowski referred to as the "imponderabilia of actual life" which he, Mead, and others captured so vividly in their tendencies toward "overwriting" (along with what Dumont calls their "underwritten" analyses [Dumont 1996]). Each captured a specific present in the life of a society and of a discipline in a particularly vital and powerful way. Each also represents the inception or culmination and clear forceful expression of a revolution-ary moment or shift in perspective, as with Kuhn's "paradigms," and is now a touchstone for the ideas that have accumulated in anthropology—or, more accurately, in the "culture" of anthropologists (Wagner 1981).

The Melanesian canon thus appears to be governed by an opposition be-tween two counterpoised creativities: that of anthropologists and that of Melanesians, one canonical and the other acanonical. The two can be com-pared in terms of the difference between their symbolic forms, overwritten accounts, and "underwritten" models, on the one hand, and the cultural cre-ativity, generativity, and lives that they endeavor to present and invoke, on the other. Seen in this way, the Melanesian canon and Melanesians both employ participatory techniques to devise and deploy glosses or symbolic forms to depict and present or summon sociality and conjure creative gener-ating powers. Melanesian societies depend upon this nexus between sym-bolic forms and generative powers, and anthropological writing and modeling are likewise predicated upon devising and formulating the most sympathetic, accurate, "true," and coherent depictions, glosses, and paradigms of culture and behavior.

In addition, however, both Melanesian cultures and the Melanesian canon have an essential "outside" or alterity, that is, something that eludes their grasp and escapes symbolic presentation and depiction. For Melanesians, this "mystical" alterity is the invisible, intangible realm in which the spirits and unknown, corporeally embodied, cosmological powers dwell, powers whose capacities Melanesians endeavor to elicit and invoke. The difference between these powers and the cultural and symbolic constructions that elicit them make Melanesian societies creative, improvisatory, self-transformative, and acanonical. The conditional and contingent, arbitrary, changeable charac-ter of Melanesians' symbolic constructs are signs of a radical finitude which makes for cultural differences and "otherness."

But Melanesian cultures endeavor to celebrate and understand another "outside" as a part of the life-giving generativity which they otherwise sym-bolically elicit: death. Indeed, a great many Melanesian religious practices focus on funerary rites and invoking ancestors. Death is an "outside," un-presentable force which disrupts generativity and interrupts every possible symbolic elicitation of mystical forces. Yet death is also the very condition of this generativity: Melanesian cultures are predicated upon the moral im-perative of giving and expenditure within kin groups whereby lines of kin are able to grow as one generation passes on its life energies to its progeny and community. These celebrations of death (Huntington & Metcalf 1991), of the life given through death, and of the irreducible inseparability of life and death underscore the contingent and ephemeral nature of human symbolic creations and help make Melanesian cultures improvisatory and acanonical.

Herein, then, lies the difference between Melanesian cultures and Western canons for, like the archive, the canon is constructed to overcome and deny death. As Derrida says,

> if there is no archive without consignation in an external place which assures the possibility of memorization, or repetition, of reproduction, or of reimpression, then we must also remember that repetition itself, the logic of repetition, indeed the repetition compulsion, remain, according to Freud, indissociable from the death drive. And thus from destruction. . . . The death drive is not a principle. It even threatens every principality, every archontic primacy, every archival desire. It is what we will call . . . *le mal d'archive*, archive fever. (Derrida 1995:14)

Like the archive, the Western canon is a consignation—a gathering together of signs or works that immortalizes them into a single corpus and assigns them to a particular historical place that precludes and refuses death. What Derrida calls "the archive drive" or "archive fever" we might call "the canon drive" or "canon fever." Again, citing Derrida,

> There would indeed be no archive desire without the radical finitude, without the possibility of a forgetfulness which does not limit itself to repression. Above all, and this is the most serious, beyond or within this simple limit called finiteness or finitude, there is no archive fever without the threat of this death drive, this aggression and destruction drive. This threat is in-finite, it sweeps away the logic of finitude and the simple factual limits, the transcendental aesthetics, one might say, the spatio-temporal conditions of conservation. . . . There is not one mal d'archive, one limit or one suffering of memory among others: enlisting the in-finite, archive fever verges on radical evil. (Derrida 1995:19)

"Canon fever," like "archive fever," can thus be viewed as a drive to overcome death or, rather, the drive toward death and toward giving, sacrifice, and in-finite expenditure whereby life is predicated upon and equated with death and mortality. The desire for immortality gained through the repetition and memory which motivates the canon becomes a kind of "canon fever" because it is haunted and made unwell by the alterity and "otherness" or "outside" that it represses and denies, that is, death, and the paradoxes whereby death and life are identical.

Nonetheless it is easy to demonstrate that any canon and any archive is founded on such terminal paradoxes. Canons are meant to fix and immortalize works; but their very fixing gives them new life by enabling continual interpretation. The continued life of any text, particularly any text that deserves canonization, is its capacity to be reinterpreted, reread, and given new meaning in the present, which is found in its "overwriting," its "imponderabilia," and its ambiguities and uncertainties. The success of any text or canon, moreover, is in its dissemination and far-reaching effects on other works whereby

it obtains new and different expression, which is also its dissipation, muta-
tion, and therefore loss or failure as a permanent singular expression of certain revealed truths. The successful canon, in other words, is only successful
by virtue of the fact that it gives rise to new expressions and a new language
which assuredly replaces it while making it both obsolete and fundamental.

Seen in this way, and despite itself, this paradoxical canon does not deny
or preclude loss and death but instead is founded on it. In other words, the
canon is situated within the enigma whereby its continuance and immortality
are dependent upon its transmutability into other forms. Yet the canon is
predicated upon the fixing of forms and expressions, and its transmutability
is therefore tantamount to its death as a type of immutable expression. The
continued life of the canon is therefore based on, in this sense, its own death.
If the canon can thus be said to be a celebration of death instead of its denial, it is in this way like the cultures of Melanesia. Like the successful canon,
Melanesian cultures have been described in ways indicating that they institute their own creative mutability: ethnographers have found these cultures
to be "underdetermined," full of "partible" and decomposable people, organized into "contingent" or "contested" clans or other groups, which are construed in relation to an "empty place" or "presence-absence" in aesthetically
sublime, symbolic presentations of "pathos" and "sorrow" (Schieffelin 1976;
Strathern 1988; Lederman 1989; Battaglia 1990; Weiner 1991; Strathern &
Stewart 1999; R. Wagner pers. comm.).

These findings indicate that the Melanesian canon has succeeded in anthropology largely because of its "overwriting" and suggestive abstract theorizing rather than its formulaic models or social scientific laws. If any canon
must be haunted by the specter of the sublimated force and violence that must
also remain unarticulated and implicit (lest its authority be undermined), this
force is undermined through the Melanesian canon's "overwriting" and its
success by means of its own dissemination and dissimulation. Melanesia's
role in the anthropological canon has thus been to ferment a kind of "mal du
canon."

Conclusion: Writing between Can(n)ons

I began this essay with the question of why Melanesia has played so prominent
a role in the anthropological canon, suggesting that the Melanesian canon is
involved in a conundrum between Melanesian defamiliarization of Western
culture and assimilation of Melanesians to the Western epistemic order embodied by the canon. In a review of the historical development of the Melanesian ethnographic canon, I pointed out how it has also been predicated upon
the conflict between not only Melanesian heterogeneity and fluidity, on the

one hand, and Western evolutionary and social structural laws, on the other, but also between, one, idealistic notions of "truth" and "native" interests and viewpoints and, two, "realpolitik." Drawing upon two essays by Derrida, I then analyzed the Western idea of the "canon" and found it to entail sublimated force and argued that, through "overwriting," the role of Melanesian ethnography has nevertheless been to subvert the force of the Western canon, and that the ambiguities and uncertainties of "overwriting" have been necessary to its success.

I have presented the case that the canon and Melanesian anthropology's place in it is subject to a number of interrelated conundrums or dilemmas in which two principles are inimical, yet mutually implicate and entail one another. I have furthermore claimed that in the case of the Western notion of the canon, while the ideals of truth and justice have been demarcated from, and thus have masked, their own requisites of force and violence, these two sets of ideas are nonetheless inseparable. It is possible, however, analytically to separate the two sides of this predicament in order to comprehend their historical influences on the emergence of Melanesia as a central place in anthropology and their roles in the dilemmas of the Melanesian canon. We may thus be in a better position to understand the historical forces that made Melanesian ethnography so important in the anthropological canon.

One factor in the centrality of Melanesia in the anthropological canon is the political and geographic location of Melanesia near Australia, and the need for Britain and Australia to maintain territorial sovereignty there against other colonial powers. These historical, territorially based political alignments created a greater need for Western (British, Australian, Dutch, German, and American) anthropological knowledge of these areas and their societies. The Dutch proclaimed possession of western New Guinea in 1828 and formally annexed it in 1850. Britain established a Protectorate over the south coast of eastern New Guinea, and Germany took possession of northeast New Guinea territories in 1884. With definite political interests and economic stakes involved, one reason for the anthropological work in Melanesia has to do with can(n)ons—written canons and military cannons. Those two homonyms here apparently serve the same ends: the furtherance of state territorial interests. One might say that "canon fever" here takes the form of the drive to maintain and extend European state power and boundaries over and against mortality, death, and the death drive.

Second, however, the allure of antipodal people of the "Papuan" race where one might be able to discover the fundamental, original principles of human culture and society, and the discovery of a million "stone-age" people not previously known to exist drew anthropology into the Melanesian arena. Here Europeans could peer through a window into human origins, and fascinated anthropologists could pursue the rudiments and bases of culture or ready-made experiments in human diversity. Unlike the force of state territorial concerns, however, these written canons do not always fit very happily with political designs and military cannons. Anthropological texts indeed have often attempted to resist and write against state or colonial intrusions in the lives of local peoples. One might therefore conclude that anthropologists are caught between canons and cannons, pursuing the former to subvert the latter, upon which they were nevertheless dependent. As Asad (1991:315) points out, though, even "if the role of anthropology for colonialism was relatively unimportant, the reverse proposition does not hold."

While anthropologists have thus attempted to resist and escape the implications of the state interests and force that I have argued are inseparable from the establishment and maintenance of the Western canon, and as indeed happened in the English language in early modern Europe, such a separation must be recognized as impossible. Having thus analytically segregated the two sides of the dilemma facing anthropologists, I find it necessary to appreciate the specific form of their interrelation, despite the fact that anthropologists sometimes focus on one side to the exclusion of the other. Although anthropologists often defend local peoples against state-sponsored enterprises, they cannot avoid being emissaries of Western culture and society to local peoples and or serving as sources of information about those people to colonial states and, in this way, wittingly or not, acting in complicity with colonial state interests by helping bring Western culture to local peoples. Therefore, when anthropologists focus on Melanesia as a place in which to pursue the truth of human origins and diversity, the canon is involved in relegating to obscurity and forgetting the originating force that gives form to its mystical foundations, much as the force and violence that support and underlie the written law and canon were ideologically disguised in early modern Europe when written canons were separated from military cannons by one silent letter.

Melanesian anthropology would therefore appear to be caught not so much between canons and cannons or truth and politics — one territorially politically determined and the other an enchantment, the founding violence underpinning the canon and its mystical foundations — but within can(n)ons, that is, within the dilemma between the mute obscuring and the clear understanding of force and violence inherent in any attempt to write the definitive canon. This understanding requires us to address the irreducible force that underwrites the canon. The lesson here is to point out the need for a kind of writing which considers its own formulations and expressions to be historically ephemeral and contingent so as to mitigate the irreducible force of the canon. Truth and justice require, in other words, an eternal vigilance against reification, which amounts to an infinite demand to pursue these ends without supposing that we shall ever have attained them.

Melanesian anthropology continues to inhabit the "savage slot" in the discipline at large and to provide the Western imagination with images of the most primordial customs. New Guinea cultures still find their status in introductory textbooks to be that of exemplars of timeless ahistorical societies with the most "primitive" of cultures. The century-old Western assumptions about "Papuans" that once lured anthropologists seeking ethnographic "truth" to the region apparently still inhabit the general introductory textbook idea of Melanesian cultures today. What once made Melanesian ethnography central to the anthropological canon, however, now marginalizes it, for the concerns of the discipline have moved on to national and transnational global historical processes.

In the last decade or so Melanesian anthropology has produced many fine, intensive ethnographic studies of change and transformation in the modern world. Melanesians appear in most cases to be, as Robbins terms the Urapmin, "modernist"—seeking the "new" (1999:83). The Kaluli no longer practice the Gisaro (Schieffelin 1981), the Arapesh have disbanded their tambaran cult (Tuzin 1997), the Daribi have probably forgotten the Habu ceremony (R. Wagner pers. comm.), and Rawa speakers no longer practice the Yambourote pig feast while, like local Rawa currencies, other pig feasts and currencies have been inflated, commercialized, and amplified, and the competition and conflict they involve has intensified—leading, I argue, to an increase of sublime pathos as well (Dalton 1996). Because of these transformations, the Melanesian canon now includes works that concern colonialism, modernism, and change, topics of great interest in anthropology.

Since the modern nation-state of Papua New Guinea obtained its independence in 1975, studies of change and development have been more imperative. Yet as Robbins says, "Even if all of our efforts were trained on these matters, the absence in most cases of time depth and rich historical archives makes it unlikely that work done in Melanesia will become standard-bearers on these topics" (1998:90). Given that Melanesian cultures have been found to be open-ended, improvisatory, and self-transforming, this situation is paradoxical to say the very least.

In a recent article comparing anthropological culture theory and cultural studies, Handler finds that the latter has devoted itself largely to an aspect of culture often ignored by anthropologists: where anthropologists have used "culture" to "relativize any and all foundational assumptions" of nature and biology (1998:459), cultural studies practitioners have concerned themselves with the relation of hegemonic, albeit internally differentiated, varieties of culture to "social stratification in modern societies along axes of class, race, and gender" (458). He suggests that fin-de-siècle U.S. anthropology has reached a crossroads and that, without cultural studies, the reified anthropological culture concept may not be able to relativize the ideas of race with which it shares certain ontological assumptions, as happened in French anthropology at the beginning of the last century (Stocking 1968d).

I have suggested that Melanesian anthropology has reached a similar impasse or perhaps a terminal paradox in which it must navigate between relativization and reification. I have also claimed that the qualities of Melanesian cultures have made them more suitable for challenging Western reifications of race, culture, and society than to support them in the history of the anthropological canon. Nevertheless, it remains to be seen if studies of cultural transformation in Melanesia come to rely on such reifications or to contest them.

Acknowledgements

The original version of this paper was presented at the 1997 Annual Meeting of the American Ethnological Society in a session organized by Peter Metcalf entitled "New Guinea : Borneo :: Canon : No Canon," and it has benefited from the comments and encouragement made in the discussions following that session, particularly those by Rena Lederman, Nahum Chandler, Jean-Paul Dumont, Jeannette Mageo, and Malcolm Blincow. It has also benefited from subsequent discussions with Dan Jorgensen and Sandra Bamford, the advice and encouragement of Charlie Piot and Richard Handler, etymological help from Frank Dalton, and from the critical assessment of one anonymous reviewer.

References Cited

Asad, T. 1991. Afterword: From the history of colonial anthropology to the anthropology of Western hegemony. In *Colonial Situations: Essays on the Contextualization of Ethnographic Knowledge*, ed. G. W. Stocking, Jr., HOA 7:314–24.

Barnes, J. A. 1962. African models in the New Guinea highlands. *Man*, n.s., 62:5–9.

Bateson, G. 1958. *Naven: A survey of the problems suggested by a composite picture of the culture of a New Guinea tribe drawn from three points of view*. Stanford, Calif.

Battaglia, D. 1990. *On the bones of the serpent: Person, memory, and mortality in Sabarl Island society*. Chicago.

Clastres, P. 1989. *Society against the state: Essays in political anthropology*. Trans. R. Hurley & A. Stein. New York.

Clifford, J. 1982. *Person and myth: Maurice Leenhardt in the Melanesian world*. Berkeley, Calif.

Codrington, R. H. 1891. *The Melanesians: Studies in their anthropology and folklore*. New York.

Dalton, D. M. 1996. The aesthetics of the sublime: An interpretation of Rawa shell valuable symbolism. *American Ethnologist* 23:393–415.

Derrida, J. 1978. *Edmund Husserl's Origin of Geometry: An introduction*. Trans. J. P. Leavey, Jr. Lincoln, Nebr.

Derrida, J. 1992a. *The other heading: Reflections on today's Europe.* Trans. P-A. Brault & M. B. Naas. Bloomington, Ind.

Derrida, J. 1992b. Force of law: The "Mystical Foundations of Authority." In *Deconstruction and the possibility of justice,* ed. M. Rosenfeld, D. Cornell & D. G. Carlson, 3–67. New York.

Derrida, J. 1995. Archive fever: A Freudian impression. *Diacritics* 25:9–63.

Dumont, J-P. 1996. Writing matters: Ethnographic overwriting and anthropological underwriting. Paper presented at the annual meeting of the American Anthropological Association, 20–24 November, San Francisco.

DuToit, B. M. 1962. Structural looseness in New Guinea. *Journal of the Polynesian Society* 71:397–99.

Errington, F., & D. Gewertz. 1987. *Cultural alternatives and a feminist anthropology: An analysis of culturally constructed gender interests in Papua New Guinea.* Cambridge.

Evans-Pritchard, E. E. 1940. *The Nuer: A description of the modes of livelihood and political institutions of a Nilotic people.* Oxford.

Fabian, J. 1983. *Time and the Other: How anthropology makes its object.* New York.

Firth, S. 1972. *New Guinea under the Germans.* Carlton, Victoria (Aus.).

Forge, A. 1972. The golden fleece. *Man,* n.s., 7:527–40.

Gates, H. L., Jr. 1992. *Loose canons: Notes on the culture wars.* Oxford.

Godelier, M. 1982. *The making of great men: Male domination and power among the New Guinea Baruya.* Trans. R. P. Swyer. Cambridge.

Godelier, M., & M. Strathern, eds. 1991. *Big men and great men: Personifications of power in Melanesia.* Cambridge.

Haeckel, E. H. 1876. *The history of creation, or, The development of the earth and its inhabitants by the action of natural causes: a popular exposition of the doctrine of evolution in general, and of that of Darwin, Goethe and Lamarck in particular.* 2 vols. Trans. Sir E. Ray. London.

Handler, R. 1998. Raymond Williams, George Stocking, and fin-de-siècle U.S. anthropology. *Cultural Anthropology* 13:447–63.

Herdt, G., & M. Stephen, eds. 1989. *The religious imagination in New Guinea.* New Brunswick, N.J.

Huntington, R., & P. Metcalf. 1991. *Celebrations of death: The anthropology of mortuary ritual.* Cambridge.

Husserl, E. 1970. *The crisis of European sciences and transcendental phenomenology.* Trans. D. Carr. Evanston, Ill.

Jorgensen, D. 1980. What's in a name: The meaning of meaninglessness in Telefolmin. *Ethos* 8:349–66.

Jorgensen, D. 1985. Femsep's last garden: A Telefol response to mortality. In *Aging and its transformations: Moving toward death in Pacific societies,* ed. D. A. Counts & D. Counts, 207–26. New York.

Kaplan, M. 1995. *Neither cargo nor cult: Ritual politics and the colonial imagination in Fiji.* Durham, N.C.

Keesing, R. M. 1992. *Culture and confrontation: The Kwaio struggle for cultural autonomy.* Chicago.

Kundera, M. 1986. *The art of the novel.* Trans. L. Asher. New York.

Lawrence, P., & M. J. Meggitt. 1965. Introduction. In *Gods, ghosts and men in Melanesia*, ed. P. Lawrence & M. J. Meggitt, 1–26. London.

Lederman, R. 1989. Contested order: Gender and society in the southern New Guinea highlands. *American Ethnologist* 16:230–47.

Leenhardt, M. 1979. *Do Kamo: Person and myth in the Melanesian world*. Trans. B. M. Bulati. Chicago.

Lévy-Bruhl, L. 1975. *The notebooks on primitive mentality*. Trans. P. Riviere. New York.

Lipset, D. 1980. *Gregory Bateson: The legacy of a scientist*. Englewood Cliffs, N.J.

Malinowski, B. 1931. A plea for an effective color bar. *Spectator* 146:999–1001.

Marett, R. R. 1909. *The threshold of religion*. London.

Mauss, M. 1967. *The gift: Forms and functions of exchange in archaic societies*. Trans. I. Cunnison. New York.

Meggitt, M. J. 1969. Introduction. In *Pigs, pearlshells, and women: Marriage in the New Guinea highlands*, ed. R. M. Glasse & M. J. Meggitt, 1–15. Englewood Cliffs, N.J.

Mikloucho-Maclay, N. 1975. *New Guinea diaries, 1871–1883*. Trans. C. L. Sentinella. Madang, Papua New Guinea.

Mimica, J. 1988. *Intimations of infinity: The mythopoeia of the Iqwaye counting system and number*. Oxford.

Rappaport, R. A. 1968. *Pigs for the ancestors: Ritual and ecology of a New Guinea people*. New Haven, Conn.

Rivers, W. H. R. 1914. *The history of Melanesian society*. 2 vols. Cambridge.

Robbins, J. 1998. Between reproduction and transformation: Ethnography and modernity in Melanesia. *Anthropological Quarterly* 71:89–98.

Robbins, J. 1999. "This is our money": Modernism, regionalism, and dual currencies in Urapmin. In *Money and modernity: State and local currencies in Melanesia*, Association for Social Anthropology in Oceania Monograph Series, No. 17, ed. D. Akin & J. Robbins, 82–102. Pittsburgh, Penn.

Schieffelin, E. L. 1976. *The sorrow of the lonely and the burning of the dancers*. New York.

Schieffelin, E. L. 1981. The end of traditional music, dance, and body decoration in Bosavi, Papua New Guinea. In *The plight of peripheral peoples in Papua New Guinea*. Vol. 1: *The inland situation*, ed. R. Gordon, 1–22. Cambridge, Mass.

Spencer, H. 1855. *The principles of psychology*. London.

Stocking, G. W., Jr. 1968a. Matthew Arnold, E. B. Tylor, and the uses of invention. In 1968e:69–90.

Stocking, G. W., Jr. 1968b. "Cultural Darwinism" and "Philosophical Idealism" in E. B. Tylor. In 1968e:91–109.

Stocking, G. W., Jr. 1968c. Franz Boas and the culture concept in historical perspective. In 1968e:195–233.

Stocking, G. W., Jr. 1968d. French anthropology in 1800. In 1968e:13–41.

Stocking, G. W., Jr. 1968e. *Race, culture, and evolution: Essays in the history of anthropology*. New York.

Stocking, G. W., Jr. 1987. *Victorian anthropology*. New York.

Stocking, G. W., Jr. 1989. The ethnographic sensibility of the 1920s and the dualism of the anthropological tradition. In *Romantic motives: Essays on anthropological sensibility*, ed. G. W. Stocking, Jr., HOA 6:208–76.

Stocking, G. W. Jr. 1991. Maclay, Kubary, Malinowski: Archetypes from the dream-time of anthropology. In *Colonial situations: Essays on the contextualization of ethnographic knowledge*, ed. G. W. Stocking, Jr., HOA 7:9–74.

Stocking, G. W., Jr. 1995. *After Tylor: British social anthropology, 1888–1951*. Madison, Wis.

Strathern, A. 1971. *The rope of Moka: Big-Men and ceremonial exchange in Mount Hagen New Guinea*. Cambridge.

Strathern, A., & P. J. Stewart. 1999. Objects, relationships, and meanings: Historical switches in currencies in Mount Hagen, Papua New Guinea. In *Money and modernity: State and local currencies in Melanesia*. Association for Social Anthropology in Oceania Monograph Series, No. 17, ed. D. Akin & J. Robbins, 164–91. Pittsburgh, Penn.

Strathern, M. 1988. *The gender of the gift: Problems with women and problems with society in Melanesia*. Berkeley, Calif.

Thomas, N. 1989. The force of ethnology: Origins and significance of the Melanesian/Polynesia division. *Current Anthropology* 30:27–34.

Turner, V. 1974. *Dramas, fields, and metaphors: Symbolic action in human society*. Ithaca, N.Y.

Turner, V. 1982. *From ritual to theatre: The human seriousness of play*. New York.

Tuzin, D. 1997. *The cassowary's revenge: The life and death of masculinity in a New Guinea society*. Chicago.

Tylor, E. B. 1871. *Primitive culture: Researches into the development of mythology, philosophy, religion, language, art, and custom*. 3d ed. New York (1889).

Wagner, R. 1967. *The curse of Souw: Principles of Daribi clan definition and alliance in New Guinea*. Chicago.

Wagner, R. 1977. Analogic kinship: A Daribi example. *American Ethnologist* 4:623–42.

Wagner, R. 1981. *The invention of culture*. 2d ed. Chicago.

Wagner, R. 1986. *Symbols that stand for themselves*. Chicago.

Wallace, A. R. 1869. *The Malay archipelago, the land of the orang-utan and the bird of paradise; a narrative of travel, with studies of man and nature*. New York (1962).

Watson, J. B. 1964. Loose structure loosely construed: Groupless groups in Gadsup. *Oceania* 35:267–71.

Watson, J. B. 1970. Society as organized flow: The Tairora case. *Southwestern Journal of Anthropology* 26:107–24.

Webster, E. M. 1984. *The moon man: A biography of Nikolai Miklouho-Maclay*. Carleton, Victoria (Aus).

Weiner, A. B. 1976. *Women of value, men of renown: New perspectives in Trobriand exchange*. Austin, Tex.

Weiner, J. F. 1991. *The empty place: Poetry, space, and being among the Foi of Papua New Guinea*. Bloomington, Ind.

Index